Introduction to Client/Server Networking

Bruce Hallberg
Jane and Chuck Holcombe
Rich McMahon
Mike Meyers
Syngress Media
Toby Velte
Alan Simpson
Rory McCaw
Kenneth Rosen
Douglas Host

McGraw-Hill Technology Education

Burr Ridge, IL Dubuque, IA Emeryville, CA New York San Francisco
Bangkok Bogotá Caracas Lisbon London Madrid
Mexico City Milan New Delhi Seoul Singapore Sydney Taipei Toronto

The McGraw·Hill *Companies*

Technology Education

1333 Burr Ridge Parkway
Burr Ridge, Illinois 60527
U.S.A.

Introduction to Client/Server Networking

For information on translations or book distributors outside the U.S.A., please see the International Contact Information page immediately following the index of this book. Some ancillaries, including electronic and print components, may not be available to customers outside the United States.

1 2 3 4 5 6 7 8 9 0 QPD QPD 0 1 9 8 7 6 5 4 3

ISBN 0-07-225455-6

This book was composed with Corel Ventura™ Publisher.

www.mhteched.com

Editorial Director
TRACY DUNKELBERGER

Project Manager
MARK KARMENDY

Project Editor
EMILY RADER

Copy Editor
ANDREA BOUCHER

Proofreaders
LINDA MEDOFF
PAUL MEDOFF

Indexer
VALERIE HAYNES PERRY

Composition
CARIE ABREW
ELIZABETH JANG

Illustrators
KATHLEEN EDWARDS
MELINDA LYTLE

Series Design
JOHN WALKER
PETER F. HANCIK

Cover Series Design
GREG SCOTT

Contributor
HURIX SYSTEMS PRIVATE LIMITED

About the Authors

Bruce Hallberg has consulted on many network system and software implementations for Fortune 1000 companies and presently works as an IT director in the biopharmaceutical industry. He is the author of more than 20 computer books on Windows NT, NetWare, Exchange Server, and other networking and computer technologies.

Jane Holcombe (A+, Network+, MCSE, CTT+, CNA, and former MCT) is a pioneer in the field of PC support training. Her introduction to computers in business began in 1983, when she installed a LAN and supported the desktop PCs for her employer. Since 1984 she has been an independent trainer, consultant, and course content author. Through the late 1980s and early 1990s she created and presented courses on PC operating systems that were taught nationwide. She also co-authored a set of networking courses for the consulting staff of a large network vendor. Beginning in the early 1990s, she worked with both Novell and Microsoft server operating systems, focusing particularly on the Microsoft operating system and achieving her MCSE certification for Windows NT 3.*x*, Windows NT 4.0, and Windows 2000.

Chuck Holcombe has a high-tech background in the use of computers in the nuclear and aerospace fields. In his 15 years at Control Data Corporation, he was a programmer, technical sales analyst, salesman, and sales manager. He ran the Executive Seminar program, was Control Data's liaison to the worldwide university community, and was a market development manager for Plato, Control Data's computer-based education system. He then spent over two decades as an independent trainer and consultant. He has authored and delivered many training courses and is a skilled writer and editor of complex materials. Jane and Chuck are a writing/editing team who authored the *MCSE Guide to Designing a Microsoft Windows 2000 Network Infrastructure* (Course Technology) and three books for McGraw-Hill/Osborne: *A+ Certification Press Lab Manual*, *MCSE Certification Press Windows 2000 Professional Lab Manual*, and the first book in the Mike Meyers Computer Skills series *Survey of Operating Systems*. They also contributed chapters to Peter Norton's *Introduction to Computers*, Sixth Edition, and *Windows 2000 Administration* for McGraw-Hill/Osborne.

Douglas A. Host is an AT&T Labs retiree, where his 29-year career most recently included responsibility for technology assessment of Intranet/Internet services. Host received masters degrees in both computer science and library science at Rutgers University.

Rory McCaw, Microsoft MVP, MCT, MCSE, CTT, is an independent trainer, consultant, and author of numerous technical books, including *Implementing a Windows Server 2003 Network Infrastructure* and *Mike Meyers' Windows 2000 Network Infrastructure Administration Certification Passport*, from McGraw-Hill/Osborne.

Richard Alan McMahon, Sr., Major (USAF Ret), is a full-time lecturer in the Finance, Accounting, and Computer Information Systems (FACIS) Department at University of Houston, Downtown, and specializes in teaching Introductory and Advanced Data Communications and Networking, Information Security Management, Systems Analysis, Project Management, Management Information Systems, and Introductory and Advanced Computer Applications, all strongly emphasizing a hands-on application approach.

Additionally, Rich is an Education Technology consultant working on LearnPoint Suite, one of the Rapid eLearning Application Development (ReAD) Enterprise Solutions from LeanForward, Inc. of Houston. Rich has written numerous other networking-related textbooks for SouthWestern Publishing, The Coriolis Group, Prentice Hall, and EMC Paradigm. Two of his textbooks, including his *Introduction to Networking*, have been nominated for the Texty Award, presented by the Text and Academic Authors Association. Rich holds an M.B.A. from Hardin-Simmons University, an M.S. from the University of Arkansas, and is currently a doctoral candidate at Argosy University, where he is working toward his D.B.A.

Michael Meyers is the industry's leading authority on A+ and Network+ certification. He is the president and cofounder of Total Seminars, LLC, a provider of PC and network repair seminars, books, videos, and courseware for thousands of organizations throughout the world. Mike has been involved in the computer and network repair industry since 1977 as a technician, instructor, author, consultant, and speaker. Author of several popular PC books and of A+ and Network+ courseware, Mike is also the series editor for the highly successful Mike Meyers' Certification Passport series as well as the new Mike Meyers' Computer Skills series, both published by McGraw-Hill/Osborne. Mike holds multiple industry certifications and considers the moniker "computer nerd" a compliment.

Kenneth H. Rosen is a Distinguished Member of the Technical Staff at AT&T Laboratories in Middletown, New Jersey. His current assignment involves the assessment of new technology and the creation of new services for AT&T. Dr. Rosen has written several leading textbooks and many articles. Rosen received his Ph.D. from MIT.

Alan Simpson (MCSA) is the author of over 80 computer books published throughout the world in over a dozen languages. His award-winning titles have sold hundreds of thousands of copies and are best known for their light, engaging style and clear, straightforward approach to technical subjects. Alan has written books on operating systems (DOS, Windows, Linux), the Internet (HTML, JavaScript), databases, spreadsheets, word processing programs, and more. Prior to becoming an author, Alan worked as a software consultant, programmer, and teacher. Alan lives in Pennsylvania with his wife and two children.

Toby J. Velte (St.Paul, MN) Ph.D., MCSE+I, CCNA, CCDA, is a technology entrepreneur in Minneapolis, MN. He has founded several technology consulting and software development firms, authored and published numerous best-selling technology volumes with Osborne/McGraw-Hill, facilitated the promotion of many local professional organizations serving business and technology (including the Minnesota High-Tech Association, and the British Business Council of Minnesota), obtained his Ph.D. in Computational Neuroscience from the University of Minnesota and then completed his post-doctoral training at Harvard University in Cambridge, Massachusetts, presented at dozens of scientific conferences throughout the nation, and published many respected articles related to his research in the field of neuroscience and its relevant concerns.

CONTENTS

INTRODUCTION

■ What Will You Learn?

In this book, you'll learn about client/server networking, in which the various underlying tasks involved in a networked environment are divided among computers that provide services (servers) and computers that consume services (clients). Client/server networking concepts are distinct from peer-to-peer networking concepts, although to some extent the two can co-exist. Generally, very small networks use peer-to-peer networking arrangements, while medium and large networks use client/server arrangement arrangements.

In addition to learning about client/server networking in general, you will learn about the key hardware and software involved in client/server networking, including Windows NT, Windows 2000, Novell NetWare, and Red Hat Linux. Finally, you will learn about some aspects of client/server networking that transcend the specific operating system a network uses, such as network security concepts and practices.

This book is organized into nine chapters:

- Chapter 1, *Designing a Network*, presents client/server and peer-to-peer networking concepts, teaches you about the key theoretical model underpinning networks, and explains the process of designing a network and estimating resource needs.

- Chapter 2, *Networking with Unix and Linux*, covers installing and configuring Red Hat Linux in both a server and a client configuration and also teaches you about the administration and use of Red Hat Linux.

- Chapter 3, *Networking with Novell NetWare 6*, discusses the installation and configuration of Novell NetWare 6, a dedicated network operating system. It also teaches you how to set up a Windows client to access a NetWare 6 server and about basic administration of NetWare 6.

- Chapter 4, *Networking with Windows NT*, gives you an opportunity to plan and perform a Windows NT Server installation. Then you will learn about configuring a network in Windows NT Server and administering a Windows NT Server system.

- Chapter 5, *Networking with Windows 2000*, provides you with a fundamental introduction to preparing to install and installing Windows 2000 Server. Next, you will learn how to administer Windows 2000 Server, share folders across a network, and install network printers. This chapter wraps up by showing you how Windows 2000 Server's built-in backup software works.

- Chapter 6, *Connecting Client Workstations*, covers a myriad of subjects involved in setting up client computers to access servers. On top of learning about networking Windows-based clients to Windows servers, you will learn different ways of accessing Windows and NetWare servers from a Macintosh, as well as accessing a Linux server from a Windows client computer.

- Chapter 7, *TCP/IP,* introduces the "mother of all Internet protocols," TCP/IP. The TCP/IP networking protocol is the foundation of how modern networks work, and understanding it in detail will vastly improve your ability to design, install, maintain, and troubleshoot virtually every type of network in the world. In addition to learning about TCP/IP itself, you will learn how TCP/IP packets get routed over complex networks and how to use TCP/IP-oriented commands in Unix or Linux.

- Chapter 8, *Configuring Hard Drives,* teaches you everything you need to know about this most important resource on any network. You will learn how hard drives work, how data is structured on them, and how to maintain and troubleshoot them.

- Chapter 9, *Securing a Network,* teaches you how to approach the subject of network security and is packed with important information to help you understand what many consider to be the most important responsibility of any networking professional: keeping the data stored on the organization's network safe and secure.

■ You Will Learn to...

Working in the networking field often requires you to have an extensive and constantly updated encyclopedia of information. Starting out that way would require you to learn networking information at an enormous rate, similar to drinking water by putting your face in front of an opened fire hydrant! Rather, you will find that this book presents just the key points about client/server networking and helps guide you as you continue to explore the specifics of the field. This book is also designed to teach you basic skills that you'll need in order to be successful as you begin working with client/server networks.

Walk and Talk Like a Pro

Each chapter starts with a list of learning objectives. These are followed by lucid explanations of each topic, supported by real-world scenarios and enhanced by liberal use of graphics and tables. To give you hands-on experience and help you "walk the walk," you'll find detailed step-by-step tutorials and short Try This! exercises that enable you to practice the concepts. To help you "talk the talk," each chapter contains definitions of networking terms, summarized in a Key Terms list. Be ready for a Key Term Quiz at the end of each chapter!

Troubleshoot Like a Pro

While there is a lot of useful information in this book, a single book simply can't give you everything you need to know about client/server networking. In addition to providing you with a solid introduction to the client/server networking field, we give you some of the tools that will help you help yourself, which is a valuable skill whether you're on the job or working at home. For example, we show you how to use help files and perform updates to your new operating systems, and we teach you how to use the Internet to find even more information that will help you with potential troubleshooting problems.

Think Like a Pro

We've also included Inside Information sidebars, which provide insight into some of the subtleties of working with networks. Notes and Tips are sprinkled throughout the chapters, and Warnings help prevent mishaps (or an emotional meltdown). At the end of each chapter, a Key Term Quiz, Multiple-Choice Quiz, and Essay Quiz help you measure what you've learned and hone your ability to present information on paper. The Lab Projects challenge you to independently complete tasks related to what you've just learned.

Resources for Teachers

Teachers are our heroes, to whom we give our thanks and for whom we have created a powerful collection of time-saving teaching tools. The following tools are available:

- An Instructor's Manual that maps to the organization of the textbook
- Testbank in Blackboard, which generates a wide array of paper or network-based tests and features automatic grading
- Hundreds of questions, written by experienced IT instructors
- A wide variety of question types and difficulty levels, allowing teachers to customize each test to maximize student progress

chapter 1

Designing a Network

In this chapter, you will learn how to

- Conceptualize client/server networking and the OSI networking model
- Discuss common network features and components
- Design a network
- Perform a disk space estimation for a new network

N etworking professionals rarely have the opportunity to walk into a company and design a new network from the ground up, but those who do are certainly lucky. While such an effort involves long hours, stress, deadlines, and the nagging worry that maybe they're forgetting something, in return they get to shape the computing environment of a large number of users, and—in many companies—set the tone for how efficiently the company itself can function in coming years.

However, most of the time you will enter a company with a functioning network that has grown organically over time and that has the capability to support a number of different applications, operating systems, hardware platforms, and design decisions woven into its fabric.

In either scenario, whether designing a new network from the ground up or taking over the evolution of an existing network, you need to have a firm grasp on how to design a network and the factors that go into network design. In this chapter, you learn about the foundations of the knowledge you need to acquire, starting with a discussion of client/server networking, which is followed by a discussion of what services most networks provide for their users, and then moves into a straight-forward approach to designing a network. This should provide you a framework into which you can fit more detailed knowledge of all the aspects that are required in detail, such as how the different operating systems work, how network protocols work, and how security in a network works.

Understanding Client/Server Networking

The term **network relationship** refers to two different concepts about how one computer makes use of another computer's resources over the network.

Two fundamental types of network relationships exist: peer-to-peer and client/server. These two types of network relationships (in fact, you could almost refer to them as different *network philosophies*) define the very structure of a network. To understand them better, you might compare them to different business management philosophies. A *peer-to-peer network* is much like a company run by a decentralized management philosophy, where decisions are made locally and resources are managed according to the most immediate needs. A client/server network is more like a company that works on centralized management, where decisions are made in a central location by a relatively small group of people. Circumstances exist where both peer-to-peer and client/server relationships are appropriate (just like different business management philosophies) and many networks have aspects of both types within them.

Both peer-to-peer and client/server networks require that certain network **layers** be common. Both types require a physical network connection between the computers and that the same network protocols be used, and so forth. In this respect, no difference exists between the two types of network relationships. The difference comes in whether you spread the shared network resources around to all the computers on the network or use centralized network servers.

Peer-to-Peer Network Relationships

A **peer-to-peer network relationship** defines one in which computers on the network communicate with each other as equals. Each computer is responsible for making its own resources available to other computers on the network. These resources might be files, directories, application programs, or devices such as printers, modems, or fax cards, or any combination thereof. Each computer is also responsible for setting up and maintaining its own security for those resources. Finally, each computer is responsible for accessing the network resources it needs from other peer-to-peer computers and

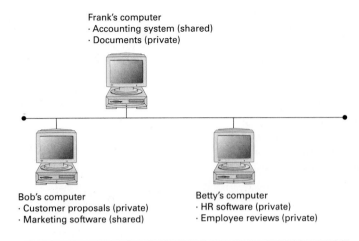

Frank's computer
· Accounting system (shared)
· Documents (private)

Bob's computer
· Customer proposals (private)
· Marketing software (shared)

Betty's computer
· HR software (private)
· Employee reviews (private)

● **Figure 1.1** A peer-to-peer network with resources spread across computers

Even in a pure peer-to-peer network, using a dedicated computer for certain frequently accessed resources is possible. For example, you might host the application and data files for an accounting system on a single workstation and not use that computer for typical workstation tasks, such as word processing, so that all the computer's performance is available for the accounting system. The computer is still working in a peer-to-peer fashion; it's just not used for any other purposes.

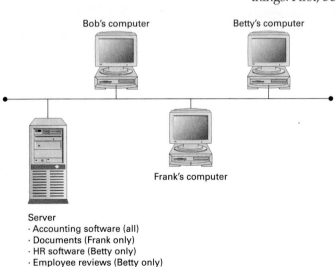

Bob's computer

Betty's computer

Frank's computer

Server
· Accounting software (all)
· Documents (Frank only)
· HR software (Betty only)
· Employee reviews (Betty only)
· Customer proposals (Bob only)
· Marketing software (all)

● **Figure 1.2** A client/server network keeps resources centralized.

for knowing where those resources are and what security is required to access them. Figure 1.1 illustrates how this works.

Client/Server Network Relationships

A **client/server network relationship** is one in which a distinction exists between the computers that make available network resources (the servers) and the computers that use the resources (the *clients*, or *workstations*). A pure client/server network is one in which *all* available network resources—such as files, directories, applications, and shared devices—are centrally managed and hosted, and then are accessed by the client computers. No client computers share their resources with other client computers or with the servers. Instead, the client computers are pure "consumers" of these resources.

The server computers in a client/server network are responsible for making available and managing appropriate shared resources, and for administering the security of those resources. Figure 1.2 shows how resources would be located in such a network.

Pros for Client/Server Networks

Client/server networks offer the opportunity for centralized administration, using equipment best suited to managing and offering each resource. Client/server networks are the type that you almost always see for networks larger than about ten users, and there are quite a few good reasons for this, as follows:

- **Very secure** A client/server network's security comes from several things. First, because the shared resources are located in a centralized area, they can be administered at that point. Managing a number of resources is much easier if those resources are all located on one or two server computers, as opposed to having to administer resources across tens or hundreds of computers. Second, usually the servers are physically in a secure location, such as a lockable server closet. **Physical security** is an important aspect of network security, and it cannot be achieved with a peer-to-peer network. Third, the operating systems on which one runs a client/server network are designed to be secure. Provided that good security and administration practices are in place, the servers cannot be easily "hacked."

- **Better performance** While dedicated server computers are more expensive than standard computer workstations, they also offer considerably better performance and they are optimized to handle the needs of many users simultaneously. They also tend to be more reliable than standard workstation computers.

- **Centralized backup**   Backing up a company's critical data is much easier when it is located on a centralized server. Often, such backup jobs can even be run overnight when the server is not being used and the data is static. Aside from being easier, centralized backups are also much faster than decentralized backups.

- **Very reliable**   While it is true more built-in redundancy exists with a peer-to-peer network, it is also true a good client/server network can be more reliable, overall. Dedicated servers often have much more built-in redundancy than standard workstations. They can handle the failure of a disk drive, power supply, or processor, and continue to operate until the failed component can be replaced. Also, because a dedicated server has only one relatively simple job to do, its complexity is reduced and its reliability increased.

Cons for Client/Server Networks

Balancing the pros of client/server networks, you also need to realize that there are drawbacks, particularly for companies that don't have their own in-house network administration, or who want to minimize the expense of the network as much as possible, as follows:

- **Require professional administration**   Client/server networks usually need some level of professional administration, even for small networks. You can hire a network administrator or you can use a company that provides professional network administration services, but it's important to remember that professional administration is usually required. Knowing the ins and outs of a network operating system is important and requires experience and training.

- **More hardware-intensive**   In addition to the client computers, you also need a server computer; this usually needs to be a pretty "beefy" computer with lots of memory and disk space. Plus, you need a network operating system and an appropriate number of client licenses, which adds at least several thousand dollars to the cost of the server. For large networks, it adds tens of thousands of dollars.

Don't confuse client/server networks with client/server database systems. While the two mean essentially the same thing (conceptually), a client/server database is one where the processing of the database application is divided between the database server and the database clients. The server is responsible for responding to data requests from the clients and supplying them with the appropriate data, while the clients are responsible for formatting, displaying, and printing that data for the user. For example, Novell NetWare or Windows 2000 Server are both client/server network operating systems (NOSs), while Oracle's database or Microsoft's SQL Server are client/server database systems.

In a nutshell, choose a peer-to-peer network for smaller networks with fewer than 10–15 users, and choose a client/server network for anything larger. Because most networks are built on a client/server concept, most of this book assumes such a network.

■ Network Features

Now that you understand the two basic ways computers on a network can interact with each other, understanding the types of things you can do with a network is important. The following sections discuss common network features and capabilities.

File Sharing

Originally, file sharing was the primary reason to have a network. In fact, small and mid-size companies in the mid-1980s usually installed networks just so they could perform this function. Often, this was driven by the need to computerize their accounting systems. Of course, when the networks were in place, sharing other types of files becomes easier as well, such as word processing files, spreadsheets, or other types of files to which many people need regular access.

File sharing requires a shared `directory` or `disk drive` to which many users can access over the network, along with the logic needed to make sure more than one person doesn't make different conflicting changes to a file at the same time (called *file locking*). The reason you don't want more than one person making changes to a file at the same time is that they might both be making *conflicting* changes simultaneously, without either person realizing the problem. Most software programs don't have the ability to allow multiple changes to a single file at the same time and to resolve problems that might arise. (The exception to this rule is that most database programs allow multiple users to access a database simultaneously.)

Additionally, network operating systems that perform file sharing (basically, all of them) also administer the security for these shared files. This security can control, with a fine level of detail, who has access to which files and what kinds of access they have. For example, some users might have permission to view only certain shared files, while others have permission to edit or even delete certain shared files.

Printer Sharing

A close runner-up in importance to file sharing is printer sharing. While it is true that laser printers are currently so inexpensive you can afford to put one in every office, if you wish, sharing laser printers among the users on the network is still more economical overall. Printer sharing enables you to reduce the number of printers you need and also enables you to offer much higher-quality printers. For example, a high-end color laser printers costs about $5,000. Newer digital copiers that can handle large printouts at more than 60 pages per minute can cost more than $30,000. Sharing such printers among many users makes sense.

Printer sharing can be done in several different ways on a network. The most common way is to use `printer queues` on a server. A printer queue holds print jobs until any currently running print jobs are finished and then automatically sends the waiting jobs to the printer. Using a printer queue is efficient for the workstations because they can quickly print to the printer queue without having to wait for the printer to process their job. Another way to share printers on a network is to let each workstation access the printer directly (most printers can be configured so they are connected to the network just like a network workstation), but each must wait its turn if many users are vying for the printer at once.

Networked printers that use printer queues always have a `print server` that handles the job of sending each print job to the printer in turn. The print server function can be filled in a number of ways:

- By a file server with the printer connected directly to it (this option is not usually recommended because it can adversely affect the file server's performance).

- By a computer connected to the network, with the printer connected to that computer. The computer runs special print server software to perform this job.

- Through the use of a built-in print server on a printer's network interface card (NIC). For example, nearly all Hewlett-Packard LaserJets offer an option to include a network card in the printer. This card also contains the computer necessary to act as a print server. This is far less expensive than the previous option.

- Through the use of a dedicated network print server, which is a box about the size of a deck of cards that connects to the printer's parallel or USB port (or even a wireless 802.11a or 802.11b connection) on one end and the network on the other end. Dedicated print servers also contain the computer necessary to act as a print server.

Application Services

Just as you can share files on a network, you can often also share applications on a network. For example, you can have a shared copy of Microsoft Office, or some other application, and keep it on the network server, from where it is also run. When a workstation wants to run the program, it loads the files from the network into its own memory, just like it would from a local disk drive, and runs the program normally. Keeping applications centralized reduces the amount of disk space needed on each workstation and makes it easier to administer the application (for example, with some applications you have to upgrade only the network copy; with others you also must perform a brief installation for each client).

Another application service you can host on the network is a shared installation point for applications. Instead of having to load a CD-ROM onto each workstation, you can usually copy the contents of the CD-ROM to the server, and then have the installation program run from the server for each workstation. This makes installing the applications much faster and more convenient.

E-Mail

An extremely valuable and important network resource these days is e-mail. Not only can it be helpful for communications within a company, but it is also fast becoming a preferred vehicle to communicate with people outside a company.

E-mail systems are roughly divided into two different types: *file-based* and *client/server.* A file-based e-mail system is one that consists of a set of files kept in a shared location on a server. The server doesn't actually do anything beyond providing access to the files. Connections required from a file-based e-mail system and the outside (say, to the Internet) are usually accomplished with a stand-alone computer—called a gateway server—that handles the e-mail interface between the two systems using gateway software that is part of the file-based e-mail system.

A client/server e-mail system is one where an e-mail server contains the messages and handles all the e-mail interconnections, both inside the company and to places outside the company. Client/server e-mail systems, such as Microsoft Exchange or Lotus Notes, are more secure and far more powerful than their file-based counterparts. They often offer additional features that enable you to use the e-mail system to automate different business processes, such as invoicing or purchasing.

Unless a company has at least 50 employees, though, e-mail servers or dedicated e-mail systems are usually overkill and are too costly to purchase and maintain. For these smaller companies, e-mail is still just as important, but there are other strategies to provide e-mail these days that do not require that you run your own internal e-mail system (whether it be file-based or client/server). For example, many small companies instead simply set up a shared connection to the Internet that all of their computers can access, and then set up e-mail accounts either through their `Internet service provider (ISP)` or through a free e-mail service such as Yahoo! Mail or Hotmail.

Remote Access

Another important service for most networks is `remote access` to the network resources. Users use this feature to access their files and e-mail when they're traveling or working from a remote location, such as their homes. Remote access systems come in many different flavors. Some of the methods used to provide remote access include

- Setting up a simple `remote access service (RAS)` connection on a Windows 2000 Server, which can range from using a single modem to a bank of modems.

- Using a dedicated remote access system, which handles many modems and usually includes many computers, each one on its own stand-alone card.

- Employing a workstation on the network and having users dial in using a remote control program like PC Anywhere.

- Setting up a `virtual private network (VPN)` connection to the Internet, through which users can access resources on the company network in a secure fashion through the Internet.

- Installing Windows Terminal Services (on Windows 2000) or Citrix MetaFrame, both of which allow a single Windows 2000 Server to host multiple client sessions, each one appearing to the end user as a stand-alone computer.

As you can see, there are many ways to offer remote access services to users of the network. The right solution depends on what the users need to do remotely, how many users exist (both in total and at any given time), and how much you want to spend.

Wide Area Networks

You should think of a `wide area network (WAN)` as a sort of "metanetwork." A WAN is simply the connection of multiple `local area networks (LANs)` together. This can be accomplished in many different ways, depending on how often the LANs need to be connected to one another how much data capacity (bandwidth) is required, and how great the distance is between the LANs. Solutions range from using full-time leased telephone lines that can carry 56 Kbps of data, to dedicated `DS1` `(T-1)` lines carrying 1.544 Mbps to DS3 lines carrying 44.736 Mbps to other solutions (like private satellites) carrying even higher bandwidths. You can also create a WAN using VPNs over the Internet (although this method usually offers inconsistent bandwidth, it's often the least expensive).

A WAN is created when the users of one LAN need frequent access to the resources on another LAN. For example, a company's `enterprise resource planning (ERP)` system might be running at the headquarters' location, but the warehouse location needs access to it to use its inventory and shipping functions.

As a general rule, if you can design and build a system that doesn't require a WAN, you're usually better off because WAN links are often expensive to maintain. However, the geographic and management structure of a particular company can dictate the use of a WAN.

Internet and Intranet

There's no way around it these days: The `Internet` has become vital to the productivity of most businesses, and handling Internet connectivity on a network is often an important network service. Many different types of services are available over the Internet, including e-mail, the Web, and Usenet newsgroups.

An Internet connection for a network consists of a telecommunications network connection to an ISP, using a connection such as a leased 56 Kbps line, an ISDN line, or a fractional or full DS1 (T-1) connection. This line comes into the building and connects to a box called a `CSU/DSU (channel service unit/data service unit)`, which converts the data from the form carried by the local telephone company to one usable on the LAN. The CSU/DSU is, in turn, connected to a router that routes data packets between the local network. Internet security is provided either by filtering the packets going through the router or by adding a firewall system. A firewall system runs on a computer (or has a computer built into it if it's an appliance device) and offers the highest level of security and administration features.

An `intranet`, as its name suggests, is an internally focused network that mimics the Internet itself. For example, a company might deploy an intranet that hosts a `web server`, and on that web server, the company might place documents such as employee handbooks, purchasing forms, or other information that the company publishes for internal use. Intranets can also host other Internet-type services, such as FTP servers or Usenet servers, or these services can be provided by other tools that offer the same functionality. Intranets are usually not accessible from outside the LAN (although they can be) and are just a much smaller version of the Internet that a company maintains for its own use.

Network Security

Any time you share important and confidential information on a network, you have to carefully consider the security of those resources. Users and management must help set the level of security needed for the network and the different information it stores and they need to participate in deciding who has access to which resources.

Network security is provided by a combination of factors, including features of the network operating system, the physical cabling plant, how the network is connected to other networks, the features of the client workstations, the actions of the users, the security policies of management, and how well the security features are implemented and administered. All of these things come together into a chain, and any single weak link in the chain can cause it to fail. Depending on the company, any failures of network security can have severe consequences, so network security is usually an extremely important part of any network.

■ The OSI Networking Model

The `Open Systems Interconnection (OSI) model` defines all the methods and protocols needed to connect one computer to any other over a network. The OSI model is a conceptual model, used most often in network design and in engineering network solutions. Generally, real-world networks conform to the OSI model, although differences exist between the theory of the OSI model and actual practice in most networks. Still, the OSI model offers an excellent way to understand and visualize how computers network to each other, and it is required knowledge for anyone active in the field of networking. Just about all employers expect networking professionals to be knowledgeable about the OSI model, which defines a basic framework for how modern networks operate. The model also forms a key part of most networking certification tests. Dry the model might be, but it's important to learn it!

The OSI model separates the methods and protocols needed for a network connection into seven different *layers.* Each higher layer relies on services provided by a lower-level layer. As an illustration, if you were to think about a desktop computer in this way, its hardware would be the lowest layer and the operating system drivers—the next-higher layer—would rely on the lowest layer to do their job. The operating system itself, the next-higher layer, would rely on both of the lower layers working properly. This continues all the way up to the point at which an application presents data to you on the computer screen. Figure 1.3 shows the seven layers of the OSI model.

For a complete network connection, data flows from the top layer on one computer, down through all the lower layers, across the wire, and back up the seven layers on the other computer. The following sections discuss each layer in turn, making comparisons to real networking systems as appropriate.

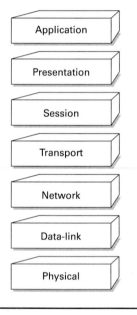

● **Figure 1.3**   The seven layers of the OSI model

The OSI model is sometimes called the `seven-layer model`. It was developed by the International Standards Organization (ISO) in 1983 and is documented as standard 7498.

Physical Layer

The first layer, the `physical layer`, defines the properties of the physical medium used to make a network connection. The physical layer specifications result in a physical medium—a network cable—that can transmit a stream of bits between nodes on the physical network. The physical connection can be either point-to-point (between two points) or multipoint (between many points, such as from one point to many others), and it can consist of either *half-duplex* (one direction at a time) or *full-duplex* (both directions simultaneously) transmissions. Moreover, the bits can be transmitted either in series or in parallel (most networks use a serial stream of bits, but the standard allows for both serial and parallel transmission). The specification for the physical layer also defines the cable used, the voltages carried on the cable, the timing of the electrical signals, the distance that can be run, and so on. A NIC, for example, is part of the physical layer.

Data-Link Layer

The `data-link layer`, layer 2, defines standards that assign meaning to the bits carried by the physical layer. It establishes a reliable protocol through the physical layer so the network layer (layer 3) can transmit its data. The data-link layer typically includes error detection and correction to ensure a reliable data stream. The data elements carried by the data-link layer are called *frames*. Examples of frame types include X.25 and 802.*x* (802.*x* includes both Ethernet and Token Ring networks).

The data-link layer is usually subdivided into two sublayers, called the `logical link control (LLC)` and `media access control (MAC)` sublayers. If used, the LLC sublayer performs tasks such as call setup and termination (the OSI model can be applied to telecommunications networks as well as LANs) and data transfer. The MAC sublayer handles frame assembly and disassembly, error detection and correction, and addressing. The two most common MAC protocols are 802.3 Ethernet and 802.5 Token Ring. Other MAC protocols include 802.12 100BaseVBG, 802.11 Wireless, and 802.7 Broadband.

On most systems, drivers for the NIC perform the work done at the data-link layer.

Network Layer

The `network layer`, layer 3, is where a lot of action goes on for most networks. The network layer defines how data *packets* get from one point to another on a network and what goes into each packet. The network layer defines different packet protocols, such as `Internet Protocol (IP)` and `Internet Protocol Exchange (IPX)`. These packet protocols include source and destination routing information. The routing information in each packet tells the network where to send the packet to reach its destination and tells the receiving computer from where the packet originated.

The network layer is most important when the network connection passes through one or more `routers`, which are hardware devices that examine each packet and, from their source and destination addresses, send the packets to their proper destination. Over a complex network, such as the Internet, a packet might go through ten or more routers before it reaches its destination. On a LAN, a packet might not go through any routers to get to its destination or it might go through one or more.

Note that breaking the network layer (also known as the *packet layer*) into a separate layer from the physical and data-link layers means the protocols defined in this layer can be carried over any variations of the lower layers. So, to put this into real-world terms, an IP packet can be sent over an Ethernet network, a Token Ring network, or even a serial cable connecting two computers to one another. The same would hold true for an IPX packet: If both computers can handle IPX, and they share the lower-level layers (whatever they might be), then the network connection can be made.

Transport Layer

The transport layer, layer 4, manages the flow of information from one network node to another. It ensures that the packets are decoded in the proper sequence and that all packets are received. It also identifies each computer or node on a network uniquely. Different networking systems (such as Microsoft's, or Novell's) implement the transport layer differently, and, in fact, the transport layer is the first layer where key differences occur. Unique at this layer are Windows NT networks, Novell NetWare networks, or any other networking system. Examples of transport layer protocols include Transmission Control Protocol (TCP) and Sequenced Packet Exchange (SPX). Each is used in concert with IP and IPX, respectively.

Session Layer

The session layer, layer 5, defines the connection from a user to a network server, or from a peer on a network to another peer. These virtual connections are referred to as sessions. They include negotiation between the client and host, or peer and peer, on matters of flow control, transaction processing, transfer of user information, and authentication to the network.

Presentation Layer

The presentation layer, layer 6, takes the data supplied by the lower-level layers and transforms it so it can be presented to the system (as opposed to presenting the data to the user, which is handled well outside of the OSI model). The functions that take place at the presentation layer can include data compression and decompression, as well as data encryption and decryption.

Application Layer

The application layer, layer 7, controls how the operating system and its applications interact with the network. The applications you use, such as Microsoft Word or Lotus 1-2-3, aren't a part of the application layer, but they certainly benefit from the work that goes on there. An example of software at the application layer is the network client you use, such as the Windows Client for Microsoft Networks, the Windows Client for Novell Networks, or Novell's Client32 software. It also controls how the operating system and applications interact with those clients.

Understanding How Data Travels Through the OSI Layers

As mentioned earlier in this section, data flows from an application program or the operating system, and then goes through the protocols and devices that make up the seven layers of the OSI model, one by one, until the data arrives at the physical layer and is transmitted over the network connection. The computer at the receiving end reverses this process, with the data coming in at the physical layer, traveling up through all the layers until it emerges from the application layer and is made use of by the operating system and any application programs.

At each stage of the OSI model, the data is "wrapped" with new control information related to the work done at that particular layer, leaving the previous layers' information intact and wrapped within the new control information. This control information is different for each layer, but it includes `headers`, `trailers`, `preambles`, and `postambles`.

So, for example, when data goes into the networking software and components making up the OSI model, it starts at the application layer and includes an application header and application data (the real data being sent). Next, at the presentation layer, a presentation header is wrapped around the data and it is passed to the component at the session layer, where a session header is wrapped around all of the data, and so on, until it reaches the physical layer. At the receiving computer, this process is reversed, with each layer unwrapping its appropriate control information, performing whatever work is indicated by that control information, and passing the data onto the next higher layer. It all sounds rather complex, but it works very well in practice.

Network Hardware Components

This chapter is really about understanding and designing networks, with a "view from 30,000 feet." However, before jumping off into designing a network, it's important to complete this discussion with an overview of the specific hardware that makes networks operate. Understanding the general types of devices you typically encounter in a network is important, not only for planning a network but also for troubleshooting and maintenance.

Servers

A *server* is any computer that performs network functions for other computers. These functions fall into several categories, including

- **File and print servers**, which provide file sharing and services to share network-based printers.

- **Application servers**, which provide specific application services to an application. An example is a server that runs a database that a distributed application uses.

- **E-mail servers**, which provide e-mail storage and interconnection services to client computers.

- **Networking servers**, which can provide a host of different network services. Examples of these services include the automatic assignment of **TCP/IP addresses** (DHCP servers), routing of packets from one network to another (routing servers), encryption/decryption and other security services, VPN servers, and so forth.

- **Internet servers**, which provide Web, Usenet News (NNTP), and Internet e-mail services.

- **Remote access servers**, which provide access to a local network for remote users.

Servers typically run some sort of NOS, such as Windows 2000 Server, Novell NetWare, or UNIX. Depending on the NOS chosen, all the functions previously listed might all be performed on one server or distributed to many servers. Also, not all networks need all the previously services listed.

A number of things distinguish a true server-class computer from a more pedestrian client computer. These things include built-in redundancy with multiple power supplies and fans (for example) to keep the server running if something breaks. They also include special high-performance designs for disk subsystems, memory, and network subsystems to optimize the movement of data to and from the server, the network, and the client computers. Finally, they usually include special monitoring software and hardware that keeps a close eye on the health of the server, warning of failures before they occur. For example, most servers have temperature monitors in them; if the temperature starts getting too high, a warning is issued so the problem can be resolved before it causes failure of any of the hardware components in the server.

Hubs, Routers, and Switches

Hubs, routers, and switches are the most commonly seen "pure" networking hardware. (They're "pure" in the sense that they exist only for networking and for no other purpose.) Many people refer to this class of equipment as "internetworking devices" because that's what they're for. These are the devices to which all the cables of the network are connected and that pass the data along at the physical, data-link, or network layers of the OSI model.

A **hub**, sometimes called a *concentrator*, is a device that connects a number of network cables coming from client computers to a network. Hubs come in many different sizes, supporting from as few as two computers, up to large hubs that can support 60 computers or more. (The most common hub size supports 24 network connections.) All the network connections on a hub share a single **collision domain**, which is a fancy way of saying all the connections to a hub "talk" over a single logical wire and are subject to interference from other computers connected to the same hub. Figure 1.4 shows an example hub and how it is logically wired.

A **switch** is wired very similarly to a hub, and actually looks just like a hub. However, on a switch all of the network connections are on their own collision domain. The switch makes each network connection a private one, and then collects the data from each of the connections and forwards it to a network backbone, which usually runs at a much higher speed than the individual switch connections. Often, switches will be used to connect many hubs to a single network backbone. Figure 1.5 shows a typical switch and hub wiring arrangement.

A *router* routes data packets from one network to another. The two networks connect to the router using their own wiring type and connection type. For example, a router that connected a 10Base-T network to an ISDN telephone line would have two connections: one leading to the 10Base-T network and one leading to the ISDN line provided by the phone company. Routers also usually have an additional connection that a terminal can be connected to; this connection is just used to program and maintain the router.

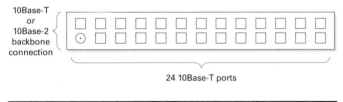

10Base-T
or
10Base-2
backbone
connection

24 10Base-T ports

● **Figure 1.4**   A typical network hub

Cabling and Cable Plants

Many types of network cable exist, but you need to be concerned with only a few of the more common ones. The most common network cable for LANs is `Category 3 (Cat-3)` twisted-pair cable. This cable carries the network signal to each point through four wires (two twisted-pairs). Cat-3 cable is used to support 10Base-T Ethernet networks.

Higher in quality and capability than Cat-3 cable is `Category 5 (Cat-5)` cable. This is similar cable, made up of sets of twisted-pairs, but it contains twice as many pairs as Cat-3 cable. Cat-5 cable is required for 100Base-T networks. You can also use Cat-5 cable to carry two simultaneous Cat-3 network connections.

`Coaxial cable` (called `coax`) is

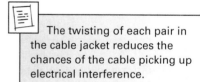

● **Figure 1.5**   Using switches and hubs in concert

not currently used for new cable installations, but you might still come across it in older buildings. Coax cable has a center core of copper (called the `conductor`) surrounded by a plastic wrapper, which is in turn wrapped with braided metal, called the `shield`, and then finally an outer plastic coating. For example, the cable that you use to connect a television to a cable TV network is a type of coax cable (the same coax is used for cable modems, by the way). Most coax cable used for networks is a type called RG-58, which is used for 10Base-2 (thin Ethernet) networks. Another is RG-56, used for ARCnet networks. The different types of coax cable refer to the specifications of the cable, which determines whether a particular network type can make use of the cable. You cannot mix different types of coax cable in a single network, and you must use the correct type for the network you are building.

> The twisting of each pair in the cable jacket reduces the chances of the cable picking up electrical interference.

The term `cable plant` refers to the entire installation of all your network cable. It includes not only the cable run throughout a building, but also the connectors, wall plates, patch panels, and so forth. It's extremely important that a new installation of a cable plant be performed by a qualified contractor trained to install that type of cable. Despite the apparent simplicity of cable, it and its installation are quite complex.

Workstation Hardware

Any computer on a network that is used by people is usually referred to as a `network workstation`. Sometimes such workstations are also called `network clients`. Usually, a network client is an Intel-based PC running some version

Don't confuse a network workstation (a generic term) with workstation-class computers. Workstation-class computers are high-end computers used for computer-aided design, engineering, and high-end graphics work.

You can't design a network of any size without plenty of experience running similar networks. You can manage the overall process by understanding the methodology, but you can't create a good design without experience. If you're new to networking and you have to design a network, make sure you get experienced people on the team—either as consultants or as part of a supplier-led team—and listen carefully to their experience and knowledge. Listening well pays off with a design that will work, rather than one that might look good on paper but won't hold up to actual use.

of Windows, which has an NIC installed into it along with network client software, all of which allow the workstation to participate on the network. Network workstations can also be any other type of computer that includes the necessary network hardware and software, such as an Apple Macintosh or some form of Unix-based computer.

Designing a Network

Regardless of whether you're building a brand new network from scratch or renovating an existing network, the tools you use are much the same, and the process of designing the network is also much the same. The concept of network design is actually simple: You assess the needs that the network must meet and then you design the network to meet those needs. In practice, this process is much more involved, but the idea is straightforward. Even in an evolving network, using network planning to formulate a long-term plan to renovate the network makes sense. So, understanding what you must examine when you build or renovate a network is important.

Network design is not really an exact science. Getting it exactly right the first time is nearly impossible, even with the best design tools and resources available. This is because every network has different demands placed on it, and these demands often interact in surprising ways. Moreover, predicting what new demands will be placed on the network over time, how users will use the network resources, or what other changes you might have to make is almost impossible. The entire situation is both fluid and chaotic. The trick is to do a good job of estimating needs and then do the best job possible to create a design to meet those needs. Having fallback plans is also important, in case some part of the network doesn't perform the way you intended, of if unknown impacts to the network emerge as the business starts to use it. For example, after the network is up and running, you might find that the distribution of bandwidth across segments is poor. You want to know in advance how you can measure and address these types of problems. You might also find storage requirements are much higher or lower than you expected. You need to know what to do if this happens. The real point is this: Network design is a process, and often an iterative process. Your job as a network designer is to get as close as possible to the needed design and then fine-tune the design as needed.

A lot of the network design process is what you decide to make of it. There are simple network design processes, and there are horrendously complex processes that involve dozens of people, complex statistical modeling, and even network simulation software to test a planned design and see if it holds together. Here, you learn a relatively comprehensive process that is straightforward and simple. Using the information in this section, along with a good dose of experience, will yield a flexible network that should easily meet the needs of hundreds of users.

Assess Network Needs

The importance of doing a good job in assessing the needs that a network must meet cannot be overstated. Many adages exist concerning the importance of knowing your goals. "Measure twice and cut once," is one that carpenters use. "Ready, fire, aim," is one that pokes fun at people who don't properly set goals. And hundreds of others exist. The point is this: Before worrying about what network topology to use, what NOS platform to use, how to structure your hubs, bridges, and routers, and what grade of wiring to install, you must know what the network needs to accomplish. Doing a proper job can be tedious, but assessing needs is where you should place the most emphasis during a design process. Failing to do so almost certainly will result in a network that isn't productive for its users.

When assessing needs, you are trying to come up with detailed answers to the following questions:

- How much storage space is required?
- How much bandwidth is required?
- What network services are required?
- What is the budget for the project?

Many information systems (IS) professionals are, at heart, technologists who love to play with the latest technologies. Be careful to avoid giving in to the temptation to design the network around the "hot" technologies and then try to figure out how the needs fit into those technologies (many people mistakenly try to do this). Instead, start with the needs and then find out what technologies support those needs.

These basic questions are fairly easy to answer as a whole, but you need to break them down further to make sure no holes in the network design could lead to problems. For example, it might be easy to determine that the network must be able to support up to 100 Mbps of bandwidth, but you need to know how and when that bandwidth is used. If the accounting department is using 90 percent of the bandwidth when communicating to the accounting server, for example, then naturally you want to put the accounting system's server and its users on their own network segment. You won't recognize such issues and how to address them unless your assessment leads you to determine with some degree of detail how the network resources will be used.

The following sections discuss what you should examine as you learn what a given network must be able to do. No particular order exists in which you should examine these issues and you might find that you must cycle through the list several times to get a complete picture. You also might find a particular company's needs require more or less analysis in each category. Common sense and experience is required when you design a network. The following suggestions are guidelines to start you on the right path.

Applications

A good place to start with a network design is to list and understand the applications that will run on the network. Ultimately, a network is only as good as the work it helps people accomplish, and people do their work most directly through the application software they use. If the applications don't work right, then the users won't work right, so the network has to support the planned applications properly.

Most networks have both common applications and department- and user-specific applications. Most companies usually meet the common application needs through a suite of desktop applications, such as Microsoft Office or Lotus SmartSuite. The following is a list of applications that most companies simply install for all users, whether or not each user needs each one:

- Word processor
- Spreadsheet

- End-user database
- Presentation graphics
- E-mail
- Personal information manager (calendar, contact list, and so forth)
- Virus-scanning software

You can help reduce overall network storage requirements by establishing shared directories in which different groups of people can store and access shared files.

Your first order of business is to determine a number of things about the common applications. You need to know whether all users need to have the entire suite installed, how often different users plan to use the different applications, how many files they will create and store, how large those files might be, and how those files will be shared among users. For example, in a 1,000 user population, you might determine that 90 percent will use word processing to generate an average of ten documents a month, with each document averaging 100KB, and the users probably will want to keep two years' worth of documents on hand at any given time. Yes, these will be educated guesses, but it's important to come up with reasonable estimates. Experience with similar user populations and companies can pay off handsomely in determining these estimates. With this information alone, you know immediately that you need about 24MB of storage per user, or 21.6GB for the word processing population of 900 users, just for word processing documents. For applications where users frequently will share files, you might have to factor in that most users keep personal copies of some files that they also share with others.

Then you come up with the same estimates for the other applications, taking into account their expected size, frequency of creation, and long-term storage requirements.

Don't get bogged down in "analysis paralysis," worrying about whether you can scientifically prove that your estimates are accurate. Instead, make sure that the estimates are reasonable to other network professionals. At a certain point, you need to justify the network design and cost, and, to do this, having reasonable estimates is necessary. Just avoid overdoing it.

After determining the common applications, move on to department-specific applications. This step gets trickier for new networks in new companies because you might not know what applications will be used. For existing companies, you have the advantage of already knowing what departmental applications you need to support. Different departmental applications can have wildly different impacts on the network. For example, an accounting system designed around shared database files needs a different network design than one using a client/server database design. The former relies more on file server performance and is more likely to be bandwidth-sensitive than an efficient client/server application that runs on a dedicated server. If a departmental application is not yet selected, talk with the managers of that department to get their best estimates and then proceed.

Following are common departmental applications you should consider:

- Accounting
- Distribution and inventory control
- Manufacturing/MRP
- Information technology
- Electronic commerce
- Human resources
- Payroll and stock administration
- Publishing

- Marketing support
- Legal
- Other line-of-business applications specific to the company's industry

For each of the departmental applications you identify, you need to ask several questions: How much storage will they consume? Where will the applications be run from (from local computers with data on a server or completely centralized where both the data and the application run on a central computer)? Will they have their own dedicated servers? How much network bandwidth will the application need? How will all these factors change as the company grows?

Finally, while you might not formally include them in your plan, consider user-specific applications that might be run. For example, you might estimate that people in the company's research and development (R&D) group are all likely to run two or three unknown applications as part of their job. If you decide that user-specific applications will have a significant impact on the network, then you should estimate their needs just as you have the other types of applications. If you decide they will have minimal impact, then you might decide either to include a small allowance for them or none at all.

Step-by-Step 1.1

Performing an Application Assessment

ACME Industries is a company that manufactures a number of products, such as magnetic bird seed, giant slingshots, and fake train whistles used by coyotes in Arizona in their pursuit of roadrunners. They have two facilities: one in which all of their manufacturing and distribution is done, and a corporate headquarters that houses all of the office-based functions of the company (such as the executives, salespeople, accounting, and so forth). The company is moving both locations and you are tasked with helping to design the networks in each location. The applications in use are already selected and consist of the following:

Manufacturing Facility (25 employees)	Headquarters Facility (25 employees)
Microsoft Excel	Microsoft Word
	Microsoft Excel
	Microsoft PowerPoint

In reality, virtually any company in the world will have more complex requirements than those noted; however, the steps that you follow to assess the applications will be the same. In this exercise, you will perform an application assessment for a fictional company. To do this, you will need the following:

- A computer running Microsoft Excel or a similar spreadsheet program that you know how to use to create tabular, calculated data

Step 1

Create a table (either on paper or in Excel). In the rows, create a section for each facility, and list one application in each of the rows. For example:

Manufacturing	Headquarters
Microsoft Excel	Microsoft Word
	Microsoft Excel
	Microsoft PowerPoint

Create the following columns for the table:

- Number of users
- Number of files per user per day
- Average size of files
- Number of days to keep online

When complete, your table should resemble the one shown here.

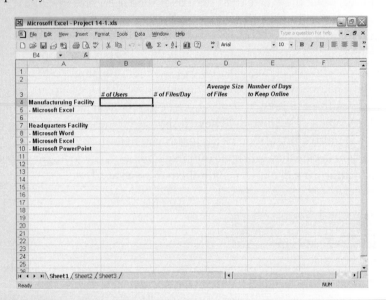

- The table after Step 2

Complete the table using the example values shown in the illustration. In a real assessment, you will need to come up with appropriate real-world estimates for these values.

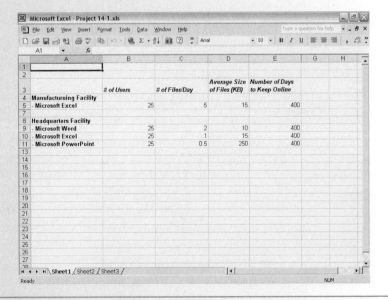

- Example values for the assessment table

Step 4

Using Excel, or a calculator, calculate the total storage requirements for each application and for each facility. The illustration shows these values. Note that in the example, size values are all in kilobytes.

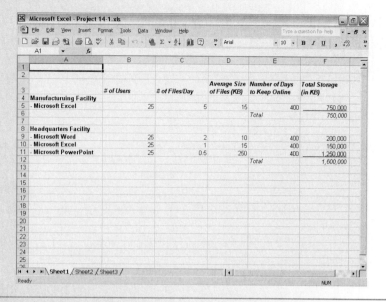

	# of Users	# of Files/Day	Average Size of Files (KB)	Number of Days to Keep Online	Total Storage (in KB)
Manufacturuing Facility					
- Microsoft Excel	25	5	15	400	750,000
				Total	750,000
Headquarters Facility					
- Microsoft Word	25	2	10	400	200,000
- Microsoft Excel	25	1	15	400	150,000
- Microsoft PowerPoint	25	0.5	250	400	1,250,000
				Total	1,600,000

- Total file storage requirements

Allowing for Growth and Model Errors

While simplified, Step-by-Step 1.1 illustrates how you can approach calculating storage requirements for a network. In the real world, you will also add in a "fudge factor" to allow for inaccuracies in your model. You will have to come up with a fudge factor that you're comfortable with for the actual environment, and this will be guided by the importance of the storage requirements, the budget available, and any other factors that you think important. I typically recommend increasing your totals by at least 50 percent. In some cases, particularly if the incremental storage cost is minimal, you might increase your totals by 100 percent.

Using the model shown in Step-by-Step 1.1, you would need a minimum of 750MB of disk storage for the manufacturing facility and 1.6GB for the headquarters facility. In the real world, you would likely purchase a file server with 2GB+ for the manufacturing facility, and 5GB+ for the headquarters facility, which should allow plenty of room for errors in the model and for unforeseen growth.

Users

After you know what applications the network must support, you can estimate how many users need to be supported and what applications each user will use. Estimating total users will likely be easier because the company should already have a business plan or long-range budget from which you can derive these estimates. Your user estimates should be reasonably granular: know the number of users in each department in the company as well as the company's total number of users.

You should estimate how many users will need to be supported immediately, in one year, in three years, and in five years. Even though five years is a distant horizon to use for an estimate, this information is important to know during the design process. Different growth rates suggest different network designs, even at the inception of the network. A company estimating it will have 100 users immediately, 115 users in one year, 130 users in three years, and 150 users in five years needs a different network design than a company estimating 100 users immediately, 115 users in one year, 300 users in three years, and 1,000 users in five years. In the latter case, you must invest more in a design that is more quickly scaleable and you are likely to spend much more at inception to build the network, even though the network will have the same number of users in the first two years.

Knowing the number of users isn't enough, though. You need to know more about the users. At a minimum, consider the following questions to determine if any of the following will be important factors for the users generally or for subgroups of the users:

- **Bandwidth requirements**   Aside from the bandwidth required to save and retrieve files, send and receive e-mail, and perform an average amount of browsing on the Internet, do any users need significant amounts of bandwidth? For example, will scientists download a fresh copy of the human genome from the Internet once a week? Will groups of users need to exchange large quantities of data among different sites? Will any users be running video conferencing software over your LAN and WAN/Internet connection? How much web browsing do you expect the network's users to do? Will people be sending large attachments frequently through Internet e-mail?

- **Storage requirements**   Will any group of users need significantly more storage capacity than the overall average you already determined? For example, will an electronic imaging group catalog millions of documents into image files on a server? If so, how many people need access to that data? Will the accounting group need to keep the previous ten years of financial information online? Will the company use or install an executive information system where all the managers have query capability into the company's accounting, distribution, and manufacturing systems, and, if so, how much additional bandwidth or server performance could that capability require?

- **Service requirements**   Will any groups of users need additional network services not needed by most users? For example, does part of the company do work of such sensitivity that it should be separated from the rest of the LAN by a network firewall? Will a subset of users need direct inward fax capability?

When examining user bandwidth requirements, remember to look at the timeliness of the bandwidth needs. If certain known activities require a lot of bandwidth and must be carried out during the normal workday, that high-bandwidth use might interfere with the performance of the rest of the network. Therefore, make sure to estimate both average and peak bandwidth needs.

Network Services

Next, you should look at the services that the network must provide. These can vary widely in different companies. A very basic network might need only file and print services, plus perhaps Internet connectivity. A more complex network will need many additional services. Consider which of the following types of services the network you are designing will need to provide, as well as any others that are specific to the company:

- File and print services
- Backup and restore services
- Internet web browsing
- FTP and Telnet
- Internet or external e-mail
- Internet security services
- Dial-out from LAN through a modem pool
- Dial-out to LAN through a modem pool
- Fax into LAN (manually distributed or automatically distributed)
- Dynamic Host Configuration Protocol (DHCP) services
- Centralized virus-protection services
- WAN services to other locations
- Streaming Internet radio and other media
- Voice over IP (VoIP)

For each service, you must answer a number of questions. First, you need to know the storage and bandwidth requirements for each service, and any other impacts they will make. For example, a fax-in service might itself require a small amount of storage space, but all the fax bitmaps that users will end up storing might have a large impact on total storage needs. Second, you need to know how the service is to be provided. Usually, this means that you need to know what server will host the service. Some services require such little overhead that you can easily host them on a server that does other jobs. A DHCP server, which requires minimal resources, is a good example of such a service. On the other hand, an e-mail system might require such high resources that you must plan to host it on its own dedicated server. Third, you need to know what users or groups of users need which services. This is because, to minimize backbone traffic, you might need to break the network down into smaller segments and locate frequently used services for a particular user population on the same segment as the users use.

Security and Safety

The preceding considerations are all related to the bits and bytes required by different parts of the network. Security and safety concern the company's need to keep information secure—both inside and outside a company—and to keep the company's data safe from loss. You need to know how important these two issues are before attempting to set down a network design on paper.

For both these considerations, a trade-off exists between cost and effectiveness. However, different companies and departments have different sensitivities to these issues, indicating that more or less money should be spent on these areas. Some applications might be perfectly well suited to keeping their data on a striped RAID 0 array of disks, where the risk of loss is high (relative to other RAID levels), because the data might be static and easy to restore from tape if the disk array is lost. Other applications might require the highest level of data-loss safety possible, with fail-over servers each having mirrored RAID 1 or RAID 10 arrays and online tape backup systems updating a backup tape every hour or for every transaction. Similarly, some companies might work with data that is so sensitive that they must install the best firewalls, perhaps even two levels of firewalls, and hire full-time professionals dedicated to keeping the data secure. Other companies might be happy if they are only reasonably secure.

The point is that you must determine how important these issues are to the company for which you are designing the network. Then, you can propose different solutions to address these needs and factor these needs into the rest of your design.

Growth and Capacity Planning

The final area to consider is the expected growth of the network, particularly if the company expects this growth to be substantial. As mentioned earlier in this chapter, a network designed for a rapidly growing company looks different from one for a slowly growing company, even if both companies start out at the same size. In the former case, you want a design that you can quickly and easily expand without having to replace much of the existing hardware and software. In the latter case, you can get by with a simpler network design.

You want to consider the impact of growth on the different parts of the network that you've already examined (applications, users, and services), because linear growth does not always mean a matching linear impact to the network. Assuming linear growth, the impact to the network might be much lower, or much higher, than the curve.

For example, Ethernet scales linearly, but only up to a point. When the network starts to become saturated, performance starts to drop rapidly because of the chaotic nature of Ethernet's collision detection scheme. Consider a 10 Mbps Ethernet network transmitting 3 Mbps of traffic. This traffic probably flows smoothly, with few collisions and few retransmissions required. Push the network demand up to 4–5 Mbps, however, and its performance grinds to a halt as the network becomes saturated and you end up with as many collisions and retransmissions as real data. In fact, the amount of good data flowing over a saturated Ethernet network will actually be less than the amount flowing over a less-saturated network.

You can also find examples where an increase in demand doesn't cause a corresponding increase in network or server load. For example, the server load for a complex e-mail system might increase only by a small amount if you doubled the number of users because the system's overhead generates

Be careful not only to consider how applications behave as they scale, but also how they behave as they are scaled in your planned network environment. Different network operating systems, network topologies, and client and server computers will all affect how well a particular application can support growth.

most of the load. Or, the storage requirements for an accounting system might not double just because you keep twice as much data in it to accommodate the overhead that might consume most of the existing space. Alternatively, that same accounting system might consume four times as much storage space if you double the data storage, because its indexing scheme is relatively inefficient. The point is that you need to know how different applications scale with increased use. The vendors of the main applications you will use should be able to provide useful data in this regard.

Step-by-Step 1.2

Developing a Scenario Plan

The preceding step-by-step showed a basic approach to assessing network storage requirements. When performing any important planning activity, you should also do something called "scenario planning," in which you explore how changes to the model will affect the answers you come up with. This lets you assess the impacts of different possible future scenarios and develop plans to meet those possibilities should they occur. To complete this step-by-step, you will need the following:

- A computer running Microsoft Excel or a similar spreadsheet program that you know how to use to create tabular, calculated data
- The spreadsheet you created in Step-by-Step 1.1

Step 1

Starting with the model you built in the preceding step-by-step, assess the different storage requirements using the following changes:

- Increase users at both locations to 100.
- Increase the size of the average PowerPoint file to 1MB.
- Increase the number of Excel files generated at the headquarters facility to three per day.

Step 2

Based on the changed resulting storage totals for each location, consider how you would meet the increased needs.

The three changes shown, all very reasonable changes that may occur after setting up a network, increase the storage requirements at the manufacturing facility by a factor of four and at the headquarters by a factor of ten. How would you address these needs if they became apparent only several months after setting up the network that you planned earlier? Many possibilities exist:

- Add additional disk drives to the servers.
- Replace existing disk drives in the servers with larger-capacity units.
- Add an external storage cabinet to any servers that already have the maximum internal storage installed.
- Install network-attached storage (NAS).
- Add incremental servers, dividing up the data that each must hold.

■ Meeting Network Needs

After you complete your assessment (by this point, you're probably sick of the assessment process!), you can then start working on finding ways to meet all the needs you've identified. This process is largely holistic and is not worked through by following a series of steps and ending up with a single answer, like an equation. Instead, you should start by mapping out the various parts of the network, considering the three main topics discussed in this section, and "build a picture" of the network design. The design that you create will incorporate all you learned during the assessment process, taking into account your experience and the advice you get to devise a concrete design that results in an equipment list, specifications, and a configuration.

Seeking criticism of your design from other network professionals, who might have valuable experience that you can then factor into your design, is important. No single networking professional exists who has seen and had to cope with all possible design needs, so you want to combine the advice of as many seasoned people as you can.

Choose Network Type

You probably want to start the design by choosing a network type. This should be a relatively straightforward decision, based on the overall bandwidth requirements for the network. For most new networks, you almost certainly will decide to use one of the flavors of Ethernet. Ethernet is by far the most common type of network installed today and it's an easy default choice.

You also need to decide what level of Ethernet you need. For wiring to the desktop, you should choose 100Base-T. It is reliable and provides plenty of capacity for most needs. For your network backbone, you can usually use a higher-bandwidth connection, such as 1000Base-T, without incurring too much additional cost.

Choose Network Structure

Next, decide how you plan to structure the network. In other words, how will you arrange and wire the various hubs, switches, and routers that the network needs? This is probably the trickiest thing to determine because it's hard to predict how much data must flow from any given set of nodes to any other set of nodes. Still, you should have estimates based on your assessment work that will help. If you can identify expected heavy traffic patterns, you should also draw a network schematic with these patterns indicated to help you sort it out. Remember the following tips:

- Ethernet's CDMA/CD collision handling means that an Ethernet network will handle only about one-third of its rated speed. In other words, a 10Base-T segment, which is rated at 10 Mbps, will handle about 3.3 Mbps in practice. The same holds true for 100Base-T, which will handle about 33 Mbps of actual data before starting to degrade.

- Whenever possible, use *"home run" wiring* for all nodes to a single wiring closet or server room. (Home run wiring means that each network cable runs from each workstation to a single location.) Doing so enables you to change the network structure more easily (for example, to break segments into smaller segments) as needs change.

- Except in the smallest networks, plan on a network backbone to which the hubs connect. An Ethernet switch rather than a non-switching hub should handle the backbone, so each hub constitutes a single segment or collision domain. You still must plan to keep each segment's traffic below the Ethernet saturation point, but this structure will give you plenty of flexibility to meet this goal.

- These days, Ethernet switches are inexpensive enough that you can actually use them as hubs. It's not at all unreasonable to use current hardware to wire everything at 100Base-T using only switches, and it's not much more expensive than using a combination of hubs and switches.

- The physical building might dictate how you structure your network. For example, a building larger than 200 meters in any dimension probably means you won't be able to employ a home-run wiring scheme for all your nodes. This is because twisted-pair Ethernet usually reaches only 100 meters (that includes routing around building obstructions, patch cables, and other things that make the actual cable distance longer than you might measure on a map of the building).

- For multifloor buildings that are too big for a home-run wiring scheme, consider running the backbone vertically from floor to floor and then have a wiring closet on each floor that contains the hubs to service that floor's nodes. The wiring from the closet on each floor then fans out to each of the nodes on that floor.

- Consider running the backbone speed at ten times the hub/desktop network speed. If you're using 10Base-T hubs to connect to the desktop computers, plan on a 100Base-T backbone. If you're using 100Base-T to the desktop, consider a gigabit network connection such as 1000Base-T for the backbone.

- Most of the time, most nodes do the majority of their communication to one or two servers on the network. If you are planning department-specific servers or if you can identify similar patterns, make sure that each server is on the same segment as the nodes that it primarily serves.

- If your servers tend not to be assigned to support departments and instead support the entire company, make sure that the servers are directly connected to the backbone's Ethernet switch.

- If you have any high-bandwidth users, consider keeping them on a segment separate from the rest of the network (if appropriate) and also consider upgrading the speed of that segment to 100 Mbps or 1,000 Mbps if needed.

- As you start to implement the network, carefully watch the ratio of collision packets to data packets. If the number of collisions on any segment climbs to 5 to 7 percent of the total number of packets, performance is starting to suffer; you need to investigate the cause and find a way to decrease this ratio. You can usually do so by breaking the segment into smaller pieces, or by configuring capable switches into what is called a virtual LAN, or VLAN, unless you know of another way to reduce the amount of traffic.

Choose Servers

When choosing servers for a network, start by determining what network operating system you will use. For PC-centric networks, the decision is usually between Novell NetWare 5 and Windows 2000 Server. Whenever possible, avoid using both, because supporting two NOS systems makes managing the servers much more difficult. You're better off compromising on a single NOS platform than trying to support both.

Next, list the various network services that your servers must provide. You need to look for efficient ways to host these various services on your servers, balancing a number of factors:

- All else being equal, using more small servers to host fewer services each is more reliable than using fewer large servers to each host many services.

- Conversely, having more small servers increases your chance of having a server fail at any given time.

- Using more small servers is more expensive and requires more maintenance than using fewer large servers.

- If you plan to use more than one server, consider which services should be redundant on another server or how you plan to deal with the failure of any server.

Using your assessment information, you can easily determine how much storage capacity your servers will need. However, it's much harder to know how capable each server should be in terms of processor power, installed RAM, and other features, such as bus configuration. For these specifications, you need to rely on the advice of the NOS vendor and the manufacturer of the servers that you are considering. Fortunately, both Microsoft and Novell have published tests and recommendations for sizing servers given different service and user loads. Many first-tier server manufacturers also have such data to help you choose an actual server model and its specifications.

Chapter I Review

■ Chapter Summary

After reading this chapter and completing the exercises, you should understand the following.

Understand Client/Server Networking

- Network relationship refers to two different concepts about how one computer makes use of another computer's resources over the network. Two types of network relationships are peer to peer-to-peer and client/server.

- A client/server network relationship is one in which a distinction exists between the computers that provide network resources (the servers) and the computers that use the resources (the clients and workstations).

- The server computers in a client/server network provide and manage appropriate shared resources. They are also responsible for the security of those resources.

- A peer-to-peer network relationship can be defined as one in which computers on the network communicate with each other as equals.

- Network layers are common in peer-to-peer as well as client/server networks. Also, it is mandatory that a physical network connection exists between computers using the same network protocols.

- Physical security is an important aspect of network security. A peer-to-peer network is not ideal for this.

- Dedicated server computers ensure good performance and are optimized to handle many users' needs in a reliable manner.

- Centralizing critical data aids in creating faster and more secure backups.

Learn Network Features

- File sharing can be facilitated by having a shared directory or disk drive that users can access over the network. It logically follows that users should be prevented from making conflicting changes to a file at the same time. File locking is a useful feature in this regard.

- A printer queue holds print jobs until any currently running print job is finished and then automatically sends the waiting jobs to the printer.

- A print server handles the job of sending each print job to the printer in turn.

- Hosting a shared installation point on the network ensures that the installation of applications is rapid.

- E-mail systems are available in two flavors—file-based and client/server.

- An Internet connection for a network comprises a telecommunications network connection to an ISP, using a connection such as a leased 56 Kbps line, an ISDN line, or a fractional or full DS1 (T-1) connection.

- An intranet is an internally focused smaller version of the Internet.

- Network security is determined by several factors, including features of the network operating system, the physical cabling plant, the connection mechanism of the network to other networks, the features of the client workstations, the actions of the users, the security policies of the management, and the degree of implementation and administration of security features.

Understand the OSI Networking Model

- The Open Systems Interconnection (OSI) model defines all the methods and protocols needed to connect one computer to any other over a network. It is used typically in network design and in engineering network solutions.

- The physical layer defines the properties of the physical medium (network cable) used to make a network connection. The physical medium transmits a stream of bits between nodes on the physical network. The bits can be transmitted in serial or in parallel.

- The transport layer manages the flow of information from one network node to another.

- The data-link layer defines standards that assign meaning to the bits carried by the physical layer. It establishes a reliable protocol through the physical layer so that the network layer can transmit data contained in it.

- The session layer defines the connection from a user to a network server or from a peer on a network to another peer. These connections are called sessions.

- The presentation layer takes the data supplied by the lower-level layers and presents it to the system.

- The application layer controls the interaction of the operating system and its applications.

Servers

- A server is any computer that performs network functions for other computers.

- File and print servers provide file-sharing and printer-sharing services.

- Application servers provide specific application services to an application.

- E-mail servers perform the task of providing e-mail storage and interconnection services to client computers.

- Networking servers provide a host of network services that include the automatic assignment of TCP/IP addresses, routing of packets from one network to another, and security services such as encryption and decryption, VPN servers, and the like.

- Remote access servers provide access to a local network for remote users.

- Gateway servers handle the e-mail interface between the two systems using gateway software. This software is part of the file-based e-mail system.

Hubs, Routers, and Switches

- A hub, sometimes called a concentrator, is a device that connects a number of network cables coming from client computers to a network.

- A switch makes each network connection a private one. It then collects the data from each of the connections and forwards it to a network backbone, which usually runs at a much higher speed than the individual switch connections. Switches are often used to connect many hubs to a single network backbone.

- A router routes data packets from one network to another. The two networks connect to the router using their own wiring type and connection type. Routers also possess an additional connection that can be used to program and maintain the router.

Cabling and Cable Plants

- Category 3 (Cat-3) cable carries the network signal to each point through four wires (two twisted-pairs). Cat-3 cable is used to support 10Base-T Ethernet networks.

- Category 5 (Cat-5) cable comprises sets of twisted-pairs but contains twice as many pairs as Cat-3.

- Coax cable has a center core of copper (called the conductor) surrounded by a plastic wrapper, which is in turn wrapped with braided metal, called the shield. The outer coating is of plastic.

- Cable plant refers to the entire installation of all the network cable. This includes the cable installed throughout a building as well as the connectors, wall plates, and patch panels.

Workstation Hardware

- Network workstation refers to any computer on a network.

- True server-class computers include built-in redundancy with multiple power supplies. They also consist of special high-performance designs for disk subsystems, memory, and network subsystems to optimize the movement of data to and from the server, the network, and the client computers. They include special monitoring software and hardware as well.

■ Key Terms

application layer (10)

application servers (11)

cable plant (13)

Category 3 (Cat-3) (13)

Category 5 (Cat-5) (13)

channel service unit/data service unit (CSU/DSU) (7)

client/server network relationship (2)

coaxial (coax) cable (13)

collision domain (12)

compression (10)

conductor (13)

data-link layer (9)

decompression (10)

decryption (10)

directory (4)

disk drive (4)

DS1 (T-1) (7)

e-mail servers (11)

encryption (10)

enterprise resource planning (ERP) (7)

file and print servers (11)

gateway server (5)

headers *(11)*
hub *(12)*
Internet *(7)*
Internet Protocol (IP) *(9)*
Internet Protocol Exchange
  (IPX) *(9)*
Internet servers *(11)*
Internet service provider *(6)*
intranet *(7)*
layers *(1)*
local area networks (LANs) *(6)*
logical link control (LLC) *(9)*
media access control (MAC) *(9)*
network clients *(13)*
network layer *(9)*

network operating system
  (NOS) *(3)*
network relationship *(1)*
network workstation *(13)*
networking servers *(11)*
Open Systems Interconnection
  (OSI) model *(8)*
peer-to-peer network
  relationship *(1)*
physical layer *(8)*
physical security *(2)*
postambles *(11)*
preambles *(11)*
presentation layer *(10)*
print server *(4)*
printer queues *(4)*

remote access *(6)*
remote access servers *(11)*
remote access service (RAS) *(6)*
routers *(9)*
session layer *(10)*
sessions *(10)*
seven-layer model *(8)*
shield *(13)*
switch *(12)*
TCP/IP addresses *(11)*
trailers *(11)*
transport layer *(10)*
virtual private network (VPN) *(6)*
web server *(7)*
wide area network *(6)*

■ Key Term Quiz

Use the Key Terms list to complete the sentences that
follow. (Not all terms will be used.)

1. <u>routers</u> are hardware devices that route data
    packets from one network to another.

2. <u>Physical Security</u> is an important aspect of network
    security that cannot be achieved with a peer-to-
    peer network.

3. File sharing requires a shared <u>directory</u> or
    <u>disk drive</u> that many users can access over
    the network.

4. Networked printers equipped with the facility of
    printer queues have a <u>Print Server</u> that sends each
    print job to the printer in turn.

5. E-mail systems are generally of two types,
    namely, <u>file based</u> and <u>client Server</u>.

6. <u>Gateway Server</u> controls the e-mail interface between
    two systems using gateway software, which is
    part of the file-based e-mail system.

7. A <u>client Server</u> comprises an e-mail server that
    holds messages and handles all the e-mail
    interconnections, both internal and external to
    the company.

8. The <u>remote access</u> feature enables users to access
    files and e-mails from a remote location or while
    traveling.

9. <u>intranet</u> are smaller versions of the Internet
    that cannot be accessed from outside the local
    area network.

10. _____ also called the _____ offers an
    excellent way to understand and visualize how
    computers network to each other

■ Multiple-Choice Quiz

1. Which layer is divided into two sublayers?

    a. Physical layer

    b. Session layer

    c. Data-link layer

    d. Network layer

2. Which of the following is true of the network layer?

    a. Handles frame assembly and disassembly,
       plus error detection

    b. Defines how data packets get from one point
       to another on a network

    c. Assigns meaning to the bits carried by the
       physical layer

    d. Presents the data provided by lower levels to
       the system

3. An NIC is part of which layer?

    a. Transport layer

    b. Physical layer

   c. Application layer

   d. Network layer

4. X.25 and 802.x are examples of what?

   a. Frames

   b. MAC protocols

   c. Sublayers

   d. Serial cables

5. What device connects a number of network cables coming from client computers to a network?

   a. Router

   b. Network

   c. Header

   d. Hub

6. What action will prevent two users from making conflicting changes to the same file?

   a. Disabling the share option of a file

   b. Reducing access levels

   c. File locking

   d. Placing files in local drive

7. What device controls print jobs until currently running ones are completed?

   a. Print server

   b. Network printer

   c. Network administrator

   d. Print queue

8. Which of the following consists of a set of files placed on a shared location on the mail server?

   a. Shared file folder

   b. File-based e-mail system

   c. Client/server e-mail system

   d. Mail folders

9. Which of the following enables users to access company resources on its network in a secure manner via the Internet?

   a. Dedicated remote access system

   b. Remote access service connection

   c. Providing users with a dial-up program

   d. Setting up a virtual private network

10. What type of network is necessary when users of one LAN require access on a frequent basis to resources located on another LAN?

   a. MAN

   b. WLAN

   c. WAN

   d. VPN

11. The OSI model separates methods and protocols into how many layers?

   a. Five

   b. Ten

   c. Seven

   d. Four

12. What performs the tasks of call setup, termination, and data transfer?

   a. Router

   b. Logical link control sublayer

   c. Media access control sublayer

   d. Hub

13. Which layer ensures that packets sent over the network are decoded sequentially and also confirms receipt of the packets?

   a. Transport

   b. Network

   c. Physical

   d. Session

14. What are virtual connections from a user to a network server called?

   a. Protocols

   b. Sessions

   c. Frames

   d. Nodes

15. What is the center core of copper in coax cables called?

   a. Connector

   b. Shield

   c. Cable jacket

   d. Conductor

■ Essay Quiz

1. Write a brief note on the functions of the network layer.

2. Providing remote access is an important service that a network needs to carry out. Give a brief description of the methods that can be used.

3. Give a brief listing of the pros and cons of using client/server networks.

4. There are many ways in which a print server function can be deployed. Briefly examine each one.

Lab Projects

• Lab Project 1.1

Perform an assessment of the application requirements for a mid-sized company that is shifting location, and hence requires creation of a new network. Keep in mind the number of users, storage requirements, duration of application use, and the like.

• Lab Project 1.2

Set up remote access for personnel who frequently travel but still need to access to network resources. Try out each of the following methods.

❶ Set up a remote access service connection on a Windows 2000 Server.

❷ Deploy a dedicated remote access system.

❸ Employ a workstation on the network and ask users to dial in with the help of a popular remote control program.

# chapter 2

Networking with Unix and Linux

In this chapter, you will learn how to

- Install and configure Red Hat Linux 7.3 server
- Employ basic Linux skills
- Manage files and folders
- Use the Gnome Desktop
- Configure Linux

The **Linux** operating system, which is essentially a version of Unix, has gained a fairly wide following in the field of networking in recent years. This is due in part to the inherent reliability and capability of Unix-type operating systems and in part to the fact that Linux is much less expensive than other alternatives. At any rate, its importance has made understanding Linux critical for networking professionals, and it is also important in the field of client/server networking. Most client/server databases, for example, offer Linux versions. The most popular version of Linux in the business world is **Red Hat Linux**, which you learn about in this chapter.

Installing and Configuring Red Hat Linux Server

A relative newcomer to the server field gives you yet another choice when selecting your networking products. Red Hat Linux worked its way into the industry by providing free software, and it has developed that product line into a very viable alternative. If you decide to use Red Hat Linux products on your network, you should acquire the latest version of the server software. Red Hat Linux 7.3 was used to demonstrate this vendor's network operating system because it's still in wide use and is very stable. At the time of this writing, Red Hat Linux 9 is available, and version 10 is in beta testing. While the installation procedures given here will not make you an expert on using Red Hat Linux products, they *will* build you an operational Red Hat Linux server.

Preparing for the Server Installation

You must carefully prepare for a Red Hat Linux server installation as you would for a NetWare or Windows server installation to avoid as many problems as possible. The Red Hat Linux installation process has most of the input screens earlier in the setup process than in either Microsoft or Novell setups, but the software setup itself is not as thorough in deciding what components make up your system so it can determine what new things it needs to install. Therefore, when getting ready to set up your server, make sure the computer meets the requirements, operates properly, and includes all the necessary drivers. This will help ensure a complete setup and consistent trouble-free operation after installation.

Checking Hardware Compatibility

As with the other two operating systems, you need a computer to act as the server. Again, because this server will be used in a classroom, it will probably be similar to your workstations and won't be as powerful as most companies would need a server to be. Like Novell and Microsoft, Red Hat Linux also gives different sets of requirements for its operating systems. Because they can also operate in just a text-only mode that doesn't need a graphical user interface, some of the Red Hat Linux requirements have minimum requirements, recommended requirements, and also text-mode requirements. Unlike the other operating systems, however, most of Red Hat's documentation is available on the company's web site. Keep this URL handy during the installation and when operating your server: `www.redhat.com/docs/manuals`.

In your lab, you will be lucky if you meet the Red Hat Linux minimum requirements, but this should not hamper your efforts. With this operating system, as with any other products you learn about in the classroom, simply seeing it run will give you important experience. The minimum requirements for a Red Hat Linux server are a Pentium class computer with a Pentium 200 MHz processor, 32MB of RAM for a text-mode installation and 64MB for graphical mode (but 96MB is recommended). The installation also requires at least 650MB of hard disk space or 4.5GB of available hard disk space for a full install (plus additional space for any files you will be storing on the server).

Red Hat Linux, like Microsoft Windows 2000, includes another product that will help you decide whether your equipment will be supported by its operating system. On its web site is a Hardware Compatibility List (HCL) at `http://hardware.redhat.com/hcl/`. That list identifies all the hardware that has passed Red Hat's `Ready Tests` (Red Hat's equivalent of Microsoft's extensive component compatibility testing) before the latest software's release. This list should be reviewed before installing a server. It lists alternative search techniques that you can use when searching through the listed products that are compatible with the latest release of the operating system.

In addition, the installation guide on the Red Hat web site includes a form that gives you a systems requirement table, listing the items you should have information about prior to beginning the installation. This form can be found in the guide at `www.redhat.com/docs/manuals/linux/ RHL-7.3-Manual/install-guide/`.

Checking Hardware Configuration

Linux recommends using a boot-enabled CD-ROM drive for installations but provides alternative boot methods as well. You will need a high-density 3½-inch floppy drive for the installation if your CD is not bootable. You also need information about your monitor and display adapter and the network operating system software that you plan to install. For the graphical installation, you should also have a mouse.

Testing Server Hardware

In order to test that your server's hardware functions properly, it is a good idea to rebuild your selected computer's hard disk drive and start with a fresh installation (a new install done so that nothing remains on your hard drive from a previous system). Although Red Hat Linux products wipe your hard drive clean by booting from the CD and building all new partitions during the installation (and deleting any unnecessary partitions to get the required free space), it is good to know how to perform these procedures for older equipment and to understand what is and is not performed automatically for you. When you do this, you will end up with the primary DOS partition being the only partition on your hard drive when you start the server installation.

Using FDISK to Remove Partitions   You should use `FDISK` (the DOS command for partitioning fixed disks) to delete all the existing partitions, including the primary DOS partition, and re-create only a primary DOS partition. When you are prompted for the size of the partition, change the setting from 100 percent to 500MB. That partition size will work no matter whether you install Linux, Novell, or Microsoft server software. However, during the server installation, all partitions in the needed space will be removed.

Removing NT Partitions   Should you decide that you want to reuse a Windows NT or 2000 server or workstation as a Linux server, you do not have to remove the NT partitions prior to installing your new operating system. You should still check your drive with FDISK to verify proper operation but you will completely remove all partitions during the Linux operating system's installation procedure.

Installing Your Drivers   You should continue to install DOS onto your rebuilt server's hard disk drive by following the simple installation steps found in the DOS 6.21 or 6.22 setup disks, and you should try out any drivers you have for your equipment. During the actual Red Hat Linux server installation, the installer uses its extensive driver base and may overwrite the drive configurations you installed as it automatically selects updated drivers.

Because Red Hat Linux server installations use CD-ROMs, you should run the installation software for your CD-ROM drive to install your CD-ROM drivers in DOS. Your installation will go more smoothly if you connect both your hard drive and your CD-ROM drive directly to your motherboard as IDE drives, rather than using the disk controller cards found in older equipment. There will be fewer configuration errors when the installer needs to know which driver to use. Your computer should also be configured so that one of its options includes booting from the CD-ROM drive. Because this connection is done inside your system unit, you should ask your instructor about how your computer is configured.

You should also load your mouse drivers to ensure that the mouse works for your **graphical user interface (GUI)**. In the past, the user interface was simply text-based, and you entered information by typing text commands into a console. Now with the more graphically oriented interfaces that are available for Red Hat Linux servers (such as Gnome and K Desktop Environment, or KDE), users are becoming more accustomed to working with graphical interfaces—pointing at icons and clicking on objects instead of typing text commands. Operating server consoles has thus become more user friendly. You'll see these newer graphical interfaces during the installation when you are asked to select the packages (which are actually sets of available applications). The Linux installer will piece together the customized environment you choose.

Your network interface card's installation disks should also be available when you start installing the server software because you may need the network card settings. You should confirm that your NIC manufacturer has an updated driver. Most manufacturers have new drivers available on the Internet, and your instructor has probably already checked the Web for your driver's availability.

Some Linux Specifics

One of the main attractions of using Linux that its supporters point to is its open source code. Not only can you view the operating system's actual programming code, but you can change it as well. Unlike Microsoft and Novell, which protect their program code, you are encouraged to look at how things work in Linux and to make changes to nearly anything you want. You are then encouraged to share your changes with all other Linux users. Because you are forbidden to sell the software, such changes are seen simply as a way of creating better software for everyone.

One result of this open source code is very evident during the installation of your server software, as you can choose the packages of applications you want to install on your server to create your desired environment. Some of the most evident choices involve the different user interfaces (text-based, Gnome, or GNU, for example), different file systems (Novell's file system or the Windows file system, for example), and different server functions (such as a news server). Each of these can be configured during setup, and your instructor will likely give you any required settings that differ from the default recommendations.

Another Linux feature is that it allows you to choose your type of **boot loader**. Boot loaders start your operating system on your hard drive, and Linux offers numerous choices, including the option to not use a boot loader at all. If one is not used, your computer should boot up using a floppy disk (which you can also choose to create during your installation).

After you decide to use a boot loader, you get to choose between the LILO (Linux Loader) and GRUB (Grand Unified Bootloader) boot loaders. Choose the older LILO to provide legacy support for older equipment or choose the newer GRUB, which is the default loader, for newer systems. You also have the choice of where you want your boot loader to be loaded from. By default, the system looks to the Master Boot Record (MBR) during startup, but you can also locate the boot loader on your computer's root partition and direct the computer to look there instead.

Linux also provides partitioning choices during installation. This used to be quite cumbersome, as you had to assign a starting point on your hard drive where your operating system and its associated storage would be located, in addition to allocating sufficient disk space to incorporate any required functionality provided for during your installation. While you can still perform this type of manual configuration using either the Disk DRUID tool (Red Hat's interactive manual disk partitioning tool) or the Red Hat FDISK option (a partitioning tool similar to the MS-DOS FDISK command), the installer now includes an automatic setup option. You should use automatic partitioning unless you are well versed in the partitioning process or you receive extensive directions from the person in charge of maintaining your computers.

Step-by-Step 2.1

Installing Linux 7.3 Server

If you have carefully prepared, your computer should be ready for the Red Hat Linux network operating system. The Red Hat Linux server setup has one installation method that includes several options for different types of installations.

Your server needs in the classroom are relatively small, so one of the simplest installations will suffice, and you will be able to simply accept most of the default settings as you create your basic server. Later, you might rebuild your server and use a more customized installation. In this exercise, you will install Red Hat Linux 7.3 from a CD-ROM, and this will erase everything on your workstation's disk drive and reformat it, configure your server to use IP, and create a new Red Hat Linux server.

Warning: *Do not proceed with this section until your instructor tells you to do so. This procedure can result in irreparable damage to someone else's files.*

To complete this exercise, you will need the following:

- Computer with a hard disk drive that can be totally erased

- Red Hat Linux network operating system software
- DOS install disks (6.22 or 6.21) if the computer does not boot from CD, or bootable floppy if DOS is not available (created using the boot.img file found in the Images directory on the Red Hat Linux operating system CD)
- CD-ROM drive with drivers if the computer does not boot from CD
- Mouse with drivers
- Network interface card and drivers
- Graphics card information
- Hub or switch
- Networking cables
- Network IP addresses and naming convention

Step 1

Insert the Red Hat Linux 7.3 operating system CD into your computer's CD drive and restart the computer by turning it off and then back on. This reboots the computer, ensures that it goes through a cold start with all settings reinitialized, and displays the first installation dialog box, where you can choose the installation mode, as shown here. If you just press ENTER, the setup will automatically start with the default settings.

```
                    Welcome to Red Hat Linux 7.3!

   -  To install or upgrade Red Hat Linux in graphical mode,
      press the <ENTER> key.

   -  To install or upgrade Red Hat Linux in text mode, type: text <ENTER>.

   -  To enable low resolution mode, type: lowres <ENTER>.
      To disable framebuffer mode, type: nofb <ENTER>.
      Press <F2> for more information.

   -  To disable hardware probing, type: linux noprobe <ENTER>.

   -  To test the install media you are using, type: linux mediacheck<ENTER>.

   -  To enable rescue mode, type: linux rescue <ENTER>.
      Press <F4> for more information about rescue mode.

   -  If you have a driver disk, type: linux dd <ENTER>.

   -  Use the function keys listed below for more information.

[F1-Main] [F2-General] [F3-Kernel] [F4-Rescue]
boot: _
```

Step 2

The Red Hat Linux setup takes you through several screens, starting with text-based line entries, then basic blue-screen dialog boxes, and finally the higher resolution graphical implementation with the Red Hat logo.

Step 3

Decide whether you want to use the Help screen during the installation, and click Next in the Welcome to Red Hat Linux dialog box to initiate the installation. The screen shots used in this exercise show the Help feature displayed. You can also display this information at any time during the installation by pressing the Help button. Use the scroll bar on the side of the screen to view additional information, and click the Hide Help button if you no longer want the Help information displayed.

When the Language Selection window appears, choose the appropriate languages and click Next.

Step 4

In the Keyboard Configuration window, select the appropriate configuration and click Next. In the Mouse Configuration window, select your mouse configuration and click Next.

Step 5

In the Installation Type window, select the Server option and click Next. In the Disk Partitioning Setup window (see next illustration), click the Help button and read the information provided. Select automatic partitioning (unless your instructor tells you to manually partition your drives and provides you with detailed instructions for either Disk DRUID or FDISK), and click Next.

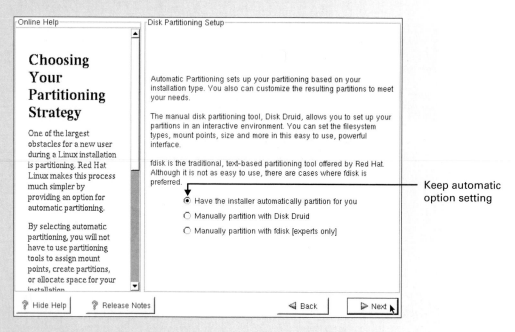

Step 6

Confirm the drive initialization by clicking Yes in the dialog box that is displayed, and then read the three partitioning options in the Automatic Partitioning window (if you chose that option earlier). These methods involve removing just the Linux partitions, removing all partitions, or leaving all partitions intact so that your new installation is built in a new partition using any free space that exists on your hard drive. Unless your instructor tells you otherwise, you should select the Remove All Partitions on This System option. After you have made your selection, click Next.

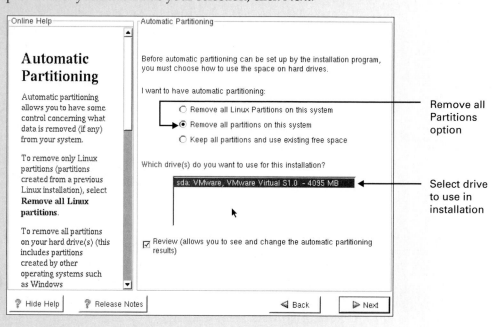

Step 7

If the option you selected involves removing partitions, click the Yes button to confirm that you want to go ahead. In the Disk Setup window, verify the location where you want Red Hat Linux installed, and click Next.

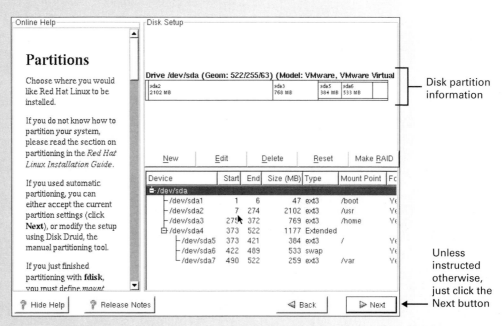

Step 8

Unless your instructor tells you otherwise, keep the default settings in the Boot Loader Configuration window, and click Next. This keeps GRUB as your boot loader and locates it in the Master Boot Record using the filename displayed in the following illustration.

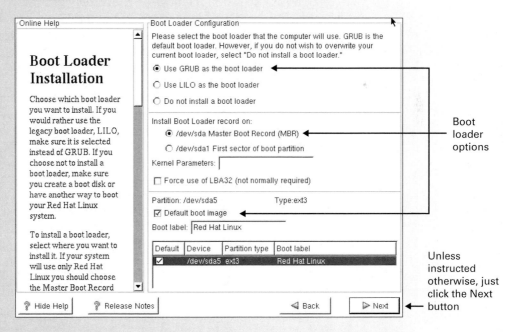

Step 9

In the Boot Loader Password Configuration window, type and verify a boot loader password if you intend to use one, and click Next. Assigning a password to the boot loader feature ensures that users are not able to reboot your computer without authorization.

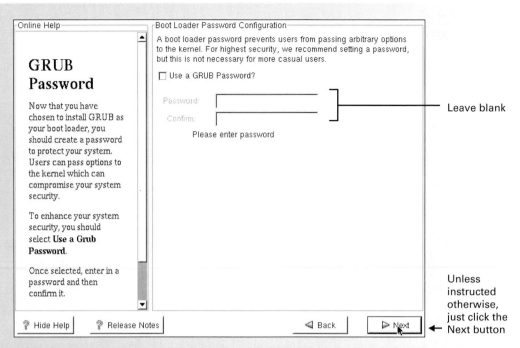

Warning: *Be sure to remember your password. You may have to completely rebuild the computer's operating system to get past the password security if you forget the password.*

Step 10

In the Network Configuration window, select the Activate on Boot option to start your network interface card when you turn on your computer. Select the Configure Using DHCP (Dynamic Host Configuration Protocol) option to allow a properly configured server to automatically assign an IP address to each networked computer. Finally, confirm or configure any remaining settings provided by your instructor, and click Next to continue. Notice in the following illustration that the configuration shows each of your network connections (eth0 in this example) in its own window and lets you set up each one separately. If your network will use static IP addresses, uncheck the DHCP option and insert any information provided by your instructor in the applicable remaining fields.

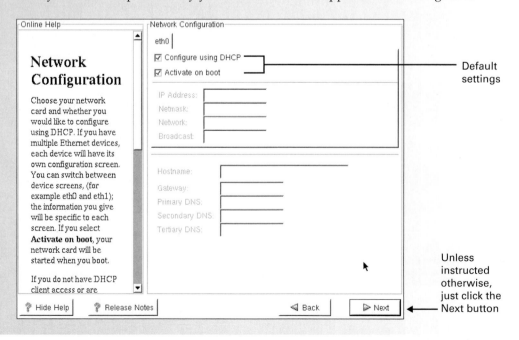

Step 11

In the Firewall Configuration window, confirm or configure your settings. Clicking the Help button displays the Firewall Help information shown in the following illustration, which includes the definition of and uses for a firewall. As shown, your server will use a medium security firewall with a set of customized rules that allows incoming DHCP requests to be accepted by your server. Remember that a firewall keeps unwanted connections out of your network and only allows those connections you specify— DHCP requests in this case. Notice too that you can turn the firewall completely off, or you can increase the security level and even use a default set of rules. Your firewall decisions should be verified with your instructor before making any changes. Click Next to continue.

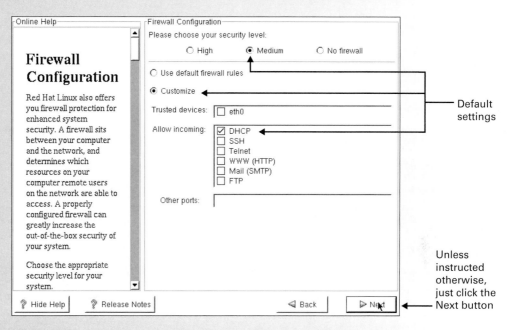

Step 12

In the Additional Language Support window, verify or select your configuration and click Next. In the Time Zone Selection window, select your time zone and click Next.

Step 13

In the Account Configuration window, enter and verify your root administrator password. Then click Add to create a new login account for yourself, enter the appropriate information, and click OK and then Next. As you can see from the Help information for this window, setting up this account (and its password) is one of the most important aspects of your installation. The root user account has complete control of the system, and with it you can install the packages (applications) that control and run on your system. Because this account is so powerful, you should use the root user account only when administration activities are necessary. Unauthorized use of that account will then be less likely because of its less frequent use.

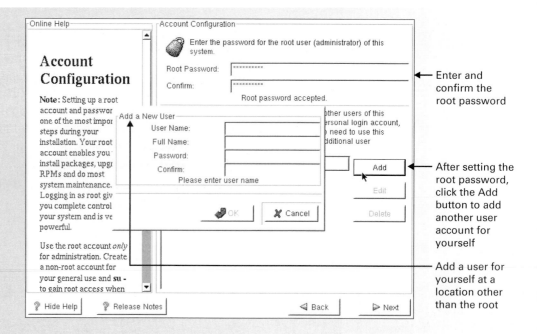

Enter and confirm the root password

After setting the root password, click the Add button to add another user account for yourself

Add a user for yourself at a location other than the root

Step 14

In the Package Group Selection window, select the package groups (or applications) that will be installed when creating your server. Linux calls its graphical interface the *X Window System* (commonly referred to as **X Windows**), and that interface must be used with either the Gnome or the KDE graphical user interfaces, as they simulate the Windows desktop environment. Notice that you also get to choose between the different types of server application packages that you wish to use on your computer (such as the news server or various file servers). Click Next to continue.

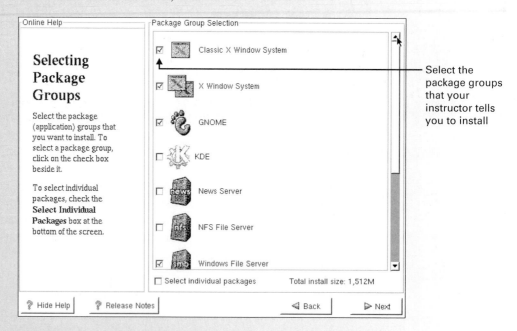

Select the package groups that your instructor tells you to install

Step 15

In the Graphical Interface (X) Configuration window, use the vendor selection triangles and the scroll bar to locate and verify that the appropriate graphics adapter has been selected for your server. If the correct information has not automatically been configured, select the appropriate adapter and specify the amount of RAM contained on your video card. This is an important step—your video configuration must be correct or the graphical user interface will not function properly. Notice, the Skip X Configuration check box at the bottom of the window. This option is used if you want to use only a text-based user interface and do not wish to activate any GUI environments. Click Next to continue.

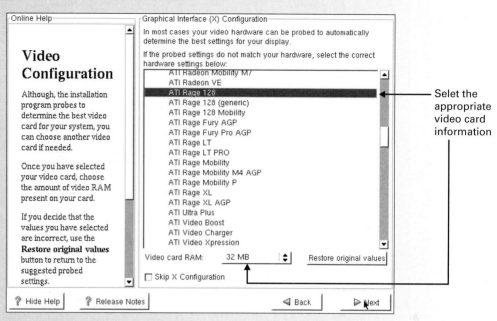

Step 16

In the About to Install window, click Next to start the actual server installation. Monitor the installation on the Installing Packages screen. When the first installation CD is completed, remove it, replace it with the second CD, and click OK.

Step 17

When the Boot Disk Creation window is displayed, insert a non-write-protected blank 3 ½-inch HD diskette into your floppy disk drive and click Next to have the system create a boot disk. Remember to remove the disk when it is completed. You should take this opportunity to create a boot disk in case there are startup difficulties later. Should your server fail to start, you can insert this boot disk and perform an emergency startup.

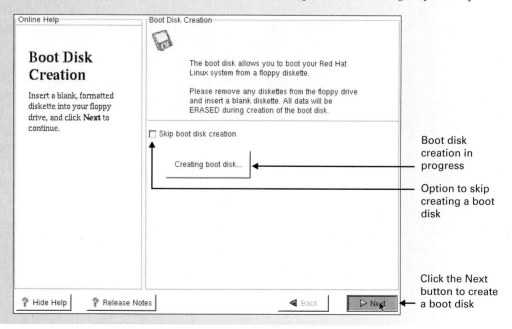

In the Monitor Configuration window, select your monitor and click Next. When the Customize Graphics Configuration window appears, you can set or test your graphics configuration, choose your desktop environment (if there are multiple choices available), and choose your login type. This is another point at which you can decide whether to use GUI or text-based operations—during startup in this instance. This window also lets you sample different screen resolutions and color depths to see the display that best suits your needs and to test those configurations prior to completing the software installation. When you are satisfied, click Next to continue.

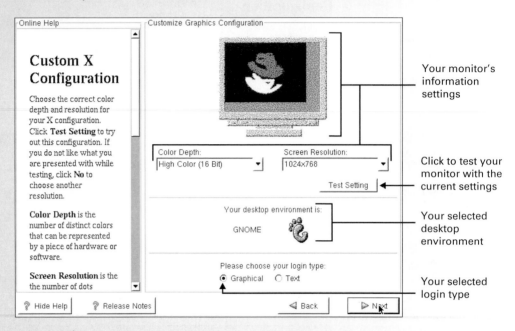

In the Congratulations window, click the Exit button. Upon restarting your computer, your server will offer you a choice of available installation options that you can highlight and press ENTER to select. The default settings will automatically be selected if you do not make a selection. Your server will provide you with either the graphical logon screen or, as shown here, a text-based logon to your new server.

■ Installing and Configuring Red Hat Linux Workstation

Ricky likes working with the Red Hat Linux server, and because both server and workstation software are on the same Red Hat Linux installation CD, he wants everyone at SinkRSwim Pools to be aware that an alternative workstation is available for networked users. Therefore, he intends to add several Red Hat Linux workstations in various locations around the company.

Ricky realizes that a major drawback to using Linux as the workstation operating system is that he will not be able to install the same applications his workers currently use on their Windows workstations. Still, he believes it is important that the workers have additional options.

He already has the latest version of the software and, like you, he is experienced with the Red Hat Linux installation procedures. Although he does not consider himself an expert, he is comfortable that the knowledge gained building his server will be useful when he creates the workstations. You, too, will see that the procedures are extremely similar, and you should have no trouble at all installing a Red Hat Linux workstation.

Preparing for the Workstation Installation

In order for the installation to go as smoothly as possible, you must carefully prepare for a Red Hat Linux workstation installation. You should make sure that your hardware meets the program requirements, operates properly, and includes all the necessary drivers. This will help ensure a complete setup and consistent, trouble-free operation afterward.

Checking Hardware Compatibility

As with the other operating systems you have already installed, you need a computer on which to install this software, and because it is for classroom use, it won't need to be as powerful as the workstations used in most companies. As with Red Hat servers, Red Hat Linux workstation also has a text-only mode (that does not use a graphical interface), so minimum requirements, recommended requirements, and text- mode requirements are necessary for the hardware.

Unlike that of other operating systems, most of Red Hat's documentation is available on the company's web site. Use the following link to get the documentation: www.redhat.com/docs/manuals.

For a Red Hat Linux workstation used in a classroom setting, the vendor's minimums require the use of a computer with a Pentium 200 MHz processor and 32MB of RAM for a text-mode installation or 64MB for graphical mode (96MB is recommended). The installation also requires at least 650MB of hard disk space or 4.5GB of available hard disk space for a full install, plus additional space for any files you will be storing on the server.

As you did before you installed the Red Hat Linux server, you should visit the section of Red

 Try This!

Red Hat Online Documentation

Red Hat provides you with online documentation for its products. You can locate information on its web site about the different types of installations (called *classes*) that you can install using the latest Red Hat software. To view information about the different classes, try this:

1. Log on to your Windows XP Professional client and open your browser.

2. Go to the following link: www.redhat.com/docs/manuals.

3. Click the Red Hat Linux link, scroll through the available manuals, and then locate and click the link to the *x*86 Installation Guide. Note that if you want to download a copy of the manual to your desktop, you could right-click the PDF link (located right below the filename) and save the entire Installation Guide's file to your desktop for later use.

4. In the Red Hat Linux Table of Contents, scroll down to "Which Installation Class Is Best For You?" in section one, and click that link.

5. Read the section and decide which installation class you will be using for your classroom computers.

Hat's web site that posts the Hardware Compatibility List (HCL): `http://hardware.redhat.com/hcl/`. That list identifies all the hardware that passed Red Hat's Ready Tests prior to the latest software's release. You should review that updated version of the list before you install the workstation operating system. In addition, remember that a systems requirement table lists the things you should know before beginning the installation. This table can be found in Chapter 2 of the Installation Guide.

Checking Hardware Configuration

As you'll remember from your Linux server installation, Red Hat recommends using a boot-enabled CD drive for all installations of its software, but it provides alternative boot methods as well. You will need a high-density 3½-inch floppy drive if your CD is not bootable or is not being used for the installation.

You will also need information about your monitor and display adapter. For the graphical installation, you should also have a mouse.

Testing Workstation Hardware

In order to test your workstation's hardware, it is a good practice to rebuild your selected computer's hard disk drive and start with a fresh installation rather than an update. However, as you know from your server installation, Red Hat Linux products wipe your hard drive clean by booting from the CD and building all new partitions during the installation. Unlike the server installation (which you could also use when installing a workstation), where you used FDISK manually, removed the NT partitions, and installed DOS, in this installation you will use an alternative method where you simply use the Red Hat Linux CD to initiate your installation.

Step-by-Step 2.2

Installing Linux 7.3

If you have carefully prepared, the computer you selected for this workstation should now be ready for the Red Hat Linux workstation operating system. You are already familiar with how the Red Hat Linux setup process has one installation method with several options, and once again, you will use the simplest installation. In this exercise, you will perform a CD-based installation that will erase everything on your workstation's disk drive and reformat it, configure your workstation to use IP, and create a new Red Hat Linux workstation.

Warning: Do not proceed with this section until your instructor tells you to do so. This procedure can result in irreparable damage to someone else's files.

To complete this exercise, you will need the following:

- Computer with a hard disk drive that can be totally erased
- Red Hat Linux operating system software
- Bootable floppy disks if DOS is not available, created using boot.img found in the Images directory on the Red Hat Linux operating system CD
- CD drive (with drivers if the computer does not boot from CD)
- Mouse for the graphical configuration
- Network interface card
- Graphics card information
- Network IP addresses and naming convention

Step 1

Insert the Red Hat Linux operating system CD into your computer's CD drive and re-start the computer by turning it off and then back on. This reboots the computer, ensures that it goes through a cold start with all settings reinitialized, and brings up the first installation dialog box where you can choose the installation mode. If you do not make a selection, the setup process will automatically start with the default settings.

Note: Because you have already completed a Red Hat Linux installation and most of the screens are the same, only those specifically applicable to a workstation's installation will be provided in this step-by-step procedure.

Step 2

The Red Hat Linux setup process displays several initial screens starting with text-based line entries, then basic blue-screen dialog boxes, and finally the higher resolution graphics implementation shown using the Red Hat logo.

Step 3

Decide whether you want to use the Help screen during the installation. You may not need it for this installation (because you have done the server installation), so you can click the Hide Help button in the Welcome dialog box. You can always click the Show Help button at any point during the installation should you feel you need that added assistance. Click Next to initiate the installation.

Step 4

In the Language Selection window, choose the appropriate languages and click Next. In the Keyboard Configuration window, highlight the appropriate configuration and click Next. In the Mouse Configuration window, highlight your mouse configuration and click Next.

Step 5

In the Installation Type window, select Workstation and click Next.

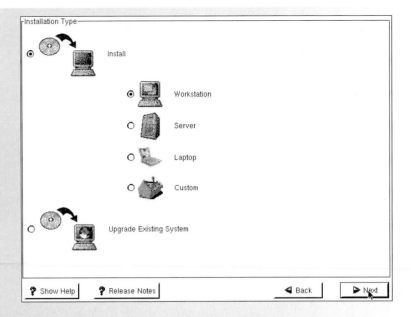

Step 6

In the Disk Partition Setup window, choose the way you want partitioning set up and click Next. Click Yes to confirm that you want to initialize the drive.

In the Automatic Partitioning window, choose the method you want used for automatic partitioning, and click Next. Click Yes to confirm that you want to remove the partition.

Step 7

In the Disk Setup window, verify the location where you want Red Hat Linux installed, and click Next. Verify the information in the Boot Loader Configuration window, and click Next. In the Boot Loader Password Configuration window, type and verify a boot loader password, and click Next.

Step 8

In the Network Configuration window, keep the default settings of Configure Using DHCP and Activate on Boot, as shown here, and click Next.

In the Firewall Configuration window, confirm or configure your settings, and click Next. In the Additional Language Support window, verify or select your configuration, and click Next. In the Time Zone Selection window, confirm or select your time zone, and click Next.

In the Account Configuration window, enter and verify your root administrator password. Create an additional new user login account for yourself, and click OK. Click Next to continue.

In the Package Group Selection window, select the Gnome and KDE packages to be installed on your workstation, as shown here, and click Next.

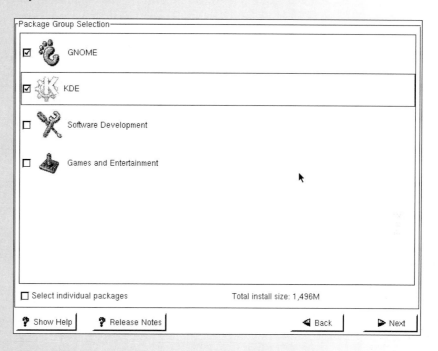

In the Graphical Interface (X) Configuration window, use the small triangle next to your vendor's selection and the scroll bar to locate the appropriate graphics adapter for your workstation. Specify the amount of RAM on your video card, and click Next to continue.

In the About to Install window, click Next to start the actual installation, and monitor the installation on the Installing Packages screen. When the first installation CD is completed, replace it with the second installation CD, and click OK.

When you come to the Boot Disk Creation window, if you need a floppy boot disk, insert a non-write-protected blank 3½-inch, high-density disk into your floppy disk drive, and click Next. If you don't need a floppy boot disk, click the Skip Boot Disk Creation option and click Next. If you create one, remember to remove the boot disk when it is completed.

In the Monitor Configuration window, locate and highlight your monitor, and click Next.

In the Customize Graphics Configuration window, set or test your graphics configuration, choose your login type, choose your desktop environment if multiple choices are available, and click Next. When the Congratulations window appears, click the Exit button.

| **Step 15** | Upon restarting, your workstation will offer you a choice of available installation options that you can highlight and press ENTER to select. The default setting will be selected automatically if you simply press ENTER without making another selection.

Your system will provide you with either the graphical logon or a text-based logon to your new workstation. |

Inside Information

Root Account

The `root account` is the most powerful account on a Linux/Unix computer. It is capable of doing anything. Be very careful with your use of root. Log in as root only when you need to perform system maintenance tasks.

In your encounters with Linux, you may see the term superuser. *The superuser is not a guy in tights; superuser is simply another name for* `root` *, the administrator's log in. This name still appears in Unix help pages and chat rooms, and if you're going to be cruising these Internet spots, you need to be savvy about the vocabulary.*

▪ Basic Linux Skills

There are some basic Linux skills and concepts that everyone working with Linux should know. In this section you will practice these skills, including logging in and out, working with Linux commands at the Linux prompt, and shutting down the computer.

Getting Access to Linux

Linux has security components that require authentication of each user with a login using a Linux `user account`. When you start a Linux computer, it will display the login prompt. Just as in other OSs, you must provide a valid username and password.

Step-by-Step 2.3

Logging In and Out

In this exercise, you will log in to your computer. You need the following:

- A computer with Linux installed

- A username and password that will allow you to log in to your computer

| **Step 1** | To log in to the Linux computer, type the username and press ENTER. You will be prompted for a password. Type your password and press ENTER. You will not see the password as you type. If all is correct, you will see the Linux prompt. The prompt typically includes your username followed by *machine* | ```
Red Hat Linux release 7.3 (Valhalla)
Kernel 2.4.18-3 on an i686

localhost login: cottrell
Password:
Last login: Sat Jul 13 21:04:35 on tty1
[cottrell@localhost cottrell]$
``` |

name. The second instance of your username indicates the current folder. Finally, the $ sign is the traditional end of a Red Hat Linux prompt. It is often called the `$ prompt`.

| **Step 2** | When you are done working in Linux, you will normally log out so that someone else can use the computer. Typing **exit** or pressing CTRL-D logs you out of Linux, which is similar to the Logout option in Windows. Type the command **exit**. You will again see the login screen. |
```

Working with Linux Commands

All right! You can now log in and out of Linux. You should feel pretty pleased. You would like to start using Linux on a daily basis but you realize that you have a lot to learn before you can be productive. Experience with DOS will be very helpful in your initial explorations of Linux because of the many similarities between them.

 Try This!

What Time Is It?

Here's a simple exercise you can do to learn how to enter commands into Unix or Linux. You'll need a login name and you may need a password. Try this:

1. At the login prompt (Login:), type in your login account and press ENTER.

2. Type the command **date** and press ENTER. This will display the date.

3. Now type the command **cal** and press ENTER. This will display the current month's calendar.

The Command Syntax

The Linux command syntax is pretty basic. All lines start with a Linux command. Then, separated by spaces, are optional parameters and switches. Order is usually of little importance, but the space between the commands, parameters, and switches is crucial. However, if you want to use multiple switches for a command, you can combine them into one long switch. For example, consider the Linux command **ls**, which lists files in a folder. The **ls** command has several switches, two of which are **a** and **l**. To use **ls** with the a switch, enter **ls –a**. To use both switches, enter either **ls –al** or **ls –la**—either will work. If you want to use a switch and list the /etc folder, you can enter **ls –a /etc**. In all cases, spaces separate the portions of the command line.

 A switch changes the way that a command works. Parameters are data that the command works on. In general, the command syntax in Linux follows the format *command –switch parameter*.

Differences Between DOS and Linux

There are five primary differences between working with DOS and working with Linux.

 The developers of Linux were also users of DOS, and they included several DOS commands in Linux. In particular, the **dir** command works in Linux—that is, you can use **dir** instead of **ls**. However, **dir** in Linux supports the same switches as **ls** rather than the DOS switches you may be more familiar with.

Case Sensitivity

The first difference is case sensitivity. An operating system that is case sensitive treats *A* differently then *a*. DOS is case insensitive. Thus, **DIR** is the same command as **dir**. Linux is case sensitive. The command **exit** is much different than **EXIT** (which is not a command).

Designation of Switches

The second difference is the way switches are designated. A switch changes the way that a command runs. For example, in DOS, **dir /w** displays the files in a folder in a wide column layout. The / indicates the switch. Linux switches

 Try This!

Test Linux's Case Sensitivity

If you have access to a computer with Linux, test its case sensitivity. Try this:

1. Log in to Linux and type **MAN LS**.

2. Notice that you get an error message.

3. Look at help for the **man** command and find a subcommand that requires an uppercase, and test it.

4. When you have successfully run an **ls** subcommand requiring uppercase, log off.

```
[root@localhost root]# shutdown-h now
bash: shutdown-h: command not found
[root@localhost root]#
[root@localhost root]#
[root@localhost root]# shutdown -hnow
shutdown: invalid option -- o
Usage:    shutdown [-akrhfnc] [-t secs] time [warning message]
                    -a:      use /etc/shutdown.allow
                    -k:      don't really shutdown, only warn.
                    -r:      reboot after shutdown.
                    -h:      halt after shutdown.
                    -f:      do a 'fast' reboot (skip fsck).
                    -F:      Force fsck on reboot.
                    -n:      do not go through "init" but go down real fast.
                    -c:      cancel a running shutdown.
                    -t secs: delay between warning and kill signal.
                    ** the "time" argument is mandatory! (try "now") **
[root@localhost root]# _
```

• **Figure 2.2**   Example of a bash error

```
[cottrell@localhost cottrell]$ mv a.out hello.exe
[cottrell@localhost cottrell]$
[cottrell@localhost cottrell]$
[cottrell@localhost cottrell]$ mv a.out hello.exe
mv: cannot stat `a.out': No such file or directory
[cottrell@localhost cottrell]$ _
```

• **Figure 2.1**   Linux messages

start with a hyphen (–) character. For example, the **shutdown –h now** command uses the **–h** switch.

Use of Spaces

The third difference between DOS and Linux syntax is the use of spaces. DOS allows you to forget a space. For example, **dir /ad** works with or without a space before the /. In Linux, all parts of the command line must be separated by a space. For example, neither of these commands will work in Linux:

```
shutdown-h now
shutdown -hnow
```

Figure 2.1 shows the error messages each command will generate.

Paths

The fourth difference is the way the paths are built. In DOS and Windows, a path to a folder is built using the backslash (\) character. Thus, a valid path is C:\Winnt\System32. In Linux, you use the forward slash (/) character to indicate a folder. A valid path is /etc/gtk.

Linux Feedback

The fifth difference between DOS and Linux commands is that Linux communicates with you only if there is a problem. In Linux, commands entered will not report that they are successful, though you're warned if the command is incorrect. Figure 2.2 illustrates this trait of Linux. The first command successfully renames a file. Notice that no message is returned to the user. The second command returns an error message. Linux talks back only if you enter a command incorrectly.

In addition to providing little feedback, Linux provides only the bare minimum output. For example, **ls** is the Linux equivalent of the DOS **dir** command. Whereas **dir** returns considerable information about the files it finds, ls returns only the file names. If you want more information, you need to enter a switch. Figure 2.3 shows the results of two different ls options. The first command, **ls**, simply lists the files. The second command returns a long listing that includes the file attributes. You'll learn more about the **ls** command later.

Shutting Down a Linux Computer

If you want to turn off your computer, you should shut down Linux correctly. To do this, you need to log in as root. Shutting down Linux is an important task and so it is a task for root. The command to shut down the computer is

```
shutdown -h now
```

This command tells Linux to shut down immediately and to halt after shutting down. The process will take a few minutes. The **shutdown** command has several other switches that can be used in place of the **–h** and **now** options. One option is the **–r** switch. This will reboot the system after the shutdown. For a complete list of switches, type **man shutdown** at a Linux prompt.

```
[cottrell@localhost cottrell]$ ls
hello.exe   lee.cpp   nsmail     page.html   pay.pl   pool.cpp   tile.cpp
hello.pl    letter    ntp.conf   passwd      perl     stick.png
[cottrell@localhost cottrell]$ ls -l
total 68
-rwxrwxr-x    1 cottrell cottrell    14541 Jul 17 22:26 hello.exe
-rw-rw-r--    1 cottrell cottrell       48 Jul 16 22:38 hello.pl
-rw-rw-r--    1 cottrell cottrell      147 Jul 17 22:25 lee.cpp
-rw-rw-r--    1 cottrell cottrell      186 Aug 17 00:38 letter
drwx------    2 cottrell cottrell     4096 Jul 16 22:43 nsmail
-rw-r--r--    1 cottrell cottrell     2794 Jul 13 22:29 ntp.conf
-rw-rw-r--    1 cottrell cottrell      172 Jul 13 22:10 page.html
-rw-rw-r--    1 cottrell cottrell     1322 Jul 16 22:07 passwd
-rw-r--r--    1 cottrell cottrell      238 Jul 13 23:12 pay.pl
drwxr-xr-x    2 cottrell cottrell     4096 Jul 16 22:39 perl
-rw-rw-r--    1 cottrell cottrell      257 Jul 19 21:51 pool.cpp
-rw-rw-r--    1 cottrell cottrell     7064 Jul 14 00:47 stick.png
-rw-rw-r--    1 cottrell cottrell      256 Jul 13 23:31 tile.cpp
[cottrell@localhost cottrell]$
```

Managing Files and Folders

• **Figure 2.3**   Output from the **ls** and **ls –1** commands

File management is one of the most important tasks to learn for any operating system. In Linux, everything is treated as a file. Web pages and games are files. Folders are files. Even the keyboard and monitor are treated as files. Learning how to create, manipulate, and use files is crucial to your Linux development. In this section, you will learn the basics of a Linux command. You will create a file using **pico** (pronounced "peek-o," a simple text editor in Linux) and then copy, move, and delete this file. Finally, you will learn how to create a folder and protect the contents of that folder.

To learn the commands, you must enter them at a Linux prompt. Sit at a Linux computer while reading the following sections. The sections that follow will walk you through the basics of each command. The only goal right now is to learn the commands. After you have used all the commands, you

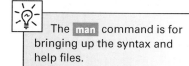

The **man** command is for bringing up the syntax and help files.

will perform an exercise similar to those you may perform on the job. Note that your screen may not look exactly like the ones shown in this book. This is okay. Table 2.1 lists commands for your reference.

Listing the Contents of a Folder

The **ls** command is the Linux equivalent of the DOS command **dir**. The **ls** command lists the contents of a folder. By default, **ls** provides only the names of visible files in the current folder. Using switches changes the way that the command runs. Table 2.2 lists the commonly used switches for **ls**. For a complete list of switches, enter the command **man ls**.

Try This!

Comparing Linux with DOS

On a Windows computer, access the DOS prompt. Run the command **dir | more**. The | will take the output of **dir** and run it through the filter command **more**. The **more** command displays its input one line at a time. Thus the | acts as a pipe to make the output of **dir** the input of **more**. Compare this output with the output for the **ls –la** command. Use the comparison to answer the first two questions.

1. What information does DOS list that is not provided by Linux?

2. What information does Linux list that is not provided by DOS?

3. What are the differences between Linux and DOS that will be the most troublesome for you to deal with?

Table 2.2	Basic File Management Commands
Command	**Description**
cd	Changes to another folder
chmod	Changes the mode or file permissions
cp	Copies a file
head	Displays the first 10 lines of a file
ls	Lists contents of a folder
mkdir	Makes a folder
more	Displays a text file, one line at a time
pico	Creates a text file
pwd	Prints the working folder
rm	Deletes a file

Table 2.1	Commonly Used Switches for the ls Command
ls Switch	**Description**
–a	Lists all files in the folder, including the hidden files. Files are hidden in Linux by making the first character a period, like this: .bash_profile.
–l	Displays a long listing of the folder. All file attributes are listed.
–F	Classifies the listing of the folder. In particular, folder names have a / character after the name.
–S	Sorts the output by size.
–t	Sorts the output by time.

If you enter the command **ls**, you will get a list of all files in the current folder. Figure 2.4 shows the contents of the /etc folder. Different colors have different meanings. White files are simple files. Dark blue files are folders. Green files are programs that you can run at the command prompt or binary files like jpgs. Light blue files are like Windows shortcuts; they are links to files in a different folder.

You might notice that details like date of creation and length were omitted from the output. You must tell **ls** that you want these details. This requires a switch. Enter the command **ls –l** to see output as shown in Figure 2.5. The first column lists the permissions on the file. The permissions indicate who can read, write, or execute the file. The next column indicates the type of file. The number 1 indicates a normal file, and 2 indicates a folder. Higher numbers indicate that the file is either a link, which is like a shortcut in Windows, or a special system file. The next two columns list the owner and last modifier of the file, respectively. The next number indicates the size of the file. The date and time columns indicate when the file was created. Last, the name of the file is shown. If a file is a link (in light blue), the link location is listed; the file after the arrow is the original file, and the light blue filename in this folder is a shortcut to the original file.

```
gnome-vfs-mime-magic  nscd.conf           ssh
gpm-root.conf         nsswitch.conf       sudoers
group                 ntp                 sysconfig
group-                ntp.conf            sysctl.conf
grub.conf             oaf                 syslog.conf
gshadow               openldap            termcap
gshadow-              opt                 updatedb.conf
gtk                   pam.d               updfstab.conf
gtk-2.0               pam_smb.conf        updfstab.conf.default
host.conf             pango               vfontcap
hosts                 paper.config        vfs
hosts.allow           passwd              warnquota.conf
hosts.deny            passwd-             wgetrc
hotplug               passwd.OLD          wine.reg
identd.conf           pbm2ppa.conf        wine.systemreg
im_palette.pal        php.ini             wine.userreg
im_palette-small.pal  pine.conf           X11
im_palette-tiny.pal   pine.conf.fixed     xinetd.conf
imrc                  pinforc             xinetd.d
info-dir              pluggerrc           xml
init.d                pnm2ppa.conf        xpdfrc
initlog.conf          ppp                 yp.conf
inittab               printcap
inputrc               printcap.local
[cottrell@localhost etc]$
```

• **Figure 2.4**   File listing of the /etc folder

Creating a File with pico

You want to write a letter to your instructor. You need to use a text editor to write the file. Several text editors exist for Linux, but **pico** is the easiest editor to use. It provides a series of commands at the bottom of the screen and allows you to use the keyboard as expected—BACKSPACE and DELETE work as usual—

and the screen will wrap when necessary. This is not true of all Linux editors. Table 2.3 lists handy **pico** commands.

Now you'll practice using **pico** to type a simple note to a teacher. You can type paragraphs and sentences just as in Word. Lines wrap properly in **pico**. Everything works as you expect it to.

Start by entering the command **pico letter**. Typically, you start **pico** with the name of the file you want to open. After **pico** has opened, type a simple letter. Figure 2.6 shows a letter to an instructor. (Saying nice things to an instructor will rarely hurt your grade!) While you are typing, look at the bottom of the screen. Some common commands are listed for your convenience. The ^ is short for the CTRL key on your keyboard. Thus, CTRL-O will save the file to disk. Press CTRL-O to save the file. You will be prompted for a name. Because you want to keep the file as is, you will simply press ENTER.

If you need help with spelling, you are in luck because **pico** includes a spell checker. Press CTRL-T to spell-check the document. You will quickly notice that the checker is not quite as nice as the spell checker in Microsoft Word.

```
-rwxr-xr-x   1 root     root           10888 Mar 24 20:23 rmdir
-rwxr-xr-x   1 rpm      rpm          1735412 Apr 18 17:35 rpm
lrwxrwxrwx   1 root     root               2 Jul  5 12:38 rvi -> vi
lrwxrwxrwx   1 root     root               2 Jul  5 12:38 rview -> vi
-rwxr-xr-x   1 root     root           54949 Apr  5 04:26 sed
-rwxr-xr-x   1 root     root           16700 Sep 17  2001 setserial
-rwxr-xr-x   1 root     root           46780 Jun 25  2001 sfxload
lrwxrwxrwx   1 root     root               4 Jul  5 12:28 sh -> bash
-rwxr-xr-x   1 root     root           11240 Apr  8 12:02 sleep
-rwxr-xr-x   1 root     root           55532 Mar 22 18:02 sort
-rwxr-xr-x   1 root     root           32552 Apr  8 12:02 stty
-rwsr-xr-x   1 root     root           19116 Apr  8 12:02 su
-rwxr-xr-x   1 root     root            9704 Mar 24 20:23 sync
-rwxr-xr-x   1 root     root          155240 Apr  9 13:39 tar
-rwxr-xr-x   1 root     root          288604 Jun 24  2001 tcsh
-rwxr-xr-x   1 root     root           24040 Mar 24 20:23 touch
-rwxr-xr-x   1 root     root            9704 Apr  8 12:02 true
-rwsr-xr-x   1 root     root           30664 Apr  1 18:26 umount
-rwxr-xr-x   1 root     root           10312 Apr  8 12:02 uname
-rwxr-xr-x   1 root     root           24590 Apr 19 12:35 usleep
-rwxr-xr-x   1 root     root          386120 Mar 27 18:20 vi
lrwxrwxrwx   1 root     root               2 Jul  5 12:38 view -> vi
lrwxrwxrwx   1 root     root               8 Jul  5 12:26 ypdomainname -> hostname
-rwxr-xr-x   3 root     root           63555 Mar 13 18:55 zcat
[cottrell@localhost bin]$ _
```

• **Figure 2.5**   File listing details

Table 2.3	Common pico Commands
pico Command	**Description**
CTRL-O	Saves the current file. If it is unnamed, you will be prompted to name the file.
CTRL-R	Opens another text file. You will need to enter the name of the file you want to open.
CTRL-T	Spell checks the current document.
CTRL-X	Exits pico. If the current file is unsaved, you will be prompted to save the file.

Try This!

Using Wildcards

Linux supports wildcards, which are characters that enable you to list a range of related files. At a Linux command prompt, try this:

1. Enter the command **ls e***. You'll see all files that begin with the letter *e*.

2. Linux supports more wildcards than DOS. You can enter a range of characters as a wildcard. Enter **ls [a-e]***. You see all files that begin with the letters *a* through *e*. The [ ] are part of a Linux feature called regular expressions.

Inside Information

Using Other Linux Editors

*The **pico** editor is an easy Linux editor to use. Several other editors exist. One of the oldest editors around is **vi**, which is a line editor. You essentially edit one line at a time. The **vi** editor has three modes: text, colon, and graphical. To use **vi**, you must master all three modes.*

Another popular Linux editor is Emacs. Emacs is especially popular with developers because it has several programming features. One of these features is called the Emacs dance. When you close a pair of quotation marks or parentheses, the cursor jumps back to the item that you are closing. This feature helps developers with complex code. A downside to Emacs is that the BACKSPACE key does not always work as expected. In a default installation, the BACKSPACE key opens help after the third use. This can be changed by root.

You should learn how to use both editors. Your future career opportunities depend on it.

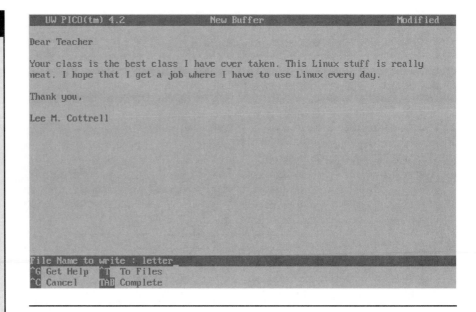

• **Figure 2.6**   Saving a **pico** file

To exit, press CTRL-X. If you have not saved the file, you will be prompted to enter a filename. If the filename shown is correct, simply press ENTER. Type **ls** at the $ prompt, and you will see the file you created.

Step-by-Step 2.4

Displaying the Contents of Files

A typical Linux folder contains many files. You often need to know what is in the files. Linux has several commands that allow you to see the contents of a file. In this exercise, you practice using two commands to list the contents of files: the **more** command and the **head** command.

To complete this exercise, you will need the following:

- A Linux computer.
- A file called letter. The letter you wrote to your instructor will work nicely.

Step 1

Enter the command **more letter**. This command displays the contents of the file one page at a time. Because the letter document is small, the entire file is displayed at one time.

Step 2

Now enter **more /etc/ntp.conf**. You will see a screen like the one shown next. To move through the file, use the SPACEBAR to jump one page at a time.

```
[cottrell@localhost cottrell]$ more /etc/ntp.conf
# Prohibit general access to this service.
restrict default ignore

# Permit all access over the loopback interface.  This could
# be tightened as well, but to do so would effect some of
# the administrative functions.
restrict 127.0.0.1


# -- CLIENT NETWORK -------
# Permit systems on this network to synchronize with this
# time service.  Do not permit those systems to modify the
# configuration of this service.  Also, do not use those
# systems as peers for synchronization.
# restrict 192.168.1.0 mask 255.255.255.0 notrust nomodify notrap


# --- OUR TIMESERVERS -----
# or remove the default restrict line
# Permit time synchronization with our time source, but do not
# permit the source to query or modify the service on this system.

# restrict mytrustedtimeserverip mask 255.255.255.255 nomodify notrap noquery
--More--(29%)
```

Step 3 Try the command **head /etc/ntp.conf**. Notice that only the first ten lines are shown. The **head** command displays just the first ten lines of a file, which is helpful in occasions when you don't want to see the entire file. Often, the first few lines suffice.

Note that the **more** and **head** commands are not the only commands that display a file. The commands **less**, **tail**, and **cat** also display files. The **less** command is nearly equivalent to the **more** command. The difference is that the **less** command allows you to move forward and backward in the file, whereas the **more** command allows you to only move forward. Thus, the **less** command has more features than the **more** command. (This is more Linux humor.) The **tail** command displays the last ten lines of a file. The **cat** command displays the entire contents of a file. Be careful with the **cat** command because "catting" a large file can take some time.

Copying Files in Linux

Like DOS and Windows, Linux allows you to copy files. The command to copy a file in Linux is **cp**. If you are wise, you will make a copy of a file before you change it. This allows you to go back and recover from any changes you make.

The **cp** command requires two parameters. The first is the source file, which can be a file in the current folder or a file in another folder. The second parameter is the location to copy to, which again can be the current folder or a different folder.

As you can see in Figure 2.7, the file ntp.conf has been copied to the current folder. The period at

> ⚠️ A file you may want to copy is your .bash_profile file. This file is run when you log in to Linux. A mistake in this file can cause Linux to not work. By creating a copy of the file, you can recover if you make a mistake when changing this file.

Try This!

Finding Hidden Files

There is another way to use the **ls** command to see files in Linux. Try this:

1. Enter the command **cd** to return to your folder.

2. Enter **ls –a** to see the contents of your folder. Notice that several files begin with a period. This is how Linux hides files.

3. Practice using the **more** and **head** commands to display these files.

```
[cottrell@localhost cottrell]$ cp /etc/ntp.conf .
[cottrell@localhost cottrell]$ ls
ntp.conf   page.html   perl
[cottrell@localhost cottrell]$
```

the end represents the current folder. The file ntp.conf resides in the /etc folder. Notice that Linux does not report that it copied a file. You can use the **ls** command to verify that the file exists.

• **Figure 2.7**   Copying the ntp.conf file

You may not have the perl folder shown in Figure 2.7.

Deleting Files in Linux

Often you will find you no longer need a file. Deleting unnecessary files frees disk space. The command to delete a file is **rm**. The **rm** command requires at least one parameter: the name of the file to delete. If you include more than one filename each file will be erased.

Renaming or Moving Files in Linux

The **cp** command allows you to have two versions of a file. There are times when you want to rename a file. The net result is one copy of the file. Copying the file and then deleting the original file can accomplish this. However, Linux also provides the **mv** command. The **mv** command can rename a file in the current folder or move the file from the current folder to a different folder.

The **mv** command requires two parameters: the name of the original file and the new name or location of the file. If the original file does not exist, then you will get an error message. If you cannot delete or change the original file, then **mv** will generate an error message.

Working with Folders in Linux

Linux relies heavily on a folder structure. The structure is similar to that used by Windows XP, which has several predefined folders that are needed by the system. Some hold important system files, and others hold user data. Linux is very similar. It has several folders for system files and an organized series of home folders for each legitimate user.

If you want to work with Linux, you will have to understand the Linux folder structure. The folders can be categorized into two types. The first type consists of folders that you are allowed to change. These are called home folders. Your home folder is the one place in Linux where you have full control over files. By default, the other folder category consists of folders that you cannot change. These are often system folders, such as /etc and /bin, or other user's home folders.

The terms *folder* and *directory* are synonymous in Linux.

When you log in to Linux, you are automatically placed in your home directory. This is the place in the Linux computer where you can save your files. Every user has a home folder. Unless you take special steps, your home folder is readable by everyone else on the system. If you installed Linux with the defaults, your home directory path is /home/username. A shortcut for this is ~.

Try This!

Deleting Files

Practice deleting files. Try this:

1. Enter the command **cp letter oldletter**. Enter **ls** to list your files to verify that the copy operation worked. Then enter the command **rm oldletter**. Again enter **ls** to verify the operation.

2. To delete the files you copied earlier, enter the command **rm ntp.conf.** You can delete several files at a time just by listing them with a space between them.

The default installation includes several other folders. The /bin folder contains many of the Linux commands. To see the contents of this folder, enter the command **ls /bin**. Notice that the **ls**, **cp**, and **more** commands are stored in this folder.

The /etc folder contains settings and configuration data for your Linux computer. Do not change anything in this folder unless you know what you are doing. To see the contents of this folder, enter the command **ls /etc**.

The /etc and /bin folders are not the only folders included with a Linux installation. Spend some time exploring your Linux computer to see others. Some have pretty strange names.

Try This!

Renaming a File

Practice renaming a file. Try this:

1. Log in as a regular user, not root. Use **mv** to rename your letter. Enter the command **mv letter teacher_letter**. Then list your files. What happened to the letter file?

2. Intentionally generate an error message with **mv**. You are trying to move the termcap file to your home folder.

3. Enter the command **mv /etc/termcap ~/termcap**. What happens?

Changing to a Folder

As in DOS, the command to change a directory in Linux is **cd**. The **cd** command requires just one parameter to run: the name of the folder. If the folder is a child of the current folder, then only the name is needed to change to this folder. For example, suppose that in your home folder you have a child folder called private. To change to this folder, you enter **cd private**. If the folder is not a child of the current folder, you will need to enter the path to the folder. Typically, the path will start with / (the root folder). Each folder in the path is listed after the / and separated by another /. For example, to change to the sbin folder under the /usr folder, you would enter **cd /usr/sbin**.

When you correctly use **cd** to change to a different folder, you are rewarded with a change in your prompt. In Figure 2.8 the user started in the cottrell folder and changed to the sbin folder. The prompt changed to reflect the new folder.

Unfortunately, unless you adjust your settings, Linux does not provide the entire path, unlike DOS. If you are unsure what path you are in, use the command **pwd**. The **pwd** command stands for print working directory. When entered, the **pwd** command simply prints the path to the current folder.

```
[cottrell@localhost cottrell]$ cd /usr/sbin
[cottrell@localhost sbin]$
```

• **Figure 2.8**   Changing directories

Creating Folders

Creating a folder in Linux is simple. The command to do so is **mkdir**. The **mkdir** command requires at least one parameter: the name of the folder to create. For ex-

Try This!

Using Multiple Switches

The following exercise will demonstrate that Linux allows you to use multiple switches at one time. Try this:

1. Enter the command **ls /etc**.

2. Notice that **ls** defaults to column output.

3. To get a long listing of this folder, enter **ls –l /etc**. This runs the –l switch on the /etc folder.

4. Now enter **ls –la /etc**. This provides a long listing for all files in the /etc folder.

Using Relative Path Statements

This exercise will provide practice in using the relative path symbols in Linux. Enter the following **cd** commands and record what happens. In particular, record the change in your prompt and use **pwd** to record the full path. Try this:

1. **cd /etc**

   _____

2. **cd ..**

   _____

3. **cd**

   _____

4. **cd ../../etc**

   _____

5. **cd ~**

   _____

6. **cd .**

   _____

Web Pages and Unix/ Linux

In the early days of the Web, most webmasters had little knowledge of how Unix worked. They simply knew that they could post their pages on a Unix computer, and the world could read them. Unfortunately, many did not pay close attention to the modes of the files. Typically, the webmaster set the permissions as 777. This, of course, allowed anyone to change the files.

Several famous web pages were hacked because of this lack of care. Two that stand out as gutsy moves on the part of the hacker were the FBI's web page and the Pentagon's. Both were hacked in a very visible manner. If you start writing web pages on a Linux or Unix computer, be sure to set permissions for your pages to 755. This lets the world read and execute the page, but the world cannot change the files.

ample, to create a folder called junk, enter the command **mkdir junk**. Because Linux gives you no feedback after you create a folder, use **ls** to verify that the folder was built.

If more than one parameter is listed, then a folder will be created for each. Therefore, to create several folders at once, enter the command **mkdir perl html bin data**. Again use **ls** to verify that the folders were built.

Changing File Permissions

One of the benefits of Linux is the great security. However, unless you implement the security features, anyone can access anyone else's folders and files on the Linux computer. To secure your files, you need to decide which files you want to secure.

To implement security for a file, you must change the mode of the file. At the $ prompt, enter **ls –l**, and you'll see something similar to Figure 2.9. Compare the first columns. Notice that pool.cpp has a different set of letters than tile.cpp. These letters are the permissions on the files. The permissions are as follows:

r = read
w = write
x = execute

Pool.cpp has the same permissions repeated three times. Linux is not repeating itself; it is listing permissions for three different groups of people. The first three permissions apply to the owner of the file. Normally, if you create a file, then you are the owner. Pool.cpp and tile.cpp allow the owner to read, write, and execute this file. The second set of permissions applies to the group the user belongs to. Groups are used in the working world as a way to organize users. For example, a school may group all faculty members into a single group. This will allow teachers to create files that other instructors can read, but that students cannot read. Pool.cpp can be read by the group Cottrell belongs to, but tile.cpp cannot be read by anyone in that group. The third set of permissions is applied to other people in the world. Again, pool.cpp is readable by the world, but tile.cpp cannot be read by the world. In this example, tile.cpp is extremely secure.

The command to change a file's modes is **chmod**. The **chmod** command requires two parameters. The first parameter is the access mode number. The second parameter is the file to change.

The hard part about **chmod** is determining the access mode number. In Figure 2.9, pool.cpp has access mode number 777, and tile.cpp has access mode number 700. The number can be calculated using the values in Table 2.4. Determine the permission for each setting by adding the values together. Thus, if the owner needs to read, write, and execute a file, the first number is $4 + 2 + 1 = 7$. If the group is to also read, write, and execute the file, the second number is also 7. If a user has permission only to read and execute a file, the value is $4 + 1 = 5$.

```
[cottrell@localhost cottrell]$ ls -l *.cpp
-rwxrwxrwx    1 cottrell cottrell      257 Jul 19 21:51 pool.cpp
-rwx------    1 cottrell cottrell      256 Jul 13 23:31 tile.cpp
[cottrell@localhost cottrell]$
```

● **Figure 2.9**   Comparing file permissions

Always be sure the file owner has at least a six access mode number for a file. If the mode for the owner drops below six on some Linux installations, any future access to this file is blocked. You should rarely have a file with permissions of 777 because it means that anyone can change the file.

Table 2.4	The chmod Permissions
Permission	**Value**
Read	4
Write	2
Execute	1

Step-by-Step 2.5

Working with Folders

Imagine that you have been hired by a marketing firm that uses Linux as its primary OS. You will work with a group of users. You will need to create a series of folders that the group can see as well as a private folder that no one else but you can see. Be sure that you are logged in as a regular user. This exercise will allow you to create folders and set permissions on the folders. You will need the following:

- A Linux computer
- An account on this computer
- Read access to the /etc folder

Step 1   First create the folders needed to work. Use **mkdir** to create two folders, called wineProject and private, by entering the command **mkdir wineProject private**.

Step 2   Set the permissions on the folders. The private folder needs to be accessed by only you, and the wineProject folder needs to be read and written to by users in your group. Set the permissions appropriately. Enter these two commands: **chmod 700 private** and **chmod 760 wineProject**.

Step 3   You will start populating the wineProject folder with files. A file called wine.reg has been provided for you to start working with. You will need to copy this file to your wineProject folder. Change to the wineProject folder by entering the command **cd wineProject**. Then copy the wine.reg file. For the purposes of this assignment, you can copy the file from the /etc folder. Enter the command **cp /etc/wine.reg**.

Step 4   You have been asked by your boss to keep a daily journal. Naturally, this is private information and will be stored in the private folder. You need to change to this folder. One method is to enter the command **cd ~/private**. Then enter **pico journal** to start your journal. Make an entry for today and then save it by pressing CTRL-O.

Using the Gnome Desktop

You are showing Linux to your client Laurie one day. Laurie likes computers but does not want to type everything at a prompt. She complains that Linux should be as easy to use as Windows.

Laurie is not alone. Most users at some point complain about the command prompt. Visual interfaces are much easier to use, but at a cost. It typically takes longer to perform a task in a GUI than it does to perform the same task at a command prompt. However, some actions are better performed in a GUI.

Linux includes a GUI. Recall that during the installation process, we selected the **Gnome** desktop. This is a version of X Windows, which is similar to Microsoft Windows. There is a start button and a trash can, and you can use a mouse. To start the Gnome, type **startx** at a command prompt. After a delay, you will see a screen like Figure 2.10.

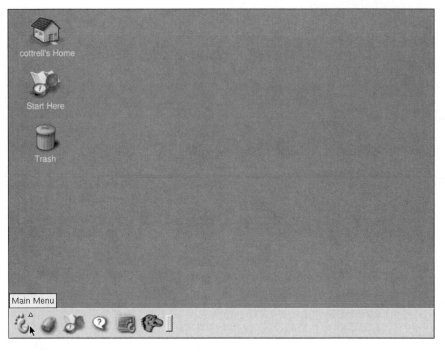

• **Figure 2.10**   The Gnome desktop

The start button is referred to as the *panel*. After you start Gnome, you will log off using the Panel. Shutdown can be accomplished as well, without logging in as root.

If you have worked with computers for any time, you may have noticed that you open applications in certain groupings. For example, when you write, you may have Word and a music program open. When you are programming, you may have Access, Word, Visual Studio, a music program, and Internet Explorer open. In Windows, you need to open each program independently. The Gnome, through the Gnome Window Manager, lets you have the applications open and easily accessible, but not always visible. The manager allows you to keep several sets of applications open. To switch between sets, you simply need to switch to different screens.

To understand the manager, think of the traditional Windows desktop. All open applications are accessible through the desktop. The Gnome Window Manager provides you with four desktops. Each desktop can have applications open. To switch to a different application set, you simply need to switch desktops.

The Gnome Window Manager is located in the lower-right corner of your screen. By default, the upper-left box is selected. The other boxes can be used to hold application sets.

Inside Information

X Windows and NeXTSTEP

The Gnome desktop is an implementation of X Windows that has been around for some time. It has its proponents and detractors. One famous detractor is Steve Jobs. In the early 1990s, Jobs, after leaving Apple computer, founded a new computer company called NeXT, intending to build high-powered graphic workstations. In his search for an operating system, Jobs tried X Windows. He publicly declared it "brain dead." He decided to create a new operating system called NeXTSTEP. While NeXTSTEP was a good OS running on a wonderful computer, it failed, leaving the "brain dead" X Windows surviving.

Part of the problem with NeXTSTEP was it was way ahead of its time. The operating system was a dream to work with, and the hardware was exceptional. However, the newest and greatest is not necessarily the best choice for the job at hand. What is important is to pick technology that solves your problems now.

Managing Windows in the Gnome

This exercise will set up two different screens with applications. You will need the following:

- A computer with Linux installed
- The Gnome installed

Step 1

If you have not already started the Gnome, run **startx**. After a few minutes, the Gnome desktop will be loaded on your screen. Leave the default desktop as is; you will create desktops for the bottom two squares.

Step 2

Click the square in the lower-left of the square group. You will be rewarded with basically the same screen you had, but with the square pushed in. You will run gedit in this desktop. Choose Panel | Games | Applications | gedit.

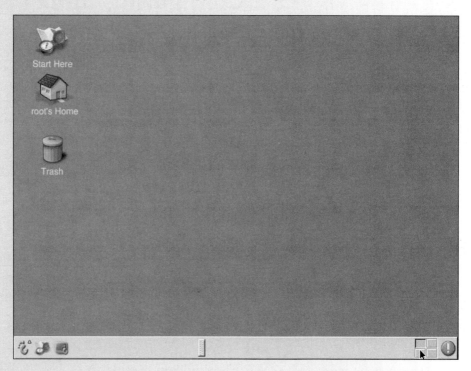

Step 3

You will now set up the lower-right desktop to run freecell. Click the lower-right square. Gedit will disappear, and the square with gedit will have changed. The lower-left square now has an additional square, indicating a running application. Start freecell by choosing Panel | Programs | Games | Freecell.

Step 4

Click back and forth between gedit and freecell. Any changes made to either desktop will reappear when that desktop is activated.

Step 5

Save your changes and exit. Click the Save Current Setup check box to keep your desktops active. The next time you start the Gnome, these applications will open for you. Unfortunately, the Gnome will not place them in separate desktops.

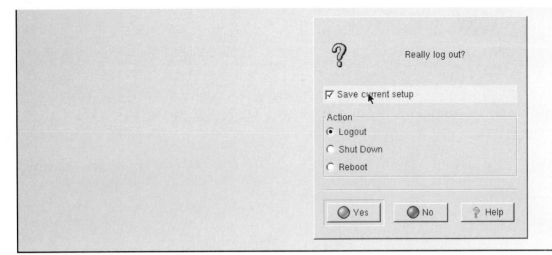

Configuring Linux

One of the most important tasks you can learn is how to configure an operating system. Rarely will an operating system work for a user without some adjustments. You usually need to add printers or software or change settings. Linux allows most of these changes to be made by the superuser, root. If you have not already done so, log in as root.

While logged in as a regular user, you can log in as root without logging out. Enter the command **su root** and then enter the root password. You will have root permissions. The **su** command stands for substitute user. It allows you to substitute the current user with any other user. If no username is specified, then root is loaded by default.

> ⚠ Be careful when logged in as root. You have the ability to do anything you want to the system. Remember that Linux does not warn you when you are deleting files. This behavior is especially dangerous when you are logged in as root.

Managing Users

Linux, like Windows 2000 and Windows XP, allows several users to use one computer. Each user should have a unique username, which allows the user to save files in an individual folder that can be protected using **chmod** to hide files from other users.

To manage users, you will need to learn how to create users, delete users, and change user passwords. For speed, we will create users at the command prompt. We find it faster and more convenient to add and change users at the prompt than to do so using the Gnome. Table 2.5 lists some useful commands for managing users.

Table 2.5	Common User Commands
Command	**Description**
useradd	Adds a user to the system
userdel	Removes a user from the system
passwd	Changes a user's password
rm	Removes files
rmdir	Removes an empty directory
finger	Finds a username

Try This!

Creating New Users

If you become a system administrator, you will eventually have to create new users. So why not start now? In this quick exercise, you'll create four users: brenda, chris, laurie, and lizzie. Try this:

1. Log in to the system as root. Start by creating one user, brenda.

2. Enter the command **useradd brenda**.

3. Test that the account was added by entering the command **finger brenda**. The **finger** command searches the user database for any part of a username or real name. User brenda should have been added.

4. Now add the remaining three names.

Creating Users

Use the **useradd** command to create a user. This command requires at least one parameter, the username to be added. Several users can be added at one time. The syntax is as follows:

```
useradd username1, username2, username3
```

Changing User Passwords

Setting up a user without a password is a bad idea. The password proves that it is truly user brenda who is logging in. Changing a user's password involves the command **passwd**. Entering **passwd** without any additional parameters will let you change your password. Enter the original password and then add a username after the command to change the password. For example, entering **passwd brenda** will change the password for the brenda account. If you are not logged in as root, you cannot change another person's password.

Note that selecting passwords can be difficult. Linux will force the password to be complex. No password based on a word or popular character from fiction will work. We like to use the names of bands and albums. For example, Pink Floyd's *Dark Side of the Moon* is a nice basis for a password. Use the first letters of each word and capitalize one word to get pfDsotm. This password is very hard to guess, and if you pick an album you like, you are unlikely to forget it.

Deleting Users

In any organization, employees leave. For security reasons, these accounts should be removed from the system shortly after the employee leaves. The command **userdel** allows you to remove a user from a Linux account.

Try This!

Change a Password

In the previous exercise, you created an account for brenda, chris, laurie, and lizzie. In this exercise, you will change their passwords. You will need to log in as root to perform these changes. Try this:

1. Change the passwords for brenda, chris, laurie, and lizzie. Use the **passwd** command individually for each account.

2. Change the password for the root account. Enter the command **passwd** with no username.

Linux does provide several switches with the **rm** command that should remove directories. In theory, the command **rm –fdr foldername** should remove the folder without any prompting or error. In practice, this often results in a "Directory cannot be unlinked" error message.

The syntax for **userdel** is similar to that for **passwd** and **useradd**. You use this format:

```
userdel username
```

For example, you can remove the brenda account with the command **userdel brenda**.

Recall that every user gets a home folder to store his or her files. This folder is not removed when the user is deleted—you must remove these files manually. Linux does not provide a good command that handles this. You will need to delete the files in the home folder first. Then delete the folder.

Step-by-Step 2.7

Deleting an Account

In this exercise, you will delete the account brenda. You will need the following:

- An account on the system named brenda
- The root password

Step 1

Log in to the Linux system as root. Delete the user by entering the command **userdel brenda**. Wait for a moment while the command executes.

Step 2

You will need to change to user brenda's folder. In a default installation of Linux, the home folder for the brenda account will be /home/brenda. Change to this folder with the command **cd /home/brenda**. Enter **pwd** to verify that you have successfully changed to user brenda's folder.

Step 3

List all of user brenda's files. Be sure to include the hidden files. Enter the command **ls –a** to see all files.

Step 4

Delete all of brenda's files. The **rm** command deletes files. You need to enter **rm *.*** to delete all files. Recall that * is a wildcard that stands for any character or word. Thus, *.* means "any word.any word," or any possible file in the folder. Reenter **ls –a** to verify that all files are gone. The directories . and .. should remain visible.

If the brenda folder had subfolders, you would need to change into these folders and delete all files in them as well. After the files were deleted, you would need to delete each folder with the **rmdir** command. The syntax for **rmdir** is as follows:

```
rmdir foldername
```

In our case, the brenda folder had no subfolders, so you can move on to the last step.

Step 5

You now need to remove the home folder for brenda. To do so, you need to get to the parent folder of brenda, which is /home. Enter the command **cd /home**. List your files and verify that the brenda folder exists. To remove the folder, enter the command **rmdir brenda**. Again list your files and verify that the brenda folder is gone. Change back to your home folder by entering the command **cd**.

Configuring a Printer

The users you added to the Linux computer will need some way to print. Linux supports most modern printers. Configuring printers requires the use of a program called Printtool. Like the Add Printer wizard in Windows, Printtool allows you to select the printer and the port to which the printer is attached. **Port** is a fancy name for the plug on the back of your computer to which the printer attaches. The port for most printers is LPT1, which in Linux is represented by /dev/lp0.

Printtool is best run in the GUI. Printtool is a command-line program that starts a GUI configuration program for your printer. Before you can run Printtool, you need to open a **terminal window** in Gnome. This will allow you to enter command-line Linux commands within the GUI.

Printtool provides a wizard to help you create the printer. It asks you to describe how the printer is connected to the computer and to give the printer a name. Names are typically descriptive of the type of printer. For example, you might name your printer hp842c if you have a Hewlett-Packard 842c printer. You then pick the driver for the printer. Linux will suggest what it thinks will work. Unless you know differently, you should use the driver suggested by Linux. When the wizard finishes, you should print a test page. This verifies that your printer truly works.

> Notice the path reference for LPT1. Everything in Linux is a file. Even hardware devices are treated as files.

Step-by-Step 2.8

Adding a Printer

In this exercise, you will add a Hewlett-Packard 842c printer to a Linux computer. Feel free to substitute your own printer. You will need the following:

- A Linux computer
- The root password
- A printer attached to the computer

Step 1

Log in as root and start the GUI. After the desktop loads, you will need to create the terminal window. Right-click the desktop and select New Terminal. At the prompt within the terminal window, enter the command **printtool**. After a short pause, Printtool will open. No printers have been added to this system. Click the New button at the top left of the screen to open the configuration section of Printtool. Click Next to start the configuration.

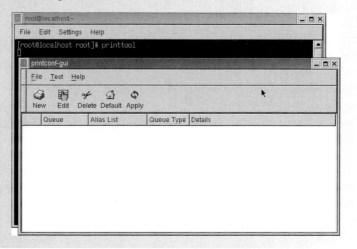

Step 2

You need to pick the type of printer. Your selection depends on the way that your printer is connected to your computer. For a printer that is directly connected to your computer, select Local. The remaining options support various networked printers. You also need to name the computer or printer to which you want to print. Unless your teacher provides different instructions, name your printer hp842c (or something similarly descriptive), select Local, and click Next.

Step 3

Linux will look on the local ports for a printer. In this example, Linux found a printer in the 840 family. In most cases, if the number reported is similar to that of the actual printer, Linux can print to the printer. Click Next to continue. If no printer is listed, then either the printer is not connected to your computer or Linux does not support it. In the second case, check the printer manufacturer's web site for an update.

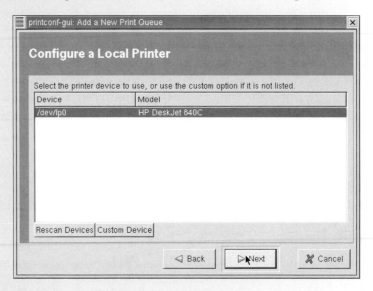

Step 4

After finding the printer, you need to select the print driver, which is the software that allows Linux to talk to the printer. The option preselected by Linux will most likely work. Other drivers may provide additional functionality. Keep the default selection and click Next. The last screen in the configuration step is simply a summary. Click Finish to build the printer. The green check mark means that the printer is the default printer.

Step 5

It is a good idea to test the printer to see if Linux has correctly configured it. Select the printer and choose Test | ASCII Test Page. This sends a small text document to the printer. If all is well, your printer will print. If you have a newer printer, you should also test the US Letter PostScript Testpage. This will send colors and a picture to the printer. It will also test your page borders. If either test fails, remove the printer and start again, selecting a different driver. Eventually, one will work correctly.

Accessing a Windows Server's Shares

Linux computers can easily access shared folders from a Windows server. Windows uses a networking protocol called Server Messaging Block (SMB) to share files. There is a freely available package called Samba for Linux that allows a Linux computer to access SMB shares. Samba will even allow a

Linux-based server to share its own folders and appear to other computers on the network as a Windows file server.

The easiest way to access a Windows share from a Linux computer is by using a program called smbclient. This program is typically found on a Linux machine in the /usr/bin/ directory.

Working with smbclient

To see what shares are accessible on a particular server on your network, enter the following command:

```
/usr/bin/smbclient -L servername
```

To access a share using smbclient, you use this command:

```
/usr/bin/smbclient   \\\\servername\\sharename
```

So, for example, if the server you are accessing is called win2k and the shared folder is called mystuff, the command would be

```
/usr/bin/smbclient   \\\\win2k\\mystuff
```

After you connect to a share with the smbclient program, you will see the smb prompt (smb: \>). Use the prompt just like you use the ftp program prompt; the commands are very similar. Enter **h** and press ENTER to see the list of commands:

```
ls          dir         lcd         cd          pwd
get         mget        put         mput        rename
more        mask        del         rm          mkdir
md          rmdir       rd          prompt      recurse
translate   lowercase   print       printmode   queue
cancel      stat        quit        q           exit
newer       archive     tar         blocksize   tarmode
setmode     help        ?           !
```

As you can see, the commands are the same as those for ftp. So, to view files in the remote share, enter the command **ls** and press ENTER. To copy a file from the remote share to your local computer, enter the command **get** *filename*. To copy a file from your local directory to the remote share, enter the command **put** *filename*. You can also change directories with the **cd** *directoryname* command.

You have to double the number of backslashes in a Linux command environment compared to the equivalent Windows command environment because otherwise Linux interprets backslashes differently. In a Linux command window, two backslashes are required for every one backslash that you would need under Windows. The server path \\win2k\mystuff under Windows instead had to be typed as **\\\\win2k\mystuff** under Linux.

The newest versions of Red Hat Linux (version 9 and higher) allow you to work with SMB shares using the Gnome graphical File Manager application, without using the smbclient program. To access an SMB share, enter the name of the share in the File Manager's address bar. For example, to access the \\win2k\mystuff folder, enter the address **smb://win2k/mystuff** and press ENTER. Notice that you use forward slashes for the address entry rather than the typical Windows backslashes.

Chapter 2 Review

■ Chapter Summary

After reading this chapter and completing the exercises, you should understand the following.

Install and Configure Red Hat Linux 7.3 Server

■ Most of Red Hat Linux's setup input screens occur early in the installation process.

■ The Red Hat Linux setup includes a text-mode installation option with separate minimum requirements.

■ Red Hat Linux offers most of the necessary documentation on its web site.

■ Red Hat Linux requires a Pentium 200 MHz processor, either 32MB or 64MB of RAM, depending on whether you do a text-mode or graphical-mode installation, and at least 650MB of available hard disk space.

■ Check the Red Hat Linux Hardware Compatibility List to ensure that your equipment will be supported by the operating system.

■ The installation guide on Red Hat's web site includes a systems requirement table listing that you can print and fill in with your system installation for use during setup.

■ Red Hat Linux can be installed using a boot-enabled CD-ROM drive or by creating a boot diskette using the tools provided on the CD.

■ Red Hat Linux includes options to install two graphical interfaces—Gnome and KDE.

■ Use the file boot.img found in the Images directory to create your bootable floppy for a Red Hat Linux installation.

Install and Configure Red Hat Linux

■ The Red Hat Linux installation CDs include both the server software and the workstation software.

■ Most of Red Hat Linux's setup input screens occur early in the installation process.

■ The Red Hat Linux setup also includes a text-mode installation option with applicable minimum requirements.

■ Red Hat offers most of the necessary documentation on its web site.

■ Red Hat Linux requires a Pentium 200 MHz processor, either 32MB or 64MB of RAM depending on whether you do a text or graphic installation, and at least 650MB of available hard disk space.

■ Check the Red Hat Linux Hardware Compatibility List to ensure your equipment will be supported by the operating system.

■ The installation guide on Red Hat's web site includes a systems requirement table that you can print and fill in with your system installation for use during setup.

■ Red Hat Linux can be installed using a boot-enabled CD drive or using the provisions on the installation CD to create a boot disk.

■ Use the boot.img file found in the Images directory to create your bootable floppy for a Red Hat Linux installation.

Describe Linux Features, Benefits, and Limitations

■ Linux, originally created by Linus Torvalds, is free, open-source software.

■ Linux is like Unix in stability and function.

■ Many versions of Linux exist.

■ Linux powers inexpensive web servers.

■ Support for Linux can be spotty.

■ There are fewer software packages for Linux than for Windows.

Work with Linux Commands

■ The command to log out of Linux is **exit**.

■ Linux listings provide little detail by default.

■ Linux switches start with a hyphen.

■ Spaces separate every portion of a Linux command line.

■ Linux is case sensitive.

■ The command to shut down Linux is **shutdown –h** now.

■ Only root can run the **shutdown** command.

Manage Files and Folders

- File management is crucial, particularly since everything in Linux is a file.

- The **pico** command allows you to create a text file and lets you use CTRL-key combinations to perform tasks.

- The **more** command displays a file one screen at a time.

- The **head** command displays the first 10 lines of a file.

- The **cp** command copies files.

- The **rm** command deletes a file.

- Your home folder is the only place you can save files.

- The **mkdir** command creates folders.

Use the Gnome Desktop

- The Gnome Desktop is based on X Windows.

- To run Gnome, enter the command **startx**.

Configure Linux

- Most configurations are handled by the root account.

- The **adduser** command creates a user at the command prompt.

- The **passwd** command changes user passwords.

- The **userdel** command deletes a user, but it does not delete the associated home folder.

- The **finger** command displays information about a user.

- The LPT1 port is represented by the file /dev/lp0.

- Installing software in Gnome is similar to installing software in Windows.

Troubleshoot Common Linux Problems

- Video problems are solved using Xconfigurator.

- The **man** command is one you can use for help.

- Displaying a binary file results in garbage on the screen.

- You must have permission to save a file in a folder.

■ Key Terms

$ prompt (50)	**home folders** (58)	**Red Hat Linux** (32)
boot loader (36)	**Linux** (32)	**root** (47)
FDISK (34)	**man** (53)	**root account** (47)
Gnome (62)	**password** (65)	**terminal window** (47)
graphical user interface (GUI) (35)	**port** (67)	**user account** (50)
home directory (58)	**Ready Tests** (34)	**X Windows** (42)

■ Key Term Quiz

Use the Key Terms list to complete the sentences that follow. (Not all of terms will be used.)

1. To access the command line in Gnome, you start a _____.

2. Gnome and KDE are examples of _____.

3. When you are logged on as a user, you enter commands at the _____.

4. When a user is created in Linux, the OS creates a _____ on disk for that user.

5. In order to log in to Linux, you need a _____.

6. The **startx** command will start the _____ GUI, provided it is installed in Linux.

7. To get help for a particular Linux command, you use the _____ command.

8. The version of Linux used in this chapter is distributed by _____.

9. The _____ will verify a user login.

10. The most powerful account in Linux is named _____.

■ Multiple-Choice Quiz

1. Which of the following is (are) not a hardware requirement when installing a Red Hat Linux 7.3 server?

a. Boot-enabled CD-ROM drive

b. Pentium 200 MHz processor

c. 128MB of RAM

d. At least 650MB of hard disk space for a full installation

2. Which of the following is not a package that you can choose on the Package Group Selection window during a Red Hat Linux workstation installation?

   a. Videos and Games

   b. KDE

   c. Gnome

   d. Software Development

3. Linux is based on which operating system?

   a. Windows

   b. Unix

   c. NT

   d. VMS

   e. CP/M

4. Which of the following are features of Linux?

   a. Fast code

   b. Very stable

   c. Runs on old computers

   d. Inexpensive

   e. All of the above

5. Who was the initial developer responsible for Linux?

   a. Ken Thompson

   b. Linus Torvalds

   c. Steve Jobs

   d. Dennis Ritchie

   e. Fred Cohen

6. Who is the user with the most power and privileges?

   a. Administrator

   b. King

   c. absolute

   d. root

   e. Linus

7. What is the command to leave Linux?

   a. **exit**

   b. **shutdown**

   c. **bye**

   d. **log off**

   e. **quit**

8. What is the Linux command to copy a file?

   a. **cpy**

   b. **rm**

   c. **mv**

   d. **copy**

   e. **cp**

9. What **ls** switch displays the file details?

   a. −C

   b. −m

   c. −l

   d. −a

   e. −d

10. What is the command to turn off Linux?

    a. **down**

    b. **shutdown**

    c. **exit**

    d. **off**

    e. **power**

11. When you are using **pico**, what is the key combination to save a file?

    a. CTRL-O

    b. CTRL-S

    c. CTRL-D

    d. CTRL-W

    e. CTRL-V

12. What command displays only the first 10 lines of a file?

    a. **more**

    b. **begin**

    c. **tail**

    d. **top**

    e. **head**

13. Why is Linux fast? Select all that apply.

    a. It uses few resources.

    b. It only runs on Pentium III or newer.

    c. Linux uses little or no graphics.

    d. It has no security.

    e. All of the above.

14. Which statements are true of Linux command syntax? Select all that apply.

   a. Order of switches and parameters must be strictly followed.

   b. Case is significant.

   c. The space is used as a separator on a Linux command line.

   d. Each line starts with a Linux command.

   e. Case is insignificant.

15. Why would you use the command line rather than the Gnome when you are creating and changing users?

   a. The command line is more intuitive.

   b. Gnome is too cryptic.

   c. The command line is faster.

   d. The command line is more secure.

   e. All of the above.

■ Essay Quiz

1. List and explain the reasons that Linux has not taken over the desktop OS market.

2. Discuss how Linux could be used in your school.

3. Discuss how open source can benefit an organization.

4. The Helping Hand, a charitable organization, has asked you to set up its computer systems. The organization has a very limited budget. Describe how Linux can allow users to be productive while costing very little.

5. You try to start the Gnome for the first time on your Linux computer, but it fails. Explain what you learned that may be the most likely problem and how you will resolve it. Be sure to explain how the tool you use works.

Lab Projects

• Lab Project 2.1

Linux and Windows products can share disks. You would like to back up your files to a Windows computer. In particular, you wish to copy the .bash_ profile file in your home folder to a Windows computer. Use **man** to learn the mtools suite. Copy the .bash_profile file to a Windows computer.

• Lab Project 2.2

Use the network configuration tool in Gnome to set up a NIC for use on a LAN. You will need to create a host name, IP address, net mask, and default gateway. Your instructor will supply you with the appropriate information for your lab. If no settings are available, use the following values for a statically set IP address:

Setting	Value
Host name	Your name
Address	192.168.110.30
Net mask	266.255.255.0
Default gateway	192.168.110.29

Networking with Novell NetWare 6

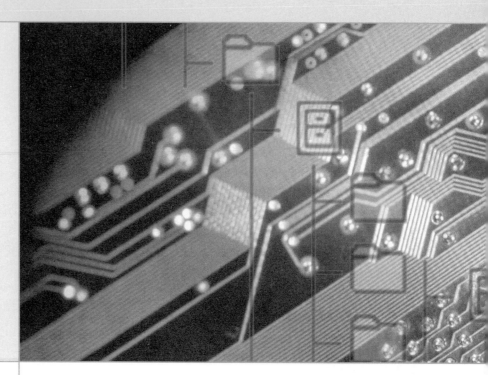

In this chapter, you will learn how to

- **Prepare a server for Novell NetWare 6 installation**
- **Install and configure Novell NetWare 6**
- **Install and configure a NetWare client**
- **Perform basic administration on a NetWare 6 server**

Now that you have a good idea about what networks are and how they can benefit you, it's time to put together your own network and get started working on it. You have information to store, multiple users, and more than one computer to share information with, so you have a need for a network.

Normally, your servers will be the strongest, fastest, and most powerful computers that your company can afford. They are the central point of all the company's users, and everyone on the network must use them for authentication, storage, retrieval, printing, and running network applications. Your servers should be fast and capable of handling high-capacity load levels. When it comes to server selection, the more powerful, the better. For your classroom servers, however, you will probably have computers similar to those at your workstations as long as they meet the minimum requirements for the particular software you are installing.

In this chapter, you will install Novell's NetWare 6, a server-only network operating system. You will work through steps to prepare your hardware for the installation: verifying its compatibility, checking its configuration, and testing its operation.

Installing and Configuring Novell NetWare 6

When you have decided to use Novell networking products, you should acquire the applicable version of the Novell NetWare network operating system. NetWare 6 is the version used here because it is currently the most recent release. While the installation procedures given here will not make you an expert on using Novell's product, their use will enable you to build an operational NetWare server.

Preparing for the Installation

Careful preparation for a server installation will make the task much easier. While servers are not the easiest things to install, making sure they meet the requirements, operate properly, and include all the necessary drivers can help ensure consistent trouble-free operation.

In nearly all Novell classes, the instructor recounts the legend of the "lost server." According to the legend, during an equipment audit done years after an office reconstruction project, a server viewable on the network was finally found inside a small walled-off room that had been thought to be empty and no longer necessary. The server was abandoned in that room but it never failed. That installation was probably accomplished using procedures like those that follow.

Checking Hardware Compatibility

First, you need a computer to act as the server. In your classroom setting, the server will probably be more powerful than the workstations, but not as powerful as would be needed in a typical company. In fact, Novell lists two sets of hardware requirements—minimum and recommended—and almost all companies use more than the recommended hardware requirements. While the minimum hardware requirements specify the absolute minimums that you must have if you want the software to operate properly, meeting the higher requirements will further reduce the possibility of your having difficulty with the operating system. Because no business's livelihood will depend on the installation you'll do in this chapter, your server will not need as much power as the recommended requirements specify. Simply getting the software running so that you can gain familiarity with its use is often sufficient in a lab situation, so you can use the lesser of the two minimums.

Novell NetWare 6's minimum requirements include a server-class computer with a Pentium II or compatible AMD K7 processor and 256 megabytes (MB) of RAM. Novell's servers also use a DOS **boot partition** (a separate section on the hard disk where the DOS startup files are located), and NetWare 6 requires its boot partition to be at least 200MB with an additional 200MB of available space. In addition, there must be at least 2GB (gigabytes) of available hard disk space for the **SYS volume** (where the system files are located).

Meeting these minimum requirements with a classroom server will be sufficient for the exercises in this text. However, most companies use

Novell's recommended hardware requirements as their real minimums. Novell's recommended hardware requirements include a Pentium III or compatible 700 MHz processor, 512MB of RAM, a boot partition of at least 1GB, and at least 4GB of available hard disk space for the SYS volume.

Checking Hardware Configuration

For any installation of NetWare 6, Novell requires a CD-ROM drive, an SVGA display adapter and monitor, and a network interface card. For NetWare 6, Novell also recommends a USB, PS/2, or serial mouse. In addition, for the workstations (typically Windows XP or 2000 Professional) supported by the network server, Novell recommends using the most recent version of its client software.

Testing Server Hardware

In order to test that your server's hardware functions properly, it is a good practice to rebuild your selected computer's hard disk drive and start with a fresh installation (a new, or clean, install) so that nothing remains on your hard drive from a previous system. The newer Novell products allow you to wipe your hard drive clean by booting from the CD and building all new **partitions** (separate storage areas on hard disk drives) during the installation, but it is good to know how to run these procedures for older equipment and to understand what the newer Novell products are performing automatically for you. Either way, you will end up with the **primary DOS partition** (the area on the hard disk that, after set to be active, is used by the operating system during computer startup) being the only partition on your hard drive when you start the server installation.

Using FDISK to Remove Partitions You should use FDISK (the DOS command for partitioning fixed disks) to delete all the existing partitions on your hard disk, including the primary DOS partitions, and re-create only a single primary DOS partition. When you are prompted for the size of the partition, change the setting from 100 percent to 500MB. That partition size will work when you install NetWare 6 as your server's network operating system. During the NetWare 6 install, the amount used will be the default 200MB.

Step-by-Step 3.1

Using FDISK

Your processor retrieves the data you store on the hard drive based on its file system. In this exercise, you will erase everything on your workstation's disk and reformat it as specified in the following steps.

Warning: Do not proceed with this section until your instructor tells you to do so. This procedure can result in irreparable damage to someone else's files.

To complete this exercise, you will need the following:

- DOS install disks (6.22 or 6.21)
- Computer with a hard disk drive that can be totally erased

Step 1

Insert the DOS diskette number 1 into the 3½-inch floppy disk drive and restart the computer by turning it off and then back on. This ensures that the computer goes through a **cold start** and that all settings are reinitialized. (This is sometimes also called a *cold boot*.)

Step 2

The computer will start up from the floppy disk, and in the Welcome to Setup screen it will warn you about backing up your files before proceeding.

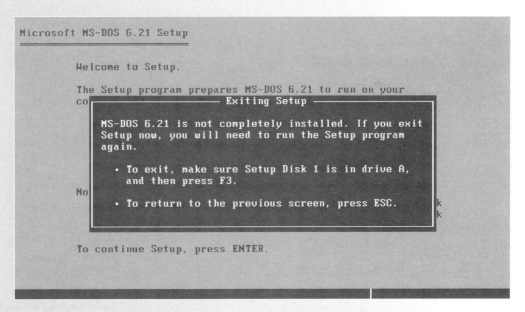

```
Microsoft MS-DOS 6.21 Setup


        Welcome to Setup.

        The Setup program prepares MS-DOS 6.21 to run on your
        computer.

            • To set up MS-DOS now, press ENTER.

            • To learn more about Setup before continuing, press F1.

            • To exit Setup without installing MS-DOS, press F3.

        Note: If you have not backed up your files recently, you
              might want to do so before installing MS-DOS. To back
              up your files, press F3 to quit Setup now. Then, back
              up your files by using a backup program.

        To continue Setup, press ENTER.



ENTER=Continue  F1=Help  F3=Exit  F5=Remove Color  F7=Install to a Floppy Disk
```

Step 3

Exit from the DOS setup by pressing F3, and exit from the Exiting Setup dialog box by pressing F3 again. You should end up at a DOS A: prompt.

```
Microsoft MS-DOS 6.21 Setup


        Welcome to Setup.

        The Setup program prepares MS-DOS 6.21 to run on your
        co┌──────────────── Exiting Setup ────────────────┐
          │                                                │
          │  MS-DOS 6.21 is not completely installed. If you exit
          │  Setup now, you will need to run the Setup program
          │  again.
          │
          │      • To exit, make sure Setup Disk 1 is in drive A,
          │        and then press F3.
        No│                                                │  k
          │      • To return to the previous screen, press ESC.  k
          └────────────────────────────────────────────────┘

        To continue Setup, press ENTER.
```

Step 4

At the A: prompt, enter the DOS command **FDISK** by typing **fdisk** and pressing ENTER. The resulting FDISK Options screen gives you options to create partitions on your **fixed disks** (your hard disk drives).

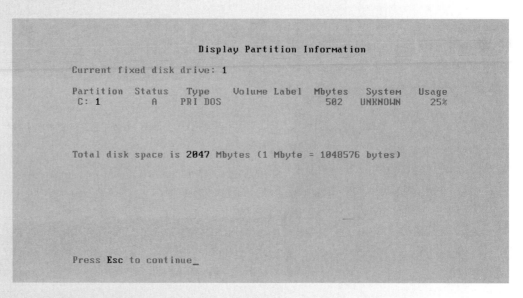

```
                          MS-DOS Version 6
                       Fixed Disk Setup Program
                  (C)Copyright Microsoft Corp. 1983 - 1993

                              FDISK Options

        Current fixed disk drive: 1

        Choose one of the following:

        1. Create DOS partition or Logical DOS Drive
        2. Set active partition
        3. Delete partition or Logical DOS Drive
        4. Display partition information



        Enter choice: [1]




        Press Esc to exit FDISK
```

Step 5

Choose option 4 to open the Display Partition Information screen, which shows information about your currently installed partitions. This exercise accomplishes only a single partition's removal, but you should delete all partitions. Note the partitions that are on your disk so that you can delete each one. Press ESC to return to the previous screen when finished.

```
                          Display Partition Information

        Current fixed disk drive: 1

        Partition  Status   Type    Volume Label   Mbytes    System    Usage
          C: 1        A    PRI DOS                    502    UNKNOWN     25%



        Total disk space is 2047 Mbytes (1 Mbyte = 1048576 bytes)




        Press Esc to continue_
```

Step 6

Choose option 1 in the FDISK Options screen, and press ENTER to get to the Delete Primary DOS Partition screen, shown here. The screen includes a warning that the data in the primary DOS partition will be lost. You have to designate the partition, enter the partition's name, and confirm this command before the computer will allow you to delete the partition.

```
                          Delete Primary DOS Partition

      Current fixed disk drive: 1

      Partition   Status    Type    Volume Label   Mbytes   System    Usage
        C: 1        A      PRI DOS                   502    UNKNOWN     25%




      Total disk space is 2047 Mbytes (1 Mbyte = 1048576 bytes)




      WARNING! Data in the deleted Primary DOS Partition will be lost.
      What primary partition do you want to delete..? [1]
      Enter Volume Label.............................? [              ]
      Are you sure (Y/N).............................? [Y]

      Press Esc to return to FDISK Options
```

Press ESC to return to the FDISK Options screen, shown in Step 4 of this exercise.

Step 7

Choose option 1 in the FDISK Options screen, which will take you to the Create Primary DOS Partition screen. Type **N** to choose a setting other than 100 percent of the drive, and press ENTER.

Step 8

In the next Create Primary DOS Partition screen, you can specify the name for and size of the partition. Type **500** for the amount of available hard disk space the computer should use for the DOS partition and press ENTER.

Step 9

Press ESC to return to the FDISK Options screen, select 2 to set an `active partition`, (the partition used for startup), and press ENTER. Note the warning that the primary DOS partition must be turned on, or active, before it can be used for startup.

Step 10

In the Set Active Partition screen, type **1** to set your new DOS partition as active, press ENTER. Then press ESC to return through the FDISK screens to the initial FDISK Options screen, and press ESC again to exit FDISK.

Removing NT Partitions   Should you decide that you want to reuse a Windows NT or 2000 server or workstation as a NetWare server, you may find it difficult to remove NT prior to reformatting the drive. You should check your NT drive with FDISK as explained in Step-by-Step 3.1 to verify whether your system is on a FAT (file allocation table) partition or an `NTFS` (NTFS file system) partition. A FAT partition should have its Windows NT boot loader removed so it can be repartitioned, and an NTFS partition should simply be removed using the install floppy disks.

Installing Your Drivers   You should install DOS onto your rebuilt server's hard disk drive using the DOS 6.21 or 6.22 setup disks and any drivers you have for your equipment. During the actual NetWare 6 installation, the special version of DOS that Novell includes with its installation software

Removing Windows NT Boot Loader on FAT Partition

If your system is on a file allocation table (FAT) partition, you must remove the Windows NT boot loader (the initial segment of the NT operating system that loads into a computer and boots the system in Windows NT) and files. To remove a boot loader on a FAT partition, follow these steps:

1. Boot the drive with a Windows 9*x* or DOS system diskette that has a SYS.COM file (the DOS file containing the operating system commands) on it.

2. Transfer the system file from the diskette to the hard drive partition by typing SYS C: (a command that directs the computer to transfer the operating system to the C: drive) from the A: prompt.

3. Remove the diskette and restart the computer.

4. Delete the following files from the C: drive:

   C:\PAGEFILE.SYS

   C:\BOOT.INI

   All files whose names begin with "NT" (i.e., NT*.*)

   C:\BOOTSECT.DOS

   The \WINNT_ROOT folder

   The \WINDOWS NT folder in the \PROGRAM FILES

package (NDOS) will overwrite the test configurations you have installed on the drive and will automatically select updated drivers. If you were to install either NetWare 5 or NetWare 4.11, you would be required to use your driver disks.

Because the NetWare operating systems we are discussing all install from CD-ROMs, you should run the installation software for your CD-ROM drive to install your CD-ROM's drivers in DOS. Your installations of DOS and NetWare will both go more smoothly if you connect both your hard drive and your CD-ROM drive directly to your motherboard as IDE drives, rather than using disk controller cards. There will be fewer configuration errors when the installer needs to know which driver to use. Because this connection is done inside your system unit, you should ask your instructor about how your computer is configured.

You should also load your mouse drivers because they are needed with NetWare 5 and NetWare 6 file servers. In NetWare 4.11 and earlier versions, the user interface was simply text-based, and you entered information through typing text commands into a console. With the advent of Windows, however, users have become accustomed to working with graphical interfaces, using a mouse to point at icons and click on objects instead of typing text commands. Novell's NetWare 5 and 6 are more graphically oriented interfaces and they include graphical user interfaces (GUIs) that involve the use of a mouse. Server console operation has thus become more user friendly.

You should also have your network interface card's installation disks available when you start the server installation because you may need your network card settings if NetWare does not automatically locate your network card. You should check whether your NIC manufacturer has an updated NetWare driver. Most manufacturers have new drivers available on the Internet, and your instructor has probably already checked the Web for your driver's availability.

Testing Other Hardware   The final hardware items you will need for your network installation are a hub and the network wiring so that you can connect the server to your other workstations. Unless you still have sufficient unused ports on hubs currently connecting your network, you will need to add any newly created classroom computers to ports on an additional hub or switch.

For each of these new connections, you will need the network wiring to join the new computers to the network. If you are connecting two computers directly to each other without an intervening Ethernet hub or switch, you will need a special Ethernet crossover cable (available at any computer parts store). Finally, you will need any other storage media planned for your network and any printers or other peripherals that will be used.

Step-by-Step 3.2

Installing NetWare 6

If you have carefully prepared for the installation, your computer should be ready for Novell's NetWare 6 network operating system. Novell's NetWare 6 has one installation method with several options for different types of installations. Your server needs for the classroom situation are relatively small, so one of the simplest installations will suffice. Later, you might rebuild your server and use a more customized installation.

In this exercise, you will install NetWare from CD-ROM, and this will erase everything on your workstation's disk drive and reformat it with a 200MB DOS partition. It will also configure your server to use the Internet Protocol (IP) and will create a new Novell Directory Services (NDS) tree.

To complete this exercise, you will need the following items:

- Computer with a hard disk drive that can be totally erased
- NetWare 6 network operating system software and sufficient licenses (evaluation copies are

available at www.novell.com/products/netware/nw6_eval.html)

- DOS install disks (version 6.22 or 6.21), if the computer does not boot from CD, or a bootable floppy if DOS is not available (created using MKFLOPPY.BAT found in the INSTALL directory of the NetWare 6 operating system CD)
- CD-ROM drive with drivers if the computer does not boot from CD
- Mouse with drivers
- Network interface card with drivers
- Hub or switch
- Networking cables
- Network IP addresses and naming convention

Warning: Do not proceed with this section until your instructor tells you to do so. This procedure can result in irreparable damage to someone else's files.

Step 1

Insert the Novell NetWare 6 operating system CD into your computer's CD drive and restart the computer by turning it off and then back on. This reboots the computer, ensures that it goes through a cold start with all settings reinitialized, and displays the first installation dialog box, where you will choose the installation language.

Note: In this first text portion of the installation process, you move around the screen using the TAB key or your arrow keys.

Step 2

Press ENTER to install in English, and press ENTER again to read the license agreement. Read the agreement and press ESC to return to the previous screen. Then scroll to the Accept License Agreement option and press ENTER.

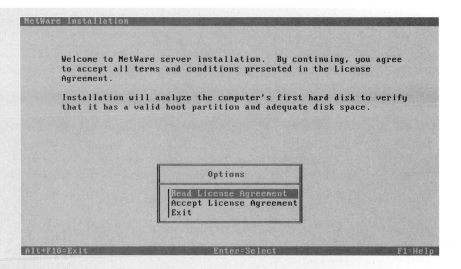

Step 3

Confirm the option to create a new boot partition by pressing ENTER.

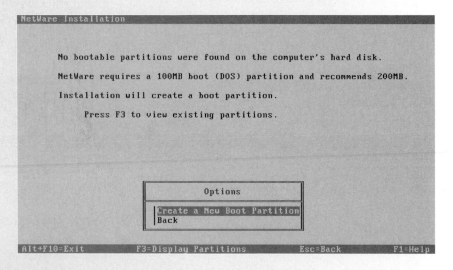

Step 4

Accept the default boot partition settings by pressing ENTER to continue. In the next window, read the warning about removing all data, volumes, and partitions on that first hard disk, and then scroll to the Continue option and press ENTER again.

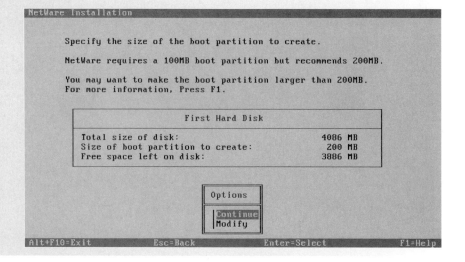

Step 5

After the default boot partition settings are implemented and a new boot partition is created, agree to the requirement to reboot by pressing any key to continue. After the computer restarts, the new boot partition will be formatted, and you are required to read the next license agreement and accept it by pressing F10.

Step 6

There are two install options—Express and Custom. To switch from one to the other, highlight the option and press ENTER. The Express install is the fastest and requires the least amount of information to be entered. However, selecting the Custom option and not changing any of the available options implements the Express setup while allowing you to verify your settings. Select Custom and press ENTER.

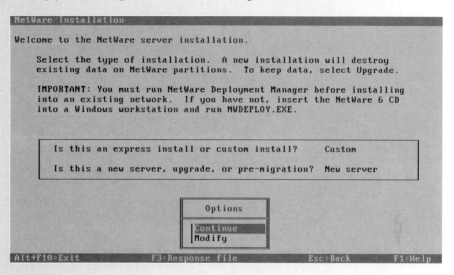

```
NetWare Installation

Welcome to the NetWare server installation.

        Select the type of installation.  A new installation will destroy
        existing data on NetWare partitions.  To keep data, select Upgrade.

        IMPORTANT: You must run NetWare Deployment Manager before installing
        into an existing network.  If you have not, insert the NetWare 6 CD
        into a Windows workstation and run NWDEPLOY.EXE.

        ┌──────────────────────────────────────────────────────────────┐
        │  Is this an express install or custom install?    Custom      │
        │                                                                │
        │  Is this a new server, upgrade, or pre-migration?  New server  │
        └──────────────────────────────────────────────────────────────┘

                            ┌──────────────────┐
                            │      Options      │
                            ├──────────────────┤
                            │ Continue          │
                            │ Modify            │
                            └──────────────────┘
Alt+F10=Exit              F3=Response file              Esc=Back      F1=Help
```

Step 7

Verify your server settings, regional information, mouse type, and video mode by selecting the Continue option and pressing ENTER in the next several windows. Monitor the small File Copy Status window on your screen as the setup copies into place the files it needs for the installation.

Step 8

Verify your device drivers and network boards by selecting the Continue option and pressing ENTER in the next several windows. Then the setup will load the drivers, save the system information, and look for the disk devices it will use for the installation.

```
NetWare Installation

The following device drivers were detected for this server.  Add, change, or
delete device drivers as needed.


┌─ Device types ───────────── Driver names ──────────────────────────────┐
│                                                                         │
│  Storage devices:           IDEHD,IDECD                                 │
│                                                                         │
│  Network boards:            CNEAMD                                      │
│                                                                         │
│  NetWare Loadable Modules:  (optional)                                  │
│                                                                         │
└─────────────────────────────────────────────────────────────────────────┘
                            ┌──────────────────┐
                            │      Options      │
                            ├──────────────────┤
                            │ Continue          │
                            │ Modify            │
                            └──────────────────┘
Alt+F10=Exit  Esc=Back                                          F1=Help
```

Step 9

Verify the volume SYS and partition size that will be used during the installation by selecting the Continue option and pressing ENTER. The system will spend several minutes performing system transfers as the installation proceeds.

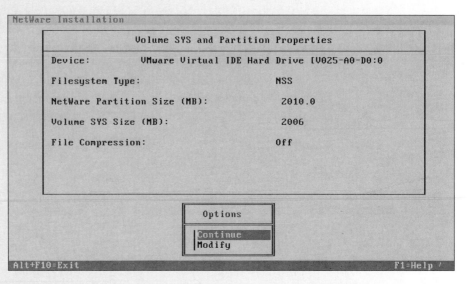

```
NetWare Installation

              Volume SYS and Partition Properties

   Device:              VMware Virtual IDE Hard Drive [V025-A0-D0:0

   Filesystem Type:                    NSS

   NetWare Partition Size (MB):        2010.0

   Volume SYS Size (MB):               2006

   File Compression:                   Off




                                   Options

                                  Continue
                                  Modify

Alt+F10=Exit                                              F1=Help
```

Step 10

At the end of this portion of the file copying process, the server reboots, leaves the text-based mode, and enters the graphical mode to finish copying files. You will notice a distinct change in the appearance of your installation screen, and your mouse will become active.

Step 11

In the Server Properties window, enter **NW6_Svr1** as the name of your server, but increase the number at the end of the server name for each additional student creating a server so that each server has a unique name in your lab. Then click Next. Use the browse button in the Encryption window to locate your operating system's license, and click Next.

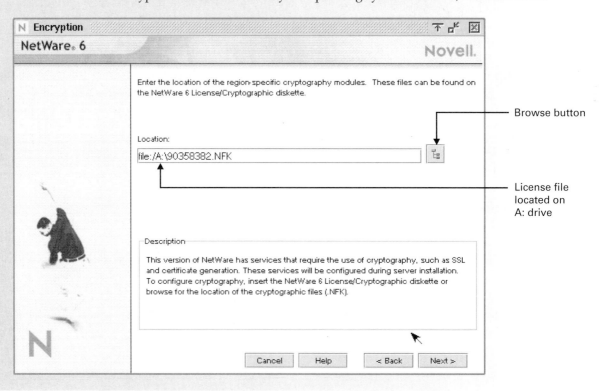

Browse button

License file located on A: drive

Step 12

In the Protocols window check the IP check box, set the IP address, subnet mask, and router IP address provided by your instructor, and click Next.

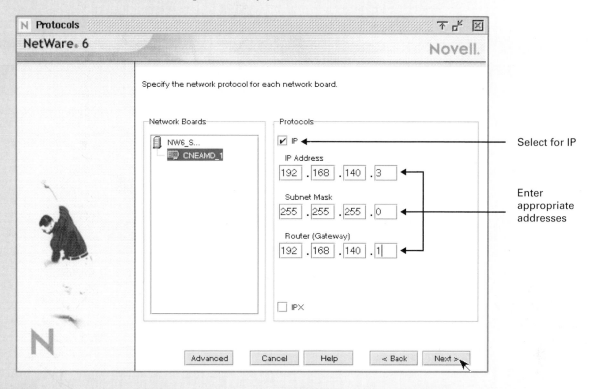

Select for IP

Enter appropriate addresses

Step 13

After setup checks for duplicate servers, you can enter your hostname, domain name, and the IP address of your name server in the Domain Name Service window. Then click Next.

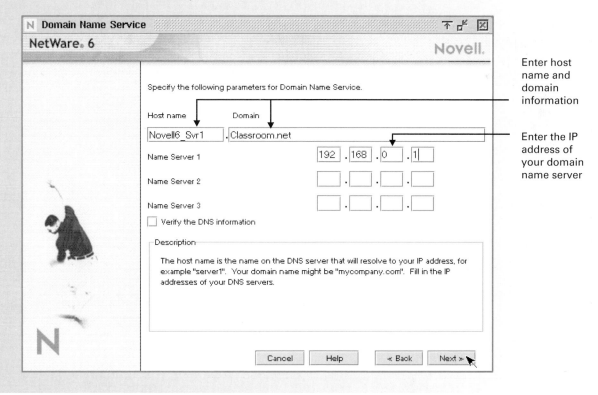

Enter host name and domain information

Enter the IP address of your domain name server

Step 14

In the Time Zone window, select your time zone and turn on the daylight saving time option if applicable by checking the check box. Then click Next. In the NDS Install window that follows, check the New NDS Tree check box and click Next.

Step 15

In the next NDS Install window, enter the information provided by your instructor for your particular server and click Next.

Caution: *Be sure to remember your* administrator password *. You may have to completely rebuild the computer's operating system to get past the password security if you forget the password.*

Tree name

Context where the server will be located

Administrator's user name

Context where the Admin user will be located

Hidden password and password verification

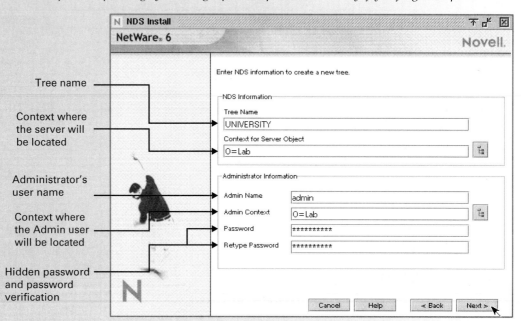

Step 16

In the final NDS Install window, confirm the information that will be used when creating your server and click Next. In the Licenses window that follows, use the browse button, if necessary, to locate the license file that will be used when creating your server. Then click Next.

Location of the license file being used

Name of the license file being used

Description of license

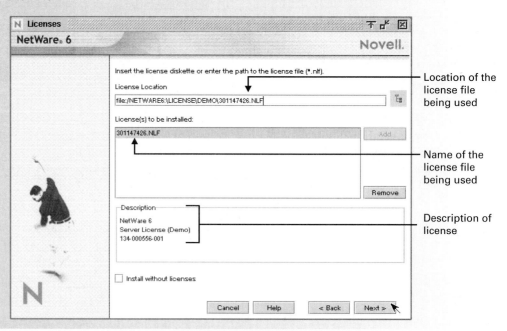

In the Summary window, confirm the products that will be installed when creating your server and click Next. The setup program will then begin creating your server and will display a progress bar to indicate its progress.

In the Installation Complete window, click Yes to restart your server. Upon restarting, your server will be operational when it displays the Novell NetWare 6 server graphical interface.

You have completed your server's installation and now have an operational Novell NetWare 6 server at your disposal. The usefulness of your new server will depend on the speed of its processor and on how much space it has remaining on its hard drive.

The server you built will be important for you during the remainder of this course, but its speed and capacity will not. Server speed and capacity, however, are very important when you create Novell NetWare servers for your future (or current) employer's environment in an actual production setting. Usually this type of server does not need rebuilding, and a newcomer may wait a long time before installing another. It is good to get the practice now.

You can get a listing of many of Novell 6's console commands by entering the command **HELP** at the System Console window and pressing ENTER. Half of the list will appear, and you can view the other half by pressing any key. Press the ESC key to exit the Help screen and return to the System Console.

Creating a User Account Using NetWare Administrator

A NetWare administrator component (called NWAdmin) provides the key to the way NetWare manages your Novell network. Users and other objects in NetWare server are managed using either NetWare Administrator or ConsoleOne. Both are user-friendly GUI programs. The NetWare Administrator executable file (Nwadmin32.exe) is located on the server but it can be run either there or from the workstation.

Try This!

Running Directory Services Repair

It is always a good idea, after building or making extensive changes to a Novell server, to run directory services repair (DSREPAIR). This NetWare Loadable Module (NLM) checks and repairs your server directory (the index inside the operating system that keeps track of your server objects). To run DSREPAIR, try this:

1. Start your new Novell server.

2. From the GUI desktop, press CTRL+ESC to go to the Current Screens window, and enter the selection number for the system console.

3. In the System Console screen, type in **DSREPAIR** and press ENTER to initiate the NLM.

4. In the Available Options window, select the Unattended Full Repair option, and press ENTER to start the repair process.

5. Watch your screen for the functionality checks that are done. The full repair should take just a few seconds to complete.

6. Press ENTER to continue, and select Yes in the Exit DSREPAIR window and press ENTER again. This will return you to the Current Screens window where you can stop or type the command **STARTX** to restart the console GUI.

Creating a User Account

In this exercise, you will create a user account on your NetWare 6 server using NetWare Administrator (Nwadmn32.exe). You will need the following:

- Operational Novell NetWare 6 server.
- Networked Windows XP Professional workstation with Novell Client installed.

Step 1

Log in to your Windows XP Professional computer and your NetWare 6 server from your workstation as an administrative user.

Step 2

Using My Computer or Windows Explorer, navigate to the location Sys:\Public\Win32\ and double-click Nwadmn32.exe to start NetWare Administrator. In Nwadmn32, right-click the container under which you want to create the user object and select New Object. In the New Object dialog box, select User and click OK.

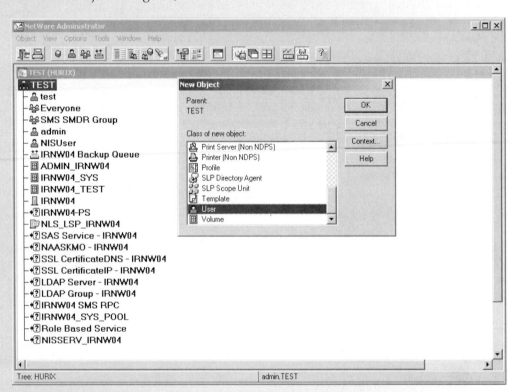

Step 3

In the Create User dialog box, fill in the Login Name and Last Name fields as instructed. Select the Create Home Directory check box and type the name of the home directory to be automatically created. Select Define Additional Properties and click Create to see additional properties you can set for the new user object.

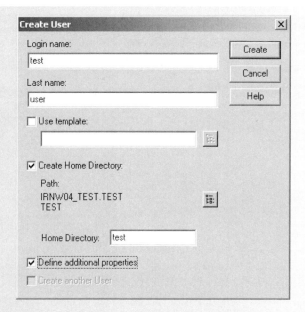

Step 4

In the Identification page of the dialog box, fill in the Given Name, Last Name, and Full Name fields with the user's information. Add any other appropriate user information and then click the Login Restrictions button to move to that page of the dialog box.

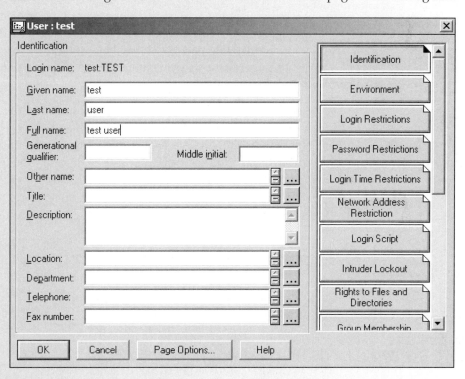

Step 5

Login restrictions are ways to control when, where, and how users can log on to your network domain. There are three buttons to control user access, as shown next.

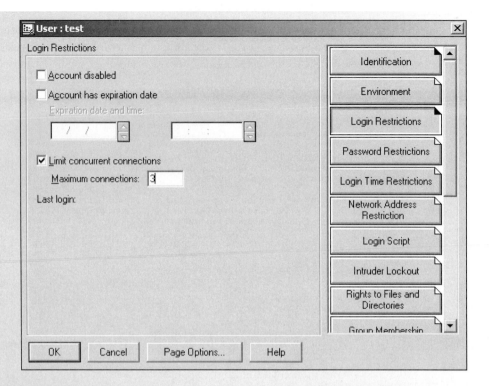

- **Account Disabled**   Disabled user accounts are user accounts that were once valid for logging on to the network but have now been invalidated. A disabled user account will be denied logon privileges if used by someone to log on. To disable or re-enable a user account, simply check or uncheck the Account Disabled box in user properties.

- **Account Has Expiration Date**   This button is useful for scenarios in which you have a temporary employee or an employee going on leave at your company. As an administrator, you can adjust this setting to the day the employee is leaving so that without administrator interference the account automatically expires and is no longer valid. You are required go back into this dialog box and extend the expiration time to retain all rights and permissions for the user.

- **Limit Concurrent Connections**   This button allows you to place restrictions on the number of simultaneous logins a particular user ID can have. The default setting is 1. You can change the default by entering a new value in the Maximum Connections field.

Make appropriate settings as suggested by your instructor and then click the Password Restrictions button to move to that page.

Step 6

The Password Restrictions page allows you to enforce password policies. Components of the page are discussed here.

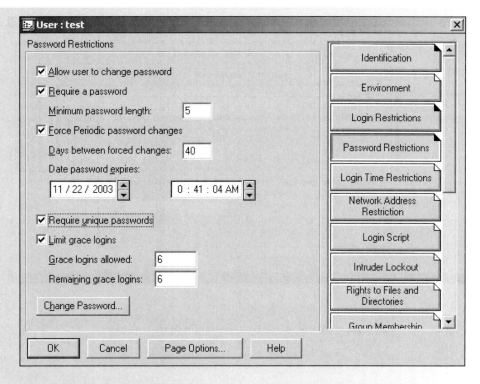

- **Allow User to Change Password**   This option enables users to change their passwords. If this option is deselected, further password restrictions policies cannot be accessed.

- **Require a Password**   Selecting this option activates the password prompt for every user. It is recommended that this always be activated.

- **Minimum Password Length**   The minimum password length should be no less than six characters. (Most companies settle on a minimum of eight characters.)

- **Force Periodic Password Changes**   When this option is active, users are prompted to change their password on a regular basis. This protects user information and prevents misuse of network passwords.

- **Days Between Forced Changes**   This option specifies the valid duration of the passwords.

- **Require Unique Passwords**   This option enforces the user to enter a new password when a password expires. This option must always remain active.

- **Limit Grace Logins**   Grace logins are the number of logins a user is permitted to log in to the system after their password expires. The number of grace logins should always be limited to prevent unauthorized access.

- **Grace Logins Allowed**   The number of permissible grace logins may be set in this option. When a password expires, it can be changed immediately by the user.

Make appropriate settings as suggested by your instructor and then click the Login Time Restrictions button to proceed.

Step 7

With the Login Time Restrictions page settings, you can prevent the user from logging on to the network at defined time periods. When you click a rectangle in the grid on this page, it turns gray. Each grid represents 30 minutes. For example, in the illustration, the login time restriction is set so that the user cannot log in to the network on Saturday and Sunday.

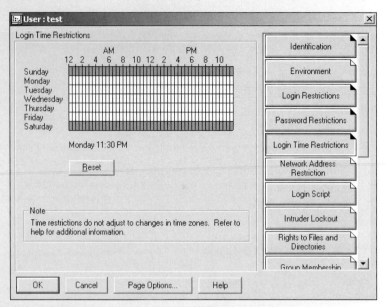

If a user is logged in, the server will warn him or her five minutes before the time restriction takes effect. The user's workstation will continue to run and save locally, but the user will not be able to use any network resources.

Make appropriate settings as suggested by your instructor and then click the Intruder Lockout button to continue.

Step 8

The Intruder Lockout page of the dialog box lets you prevent potential intruders from trying to guess user passwords by attempting multiple logins. Incorrect passwords entered by the intruder can cause the account to lock. This dialog box allows you to check any unauthorized access and unlock an account.

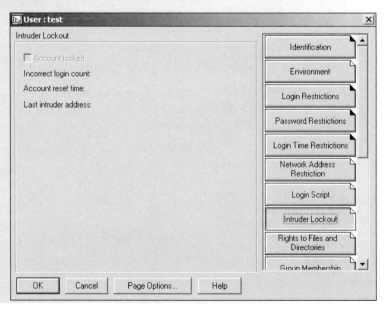

Make appropriate settings as suggested by your instructor and then click the Rights to Files and Directories button to continue.

Step 9

On the Rights to Files and Directories page, you can explicitly assign permissions that otherwise may not have been assigned through group permissions. This feature is used if permissions need to be assigned to specific users.

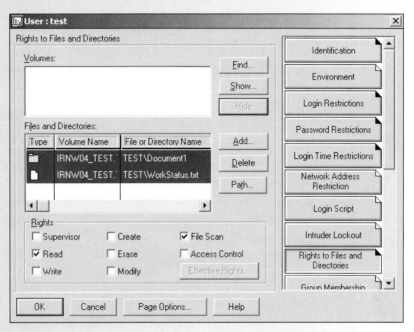

Make appropriate settings as suggested by your instructor and then click the Group Membership button to continue.

Step 10

On the Group Membership page, you assign a user account to a group and enable that user to inherit all the permissions assigned to that group.

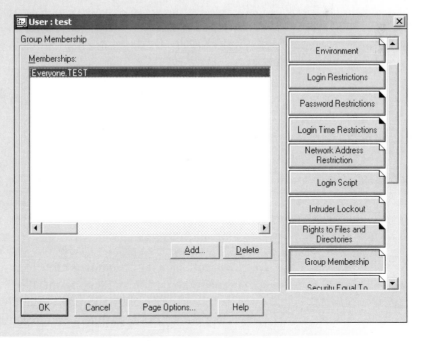

Make appropriate settings as suggested by your instructor and then click the Security Equal To button to continue.

Step 11

Security Equal To simply means that an object can be equivalent in rights to another object. This is a quick and easy function to use when you deal with a large number of users rather than a single user at a time.

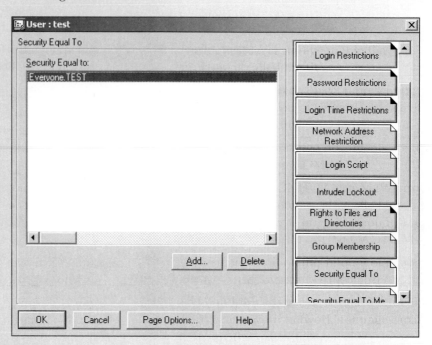

Make appropriate settings as suggested by your instructor and then click OK to create the user with all the settings you have selected in the various pages of the Create User dialog box.

Note: *Novell's ConsoleOne is another utility that is similar to NetWare Administrator but also gives you the ability to work from your workstation and conduct much of the Novell network's administration .To access ConsoleOne, log in as an administrative user. Go to Sys:\Public\Mgmt\Consoleone\1.2\bin and double-click Consoleone.exe. Browse through the various tabs available on this window. Click OK to close this utility.*

■ Installing and Configuring Novell Client

If you have a NetWare server on your network, you won't know it is there unless you either work from the server's own console or have Novell Client installed on your workstation. Novell Client software runs on Windows workstations and allows them to operate as Novell clients and connect to NetWare servers.

Lauren knew this, and that is why she instructed Ricky to first create the workstations using Windows XP Professional. Now that the workstations are operational, Ricky plans to install the Novell Client software on each one, following the very simple installation instructions. The whole process is easy if you install the client on a recently installed workstation, because during the installation process you will have already verified the computer's hardware.

Preparing for Installation

If you have just completed installing Windows XP Professional or you want to install the client on another Windows XP Professional computer, you can proceed immediately with your Novell Client installation because your hardware exceeds the requirements for the client software.

If you are about to install Novell Client on a computer running a different version of Windows, however, you should verify that your equipment meets or exceeds the minimum stated requirements before beginning any installation. This will be similar to the installation you will perform in Step-by-Step 5.02 (but using Novell Client 3.32 for Windows 95/98 software instead). That way, you will save yourself troubleshooting time when installations fail because those minimums were not met.

Checking Hardware Compatibility

The latest version of Novell Client (currently version 4.83) for Windows NT, 2000, and XP requires at least a Windows NT 4.0 operating system (with service pack 3 or later installed) and at least 24MB of RAM. Both Windows 2000 and Windows XP machines have more than these minimums, so they are also acceptable.

Checking Hardware Configuration

After you have an operational Windows XP Professional workstation connected to your classroom network, no additional hardware configuration requirements must be met prior to installing Novell Client. Although it is not needed for the client software installation, you could ensure that your NetWare 6 server is connected to your classroom network and is functioning properly.

Testing Client Hardware

The testing of the client hardware is adequately completed after you finish your Windows XP Professional installation. However, you should make sure you update your new Windows workstation with any available updates, including all service packs, prior to

 Try This!

Latest Novell Client

Although the Novell Client software used in this chapter was the latest at the time of writing, you should verify that you have the latest version available when you do your actual installations. You can locate the latest version on the Novell web site (www.novell.com/download).

To download the latest client software, try this:

1. Log on to your computer and open your browser.

2. Go to the following link: www.novell.com/download.

3. In the Search for a Product Download drop-down lists in the upper portion of the web page, select Novell Client as the product and Windows XP as the platform, and then click the Submit Search button. Alternatively, you can simply click the link to the software if it is listed in the top ten downloads section located in the lower half of the web page.

4. If you submitted the search, continue locating the latest client version; otherwise, you can usually see it in the Top 10 Product Downloads section of the main download page.

5. Follow any additional links to the desired version and then save the software to your desktop.

6. Create a new folder named Novell Client and move your newly downloaded file to that folder.

7. Open the new Novell Client folder, double-click the downloaded client file, and direct the unzipped files to be stored within your new Novell client folder.

installing your Novell Client software. Your Windows XP Professional computer coupled with the networking capability of the NetWare 6 server will allow you to utilize the powerful networking features of Novell's software.

Step-by-Step 3.4

Installing Novell Client

Your workstation computer should now be ready for installing the Novell Client software.

Warning: Do not proceed with this section until your instructor tells you to do so. This procedure may install unnecessary networking client software and affect existing users' access to their computers.

To complete this exercise, you will need the following:

- Operational Windows XP Professional computer
- The downloaded Novell Client software

Step 1

Locate and double-click the setupnw.exe file (created when you unzipped the downloaded Novell Client file) in the Novell Client folder.

Warning: You will not be able to install the Novell Client software if your Local Area Connection Properties dialog box is open. Ensure that this dialog box is closed before proceeding with your installation.

If you install Novell's client software from CD, you must choose your installation language and the proper version (Windows 9x or NT) before proceeding, as indicated in the remainder of this procedure.

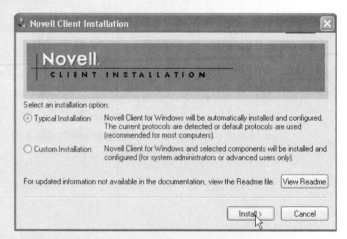

Step 2

Leave the installation option set to the Typical Installation default and click the Install button, as shown here.

Step 3

Very quickly, you will see a status window showing you that the installation is in progress. Click the Reboot button when the Installation Complete dialog box appears.

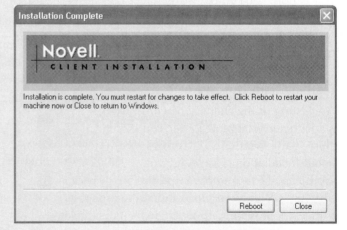

Step 4

When the computer restarts, you will be presented with the Novell Client's Begin Login screen in the middle of your blank Windows XP desktop. Press the CTRL-ALT-DELETE key combination as requested to initiate your login.

<table>
<tr><td>**Step 5**</td><td>At this point, you can simply log in to your workstation and skip the remainder of this exercise by entering your Windows XP username and password and checking the Workstation Only option before clicking OK.</td><td></td></tr>
</table>

Step 6

Since you have already built a NetWare 6 server and attached it to your network, you can log in to your server by entering your NetWare username and password. Ensure that the Workstation Only option is not selected; then click the Advanced button to reveal additional login information tabs and drop-down boxes.

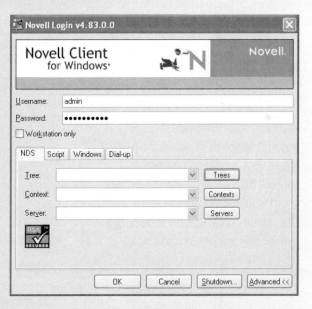

Step 7

Click the Trees button to reveal the Novell trees on your network. Highlight the tree you created when you built your NetWare 6 server, and click OK to add that tree to the Tree drop-down box in the Novell Login dialog box.

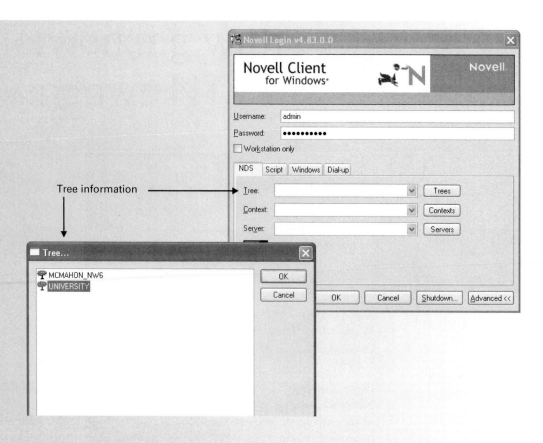

Tree information

Step 8

Click the Contexts button to reveal the context you used on your tree when creating your NetWare server. Highlight that context and click OK to add that context to the Context drop-down box in the Novell Login dialog box.

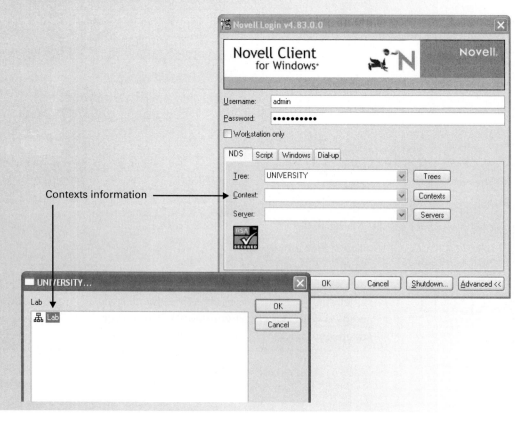

Contexts information

Step 9

Click the Servers button to reveal your NetWare server. Highlight that server, as shown here, and click OK to add that server to the Server drop-down box in the Novell Login dialog box.

Servers information ────────────→

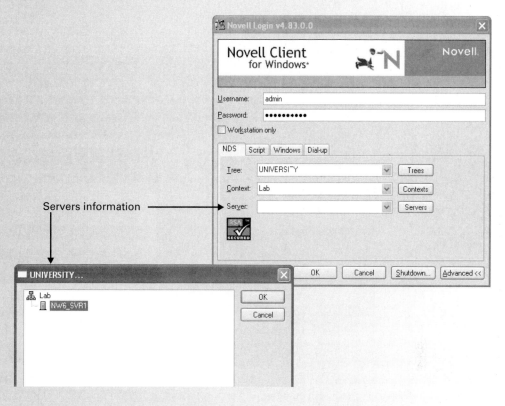

Step 10

Click the Windows tab to reveal the Windows Login Information section of the Novell Login dialog box. Enter your Windows XP Professional local username, and verify that the From box indicates the name of your local workstation. Click OK to log in to both your Novell server and your Windows XP workstation.

Tip: *If your Novell and Windows passwords are different, Novell Client will offer you the option of* **password synchronization** , *which changes your Windows password to match your Novell password. This will give you a* **one-step login** , *requiring only a single password entry for two or more logins.*

Step 11

You can verify that you are properly logged in to both systems by ensuring that your workstation now includes a **Novell Services icon** (a red *N* in the taskbar's notification area). After it is added by the installation program, you can right-click the icon to view the Novell Services shortcut menu and confirm that the client software is operating properly.

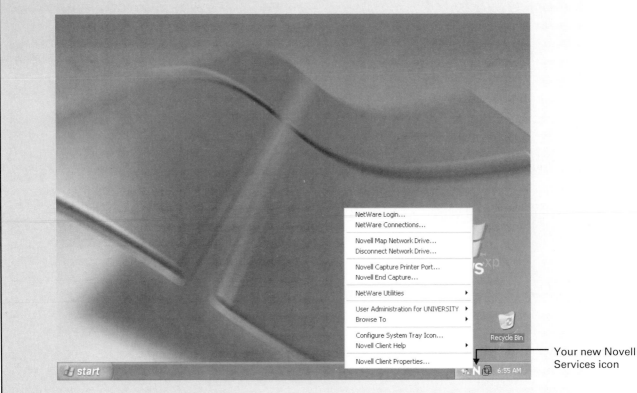

NetWare Login...
NetWare Connections...

Novell Map Network Drive...
Disconnect Network Drive...

Novell Capture Printer Port...
Novell End Capture...

NetWare Utilities ▶

User Administration for UNIVERSITY ▶
Browse To ▶

Configure System Tray Icon...
Novell Client Help ▶

Novell Client Properties...

Your new Novell
Services icon

▪ Mapping NetWare Volumes

In most networks, it is convenient for the users to access network folders through drive letter mappings. A **drive letter mapping** makes a network folder appear to the local workstation as if it is an additional hard disk, so accessing the files and folders can then be performed just as it is for real local disks. Setting up drive letter mappings for users makes it easier for them to access and use the network server's shared volumes.

Step-by-Step 3.5

Mapping a Drive Letter to a NetWare Server Volume

To complete this exercise, you will need the following:

- A functioning NetWare server connected to a LAN

- A client computer with Windows installed that also has NetWare Client installed

- A volume or folder on the NetWare server that you have network permission to access, or an administrative username and password

| Step 1 | Open My Computer or Windows Explorer and locate the Novell Connections link. (You can see this link in the left-hand pane of the illustration, near the bottom.) |

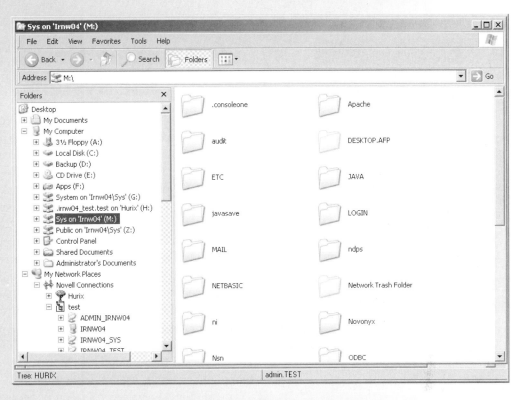

| Step 2 | Navigate to the volume or subfolder of the Novell Connections link that you want to map as a drive letter. Right-click on the resource to be mapped and choose Map Drive from the pop-up menu. You see the Map Drive dialog box shown in the illustration. |

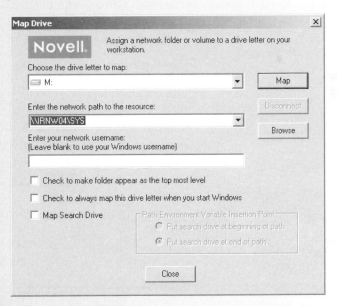

| Step 3 | Choose the drive letter to map the shared folder to. If you want the mapping to appear automatically in future sessions, you can click the Check to Always Map This Drive Letter When You Start Windows check box. |

Click the Map button to create the drive letter mapping. You can then use My Computer or Windows Explorer to navigate to the new mapped drive and explore its contents.

Inside Information

File Server Component Naming

Novell's file server components can have individual names, much like those you'd give the drawers and folders if you were storing documents in a filing cabinet. File server components must have names that make similar items distinguishable from each other. Imagine the confusion that would result if two or more drawers in a filing cabinet were labeled exactly the same way. In fact, because each named component is part of Novell's hierarchical system and is stored within NDS, each name must be unique so that the name leads to only one storage location. The convention used for creating names allows them to contain from 2 to 47 characters. The names you use for the components, however, cannot include any of the following characters:

$$= < > ? " * + , : ; \setminus / | [\;]$$

These characters can't be used because they are reserved characters, meaning they are used elsewhere in the operating system with special meaning.

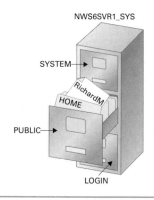

NWS6SVR1_SYS

SYSTEM

RichardM

HOME

PUBLIC

LOGIN

• A file server can be likened to a file cabinet.

Understanding Novell's Network File System

The SinkRSwim Pools users have been allowed to store things just about anywhere they wanted to on the network, and it is now time for Ricky to implement filing systems to better control, organize, and secure his users' file storage methods.

During the NetWare installation, some network files are created that are part of the operating system. These files can be configured by administrators and later employed by users. Other files created by users and stored on the NetWare servers can be shared with other users. Remember, sharing files with others was a main reason for creating networks in the first place.

The NetWare file system allows users to share their files. Users will join the network in order to gain access to the resources the network users share. They will then add more information to what already resides on the disk drives attached to the NetWare servers. The NetWare file system stores the network's data and facilitates sharing it with all the other NetWare network users. The NetWare file system also stores networked applications and shares them with network users.

NFS is on all NetWare servers. Its components include file servers, volumes, directories, subdirectories, and files. NFS provides centralized access to these components, and it coordinates efforts to share applications and data. The storage structure formed by these components is another example of NetWare's orientation toward a hierarchical filing system like that used in its implementation of NDS.

File Servers

Think of NetWare's file server as being similar in function to a typical filing cabinet. The file server, like the entire filing cabinet, is the highest level storage unit in the NFS structure. Inside the file server, all the other lower level components are organized. The file server's volumes are thus similar to the drawers used to separate stored items inside the filing cabinet. The volumes are then divided into **directories**, just as folders are used in the filing cabinet's drawers. Each directory can then be further divided into subdirectories, which would be similar to storing folders within other folders in the filing cabinet. Finally, stored inside those volumes, directories, or subdirectories are the files.

Volumes

A *volume* is a physical device used for storage and is either installed in or attached to the NetWare file server. A volume is commonly a hard disk drive, but it can also be a CD drive, a tape drive, or any other large storage device. Volumes are similar to DOS disk drives. As with DOS disks, NetWare volumes can be either entire hard drives or major subdivisions within a hard drive, divided to separate the information in one volume from everything else stored on the drive. This subdividing of a drive is similar to partitioning DOS disks with FDISK.

Your NetWare server initially boots up in the DOS partition that you created on your NetWare server—that partition contains the main server executable file (server.exe), which is the file that starts your NetWare operating system. The server.exe file loads some additional system files and then switches to the NetWare partition for all other operating system functions.

The first NetWare volume created on a server is always the SYS: volume. Each NetWare server must have at least one NetWare volume, the SYS: volume, where the operating system files that run the server are stored. Deleting or changing the name of this volume will cause the server to operate improperly and may prevent it from starting at all. Administrators should monitor the available disk space on the SYS: volume because if it becomes full, the server could crash (suffer a complete system failure), requiring the system to be rebooted and restarted.

Volumes are located on NetWare servers, and some servers may contain more than one volume. Unlike DOS drives configured using FDISK, however, a NetWare volume can span (be partially contained on) more than one physical hard drive while still being considered a single volume. The object used by NDS to represent a volume on NetWare networks is the volume object, and the system itself automatically gives the object its name. A volume object name, therefore, is a combination of the name of the server and the name of the volume, connected by an underscore.

For example, the volume object name for the volume you created in your NW6SVR1 server was NW6SVR1_SYS:, and an icon that looks like a filing cabinet represents your volume in the NDS tree. Because all servers have a SYS: volume, using this naming scheme and storing all your items in the SYS: volume will ensure that those objects are assigned unique names.

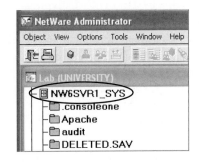

• The NetWare Administrator view of the filing cabinet icon next to the name of the server

The volume name is the highest level in NFS's directory structure on a server, much as the root directory designation is the highest storage level on DOS hard disk drives. Also, like the DOS file system structure, NetWare's file system directory structure is set up like a tree, with directories and subdirectories branching out from its root directory, and with its stored files being the lowest level object in the structure.

Directories

A directory (with a small *d*) is an object representing an area on a NetWare volume where files or additional directories (called *subdirectories*) are stored. The main reason for subdividing volumes is to increase network organization. The more you can subdivide volumes and group similar objects together, the more organized your network will be.

You can create optional directories yourself, and required directories are created for you. Both help you keep your system organized.

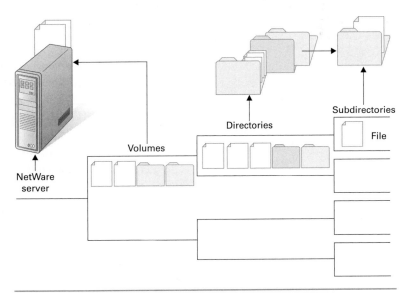

• The NetWare file server's directory structure

Verify Your Volume Object Name

The server name you used when you originally installed your NetWare 6 server should be the one displayed in your directory structure. Try this:

1. Log in to your Windows XP Professional workstation and to your NetWare 6 server as your administrative user.

2. Locate and double-click the ConsoleOne icon.

3. When ConsoleOne opens, expand NDS by clicking the small switch to the left of its icon name in the left pane. When you click the switch, its small line will point downward to expand (or open) the container object and reveal any additional container objects below it in the left pane. All of its contents (containers and files) will be displayed in the right pane.

4. Clicking the switch again will point the switch's small line to the right and collapse (or close) the container object and hide its container contents in the left pane.

5. Expand your University tree; then expand your Lab container and verify the name of your server (NW6SVR1_SYS). Click its filing cabinet icon to display its contents in the right pane without expanding its containers in the left pane.

Optional Directories When you attempt to organize the information stored on the NetWare file server that you use in this course, you will likely find that this part of a network administrator's job often involves creating and working with optional directories (those directories that you can add as you like or as they are needed). Think about the filing cabinet described earlier. Although extra drawers may not be necessary, when you wish to store and later retrieve a document easily, having things organized sufficiently by subdividing file folders makes it easier for you to locate the specific file (and then the document) you want. The same is true of your file server's storage system. In fact, most of the directories you will work with are those you or your classmates elect to create in an effort to keep your system organized. However, still other directories that you and your classmates will use are created on a server during the operating system's original installation.

Required Directories Several required directories (directories that must be on the server) are always created when a NetWare operating system is installed. They help start you off in an organized fashion when you first begin using the new NetWare server. Following are some of the required directories that NetWare automatically installs (provided you are installing NetWare 4.0 or higher). You will be working with these directories frequently as you administer your class's NetWare 6.0 network.

- **SYSTEM** The majority of the tasks you will perform on your NetWare server will use the operating system's NLM (or NetWare Loadable Module) configuration files and various other utilities that are contained in the SYSTEM directory (SYS). These items should be accessible only to those individuals designated as having administrative responsibility for the network. The majority of these files affect how your NetWare server functions, and they should be continually protected from access by unauthorized users.

- **PUBLIC** The files and programs that you want available to all users after they have logged in can be placed in the PUBLIC directory. Many of the items stored there are needed by users when gaining access to or using specific network services. By default, all users on a NetWare network are granted Read access to the PUBLIC directory.

- **LOGIN** The files located in the LOGIN directory are there to be accessed by all users prior to their logging in to the network. Merely connecting to the network gives any individual access to these files and programs. Users can see what servers are available for them to log on to and they can attempt to log on to any of those servers. Whether or not they are successful in their attempt determines whether they gain access to the network itself. Network administrators should be very careful when placing programs in the LOGIN directory because everyone (whether authorized or not) has access to those programs at all times.

Typical Directories In addition to the required directories just discussed, you will usually see several other typical directories (ones that are not required but nonetheless are used on the typical NetWare network). It may be your job, while administering the network, to create and maintain these supplementary directories.

• The server with two of the required directories displayed

■ **APPLICATION** Applications that the network administrator determines should be available to multiple users over the network are placed in an APPLICATION directory (commonly named APPS). Within the APPLICATION directory, you should create a separate directory for each application. Separate storage space for each application allows you to segregate your most frequently accessed items from other files. In case of failure or data corruption, your more important application files are not affected (just as when you segregated your SYSTEM files from all others). All users authorized to log in to the network will generally have access to these applications.

■ **USERS** Users will typically have files stored in a USERS directory that they wish to keep on the server so they can access that information from any workstation on the network. These files and the associated documents are customarily stored in each user's own HOME directory located inside the USERS directory. Think of it as the user's "home base," the location where the user gets to keep personal "possessions." When you created new users on your NW6SVR1 server, you were asked to designate their HOME directory, and you specified the USERS directory. Without creating a directory actually named HOME, the system created directories with the users' names instead.

Therefore, all users you created on your NetWare network currently have what amounts to a HOME location (considered a HOME directory by the system, but named with the user's name instead) in

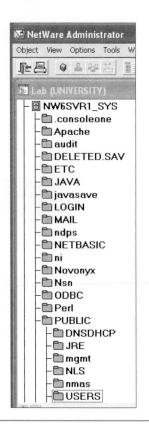

NetWare Administrator
Object View Options Tools W

Lab (UNIVERSITY)
└─ NW6SVR1_SYS
   ├─ .consoleone
   ├─ Apache
   ├─ audit
   ├─ DELETED.SAV
   ├─ ETC
   ├─ JAVA
   ├─ javasave
   ├─ LOGIN
   ├─ MAIL
   ├─ ndps
   ├─ NETBASIC
   ├─ ni
   ├─ Novonyx
   ├─ Nsn
   ├─ ODBC
   ├─ Perl
   └─ PUBLIC
      ├─ DNSDHCP
      ├─ JRE
      ├─ mgmt
      ├─ NLS
      ├─ nmas
      └─ USERS

• The NetWare Administrator view of the more typical implementation for a user's HOME directory

your PUBLIC\USERS directory. This can get confusing. Typically, a directory actually named HOME is created, and the directory named with the user's name is placed inside this HOME directory, making things easier to follow. In any case, only the users themselves will be granted access to their own HOME directory (the one with their username on it).

■ **SHARED**   Frequently, your users will also have shared files, perhaps a client database, that they wish to allow others to use over the network. Such items are usually stored in a SHARED directory created by the administrator. Users who are permitted to share all the information in the directory should be granted access to the entire SHARED directory, while other users may be granted access to individual items stored in the SHARED directory instead.

Subdirectories

A subdirectory is merely a directory stored inside another directory. Some of the directories identified previously were actually subdirectories because they were stored within other directories. Even though their names indicate that they are directories, they are actually classified as subdirectories. For example, the USERS directory you created on your NetWare server is actually a subdirectory within the PUBLIC directory on your NW6SVR1_SYS: volume. Furthermore, each of your users can have a HOME directory assigned that is actually a subdirectory of the USERS directory (or more correctly, of the USERS subdirectory).

It should be clear, then, that a subdirectory is simply a further subdivision of the information stored in its higher level directory object. In the USERS directory, for example, each user has a storage area on the network. Each user's storage area should be a separate folder within that USERS directory to separate each user's information from that of another user. Thus, each user has his or her own subdirectory within the USERS directory. As you can see, the terms *directory* and *subdirectory* are typically used interchangeably.

Step-by-Step 3.6

Changing a User's HOME Directory Location

You already created HOME directories for your network's users, but you want that location to be similar to what they will find on the typical network. You decide to create an additional subdirectory named HOME, in which you will put the system-created HOME directories (the ones with the users' names) to make the HOME directories easier to understand. In this exercise, you will use ConsoleOne first to create the new directory at your workstation, and then you will use ConsoleOne from

your server to reassign that new directory as your users' new default file-storage area.

To complete this exercise, you will need the following items:

■ Operational NetWare 6 server with the GUI operational and started

■ Networked Windows XP Professional workstation with Novell Client installed

■ ConsoleOne installed on your Windows XP Professional workstation

Step 1

Log in to your Windows XP Professional computer and your NetWare 6 server from your workstation as an administrative user.

Step 2

Double-click the ConsoleOne icon on your desktop. When ConsoleOne opens and displays the NDS and University icons, expand your University tree by clicking the plus sign (+) to the left of the icon, and then similarly expand your Lab container, NW6SVR1_ SYS server, PUBLIC directory, and USERS subdirectory.

Step 3

Right-click the USERS directory and select New | Object. Highlight the Directory folder, and click OK.

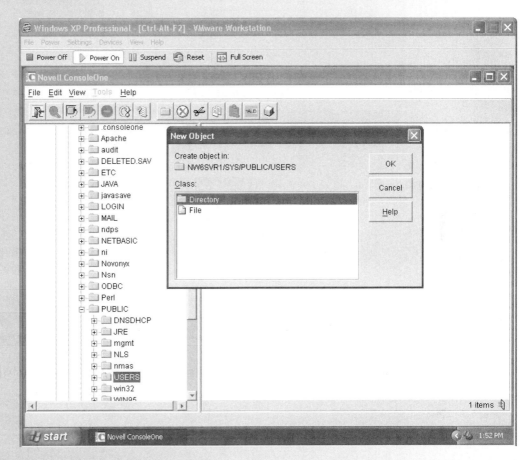

Step 4

Enter **HOME** as the directory's name, and click OK.

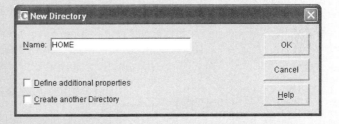

Step 5

Verify that the new HOME directory has been created in ConsoleOne's right pane.

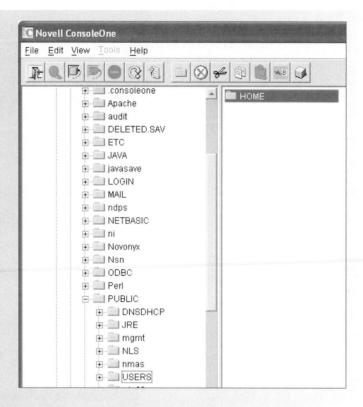

Step 6

From your server's GUI screen, click the Novell button and click ConsoleOne. When ConsoleOne starts, navigate in the left pane and highlight your LAB container object to expand it.

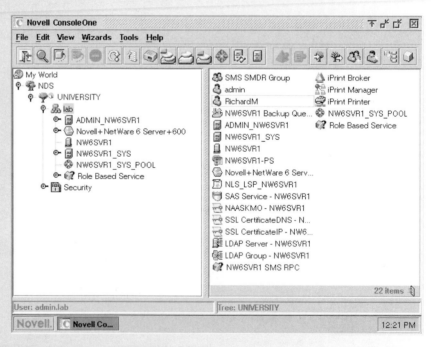

Step 7

Double-click the user object in the right pane whose HOME directory is to be changed (RichardM in this example) to open the Properties window. Click the General tab in the Properties window, and select Environment from the tab's drop-down selections. Use the Browse button in the Home Directory section to locate your newly created HOME directory, and click Apply.

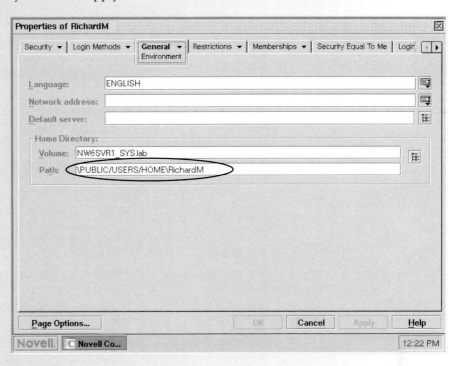

Return to ConsoleOne on your workstation and double-click your new HOME directory. Verify that the new location is now being used for your user's HOME directory.

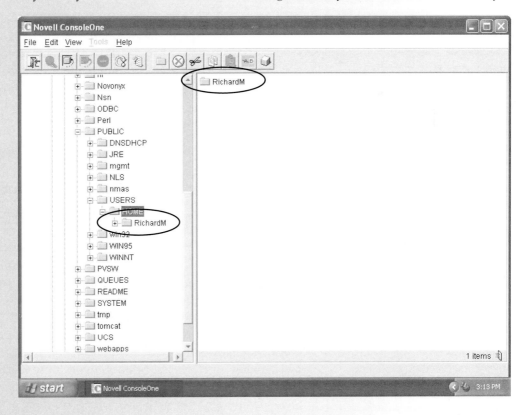

Files

Much like the documents stored in a filing cabinet, Novell uses the term file to represent a document (containing data) stored in NFS. Although files are at the end of the NFS description and may seem insignificant when viewed from that perspective, remember that the whole reason you developed your network in the first place was to allow you to share just such information (files consisting of data) with your classmates.

Files can be spreadsheets, PowerPoint presentations, Word documents, graphics files, or other individual data items. They can also be applications or any other blocks of data. You initially set out to develop a network to have somewhere to store your own files. Now, assuming you have sufficient space on your server, you have a place to store all the files you or your classmates create in this course.

Syntax

The normal syntax (or formatting structure) of the filename helps NFS locate your files. NFS requires a colon between the volume name and the directory and backslashes between subsequent directory, subdirectory, and filenames.

For example, your NetWare server and your PUBLIC directory would be identified as NW6SVR1_SYS:PUBLIC. Because the system is also aware that the NW6SVR1_SYS is the SYSTEM volume (or SYS), the same subdirectory can also be specified by the more simple name SYS:PUBLIC.

A reference to a subdirectory within its parent directory looks like this:

```
SYS:PUBLIC\USERS\HOME\RichardM
```

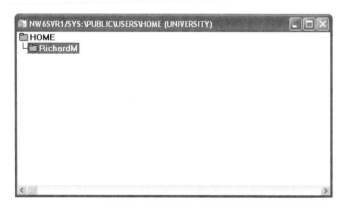

This example identifies the RichardM user's directory in the HOME directory in your NetWare server.

RichardM's HOME directory location is shown in the illustration at left, which also contains the correct syntax showing the server through file format.

• The NetWare Administrator view of RichardM's new HOME directory showing the proper filename syntax

■ Implementing Windows and NetWare Network Management

How you manage your network, and how the network's users employ the resources entrusted to them, determines the overall value of the network. If you don't properly maintain the network, the effort required to create it in the first place goes to waste.

Studying the network components discussed in the previous section will help you ensure your network's success. Regardless of the size of your network, many of the administrative responsibilities will involve managing networking functions. A healthy network's use will tend to increase rapidly, and the better your networking management skills, the better you will be able to maintain your network.

Windows Networks

When your network is operational and you are using many of the features discussed earlier in this chapter, it will become evident that the amount of storage space needed by your users seems to be ever-increasing. Microsoft makes two additional features available that will help you on the Windows portion of the network. The first, compression, helps reduce the amount of space needed for the data stored on your network. The second, quotas, lets you limit the amount of network storage space your users are authorized to use.

Compressing Data

Because you created your server and all your workstations using NTFS, you can use the Windows advanced storage feature that helps extend your network's existing storage capacity—**compression**. Compressing data reduces the size of a file so that it takes up less storage space. If you have a lot of data stored on your network, and you implement compression, you can store more in the same amount of space, making your network that much more valuable to the users without spending any money on additional storage space.

Compression is not quite as simple as it sounds—there are some trade-offs. For example, when copying a file to a compressed volume, NTFS reserves space for that file to be uncompressed, so if there is enough space for the compressed file but not enough to uncompress the file, the copy action will be disallowed. Furthermore, there is a slight decrease in performance due to the requirement to decompress a file before use.

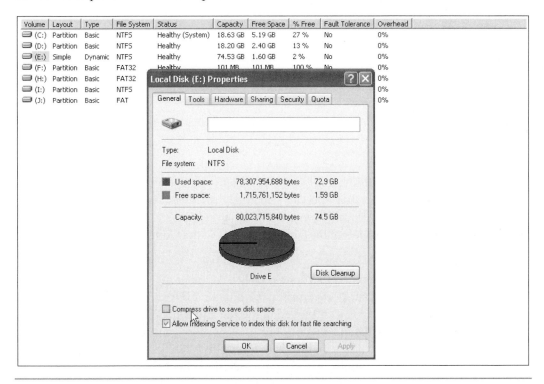

• This volume is an excellent candidate for implementing compression.

Compression Levels Compression can be initiated either at the volume level, which compresses everything on the disk drive, or at the file level. At the file level, you can select individual files you want compressed, while leaving everything else uncompressed. Compression at the file level is implemented using the object's Properties dialog box. At the bottom of the General tab, you simply click the Advanced button; and in the bottom section of the Advanced Attributes dialog box, select the Compress Contents to Save Disk Space option.

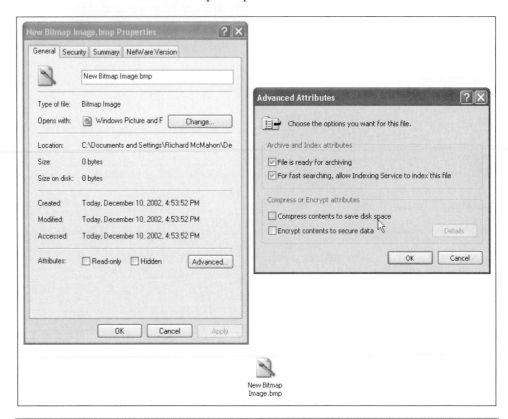

• File-level compression

At the volume level, this is reversed, and everything is compressed with the exception that you can selectively uncompress individual files. When compressing volumes, you again use the object's Properties dialog box, and at the bottom left of the General tab, select the Compress Drive to Save Disk Space option.

Compression on NTFS Volumes Only   Windows 2000 and Windows XP Professional support compression only on NTFS volumes. Whether you set compression to be employed at the file and folder level or at the entire volume level, each file on the volume has its own compressed or uncompressed condition attribute (which, when applied, results in a file's compression state). Applications using compressed files check the compression state and simply uncompress any applicable files prior to using them. All DOS- and Windows-based applications can thus use compressed files. When an application is done with a previously compressed file, or you initiate a save action, NTFS compresses the file once again.

Compression Rules   There is a general rule (with one exception) that helps explain compression attributes: A file, whether copied or moved, will inherit the compression attribute of the new folder it is being copied or moved into. The one exception is that a "move" within the same volume (partition) will not inherit the new folder's compression attribute. The reason for this exception is that the file is not actually being moved from the point of view of the operating system—only a pointer is moved, "pointing" to the original location.

An example will help explain. If you move a file from one location on an NTFS volume to another location on the same volume, the file retains its original compression state in its new location. If you copy that file from the same NTFS volume just discussed to the same new location, though, the new file acquires the compression state of the new location while the old file still remains in the original location with the same compression state.

The rule changes when using FAT partitions. When you copy or move a file from an NTFS volume to a FAT partition, the file is uncompressed first and then copied so that it matches the normally uncompressed level of the FAT partition.

When you implement compression at the directory (folder or above) level, you are given the option of leaving the object's contents in their present compression state (whether compressed or uncompressed) or imposing compression on all its contents. Additionally, once that directory-level object is marked as being in the compressed state, all objects subsequently added are immediately compressed.

Setting Quotas

A second Windows advanced storage feature that you can use on your NTFS computers allows you to share what storage you have with as many users as possible—this involves the use of quotas. Providing users a specific quota, or an assigned limit on the amount of network storage space they can use, helps ensure an equitable distribution when such networked resources are limited. The use of quotas is implemented through the Properties dialog box on each disk drive formatted with NTFS. Microsoft's quotas feature is not available on FAT partitions.

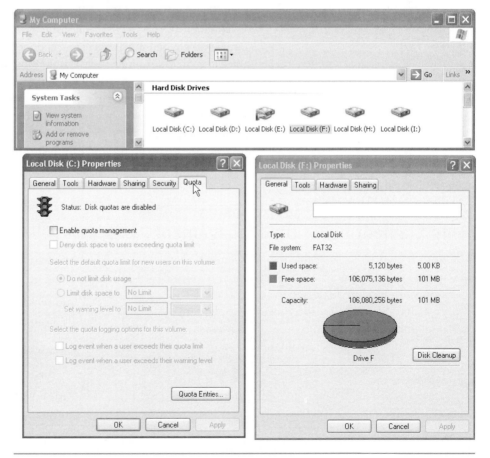

Equal Access but No Limits

Typically, when networks are first created, storage space

• Notice that the Quota tab is available on the NTFS volume but not the FAT volume.

appears unlimited and users are granted storage privileges on a first-come-first-served basis. That is, everyone has equal access to the storage, but there are no limits. What frequently happens is that some users quickly take up all the space, and those users with little (or no) space on the disks complain that such a system is not fair. If all was fair and everyone on your network was to have equal availability for storing their files, then your network's total storage capacity would have to be calculated and divided such that all users get an equal share. Keeping track of such an equitable storage solution at the network level would be burdensome.

Equal Access with Limits   All is not fair, and everyone on your network does not really need an equal amount of the total storage you have available. Nor should network management be unnecessarily burdensome. Rather, Microsoft's implementation of disk quotas lets you assign users limited storage on specified volumes anywhere on your network. The limits you place can be general, so that all users with access to a particular volume have the same amount, or they can be specific, so that some users have a higher storage limit. Thus, storage is divided at the NTFS volume level.

Setting Limits   You set limits on disk space use by implementing quotas on your NTFS volumes. After imposing the quotas, you have the choice of either enforcing their use or simply monitoring users for compliance. In addition to setting a limit on storage, you can give users a warning whenever they go beyond another, lesser, amount that you can also set. This warns users that they are running out of space and might encourage them to delete some files that they don't need to keep but haven't yet needed to delete.

You have the option of configuring quota management to halt further storage attempts when the quota is reached, or you can then have it simply send a notice to a predetermined recipient that the quota has been exceeded (usually an administrator or manager) who could then take the appropriate action—either increasing storage facilities or requesting compliance with the quota.

Another option you have when setting enforced limits is to reconfigure specific users separately. Some users may really need additional storage space, and you can increase the limits for those users on a case-by-case basis.

Step-by-Step 3.7

Implementing Quota Management

Your network storage capacity has been left open for users to store as much as they want on any of the storage devices. You decide to start monitoring potential misuse of this privilege by implementing quota management, and you want to practice on one of your network's NTFS volumes.

To complete this exercise, you will need the following:

- A Windows XP Professional workstation computer formatted using NTFS

Step 1

Log in to a Windows XP workstation as the administrative user, click the Start button, and then select Administrative Tools | Computer Management. Expand the Storage item in the left pane and select Disk Management. In the lower section of the right pane, right-click the icon of the disk that houses the volume where you will be implementing quotas, and select Properties.

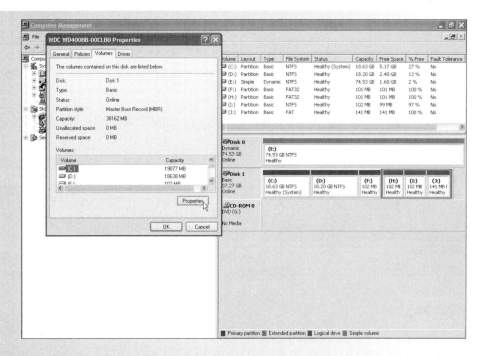

Step 2

In the Properties dialog box, click the Volumes tab and notice that you have access to all the volumes on your selected disk. In the Volumes section, scroll to and select the volume where you want quotas implemented, then click the Properties button.

Note: Accessing the entire disk drive's Properties dialog box gives you an alternative route to the Properties dialog boxes of all the volumes on that disk drive. If you are only configuring one volume, you can go directly to that volume's Properties dialog box through the My Computer window.

Step 3

In the resulting Properties dialog box, click the Quota tab and check the Enable Quota Management check box. Select the Limit Disk Space To option and set both the limit and the warning levels. Select both logging options, and click the Apply button.

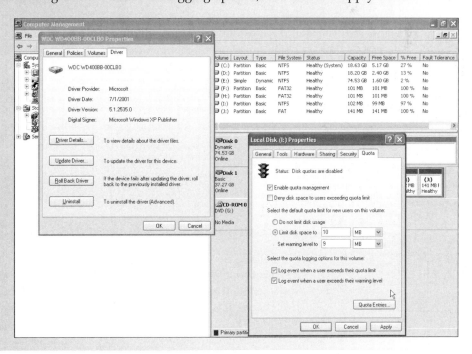

Note: If it is the first time quota management has been implemented on the volume, click OK on the Disk Quota window to enable the quota system.

Step 4

Click the Quota Entries button and observe the storage allocations currently set on the disk. In the Quota Entries window, notice that there are no imposed limits on any of the users. No limits are imposed unless you deny users additional space for exceeding their limit.

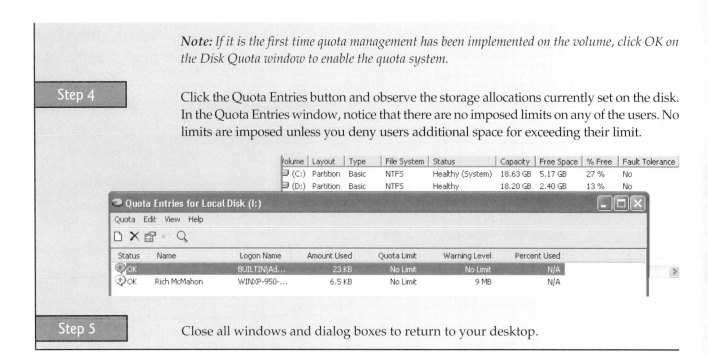

Step 5

Close all windows and dialog boxes to return to your desktop.

NetWare Networks

When it comes to managing your network components, you should consider the NetWare portion entirely on its own. This is true even though, as you have seen throughout this course, the majority of what you have done so far with your NetWare server has been accomplished from your Windows XP Professional workstation's desktop (and possibly from your Windows 2000 Server's desktop). Your NetWare 6 server offers its own, extremely detailed and oftentimes complex network management components. This course is not intended to prepare you to the point where you are an expert with these tools. Rather, the introductory nature of this course is intended to provide you with an understanding of some of the basic tools available and show you some that are comparable to those you learned about for managing the Windows portion of your network.

Using the Server Console

On large networks using most of NetWare's server capabilities, server management involves extensive communication between the administrator and the server's network operating system. This communication primarily takes the form of text-based commands and NetWare Loadable Modules (NLMs), and the majority of these are still entered or loaded by administrators using the server console. The ConsoleOne and Internet-based administration techniques, such as iManage, used in the Novell portions of this text are gaining more and more acceptance, but for now, entering text-based commands at your NetWare server's console is still the most widely used management technique.

Entering Text-Based Commands at the Console   The NetWare operating system includes numerous commands that operators use when they interface with the file server's hardware and software. The commands are part of the operating system, just as DOS commands are part of the disk operating system (DOS) or Microsoft's utilities that are built into Windows.

You must be just as careful when using NetWare commands as when working with DOS commands or Windows utilities. They will act immediately upon whatever part of the server you specify, and they will do whatever you ask of them. Some are stand-alone commands, in that they are used without any command **arguments** (parts of the command that usually tell the system what to execute the command upon). Other commands, such as the LOAD command, will not work unless the arguments are there.

If your syntax (the format of the command) is incorrect, the command may not be understood at all, or it may be misunderstood and performed by the software, returning either an error or the wrong result. On the other hand, if your syntax is correct but your command is for the wrong function, you could affect your server's health. Furthermore, in actual operation, many commands are interpreted by the system even if they are omitted. The command NAME.NLM could be executed at the console by typing **LOAD NAME.NLM** or by simply typing **NAME**. In the second instance, the system assumes you want it to LOAD an NLM and interprets your command appropriately. Therefore, typing **NAME** at the console would be an example of properly using a NetWare text-based command.

The results of using the commands are pretty easy to predict if they are used properly. The NAME command simply returns the server's name. Misspell it as NAM, however, and the system looks for a file named NAM to load. Similarly, entering the TIME command at the server console returns the system time, and entering MEMORY returns the server's total memory; on the other hand, entering the misspelled TIM looks for a file named TIM to load. Not all commands are that easily interpreted, however, and depending on how bad your misspelling is, the system could end up doing something entirely different from what you intended.

```
NW6SVR1:name
This is server NW6SVR1
NW6SVR1:time
  Time zone string: "CST6CDT"
  DST status:  OFF
  DST start:    Sunday, April 6, 2003   2:00:00 am CST
  DST end:      Sunday, October 26, 2003   2:00:00 am CDT
  Time synchronization is active.
  Time is synchronized to the network.
Wednesday, December 11, 2002   9:02:15 pm UTC
Wednesday, December 11, 2002   3:02:15 pm CST
NW6SVR1:memory
Total server memory: 261,758 Kilobytes
NW6SVR1:_
```

- Three NetWare text-based commands entered at the server console, and their results

Table 3.1 lists some commonly used commands.

Table 3.1	Common NetWare Text Commands
Command	**Description**
LOAD <NLM>	Reads the applicable NLM into the server's RAM
UNLOAD <NLM>	Removes the applicable NLM from the server's RAM
DOWN	Closes all open files/volumes and shuts down the server
SECURE CONSOLE	Removes DOS from the server; also allows loading NLMs only from SYS:SYSTEM

Table 3.1	Common NetWare Text Commands (continued)
Command	Description
MODULES	Displays currently loaded NLMs
CONFIG	Displays server's network interface card information
DISPLAY NETWORKS	Displays all networks to which the server has access
DISPLAY SERVERS	Displays all servers on which the server has information
SET TIME	Allows changing of the current system date and time
SEND	Allows transmitting message to currently logged on users

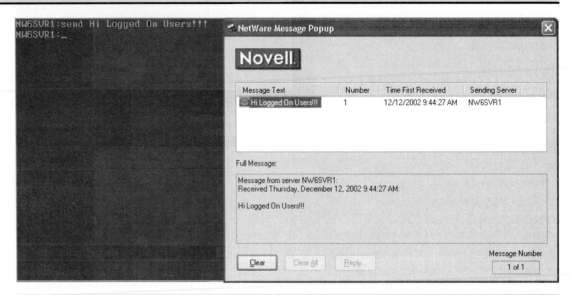

- The SEND command entered at the server console and its resulting message at the users' workstations

Using NetWare Loadable Modules   Unlike console commands, NetWare Loadable Modules (NLMs) are commands stored in locations outside the operating system. NLMs add functionality to the operating system's core capabilities, and an operator must load the NLMs into the server's memory to use them. Performing a LOAD action tells the server to read the particular module into its memory from the default SYS:SYSTEM location (unless another path is specified), and to then execute (or run) the module. The added functionality then remains in the server, provided the server continues to run, or until the operator decides to UNLOAD the NLM.

At the console prompt, type **CDROM.NLM** to prepare the server to operate the CD drive. The NLM must be loaded before running the MOUNT command when working with CDs. The MOUNT command makes a volume available for users, and it is run only once after the server is started. The MOUNT command then stays in memory until the DISMOUNT command is run (making the volume unavailable) or you DOWN the server. The NLM can be added to the startup commands so that it loads automatically whenever the server is started.

Although many of the common NLMs have an .NLM extension following the command's name, there are other extensions available such as .DSK and .LAN, as shown in Table 3.2. Table 3.3 lists some commonly used NLM modules.

Using the MONITOR NLM

MONITOR is an important NLM that you will likely use very often. If you are responsible for the overall health of your network, you will probably spend a great deal of your time reviewing the MONITOR.NLM statistics. The server's performance and operating statistics, as well as information about the connections made to the server, can be accessed by using MONITOR at your server console.

Table 3.2	NLM Types
NLM Types	**Description**
.DSK	Provides direct control of server drives (located in the DOS partition)
.LAN	Provides control drivers for network interface cards
.NLM	Adds general-purpose capabilities to the server

Running MONITOR

Typing **LOAD MONITOR** (or just **MONITOR**) at the console prompt and pressing the ENTER key will give you a screen containing several pieces of information about your server, as shown in Figure 3.1.

Table 3.3	Common NLMs
Common NLMs	**Description**
MONITOR.NLM	Provides general performance information on the server
NWCONFIG.NLM	Provides the main functions used for server configuration
CDROM.NLM	Adds CD support to the server
DSREPAIR.NLM	Allows repairs to NDS
VREPAIR.NLM	Allows repairs to specified volumes
REMOTE.NLM	Allows server operation (with password) at workstation
3C509.LAN	An example of a control driver (3Com network card)

If nothing else is entered through the console for approximately ten seconds after loading MONITOR.NLM, the General Information part of the screen opens further, as shown in Figure 3.2, and additional information is displayed. This additional information is also available in the initial screen if you press the TAB key. The TAB key also toggles you back and forth between the expanded window and the reduced initial screen.

Quick Snapshot Sometimes a quick snapshot of a network's traffic flow while the network is in actual operation will tell you if a problem exists. For example, if the total number of cache buffers (available working memory) in the General Information window falls below half of the original cache buffers, this indicates that the server is running low on memory, and you should either increase memory or decrease the demands on the amount of memory you have. Either add RAM or UNLOAD NLMs.

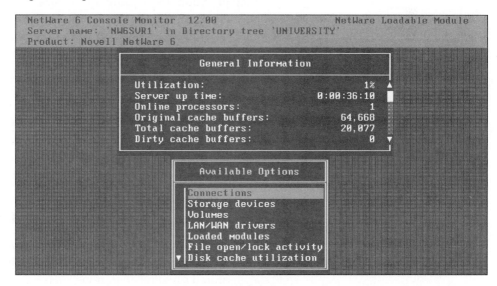

● **Figure 3.1** The initial results of running the LOAD MONITOR command at your server console

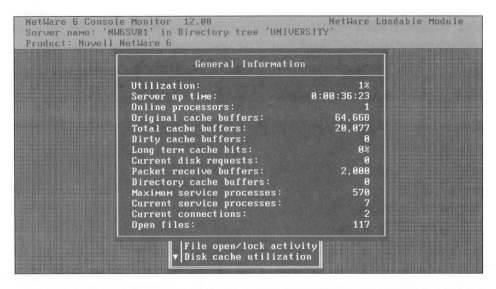

```
NetWare 6 Console Monitor   12.00              NetWare Loadable Module
Server name: 'NW6SVR1' in Directory tree 'UNIVERSITY'
Product: Novell NetWare 6

                        General Information
        Utilization:                           1%
        Server up time:                  0:00:36:23
        Online processors:                      1
        Original cache buffers:            64,668
        Total cache buffers:               20,077
        Dirty cache buffers:                    0
        Long term cache hits:                  0%
        Current disk requests:                  0
        Packet receive buffers:             2,000
        Directory cache buffers:                0
        Maximum service processes:            570
        Current service processes:              7
        Current connections:                    2
        Open files:                           117

              File open/lock activity
           ▼  Disk cache utilization
```

● **Figure 3.2**   After ten seconds of inactivity, the General Information section expands.

This course is not intended to give you a complete understanding of each of the preceding items. The goal at this introductory level is to show you where to go should you need to locate such information in times of crisis. Keeping track of the information here also lets you record trends that can help you spot potential problems as they develop.

Using the DSREPAIR NLM

Hopefully, you will *not* need to repair your NDS tree. If you must repair it, though, you should have some idea of where to go to initiate the repairs. Running the DSREPAIR NLM will help you.

You used DSREPAIR after you built your server, so you should know a little about the NLM. Occasionally running DSREPAIR will help remove small network problems before they progress any further.

Copies of NDS are located on other servers in various locations around the network, and this makes the timing of updates critical. If you are wondering whether errors in timing, and the fact that NDS is spread over several locations can cause NDS to become disjointed at times, it can. That is when DSREPAIR really comes in handy.

Unattended Full Repair   You should recall that selecting the Unattended Full Repair option in DSREPAIR and pressing ENTER immediately initiates the repair action. Depending on the size of your network, this could take some time to complete. On a small network, such as yours, the process should take only a few seconds to complete.

When the repair action is completed, a window is displayed informing you that "All automatic repair operations have been completed." It also tells you the number of errors and the total amount of repair time the operation required. It is not uncommon for DSREPAIR to uncover numerous insignificant errors, so occasionally running DSREPAIR will help keep your network operating properly. You may need to run it several times when removing errors. Provided you have the network idle time available to you, rerun the process until zero errors are found by DSREPAIR.

Advanced Options Menu   Selecting the Advanced Options Menu and pressing ENTER provides the following additional DSREPAIR options:

- **Log File and Login Configuration**   Configures options for the DSREPAIR log file. Logging in to the Directory Services tree is required by some operations.

- **Repair Local DS Database**   Repairs the Directory Services database files stored on this server.

120

- **Servers Known to This Database**   Shows the names of the servers that have performed the following operations to this server's database: time synchronization, network addresses, and server information.

- **Replica and Partition Operations**   Provides functions to repair replicas, replica rings, and server objects. This option also dynamically displays each server's last synchronization time.

- **Check Volume Objects and Trustees**   Checks all mounted volumes for valid volume objects and valid trustees on the volumes.

- **Check External References**   Checks for illegal external references.

- **Security Equivalence Synchronization**   Allows users to synchronize security equivalence attributes throughout the tree.

- **Global Schema Operations**   Provides functions to update the schema in the tree.

- **View Repair Log File**   Allows you to edit the log file, which is optionally created when repair operations are performed.

- **Create a Database Dump File**   Copies the Directory Services database files to disk in compressed format, to be used for offline repairs and diagnostics. This is not to be used as a backup method.

- **Return to Main Menu**   Exits this menu and returns to the main list.

You will probably be interested in running only the Repair Local DS Database and the Check Volume Objects and Trustees options. The first will behave in the same way as the unattended option that you ran earlier, and the second will require that your fully distinguished administrator user name and password be used for authorization. It is useful to use both of these options on an occasional basis. They should not return major errors unless there is a significant problem.

Step-by-Step 3.8

Using NWCONFIG

You should become familiar with another frequently used NLM—the NWCONFIG NLM. This is the NLM that you will use to accomplish most of the configuration options needed on your NetWare server.

To complete this exercise, you will need the following items:

- An operational NetWare 6 server
- Your administrative user information (if not already logged in to the server)

Step 1   From your NetWare 6 server's GUI desktop, press CTRL-ESC to go to the Current Screens window. Enter the selection number for the System Console.

Step 2   Type **NWCONFIG** at the server console, and press ENTER to view the options available.

Note: Most of the options listed are self-explanatory. Several options have additional features when selected, but three, Legacy Disk Options, NSS Disk Options, and License Options, tell you that they no longer work through NWCONFIG when you select them and press ENTER.

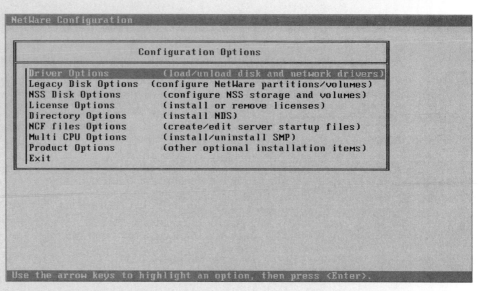

Step 3

Select Driver Options, press ENTER, and press ENTER again to view the disk drivers currently loaded on your server. You could press ENTER yet again to either search for additional drivers or load new drivers on your server. Press the ESC key twice to return to the initial NWCONFIG screen.

Step 4

Select Directory Options, press ENTER, and notice the important actions available to you here, such as installing or removing Directory Services, creating Directory backups, or extending the schema.

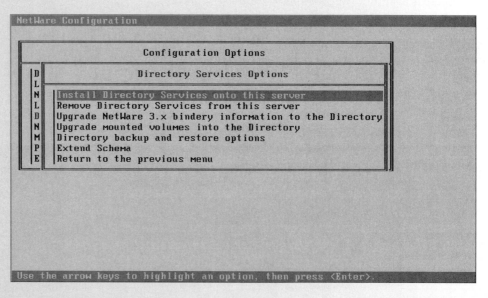

Step 5

Select Directory Backup and Restore Options, press ENTER, and press ENTER again to select the Save Local NDS Information Before Hardware Upgrade option. Read the notice that comes up on your computer screen.

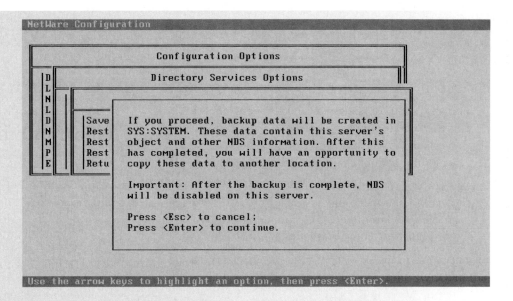

Note: If you do ever have to use this backup technique, you will be required to use your fully qualified administrative username (CN=Admin.O=LAB) and password.

Step 6

Click Cancel so you do not actually implement the backup action. You could damage your copy of NDS in the process. Press the ESC key twice to return to the initial NWCONFIG screen.

Step 7

Look through the remaining options without implementing any changes (use the same general procedures as in Steps 3 through 6). From the initial NWCONFIG screen, press the ESC key again when you are finished, and select Yes and press ENTER to exit NWCONFIG.

Chapter 3 Review

■ Chapter Summary

After reading this chapter and completing the exercises, you should understand the following.

Install and Configure Novell NetWare 6.0 Server

■ Servers are usually the fastest and most powerful computers a company can afford.

■ Novell NetWare is a server-only network operating system; Microsoft Windows 2000 Server is a server operating system that can also be used in workstation mode; and Red Hat Linux provides a low-cost alternative to using Microsoft's operating system products.

■ When preparing to install a server, check the hardware compatibility, check its configuration (possibly removing any NT partitions, if applicable), and test your hardware.

■ Novell NetWare 6 minimum hardware requirements include a Pentium II processor with 256MB of RAM and at least 2GB of available hard disk space.

■ Vendors specify their hardware requirements specifying the required minimums that you must have and recommended minimums that they think you should have.

■ When installing a server, it is a good idea to start with a fresh installation.

■ Use the DOS command FDISK when partitioning fixed disks.

■ Use a cold start when initiating a server installation to ensure all settings are reinitialized.

■ You must accept an operating system's license agreement in order to continue with the setup process.

■ The procedures you learned when installing these servers will be similar to those you will use in an employer's production environment.

Install and Configure Novell Client

■ You cannot access your server on your network from non-NetWare computers unless they have Novell Client installed.

■ Novell Client runs on Windows workstations so they can connect to Novell servers.

■ Novell Client software provides a very simple installation process.

■ Windows XP Professional more than meets the requirements for Novell Client software, so you can immediately start your client installation on a Windows XP Professional computer.

■ You can download the latest version of the client software from the Novell web site.

■ Novell Client requires at least the Window NT 4.0 operating system (with service pack 3 installed) but also installs on Windows 2000 and Windows XP computers.

■ Make sure your Local Area Connection Properties dialog box is closed before starting your Novell Client installation.

■ After completing the Novell Client installation, you are presented with a different initial login screen when you start your Windows XP Professional computer.

■ Upon logging in to your Windows XP Professional computer, you can elect to log in to just your Windows environment or choose the more extensive login that connects you to the Novell server as well.

■ When you log in to your computer through Novell Client using different passwords for Novell and Windows, you are given the option of changing your Windows password to match your Novell password for a single login entry.

Use Novell's Network File System

■ When the NetWare operating system is installed, some of the file system is created, and it gets configured by administrators and employed by users so they can share their files.

■ Accessing networked resources becomes a reason other users join the network.

■ The NetWare file system also stores and shares networked applications.

■ All NetWare servers contain NFS components, which include file servers, volumes, directories, subdirectories, and files, that together provide centralized access and coordinated sharing for users.

- Names within NFS have to be unique to allow the system to find the files; the names cannot include any reserved characters.

- A volume is a physical storage device and is similar to a DOS disk drive.

- The first volume created on a NetWare network is the SYS: volume, where the operating system files are stored.

- Although they are automatically named by the system, you can change additional volumes' names during installation or later to help clarify your system's structure.

- NFS is another tree-like hierarchical structure similar to NDS.

- Inside NFS are required directories, such as SYS, PUBLIC, and LOGIN, as well as optional directories, such as USERS, HOME, and APPS.

- Mapping a drive tells the operating system to treat the newly mapped object as a separate hard drive.

- Filename syntax is a formatting structure that helps NFS locate your files.

Implement Windows and NetWare Network Management

- Improperly maintaining networks wastes the effort required to create them.

- A healthy network's use will tend to increase rapidly.

- Compression reduces the size of files so they take up less storage space.

- Having smaller files that contain the same data means that you can store more valuable information on your network without increasing storage space.

- Compression can only be implemented on NTFS volumes.

- Compression can be implemented at the volume level with everything on that volume being stored in the compressed state, or at the file level where only specific files are compressed.

- Compression and encryption are mutually exclusive.

- Applications using compressed files check the compression state and uncompress applicable files prior to use.

- Except for FAT partitions (which are always uncompressed), moving a compressed file from one location on a volume to another location on the same volume has that file retain its original compression state, whereas copying that file to another location on the same volume has the file acquire the compression state of the receiving location.

- When implementing compression, you have the option of leaving an object's contents as they are or compressing them.

- Quota management assigns a limit on the amount of space users can use for storage on specific volumes.

- Quota management is available only on NTFS volumes.

- Quotas can be implemented as mandatory, in which case they are enforced, or as informational, which means compliance is simply monitored.

- Quota use on compressed volumes is calculated based on the uncompressed size of the stored files.

- NetWare 6 has extremely detailed, and sometimes complex, network management components.

- The NetWare server console's text-based commands are still the most widely used management technique.

- Some NetWare commands are stand-alone commands, and others require arguments.

- There are hundreds of commands available for use at the NetWare server console, and you can get information about their use by using the HELP command.

- NLMs are commands stored in locations outside the operating system.

- The NetWare MONITOR NLM is a tool for gathering and monitoring information about your network's health.

- Periodically running DSREPAIR helps maintain your system.

- NWCONFIG is another important utility used to obtain and update information about your network.

■ Key Terms

active partition *(79)*	**arguments** *(117)*	**cache buffers** *(119)*
administrator password *(86)*	**boot partition** *(75)*	**cold start** *(77)*

compression *(111)*
DSREPAIR *(87)*
FAT *(80)*
drive letter mapping *(100)*
NDOS *(80)*
NLM *(87)*
Novell Client *(94)*

Novell Services icon *(99)*
NTFS *(79)*
one-step login *(99)*
partitions *(76)*
password synchronization *(99)*
primary DOS partition *(76)*
quota *(113)*

server directory *(87)*
SYS C: *(80)*
SYS volume *(80)*
SYS.COM *(80)*
Windows NT boot loader *(80)*

■ Key Term Quiz

Use the Key Terms list to complete the following sentences. (Not all of the terms will be used.)

1. When you perform a new installation of a server's operating system, it is a good practice to check the operating system vendor's web site to see if a new _____ has been released to update your new system.

2. When installing Novell NetWare 6 on your computer, the type of partition that may need to have a Windows NT boot loader removed before it can be repartitioned is the _____ partition.

3. _____ is Novell's version of DOS and it is included with Novell's installation software package.

4. The software added to a workstation so that the computer can operate using a networked Novell server is called _____.

5. The highest-level storage unit in the _____ structure is called the file server.

6. A(n) _____ is an object representing an area on a NetWare physical network storage device where files are stored.

7. User files and associated documents are usually stored in their own HOME _____.

8. When running MONITOR on a NetWare 6 server, if the available memory, also called _____, falls below half of its original amount, a remedy could be to add RAM or UNLOAD NLMs.

9. An assigned limit on the amount of network storage a user can use is called a(n) _____.

10. The Windows advanced storage feature that helps extend your network's storage capacity by reducing the size of files is called _____.

■ Multiple-Choice Quiz

1. Which of the following is a server-only operating system?
   a. Windows 2000
   b. Novell 6.0
   c. Red Hat Linux 7.3
   d. DOS

2. Which of the following is (are) not a stated minimum requirement for a Novell 6.0 server?
   a. Pentium III processor
   b. 256MB of RAM
   c. Server-class computer
   d. At least 2GB of available hard disk space

3. Which of the following hardware items is (are) required when installing a Novell 6 server?
   a. CD-ROM drive
   b. SVGA display adapter

   c. Network interface card
   d. USB, PS/2, or serial mouse

4. Which of the following should be accomplished before initially setting up a new server?
   a. Start with a fresh installation.
   b. Rebuild your hard disk drive.
   c. Use FDISK to delete all but the primary partition.
   d. Create two primary DOS partitions.

5. Which of the following are the two install options available when installing Novell's NetWare 6?
   a. Express
   b. Full
   c. Partial
   d. Custom

6. The required boot partition needed for a Novell NetWare 6 installation is

   a. 200MB

   b. 2GB

   c. 100MB

   d. 1GB

7. What must occur after the initial file copying process of a Novell NetWare 6 installation before the installer can leave the text-based mode and enter the graphical mode to finish copying the files?

   a. Down the server.

   b. The server must reboot.

   c. You must select Text to Graphics.

   d. GNOME must be installed.

8. Which of the following protocols is (are) available during a Novell NetWare 6 installation?

   a. IPX/SPX

   b. IPX

   c. IP

   d. NETBEUI

9. Which of the following is true regarding Novell Client software?

   a. You must use the Novell Client software included on your NetWare 6 server installation CD.

   b. Novell Client software is available on a set of bootable floppy disks.

   c. Novell offers free downloads of its latest Novell Client software through its web site.

   d. Novell Client software must be loaded before installing a Windows operating system.

10. Of the following Windows operating systems, which cannot have Novell's latest client (4.83) installed?

    a. Windows XP

    b. Windows 2000

    c. Windows NT

    d. Windows 98

11. Which of the following statements is *not* true regarding Novell's client software?

    a. Novell Client is capable of creating a single-step login process, where you log in to multiple servers with one username and password.

b. Your NetWare 6 server must be operational prior to installing the latest version of Novell Client on a workstation running Windows XP Professional.

c. Using the Novell Client software gives you the option of logging in to your workstation only.

d. There are multiple versions of Novell's client software, and you should select the version applicable to your workstation's installed version of Windows.

12. Which of the following is the executable file used to install Novell Client software on your Windows XP Professional computer?

    a. setup.exe

    b. setupclient.exe

    c. setupnw.exe

    d. c483SP1e.exe

13. Which of the following is *not* true when logging on to your Windows XP Professional computer using Novell Client?

    a. On the NDS tab, you can use the Trees button to select your NDS tree.

    b. On the Windows tab, you can use the Servers button to select your Windows server.

    c. On the NDS tab, you can use the Servers button to select your Novell server.

    d. On the Windows tab, you can enter a local computer password different from the one used for your Novell login.

14. When comparing the filing cabinet to the file system used on NetWare 6 networks, which of the following components would be most like the filing cabinet's drawers?

    a. File

    b. Folder

    c. Volume

    d. Subdirectory

15. All of the following are required in the NetWare 6 operating system except which one?

    a. APPLICATION

    b. SYSTEM

    c. PUBLIC

    d. LOGIN

Essay Quiz

1. In your own words, explain how you would convince a novice networking specialist to reformat and rebuild the hard disk drive of a computer that will be used as a new server on your network.

2. Based upon your experiences with the three server installations, defend or refute the following statement: "A graphical user interface lets a user accomplish more."

3. Explain why the computer used as a server is usually the fastest and most powerful computer in an organization.

4. What is the purpose of mapping a drive?

5. When considering whether to use compression on your network servers, why is it important that you find out if encryption is being used?

Lab Projects

• Lab Project 3.1

In your position at SinkRSwim Pools, you have been asked to rebuild a server that just recently had its hard drive fail. The hardware supplier delivered the new hard drive's warranty replacement, and it has already been installed in the server. You have been asked to format the drive with a 500MB boot partition and to build a Novell NetWare 6 server using the express setup. Your server was running Novell NetWare 5 at the time it failed, so your company has decided to replace it with NetWare 6 now.

You will need the following:

- A lab computer that meets the Novell NetWare 6 minimum hardware requirements

- Novell NetWare 6 installation CD
- A set of DOS 6.21 or 6.22 diskettes
- A boot-enabled CD-ROM drive

Then do the following:

1. Use FDISK to repartition your new drive.
2. Insert the setup CD into the CD-ROM drive and reboot your system.
3. Continue the setup using the express setup procedures.
4. Test your server when it arrives at the graphical server console screen.

• Lab Project 3.2

Your TEACH organization has just recently installed a NetWare 6 server, upgraded its workstations to Windows XP Professional, and installed Novell Client software on each of the workstations. Some of your users have suggested that the login procedures they use should not include logging them into the NetWare server unless they have business on that server. They have requested training from you showing them how to change whether they log in to the server and how to browse their Windows XP Professional workstations to verify their network connection.

You will need the following:

- A lab computer with an operational NetWare 6 server

- Networked workstation computers running Windows XP Professional and Novell Client
- Access to the default administrator accounts on both the NetWare server and the local workstation

Then do the following:

1. Restart your workstation.
2. Press CTRL-ALT-DELETE at the Begin Login dialog box.
3. Observe the initial username that is displayed. Unless your default configurations have been changed, the username displayed should be the administrator account—admin.

4 Click the Workstation Only option. Notice that the username changes to the one you use when logging in to your Windows workstation. If you are still using the default accounts, this will be administrator.

5 Enter your administrator password and click OK.

6 Click the Start button and select My Computer. Notice that no Novell connections are displayed, and then close the My Computer window. Click the Start button, click the Log Off button, and click the Log Off button in the Log Off Windows dialog box.

7 Press CTRL-ALT-DELETE at the Begin Login dialog box to log in again.

8 Observe the initial username that is displayed. The username displayed should still be the administrator account—admin.

9 Ensure the Workstation Only option is not selected.

10 Enter your administrator password and click OK. You should see the Novell login screens appear as they are invoked.

11 Click the Start button and select My Computer. Notice that two default Novell connections are now displayed—System and Public. Close the My Computer window, click the Start button, click the Log Off button, and click the Log Off button in the Log Off Windows dialog box.

• Lab Project 3.3

Part two of the training you put together for your coworkers in the TEACH organization will show them how to verify their network connections from the Novell Client perspective. They have also requested training from you about how to create their own Documents folder on the NetWare server, and they want an easy way to browse directly to that folder using the Novell Services icon in their taskbar's notification area.

You will need the following:

- A lab computer with an operational NetWare 6 server

- Networked workstation computers running Windows XP Professional and Novell Client

- Access to the default administrator accounts on both the NetWare server and the local workstation

Then do the following:

1 Restart your workstation.

2 Press CTRL-ALT-DELETE at the Begin Login dialog box.

3 Ensure the Workstation Only option is not selected.

4 Enter your administrator password and click OK.

5 Right-click the Novell Services icon (the red *N*) in the taskbar's configuration area, select Browse To, and select My Computer. Notice that the same My Computer window opens as when you use the Start button on the Windows

XP taskbar. Notice also that the same two default Novell connections are displayed—System and Public. Close the My Computer window.

6 Double-click the Novell Services icon, and double-click the Novell Connections icon to display the Novell connection objects you logged in to—your server, context, and tree.

7 Double-click the server icon, double-click the SYS icon, and click the Make a New Folder option in the left panel of the SYS on NW6_ svr1 window (inserting your own server's name in place of "NW6_svr1"). Rename that new folder Rich_Documents (inserting your own name in place of "Rich"). Close the window.

8 Right-click the Novell Services icon, select Browse To, and select Edit Browseable Path.

9 In the Edit Browseable Path dialog box, click the Browse button and browse to the folder you just created, locating your server and SYS folder icons in the Network Resources window.

10 Highlight that new folder, click OK, click the Add button, and click the Close button.

11 Verify your new browse path's location operates properly by right-clicking the Novell Services icon, selecting Browse To, and selecting your new location.

12 Close the window and log off your computer.

Networking with Windows NT

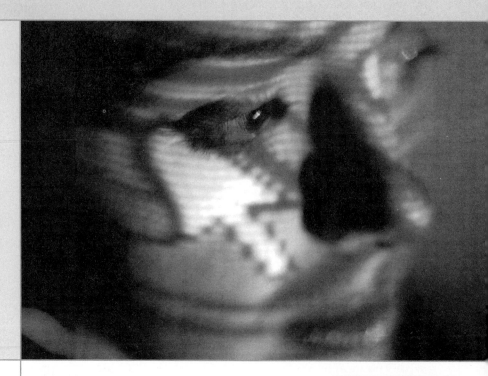

In this chapter, you will learn how to

- **Plan your Windows NT configuration**
- **Install Windows NT**
- **Determine and set Windows NT networking options**
- **Perform essential Windows NT administrative duties**

Planning and preparation are an important part of the Windows NT Server installation process. In this chapter, you will learn more about hardware requirements that need to be considered, the type of file system to be used, and the type of licensing to choose. The bulk of the chapter describes two methods you can use to install Windows NT Server 4.0: across the network using a network share or from a local CD-ROM. After a step-by-step description of the installation process, the chapter considers some special situations such as installation on a RISC computer, procedures for upgrading from a Windows NT 3.51 installation, and unattended installations. As you complete the installation, you'll need to know what protocol(s) the network will use for communication. Windows NT Server supports three protocol standards: TCP/IP, NWLink, and NetBEUI.

Another major section of the chapter deals with the maintenance and use of Windows NT in a networked environment. You learn about the use of primary domain controllers (PDCs) and backup domain controllers (BDCs) for domain management, removing Windows NT from computers, customizing the user desktop, managing Windows NT security, and mapping to shared network folders.

Planning the Hard Disk Configuration

Before you begin to install Windows NT 4.0, you must plan your hard disk partitioning scheme. Make sure to have a minimum amount of space available on the partition where you are installing Windows NT Server. You can set up a partition scheme prior to installation if you want to, or you can configure the partition scheme during installation. After the operating system is installed, systems administrators can make changes to partitions using Disk Administrator—except that the system partition must be configured during the installation process, and cannot be changed without reinstalling.

Windows NT 4.0 Server requires a minimum amount of free space on the system partition (the partition where you install Windows NT Server). The absolute minimum recommended by Microsoft for Intel x86-type computers is 124MB, but for satisfactory performance most networks require more space.

Two types of partitions are involved in Windows NT 4.0 installations: The system partition and the boot partition. It is interesting (and sometimes confusing) that the "system" partition is where the operating system boots from, and the "boot" partition is where the system files are stored. These aren't the only partitions available with Windows NT Server. Many other partitions can be set up for storing data and applications.

File System Considerations

You also need to decide how you want your file system configured. You can install Windows NT Server either with the traditional FAT (file allocation table) file system used for DOS, Windows 95, Windows 3.1, and Windows for Workgroups 3.11, or you can use the New Technology File System (NTFS) developed specifically for Windows NT. Certain hardware dictates the choice of file type. For example, you can install Windows NT on a RISC-based system, but you must use a FAT partition for the system files.

NTFS allows the administrator to set up permissions that specify who can and cannot access files or directories (folders) on the drive. In other words, selecting NTFS allows the administrator to take full advantage of Windows NT's security features, and the FAT file system does not. If security is important in your corporate environment, NTFS is the preferred file system for Windows NT Server installations.

If you decide to use NTFS for your system partition, remember that the FAT file system is kept intact until the installation is completed. The setup program does not format a new partition to NTFS. The system partition is converted to NTFS on the first boot of the server after a successful installation. If you install Windows NT Server on a FAT file partition, you have the option of converting the partition later on, using a CONVERT utility included with NT 4.0 Server that runs from a DOS session prompt.

You also need to consider whether the computer you are installing will be a *multiboot* system. Generally a Windows NT Workstation is more likely to have a multiboot configuration than an NT Server is. Operating systems such as Windows 95 and DOS cannot access NTFS drives. If you need to share information between operating systems on a multiboot computer,

FAT would be the appropriate file system choice. If you do install Windows NT as an NTFS partition, be sure that the system partition is set up as FAT so the other operating systems can boot properly. You can make a separate NTFS partition for your data by using Disk Administrator within Windows NT.

As mentioned earlier, if information security is essential in your company, then it's smart to take advantage of the NTFS security features. This also prevents someone from getting at the files on your server by using a DOS boot disk.

If you have MS-DOS and Windows 3.1 or Windows for Workgroups, you can install NT Server into the same Windows subdirectory, which will upgrade your Windows settings into Windows NT automatically. However, if you install Windows NT Server in the same subdirectory as Windows 3.1 or Windows for Workgroups, the original operating system will no longer be available. With Windows 95 and other NT operating systems (4.0 or greater) you must reinstall all your applications so they are accessible from each operating system on your hard disk.

Most of the options mentioned here can be decided during the installation process. However, it is best to prepare and plan ahead of time. Planning your installation will save time and reduce the possibility of mistakes.

Per-Server Versus Per-Seat Licensing

Another factor to consider is how your licensing will be configured. Licensing is important because it affects the cost of your network installation.

Windows NT comes with two licensing options: per-server or per-seat licensing. These options provide different types of client access.

With **per-server licensing**, your license depends upon the number of concurrent connections. If you have 100 workstations accessing your server, you would need 100 **client access licenses** and a server set up with per-server licensing. This is ideal for networks that only have one server because each workstation needs a separate client access license for each server it accesses. The server itself controls the number of connections. If you have per-server licensing set up and a 100-client access license for Windows NT Server, workstation 101 will not be able to log on when all the licenses are in use.

With **per-seat licensing**, you can set up your server so that each client has an access license for as many servers as it can access. In this case, the server doesn't control logons. Rather, you are licensed for the number of computers on the network, but the clients are not limited to one server. Each workstation can concurrently use multiple servers even though it only has one license.

During the installation process you must specify whether you want per-server or per-seat licensing. You can take advantage of the Licensing option in your Control Panel (see Figure 4.1) to tell Windows NT Server how many licenses you have. If you are unsure about which type of licensing is best for your organization, select Per Server. If per-seat licensing turns out to be what you need, you can make a one-time switch from per-server licensing to per-seat licensing.

⚠ Keep in mind that you can make that one-time switch only from the Per Server to Per Seat option. You cannot switch in the other direction.

Partitions and Fault Tolerance

When planning partitions—especially your system or boot partition—you should also consider fault tolerance and what methods you plan to use. Remember that mirroring, in which the data on one disk is exactly duplicated on a separate disk, is the only fault-tolerant scheme that can be used on the system or boot partitions.

To set up effective fault tolerance you need to keep data and fault tolerant information on a separate partition and/or disk. A good rule of thumb is to set up one partition for the system files and then keep the remaining data on a separate partition. This enables you to set up the appropriate fault tolerant scheme that you choose.

• **Figure 4.1**   The Control Panel Licensing option

Naming Conventions

When installing Windows NT 4.0 Server, it is important to understand the naming conventions. Microsoft uses a NetBIOS form of Universal Naming Convention (UNC). Everything in Windows Networking relates to naming conventions. Each computer in the domain or workgroup is given a "friendly name." Windows NT converts the friendly name into the TCP/IP address, MAC address, or other identifiable means of routing the information. The syntax for the UNC name is \computername. Because the server name is determined during the installation process, make sure to give the server a name that makes sense. Often administrators will name the server something in relation to its responsibilities. The NetBIOS name of a computer can be 15 characters in length. For example, a backup domain controller in the New York office for a company named Acme might be "AcmeNewYorkBDC." Share names, on the other hand, can be up to 255 characters in length. An example of a share name might be NT40CDROM. In this case the UNC name would be \AcmeNewYorkBDCCDROM. The slashes are important. Be sure to use the \ (backslash) and not the / (forward slash). The server (or computer) name in Windows Networking should be preceded by two backslashes, with one backslash separating the server (computer) name and share name.

Preparing for Installation

In the following exercises, you will prepare your hard disk for Windows NT 4.0 Server installation.

During the pre-installation process you can use FDISK and FORMAT from a DOS boot disk to partition and format the hard disk. For this exercise you will need a DOS boot disk with FDISK and FORMAT, as well as the installation CD and boot disks.

> ⚠️ These exercises will delete the entire contents of your hard disk. Be sure to use a computer where you can clear the hard disk!

Preparing the Hard Disk Before the Installation Process

To complete this exercise, you will need the following:

- A working computer with a hard disk installed

- A DOS boot disk with the FDISK and FORMAT commands on the diskette

Step 1

For this first exercise, use the DOS boot disk that contains FDISK and FORMAT. Insert this disk into your floppy drive and boot your new computer. Before you begin the exercise, the hard disk should have no partitions on it.

Step 2

When you get to an A:\> prompt type **FDISK**.

Step 3

You will see a menu of options. Select Option 1, Create DOS Partition or Logical DOS Drive.

```
                    Microsoft Windows 95

                    Fixed Disk Setup Program

                    (C) Copyright Microsoft Corp. 1983-1995


                          FIDISK Options

        Current fixed disk drive: I

        Choose on of the following:


        1. Create DOS partition or Logical DOS Drive

        2. Set active partition

        3. Delete partition or Logical DOS Drive

        4. Display partition information

        5. Change current fixed disk drive



        Enter Choice: [1]



        Press Esc to exit FDISK
```

• FDISK main menu

Step 4

On the second menu select option 1, Create Primary DOS Partition.

Step 5	The program asks if you want to use the entire available space on that drive to create the partition. Answer No. For this exercise, use 50 percent of the available space.
Step 6	After the partition is created, leave the DOS boot disk in the drive and reboot.
Step 7	This time when you see an A: > prompt, type **FORMAT C:**.
Step 8	You will be asked if you're sure you want to format that drive, as it will destroy all data. Answer Yes.
Step 9	After a few minutes, the drive should format. You are now ready to start Windows NT setup and installation.

Alternatively, you can partition the hard disk during the Windows NT 4.0 Server installation process. The next step-by-step shows you how to do that.

Step-by-Step 4.2

Preparing the Hard Disk During the Installation Process

To complete this exercise, you will need the following:

- A working computer with a hard disk installed

- Windows NT Server CD-ROM and installation boot diskettes

Step 1	Insert the first boot disk into the floppy drive and boot the computer.
Step 2	Insert the CD-ROM into your CD-ROM drive while disk 1 is booting up. A series of drivers loads, and you will be prompted for the second disk.
Step 3	Insert the second disk. When the option comes up, press ENTER to install Windows NT Server.
Step 4	The second screen shows what other devices were detected on the system. Your CD-ROM information should show up here. If not, you cannot continue installation unless you have the manufacturer's driver disk.
Step 5	If you have the driver disk from the manufacturer and your CD is not showing in the list, press the S key to specify additional devices. From the device list, select the option that requires a disk from the OEM manufacturer. Insert your disk and the program should load the appropriate driver into memory.
Step 6	When you are satisfied with the choices in the additional devices list, press ENTER to continue.
Step 7	You should now see the License Agreement screen. Scroll down to the end; then press F8 to agree to the license information.

| Step 8 | Next you see a summary screen containing information about your system configuration. You should see display information, keyboard information, pointing device, and so forth. |

| Step 9 | The next screen is the key screen in this exercise. This is where you select the partition where you want to install Windows NT. If partitions are already created (and of course if space permits), you can select one of them. |

| Step 10 | If you see free space without a partition type, you can select that free space; then select what type of format to apply. Your options in Windows NT are FAT and NTFS. For this exercise, select FAT. |

| Step 11 | After a few minutes, the drive should format. You are now ready to start Windows NT setup and installation. |

■ Installation Methods

When installing Windows NT Server 4.0, there are various methods one can use to configure the server. Windows NT Server comes with three boot disks and one CD. The installation files are no longer available on floppy disks. The CD contains just over 600MB of information, which would require more than 420 high-density disks! Most new computers now come with a CD-ROM drive. If not, you can add one for less than $100.

You can install over the network or from the CD. The CD install can be done one of two ways.

- The Windows NT Server 4.0 CD is a bootable CD-ROM. If your server's BIOS supports it, you can boot directly from the CD and start the installation process that way.

- If not, the three floppy disks that come with Windows NT Server are boot disks designed to allow users to start the installation process without a bootable CD-ROM drive.

The reason the boot process is so important is that the installation program runs on a low-level version of Windows NT. The installation can start in DOS, but certain related files load to allow the system to reboot and start the NT operating system.

The following sections first describe the network installation option, and then examine the CD installation process.

Network Installation

In a network installation, files are made available (shared) from another network computer, such as another server or workstation. With a network boot disk, you access the shared directory to run the setup utility. Files are then transferred across the network to the local hard disk during the installation process. Figure 4.2 illustrates this process.

Access central server to install Windows NT server

Share setup on server for installation files

New machine

Server

● **Figure 4.2**   Network installation

This isn't necessarily the best way to install across the network. Most network administrators would recommend copying the installation subdirectory to the local computer and then executing the setup file to start installation.

You can use Windows NT Client Administrator to create a network boot disk for a target computer. Step-by-Step 4.3 shows you how to configure Windows NT Client Administrator so it will install the client files and set up the share. You need to have the Windows NT Server CD in the CD-ROM drive to perform this exercise.

Step-by-Step 4.3

Configuring Microsoft Network Client Administrator

For this exercise, you will need the following:

- A computer with Windows NT Server installed
- The Windows NT Server CD-ROM

Step 1

From the Start menu, select Programs | Administrative Tools (Common).

Step 2

Click the icon for Network Client Administrator.

Step 3

When it opens, Network Client Administrator displays a screen showing four options. The option Make Network Installation Startup Disk should be selected by default. Click OK.

- Network Client Administrator

Step 4

A screen displays that gives you the option to specify the path to the client files on the Windows NT CD. The destination directory where the files will be installed is also shown, as well as the name of the share.

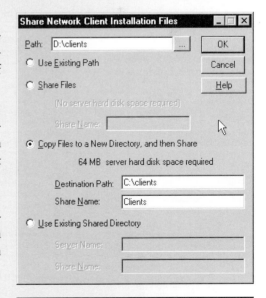

Step 5

The files on the CD are in the Clients subdirectory. Most administrators use this path on their hard disk as well. The default share name is Clients.

Step 6

Click OK. The program copies the Windows NT Client Administrator files from the CD to the hard disk and configures a network share.

- Setting up network client installation files for client installation

Now, in Step-by-Step 4.4, you will create an `installation startup disk`. This is sometimes confused with an `installation disk set`, which is a complete set of disks used to install the network client software on a PC. The installation startup disk is a single bootable disk that contains the network client software and allows you to access the network share and proceed with the installation.

Step-by-Step 4.4

Creating a Network Boot Disk Using the Windows NT Client Administrator

For this exercise, you will need the following:

- A computer with Windows NT Server installed and Step-by-Step 4.3 completed (to install the client files and set up the share on the central server)

- A blank diskette

Step 1

After the files are copied (in Step-by-Step 4.3), you are prompted for what type of boot disk you want to make. The options are Network Client 3.0 for DOS and Windows or a Windows 95 boot disk. For this exercise, select the Network Client 3.0 for DOS and Windows.

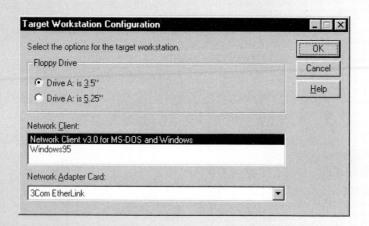

- Target workstation configuration

Step 2

Make sure you have the appropriate network card selected and that your floppy disk is in the drive. Then click OK.

Step 3

The next screen allows you to specify the computer name, domain, and protocol in use on the network. This is also where you specify the default user name to use—a name that automatically displays in parentheses during the boot process of the disk. (If you are using TCP/IP, the TCP/IP setting will not be grayed out as in the following illustration. If you are not using DHCP—Dynamic Host Configuration Protocol, you will have to specify the TCP/IP information.)

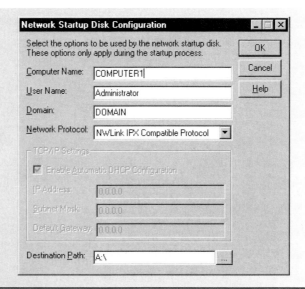

- Network startup disk configuration

Step 4

When you have entered the settings you want to use, click OK. Network Client Administrator configures the disk as a **boot disk**, which loads the network drivers, connects to the server, allows you to log on to the domain, and allows you to access shared resources.

After the boot disk is created, you'll go to the computer where you are installing the network operating system, and connect to the network. However, you must first set up a share on a central Windows NT 4.0 file server, as shown in Step-by-Step 4.5, so the new computer can access the appropriate files.

Step-by-Step 4.5

Creating a Network Share on a Central Windows NT 4.0 File Server

For this exercise, you will need the following:

- A computer with Windows NT Server installed.

- A Windows NT Server CD-ROM. At the file server, the administrator needs to share the

CD-ROM so the installation files can be accessed from a remote computer.

- The boot diskette prepared in Step-by-Step 4.4. (The administrator also needs this to load network drivers on the new computer so it can connect to the shared resource.)

Step 1

Make sure you are on a Windows NT 4.0 Server computer. You will need to log on as administrator in order to set up a share.

Step 2

Double-click the My Computer icon.

Step 3

Find the drive letter that corresponds to your CD-ROM drive (in this exercise we use D:).

Step 4

Right-click on the CD-ROM drive letter and you should see a pop-up menu, as shown in the following illustration.

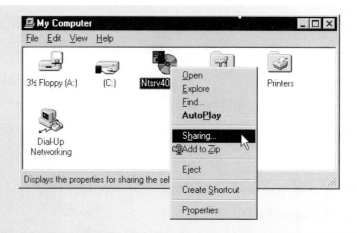

- Sharing your CD-ROM drive in Windows NT Server

Step 5

Select the Sharing option on the menu to open the Sharing window. Two options display: Not Shared and Shared As.

Step 6

Select the option and enter the name of your share. For this exercise, type **NT40CD**.

Step 7

Click OK. Record the computer name of the server and the share name you just created. You will need this information when installing the target computer with the network boot disk. (If you don't know the computer name of the server, you can find it by opening the Control Panel and selecting the network option. Click the Network Properties icon and the General tab. The computer name and domain name should be displayed there.)

When setting up the share on the server, some people suggest copying the entire contents of the CD to a directory on the hard disk and then sharing that, rather than using the CD. This can provide a faster response, due to the fact that hard disks have faster seek times than CD-ROM drives.

After your network boot disk is created and you have a share set up on a central file server, you can use the floppy disk to access the share and then install Windows NT 4.0, as shown in the remaining exercises in this section.

Step-by-Step 4.6 shows how to connect to the network drive share that contains the distribution files.

Step-by-Step 4.6

Connecting to the Network Drive Share That Contains the Distribution Files

For this exercise, you will need the following:

- A computer with Windows NT Server installed
- The diskette prepared in Step-by-Step 4.4
- A network share set up, as shown in Step-by-Step 4.5

Step 1	Insert the network boot disk created in Step-by-Step 4.4 into the floppy drive on the new computer.
Step 2	As the computer boots, you should see the network drivers load and a prompt that shows you a username. You can press ENTER to use the default user name or specify a new username at this point.
Step 3	After you enter your username, you will have to supply a password just as if you were logging on to the server in the graphical user interface (GUI).
Step 4	Upon proper connection and logon, you should see the message, "This command completed properly." This tells you that you are connected.
Step 5	At the A:> prompt, type **net use** *[drive letter]:* *servername**line sharename of Windows* **NT Server 4.0 CD**. (Specify whatever drive letter you want; the **net use** command maps a drive letter to the share set up on the server.) Also make sure there is a space between the colon after the drive letter and your *servername*.
Step 6	This should connect a network drive to whatever drive letter you specified. Change to that drive and type **dir**.
Step 7	You should see the directory of the Windows NT 4.0 Server CD.

After you have made your share on a central server and connected to that share via the network boot disk, you are ready to start the installation process on the target computer, as shown in Step-by-Step 4.7

Step-by-Step 4.7

Starting a Network Share Installation Process

For this exercise, you will need the following:

- A computer with Windows NT Server installed

- Step-by-Step 4.6 completed

Step 1	If you are on an Intel computer, you will want to copy the entire subdirectory from the CD prior to running the setup program.
Step 2	Make a directory on your local drive called i386. Change back to your local drive and type **md i386** from the root.
Step 3	Then type **copy** *[networkdriveletter:].** *[localdriveletter:].** **/s**. (The /s switch is an instruction to include all subdirectories.)
Step 4	After all the files are copied to your local i386 directory, change to your local i386 directory.
Step 5	Type **winnt /b** at the command prompt. (The /b switch indicates the install will not use floppy disks.) This starts the installation process.

You can run the setup program across the network, but the recommended procedure is to copy the files locally; then run the install. The reason for this is to prevent excess activity on the network that will affect other users. Copying the files to your local directory is faster and it does not put as much strain on the file server.

To run setup from the file server, you would complete Step-by-Step 4.6 first. Then, instead of copying files as in Step-by-Step 4.7, you would change to the i386 directory on the network drive and then type **winnt /b** there.

Step-by-Step 4.8 takes you through network installation, step by step. To perform this exercise you need to make sure, at the dedicated server, that the CD or directory containing the files is a shared resource. If necessary, refer to Step-by-Step 4.5 to do this. Also make sure that you have a network boot disk that contains the MS-DOS Network Client 3.0; the disk should be set up with the appropriate network drivers for your new computer. If necessary, refer to Step-by-Steps 4.3 and 4.4 to complete this task.

Step-by-Step 4.8

Installing Windows NT 4.0 Server on a Network

For this exercise, you will need the following:

- A computer with Windows NT Server installed
- A network boot diskette
- Completion of the preceding exercises

Step 1 Insert the disk into the floppy drive of the new computer and boot up the machine.

Step 2 Refer to Step-by-Step 4.6 to log on and set up a network drive connection to the shared directory on the server.

Step 3 Next, you will want to copy the installation files to the local drive. Refer to Step-by-Step 4.7 for information on how to copy the files and start the setup program.

Step 4 After the setup program starts, you should be prompted for the location of the Windows NT Server installation files. Confirm the default on the screen and press ENTER.

There will be instances where, as an administrator, you may have to re-create the three installation boot disks. This can be done by using the Windows NT 4.0 CD. You can use various switches in conjunction with the setup file, as shown in Table 4.1 later in this chapter. You can create the boot floppy disks from a working computer (either DOS, Windows 95, or Windows NT) with the Windows NT Server CD in the CD-ROM drive. From the command prompt you would type **Winnt /ox.** (The /ox switch tells the winnt.exe file to only create the boot floppy disks and not to continue with the remaining part of the installation.)

Step-by-Step 4.9 shows how to re-create the Windows NT boot floppy disks.

Step-by-Step 4.9

Re-creating Windows NT Boot Floppy Disks

For this exercise, you will need the following:
- A computer with Windows NT Server installed
- A Windows NT Server CD-ROM
- Three blank, formatted high-density diskettes

Step 1 On a working DOS, Windows 95, or Windows NT computer (either server or workstation), insert the Windows NT 4.0 Server CD into your CD-ROM drive.

Step 2 At the command prompt, type the driver letter of your CD-ROM drive. For example, type **D:** if your CD-ROM drive letter is D.

Step 3 Change to the subdirectory of the computer type you will be installing. In this exercise type **cd i386**. (This is for an Intel-type computer.)

Step 4 From the command prompt, type **winnt /ox**.

Step 5 Follow the prompts on the screen. The setup program should prompt you for each of the three blank disks.

Notice that the setup program creates the disks in reverse order. The third disk is created first and the first disk is created last. The setup program tells you this, but many people overlook it. *Be sure to label the disks accordingly.*

Network Installation Switches

When you install Windows NT in a network installation setting, there are various switches that can be used (see Table 4.1). These switches can make a network installation go more smoothly and quickly. In most cases, the /b switch is used in a network installation. This switch controls whether or not floppy disks are needed during the installation. In most cases, an administrator would not want to use the floppy disks if they were installing over the network.

Table 4.1	Switches Available for Winnt.exe or Winnt32.exe
Switch	**Result**
/b	Floppyless install
/c	Tells setup not to check for free disk space on setup boot floppy disks
/e	Specifies command to execute when setup is finished
/I	Specifies the name of the setup information file
/f	Tells setup to not verify files as they are copied to setup boot floppy disks
/ox	Creates the boot floppy disks only. Doesn't actually install Windows NT Server
/r or /rx	Specifies optional directory to be installed; the /RX denotes optional directory to be copied
/s	Lets the administrator specify the location of the source files (for example, winnt /s:location or \serverpath:])

| Table 4.1 | Switches Available for Winnt.exe or Winnt32.exe *(continued)* |

Switch	Result
/t	Tells setup where to put the temporary installation files (for example, winnt /t:location). This must be a local drive
/u	This is used for Unattended Installations; requires /s
/udf	Specify the Uniqueness Database File to use for unattended installation
/x	Do not create boot floppy disks

The setup program contains two parts. The installation process starts in text mode, and the second part uses the Windows NT GUI. The text part of the program:

- Identifies correct hardware
- Confirms selection of partitions
- Confirms file system to be used for Windows NT
- Confirms the directory where Windows NT Server will be installed
- Copies essentials files to hard disk so setup can start NT upon reboot

Step-by-Step 4.10 shows you how to use the text portion of the setup process.

Step-by-Step 4.10

Using the Text Part of the Windows NT Setup Program

For this exercise, you will need the following:

- A computer onto which you can install Windows NT

- A server computer running Windows NT Server, configured as shown in the preceding step-by-steps

Step 1

When you start the Windows NT Server setup process, the first screen shows the setup program loading various drivers.

Step 2

The next screen identifies all hardware in your system. Your options are

F1	Get help on installation (good for first-time installers)
ENTER	Set up Windows NT Server
R	Repair a damaged Windows NT Server install
F3	Quit without installing

Step 3

Press ENTER to continue. You will see a list of drives that Windows NT setup detects. You can press the s key if you need to specify additional CD-ROM drives or SCSI adapters. (Note: If no CD-ROM drive is displayed, setup cannot continue unless you specify more devices by pressing s. You'll need the driver disks from your CD/SCSI manufacturer to install these devices.) After you have installed the necessary devices, press ENTER to continue to the next screen.

Step 4	The next screen shows the License Agreement. Scroll down to the bottom of the agreement and press F8 to continue. F8 is the equivalent of agreeing to the License Agreement. If you don't agree with the agreement, you can press ESC; in that case, setup will not continue.
Step 5	On the next screen you should see a summary display of components on your system, including computer type, display, keyboard, keyboard layout, pointing device, and so forth. If everything looks okay, choose Accept. If something needs to be changed, use the arrow keys to scroll up to the option and make the change. When all the necessary changes have been made, press ENTER.
Step 6	The next screen allows you to specify information about the various partitions. *Be very careful on this screen: Pressing D will delete the highlighted partition!* The F1 help on this section is good.
Step 7	After you select a partition, the setup program asks what you want to do with the partition. The options are Format the partition (you can select from FAT or NTFS); Select a different partition; Convert a selected FAT partition to NTFS (if you are installing to an existing volume); Leave the current file system intact. This is a good choice, especially if you are installing for the first time.
Step 8	The next screen asks you to specify the directory where you want to install Windows NT 4.0 Server.
Step 9	Next you have an opportunity to run exhaustive diagnostics on the drive you are installing to. If you press ENTER the setup program will perform an exhaustive test of the hard disk. If you press ESC, it performs a short test of the drive and setup continues.
Step 10	In the final screen of the text section, the program copies files to the specified path. After the files are copied, setup prompts you to remove floppy disk from disk drives and the CD from the CD-ROM drive.

When all the temporary files have been copied to the appropriate subdirectories, the system reboots and the setup program continues to the graphical portion of the installation, where all the important configuration items are chosen. The graphical portion uses the Windows NT Setup wizard, which divides the installation into three sections. The first is called the Information Gathering, the second is Installing Windows NT Networking, and the final phase is Finishing Setup. Although the Windows Setup wizard proceeds directly through the three sections, each section is described in a separate exercise for your convenience.

Step-by-Step 4.11

Using the NT Setup Wizard—Information Gathering

This exercise guides you through the first section of the GUI setup, Information Gathering. You will need the following:

- A computer with a hard disk and CD-ROM drive
- A Windows NT setup CD-ROM

Step 1

When the wizard displays, click Next to proceed. The first screen you see asks you to enter your name and organization. The Name field is required, but the Organization field is optional. Click Next to continue.

Step 2

In the next screen you have to select how you want your server licensing set up. You have two options: Per Server or Per Seat. Refer to the discussion of licensing in the first section of this chapter if you need to review these options.

Step 3

The next screen asks you to enter the CD key, which is a portion of the software serial number. The CD key, as on most Microsoft software, is located on the back of the CD sleeve or back of the CD jewel case. Enter the CD key and click Next to continue.

Step 4

The next step is vital to the future of your server. This screen allows you to specify the name of the server computer. Enter the server name; then click Next to continue.

Step 5

The next screen also contains an important decision-making step. You need to choose which server role you want your server to fulfill.

Step 6

Next, you need to enter the Administrator password. *Be sure to keep this information in a secure location in case you should forget it!* You will have to enter the password twice. The password must be 14 characters or less. Click Next to continue.

Step 7

Next you must choose whether or not you want a repair disk. A repair disk is recommended for fixing crashed servers. If you don't create a repair disk now, you can use the `RDISK utility` at a later time to create or update a repair disk. Click Next to continue.

Step 8

In the next screen, you need components for the final installation, including

- **Accessories**   13 components—calculator, screen savers
- **Communications**   3 components—chat, Hyperterminal
- **Games**   4 components—FreeCell, Solitaire
- **Multimedia**   9 components—CD Player, sound schemes
- **Windows Messaging**   3 components—Internet Mail

Step 9

Choose the components you want to install; then click Next to proceed.

Step 10

A transition screen shows that you are now entering the second section of the GUI setup: Installing Windows Networking.

Using the NT Setup Wizard—Installing Windows NT Networking

This exercise guides you through the second section, Installing Windows NT Networking. You will need the following:

- A computer with a hard disk and a CD-ROM drive
- A Windows NT setup CD-ROM

Step 1

The first screen asks if your server will be wired directly to the network or be accessing the network remotely. In most cases your server will be wired directly to the network. Choose the appropriate option; then click Next to continue.

Step 2

The next screen is the Install Microsoft Internet Information Server screen. This option is not needed unless your domain is wired directly to the Internet and you will use IIS to run your web site. This can also be used for your company intranet, if you have one.

Step 3

Next you need to select the type of network adapter to be used. You can choose Start Search to have the program look for an adapter card, or choose Select From List to identify the card in use. After you have identified the appropriate card, click Next to continue.

Step 4

Next you must tell Windows NT Server what protocols the network will use to communicate. Windows NT Server can communicate with the following protocols: TCP/IP, NWLink (IPX/SPX-compatible), and NetBEUI (NetBIOS Enhanced User Interface). You can use the Select From List option to install some other protocols including DLC, PPTP, and Streams. When you finish this task, click Next to continue.

Step 5

The next screen allows you to install Network Services such as DNS Server, Windows Internet Names Service, or Remote Access Server. Choose the services you want; then click Next to continue.

Step 6

The next screen deals with the copying of network components. You may see one of several screens, depending on what protocols you selected previously.

- If you selected NWLink (IPX/SPX-compatible transport), you will be prompted for the frame type you want to use.

- If you selected TCP/IP, you will see a question about DHCP as well as a screen to specify the TCP/IP properties.

Step 7

Answer the questions; then click Next to proceed.

Step 8

Next you see a screen on network bindings. In most cases, the defaults are fine unless you need to remove or add something specific. Click Next to continue.

Step 9

Now you have two choices. You can click Next to start the network and continue setup or you can click Back to stop the network if it is running. You have to choose Next to complete setup. If Windows NT Server is successful in starting the network, the setup program will continue to copy files. If starting the network is unsuccessful, you will be prompted to change to configuration of the network adapter—for example, its IRQ (interrupt request identifier) or base port address.

Step 10

The next screen varies according to the type of server you are installing. If you are installing a primary domain controller, you simply have to specify the computer name and the domain name. If you are installing a backup domain controller or a stand-alone server, you will have four fields to complete: Computer Name, Domain Name, Administrator User Name, and Administrator Password. You need the administrator's username and password so the backup domain controller can be added to the domain. If the username and password you specify do not have administrator privileges, the computer will not be added to the domain.

Step 11

A transition screen shows that you will now enter the third phase of the graphical portion of setup: Finishing Setup.

Step-by-Step 4.13

Using the NT Setup Wizard—Finishing Setup

This exercise guides you through the final section of the wizard, Finishing Setup. You will need the following:

- A computer with a hard disk and a CD-ROM drive
- A Windows NT setup CD-ROM

Step 1

During this final phase you will see a series of screens that show the copying of files, setup of program groups, and so on.

Step 2

If you installed Internet Information Server 2.0, you will be prompted to verify the directory names for this application.

Step 3

Next you will be asked to set up the time, time zone, and date information.

Step 4

Next you will have an opportunity to adjust your display properties. The setup program should check your system for the appropriate video adapter and install the driver. You may find that the setup program installs a standard VGA driver. If this occurs, all you have to do is change it after setup is completed.

Step 5

The next screen you see depends on whether you chose to create a repair disk earlier in the setup process. If so, this is the place where the disk is created. If not, you can still create the repair disk at a later time with the RDISK utility.

Step 6

Next you see the final copying of files for Windows NT Server.

Step 7

Finally, Windows NT Server setup configures Windows Messaging and saves the final configuration. (Note: If you decide to install Windows NT Server on an NTFS partition you will see the format and installation take place on a FAT partition. After a successful installation Windows NT Server converts the partition to NTFS. The setup program ensures that everything was successful before it continues.) You should see a successful message; then the system reboots.

CD-ROM Installation

If the computer you are configuring has the option, you can boot directly from the Windows NT Server CD-ROM. The option to boot from the CD-ROM drive is configured from within the computer's BIOS. If you are installing directly from the CD you should make sure that the CD-ROM drive is compatible with Windows NT. If the CD-ROM drive is not supported, you could run into problems later on if you try to configure Windows NT and the operating system prompts you for the CD. If your CD is unsupported under Windows NT Server 4.0, you should copy the contents of the appropriate subdirectory to your hard disk prior to installation and run the setup program from there.

Step-by-Step 4.14 shows how to start a CD-ROM installation without floppy disks. For this exercise, you will need the Windows NT 4.0 Server CD.

Step-by-Step 4.14

Starting a CD-ROM Installation Without Floppy Disks

For this exercise, you will need the following:

- A computer with a hard disk and a CD-ROM drive

- A Windows NT setup CD-ROM

Step 1   Be sure that the computer you are installing has the CD-ROM drive set up as a bootable device. In order to work properly, this drive should be ahead of your hard disks in the boot order.

Step 2   With the CD in the CD-ROM drive, reboot or turn on your computer.

Step 3   Upon booting from the CD the installation program will start automatically.

Installing NT on RISC-Based Computers

One of the nice things about Windows NT Server is the fact that you can install it on multiple platforms. You can install Windows NT on a RISC-based system, but you must use a FAT partition for the system files. With RISC-based systems, the partitions must be set up ahead of time. Windows NT cannot set up and configure RISC partitions.

Upgrade Installation

If you currently have a server running Windows NT 3.51, you can install NT 4.0 Server as an upgrade. You can also upgrade from DOS, Windows 3.1,

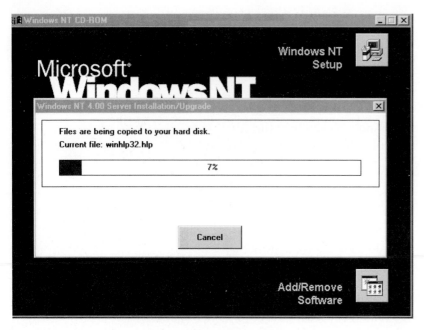

- **Figure 4.3** Windows NT Upgrade copies installation files to a temporary folder on the hard disk.

Windows NT 4.00 Server Installation/Upgrade

This portion of Setup has completed successfully. You must restart your computer to continue with the installation.

When you restart your computer, Setup will continue.

[**R**estart Computer]   [Exit to Windows **NT**]

- **Figure 4.4** Rebooting during the upgrade

Windows for Workgroups 3.11, and Windows 95. One important note: Later releases of Windows 95 use the FAT32 file format, so make sure you are not trying to upgrade in a FAT32 environment. Windows NT 4.0 cannot access the FAT32 file system.

To upgrade from a previous version of Windows NT, you run the Winnt32.exe file. The first part of the upgrade process is the same as the normal installation. The setup program copies files from the CD into temporary directories on the hard disk (see Figure 4.3).

After the files are copied to the temporary directory, you will be prompted to reboot or stay in the current version of Windows NT (see Figure 4.4).

You will have the option to overwrite the existing operating system or install a dual-boot computer. If you choose to have a dual-boot machine, the boot loader menu will have a selection that allows you to choose the original operating system.

Of course, when upgrading you want to be sure and have a complete server backup available in case the setup fails to complete and you have to revert to the original version. The following case study recounts an instance where a known good backup saved a company thousands!

A medical center had a Microsoft Windows NT 3.51 Server with various NT Workstations and Windows for Workgroups clients. This particular server was a Compaq ProLiant with a built-in CD-ROM drive and a Plextor 8 CD attached to it. An upgrade was scheduled for Saturday. Halfway through the installation, the server rebooted and the drive letters changed—which caused the entire upgrade to come to a screeching halt. Trying to reboot the server into Windows NT 3.51 did not work.

The only option was to reinstall Windows NT Server 3.51; then restore from backup. Then we started over on the upgrade. However, this time we disconnected the Plextor so that no drive letters would be changed in the middle of the installation process!

When upgrading from Windows NT 3.51 to Windows NT 4.0 you should be aware that the two products do not use the same default directory. By default, Windows NT 3.51 is installed in the directory and Windows NT 4.0 uses the directory. However, to maintain desktop, applications, and user information it is a good idea to put the upgrade files into the directory where the original version of NT had been located on that computer (in other words, in directory \NT351, *not* \WINNT). If you do not specify this directory when upgrading, you will end up with a dual-boot computer.

Of course the other big change with the transition from Windows NT 3.51 to Windows 4.0 is the GUI. The desktop and the product "look and feel" of Windows NT 4.0 is more like Windows 95. The change is similar to going from Windows 3.1 or Windows for Workgroups 3.11 to Windows 95. If your organization is used to the Windows 3.1 look of NT 3.51 it is essential to plan some training before the upgrade, to make end users comfortable with the new interface.

Unattended Installation

If you are deploying a large network with many servers and workstations, an unattended installation can make the operation much more efficient. Windows NT Server gives you the option to create an unattended answer file. Windows NT Server 4.0 CD contains a utility in the support <computer type> subdirectory called SETUPMGR (see Figure 4.5). This is a GUI program that will help you set up answer files for unattended installation.

There are three groups of options: General Setup, Network Setup, and Advanced Setup. The following sections describe how to set the options in each category.

General Setup Options

The General Setup Options screen covers basic information about the installation. The first tab is the User Information tab, shown in Figure 4.6, which includes User Name, Organization, Computer Name, and Product ID.

The General tab includes basic information about how setup will run in unattended mode. For example, you can specify that you want setup to confirm hardware during setup and you can list upgrade options. You can even specify that you want to run a program during setup.

On the Computer Role tab you choose one of the following as a role for the computer:

- Primary Domain Controller
- Backup Domain Controller
- Stand Alone Server in Domain
- Stand Alone Server in Workgroup
- Workstation in Domain
- Workstation in Workgroup

Along with the computer role, you can specify the Workgroup name, if applicable, or the Account Name, if appropriate.

The License Mode lets you specify the license mode if the Computer Role tab indicates the computer is being set up as a server or domain controller. If you have Workstation in a Workgroup or Domain, you do not need to complete the License Mode tab.

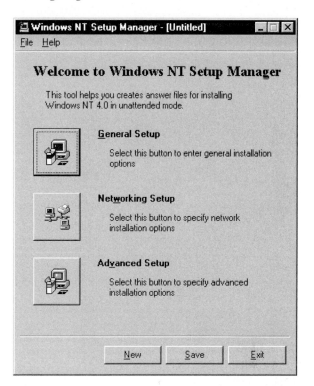

• Figure 4.5 Setup Manager

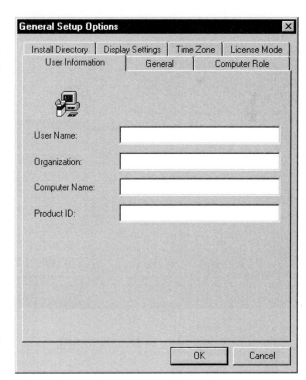

• Figure 4.6 General Setup Options window in SETUPMGR

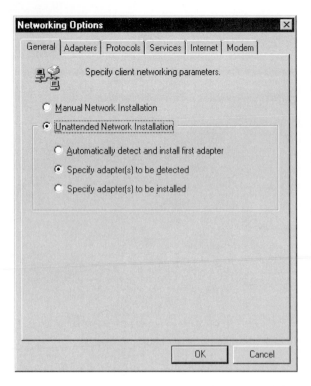

The Time Zone tab is self-explanatory—it lets you select the time zone where the computer is located.

The Display Settings tab enables you to configure Display Properties during installation. You can set up refresh rate, horizontal and vertical resolution, bits per pixel, and various flags.

The Install Directory tab lets you specify where the installation files will be located. Choices here include Use Default Directory, Prompt User for Installation Directory, and Specify Installation Directory Now.

Networking Options

The Networking Options area includes information on network adapter card configuration, bindings, protocols, Internet, and modem. The General tab, shown in Figure 4.7, allows you to specify whether you want a manual network installation or an unattended network installation. As part of the Unattended option, you can ask setup to detect and install the first network adapter it finds or you can ask it to detect specific adapters. Alternatively, you can bypass the detection stage and specify what adapters to install.

On the Adapters tab, you can specify the network adapters to install.

- **Figure 4.7**   General tab of Networking Options window in SETUPMGR

On the Protocols tab, you can specify what protocols to load and install. Only the three basic Windows NT networking protocols are listed in this section: TCP/IP, NetBEUI, and NWLink (IPX/SPX-Compatible Transport).

The Services tab allows you to specify which network services to install. The available options by default include SNMP (Simple Network Management Protocol), Client Services for NetWare, and RAS (Remote Access Service).

The Internet tab is accessible only if the computer role in the General Setup section is set up as a server. If it is, this tab tells the setup program to install Internet Information Server (IIS) and gives configuration information for it. For example, you can tell setup where to install IIS and what subdirectories to set up for FTP, WWW, and Gopher. You can choose which options you want installed: Internet Service Manager (ISM), HTMLA (an HTML version of ISM), and sample web pages. You can also specify the guest account username and password to set up.

The Modem tab must be completed only if the Remote Access Service is selected in the Services tab. You can specify the COM port, modem type, manufacturer, provider, as well as the driver to install.

Advanced Options

The Advanced Options window allows advanced users to specify additional information for the unattended installation process. The General tab in the Advanced Options, shown in Figure 4.8, lets you specify information on the Hardware Abstraction Layer (HAL), the keyboard layout, whether or not to reboot after text and graphic setup sections, and whether to skip the Welcome Wizard page and Administrator Password wizard.

The File System tab allows you to select whether you want to leave the current file system intact or convert the file system to NTFS. You also have the option here to extend the partition beyond two gigabytes (a FAT limitation), if you convert to NTFS.

The Mass Storage tab allows you specify additional mass storage devices to install drivers for during installation.

The Display tab, Pointing Device tab, and the Keyboard tab all let you specify display drivers for the installation process.

The Advertisement tab lets you customize the banner text, logo, and background information for your installation. This is a spot where network administrators can gratify their egos by personalizing an unattended installation.

The Boot Files tab allows you to specify a list of boot files.

After you've supplied the appropriate information, click the Save button in the main SETUPMGR window. You can give the file any name you want; it will have a .txt extension. There is also a New button on the main window, which clears all the information in the highlighted section so you can start over.

Step-by-Step 4.15 describes how to create an unattended answer file.

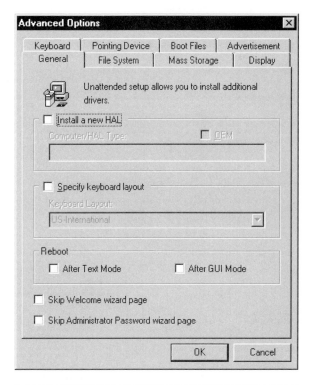

● Figure 4.8   General tab of Advanced Options window in SETUPMGR

Step-by-Step 4.15

Creating an Unattended Installation Answer File

For this exercise, you will need the following:

■ A computer with Windows NT Server installed

Step 1

To become familiar with the SETMGR, use the following scenario to create an answer file that will set up a server in a domain:

- **Username**   Bill Byttes

- **Organization**   Acme Inc.

- **Computer Name**   Bill's Machine

- Be sure to confirm the hardware during setup.

- Use the default install directory.

- Configure the graphics device at logon.

- Have setup choose the Bogota, Lima time zone.

- Convert the existing file system to NTFS.

- Add a 3COM Etherlink III Adapter.

- You need to have TCP/IP and NWLink IPX/SPX loaded.

- Be sure to skip the Welcome Wizard page.

- Set up per-server licensing with 100 licenses.

- You have Novell workstations on your network, so be sure to add Client Services for Netware.

Step 2   Save the file; then try using it in an unattended installation. Remember to use the /u switch.

After you've created the answer file, you have to tell setup where to get the file when the installation process begins. As mentioned earlier, the switch to use for an unattended answer file is /u. For example you would type **winnt /u:unattend.txt /s:source**.

Unattended Setup and the Uniqueness Database File

When deploying large networks, the unattended answer file is a great tool for speeding up the installation process. When you have ten or more machines to set up and install on your network, creating an answer file for each can be tedious. Windows NT allows the creation of what is called a **Uniqueness Database File (UDF)**.

A UDF allows an administrator to specify information for each individual workstation or server that is being installed. Items such as computer name, IP address (in a static IP environment), time zone, and other information can be specified on a per-machine basis. To use a UDF, a valid answer file must already exist.

The UDF is created as a text file that contains information to be merged into the default answer file. This is done through the use of specific switches with winnt.exe or winnt32.exe.

An example of a command-line use:

winnt /u:unattend.txt /s:d:/t:c: /udf:useridl,z:.txt

■ Server Roles

One of the most common concepts you will hear throughout your studies will be that of the **domain**. A domain, as shown in Figure 4.9, is a group of computers containing domain controllers that share account information and have one centralized accounts database. An administrator needs to determine what role the server or servers will play in the domain model. This is an important step in the installation process. A server can belong to only one domain.

The Windows NT operating system has various roles a server can play. Remember, each server can fulfill only one role. The three possibilities are primary domain controller (PDC), backup domain controller (BDC), or member server (MS). Choosing whether the server will be a domain controller is a very important decision in the installation process. At the beginning of an installation, you must choose a role for the server you are setting up. If you make a mistake, you will have to restart the installation process.

Security is an important consideration when designing your network. An important role of domain controllers is to maintain security information—

accounts information and the accounts database—for the domain. Domain controllers share a common security policy. The domain can also contain stand-alone (member) servers that do not maintain account and security information.

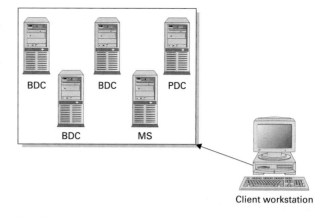

Primary Domain Controller

A **primary domain controller (PDC)** is the central server in the network. There must be one—and only one—PDC per domain. If the server you are installing is the first computer in the domain, it will be installed as a PDC. If you are not installing a PDC, another PDC must already be connected to the network.

• **Figure 4.9**   Simple domain model showing various server roles

When installing the PDC you have the opportunity to name the domain. This is an important step because it affects how the remaining servers and workstations will be named. When other servers and workstations are added to the domain, the domain name—the name you assigned when you set up the PDC—will become part of each server or workstation name.

The master accounts database resides on the PDC. Synchronization is the process of copying the security information (accounts and permissions) to the BDCs and performing periodic updates to keep the information up-to-date. This database is synchronized on the BDCs only. The domain administrator sets up synchronization and specifies how often it will occur.

Backup Domain Controller

A **backup domain controller (BDC)** serves multiple purposes in a Windows NT domain. The rule of thumb is to have at least one BDC per domain. As mentioned in the preceding paragraph, the BDC is responsible for helping maintain user account database information. When installing the BDC, you must know the name of the domain to which you are assigning it. Whoever installs the BDC must have administrative privileges in the domain. Because BDCs cannot be added to the network prior to installation, administrative privileges are needed to add machines to the network.

When a nondomain controller computer starts up, it goes through a process called **discovery**. That means the workstation looks across the network for a domain controller in its domain (and in all "trusted" domains). After the workstation locates a domain controller, it uses that BDC or PDC for subsequent authentication.

BDCs can authenticate users when they log on to the domain. If the BDC fails to authenticate the user; then the logon request is passed to the PDC for authentication.

Another function of the BDC is to back up the PDC in the event of a PDC crash. Promotion of a BDC to a PDC by the domain administrator allows the BDC to take over the primary roll in the domain. This is the only type of server within Windows NT that can be changed without reinstalling.

Member Server

A **member server** (sometimes referred to as a *stand-alone server*) is not a domain controller. Member servers have no responsibility in the accounts database and security information. They are used for application servers, print servers, or SQL servers. They are dedicated to process high-end searches and non-security type functions. They help take the load off your domain controllers, which can concentrate on security and account information processing.

Server Promotion Rules

When something happens to the PDC, such as a crash or being taken offline for an upgrade, the administrator must decide how the domain will function. If the PDC will be offline for an extended period, a BDC can be promoted to a PDC to take over the domain. When you try to bring a PDC back online, it will check the domain. If another BDC has been promoted to PDC, the original PDC will not be able to log on to the network. The administrator will have to use the Server Manager to demote the original PDC. (The Promote option on the Computer menu in Server Manager changes to a Demote option if the original PDC is highlighted on the list of computers in the domain.)

Stand-alone servers cannot be promoted or demoted. The only way to change the role of a member server is to reinstall Windows NT Server on the machine. The same applies to PDCs and BDCs. If an administrator wants to change an existing domain controller to a member server, the operating system must be reinstalled on that particular machine.

When promoting a BDC to a PDC there are two distinct possible scenarios. The BDC can be promoted while the existing PDC is still online or it can be done after the PDC has been taken offline.

If administrators know the current PDC will be offline, they can promote a BDC to a PDC to keep the domain alive. This is only recommended if the PDC will be down for an extended period. The master accounts database is synchronized on the BDC being promoted. When the BDC is promoted, the operating system automatically "demotes" the PDC, because there can't be multiple PDCs in the domain.

If a PDC is in danger of crashing, the domain administrator must decide how to maintain the domain. If the BDC is promoted while the PDC is already offline, the BDC uses the most recent update it has for the account database. If a domain synchronization hasn't been done for a while and users have been added at the PDC, *those users will be lost*. When the original PDC returns to service, it will have to be demoted before it can return to the domain. This is done with the Demote option on the Computer menu of the Server Manager utility, shown in Figure 4.10. Remember, the user who performs this activity must have domain administrator permissions.

> Make sure you have a clear understanding of the promotion/demotion process. A backup domain controller can be promoted to a primary domain controller if the current PDC is going to be taken offline or if it has already been taken offline. If taken offline, the original PDC will have to be demoted before it can return to the domain. If the PDC is online when the BDC is promoted, the demotion takes place automatically. If the PDC is already offline when the BDC is promoted, the systems administrator will have to user the Server Manager utility to demote the old PDC. Stand-alone or member servers cannot be changed to a domain controller without reinstalling Windows NT Server. Similarly, a domain controller cannot be converted to a member server without reinstalling.

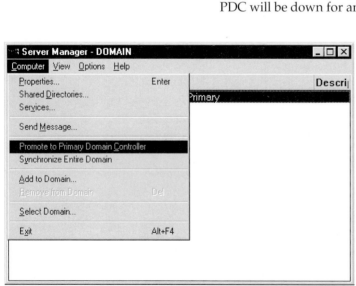

• **Figure 4.10**   Server Manager with Promote to PDC highlighted

Removing Windows NT

If you replace your server, you may want to remove Windows NT Server from the hard disk of the old server. There are a couple of ways to do this. You can delete the partition or you can simply delete the system files. The second method is better because it keeps other data intact.

Deleting FAT Partitions

You can use FDISK from DOS or Windows 95 to delete a FAT partition. Some administrators think they can use Windows NT Disk Administrator to remove the system partition. This is incorrect. Disk Administrator lets you delete partitions, but *not* the system partition. Step-by-Step 4.16 shows you how to delete a FAT partition.

Step-by-Step 4.16

Deleting a FAT Partition

For this exercise, you will need the following:

- A computer with Windows NT installed
- A DOS or Windows boot diskette with FDISK.EXE and FORMAT.COM on it

Step 1	Boot your server with a DOS or Windows 95 boot disk that contains FDISK.EXE and FORMAT.COM.	Microsoft Windows 95 Fixed Disk Setup Program (C) Copyright Microsoft Corp. 1983-1995
Step 2	When you see the A:> prompt, type **FDISK**.	FIDISK Options Current fixed disk drive: 1
Step 3	You will see a menu that looks like that on the right.	Choose on of the following:
Step 4	Choose option number 3: Delete partition or Logical DOS drive. You will see a list of partitions currently on your drive.	1. Create DOS partition or Logical DOS Drive 2. Set active partition 3. Delete partition or Logical DOS Drive 4. Display partition information 5. Change current fixed disk drive
Step 5	When you select a partition to remove, you will be prompted for the partition name, to make sure you selected the appropriate one.	Enter Choice: [1]
Step 6	After the partition is removed, you need to reboot so the changes will take effect. Keep the floppy disk in the drive and reboot to the boot machine.	Press Esc to exit FDISK

- FDISK menu (Windows 95 version)

Step 7	When you get to the A:> type **FDISK** to get back into FDISK. This time you will have to select option number 1 to create a new DOS partition to replace the old one. You will have to reboot one more time.
Step 8	When you are back at the A:> prompt, type **Format <driveletter>:**.
Step 9	You will be prompted to be sure that you want to destroy all data on that drive.
Step 10	After the drive is formatted it will be blank. You can now install a different operating system on it.

Deleting NTFS Partitions

You cannot use the FDISK utility from the DOS and Windows 95 operating systems to delete NTFS partitions because DOS and Window 95 do not recognize NTFS partitions. A utility such as DELPART, found in the Windows NT Resource Kit CD, can be used. DELPART is also available for download from the Internet. Use one of the major search engines, such as Yahoo or Excite, to locate it.

One other option for deleting an NTFS partition is to use the OS/2 version of FDISK. You can use the /D option to delete a partition.

If installing MS DOS 6 or later, you can go through the installation process to remove Windows NT and set up a new master boot record. Boot with the first disk of the installation set. When prompted, choose the Remove files option.

One final way to delete an NTFS partition is to initiate a new Windows NT Server installation and choose Delete Partition in the text portion of the setup process.

Removing Windows NT from a FAT Partition

If you don't want to destroy the data on your drive but want to remove Windows NT Server 4.0, you can delete certain system files. There are hidden, read-only system files on the drive root that you need to remove. You also need to remove some files in the Windows NT root (the subdirectory where you installed Windows NT Server—the default location is c:). This procedure, described in Step-by-Step 4.17, will work only if the partition is FAT, not NTFS.

Step-by-Step 4.17

Deleting the System Files to Remove Windows NT from a FAT Partition

For this exercise, you will need the following:

- A computer with Windows NT previously installed on it

Step 1	Boot to a DOS boot disk that has ATTRIB.EXE, SYS.COM, and DELTREE.EXE from DOS or Windows 95.
Step 2	When you are at the A:\> prompt, type **DELTREE c:** If WINNT is the Windows NT root (the directory where you installed Windows NT 4.0 Server).
Step 3	There will probably be a file named pagefile.sys on the drive root. This file will also have to be deleted. Type **DEL c:pagefile.sys**.
Step 4	There are a handful of other files you need to delete as well, but they are hidden system files. Type **ATTRIB c:<*filename*> –h –r –s**. This will have to be done for the following files: ■ NTLDR ■ BOOT.INI ■ BOOTSECT.DOS ■ NTBOOTDD.SYS ■ NTDETECT.COM
Step 5	After you have changed the attributes of the preceding files, you can go ahead and delete them. Type **DEL c:<*filename*>** for each of the files, to delete it.
Step 6	The final step to uninstalling Windows NT Server is to restore the DOS Master Boot Record. Type **SYS c:** and reboot.
Step 7	Upon rebooting, you should see a C:> prompt where you can load your new operating system.

Changing the Boot Loader in an Existing FAT Partition to MS-DOS

When Windows NT Server installs the master boot record on the drive is changed. In the event that a server needs to be set up with a different operating system, you need to make sure that the master boot record is rewritten for the operating system you have chosen. There are a couple of ways to do this. The first is shown in Step-by-Step 4.18, which shows you how to change the boot loader in an existing FAT partition to MS-DOS.

Step-by-Step 4.18

Changing the Boot Loader in an Existing FAT Partition to MS-DOS

For this exercise, you will need the following:

■ A computer that has had Windows NT installed onto it

Step 1	Use a DOS/Windows 95 boot disk and the SYS utility to configure the master boot record.
Step 2	Insert the boot disk in the drive. Be sure that this disk has the file SYS.COM.
Step 3	At the A:\> prompt type **SYS C:**.
Step 4	Reboot the machine. Now you should boot to a C:\> prompt.

If you do not want to remove Windows NT Server and simply want to make MS-DOS your default operating system, you can change the startup process within Control Panel. Changing the default operating system in this way leaves Windows NT fully functioning and easy to start when you want. The procedure for doing this is described in Step-by-Step 4.19.

Step-by-Step 4.19

Setting MS-DOS as your Default Operating System

For this exercise, you will need the following:

- A computer with Windows NT installed on top of a previous DOS installation

Step 1	Select Start	Settings	Control Panel.
Step 2	In Control Panel, select the System icon.
Step 3	In the System properties window, select the Startup tab.
Step 4	In this window, select MS-DOS in the startup box and enter the number 0 in the Show List For box.

■ Troubleshooting the Installation Process

During installation you may have to do some troubleshooting if your installation doesn't go smoothly. Here are some of the most common troubleshooting problems.

Faulty media is a common problem. The boot disks may have one bad disk or the CD itself may not be functioning correctly. There have also been many documented cases of insufficient disk space problems. These simple problems can cause financial headaches for companies, because it can take hours to track them down and resolve them.

Another item that can cause problems with configuration is an incompatible SCSI device, or a third-party drive like a Zip or Jaz drive. SCSI adapters devices (which is what most hard drives in servers are) can be one of the more challenging devices to get to work with Windows NT. The recommended method, of course, is to consult the latest edition of the Hardware Compatibility List (HCL). Microsoft Technical Support will not support you if you are having a problem with a device that is not on the HCL.

Another simple mistake—such as a wrong username, domain name, or protocol—can make it seem that the machine you are configuring is not connecting. Oversights such as usernames and domain names, if not checked, can be mistaken for hardware problems. It's much more economical to spend 15 minutes troubleshooting the basic network configuration than it is to buy a new NIC and toss the old one out.

Here's a real-life example. A network engineer, when setting up a new PDC and various workstations, named the domain MainOffice1. In the course of setting up the network, one of the workstations was also named MainOffice1. This network is part of a WAN environment, with other domain controllers set up in trusted relationships. When finalizing all the machines and rebooting the PDC and workstations, the engineer encountered an error message. What do you think it was?

Right: duplicate names. This is a classic case of mere oversight. You always have to make sure that any and all names are unique. Whether it is a domain name or a computer name, it must be unique in the network.

Preparing for Windows NT 4.0 Workstation Installation

Before you install Windows NT, or any OS, you need to prepare the hardware, determine the method of installation, and gather the materials (disks, drivers, applications, and so on) you'll need to complete the installation.

Prepare the Hardware

To install Windows NT on a computer hard disk, you must be sure that the computer is physically ready for the installation: that is, ensure that the computer is a complete system, with at least the minimal hardware recommendations, and that all of the hardware is compatible with Windows NT 4.0. You also need to ensure that all necessary connections are in place for the installed components and that the computer is plugged into a power outlet. The computer hard disk does not have to be specially

Try This!

Check Out the Compatible Products

To complete this task, you will need a computer with an Internet connection and a web browser. Try this:

1. Point your web browser at www.microsoft.com/windows/compatible/default.asp.

2. From the Operating System drop-down list, select Windows NT.

3. From the Product Category drop-down list select 1394 Controller.

4. Leave Company Name set to All and click Go to begin a search.

5. The search results will show you the manufacturer and model name of any 1394 controller tested to work with Windows NT.

6. Click the Back button in your browser to return to the Compatible Products page. Confirm that Windows NT is still selected and then select Network/Wireless from the Product Category list. Leave Company Name set to All. Then click Go.

7. Unless you want to search for more hardware or software, close your web browser.

prepared for Windows NT installation because the Windows NT setup program can prepare the hard disk.

Determine the Service Pack and Updates to Use

After any software company releases complex software such as Windows NT, the programming staff continues to work on the software. Programmers receive feedback about problems from customers, and they re-create the problems and come up with software fixes. We may call these **patches** or **updates**. Those that solve security problems and/or problems that can potentially cause major failures are now called critical updates.

What Do I Need and Where Do I Look?

Microsoft releases updates individually, as they are completed, and the company also periodically bundles together a series of accumulated updates into a larger package called a service pack. These, in turn, are made available in versions, or levels, such as Service Pack 1 and Service Pack 2. NT 4.0's service packs were numbered through 6a (a post–Service Pack 6 release), which was followed by the Post–SP6a Security Rollup Package (SRP). You can find out more about the updates and service packs for Windows NT 4.0 Professional at www.microsoft.com/ntworkstation.

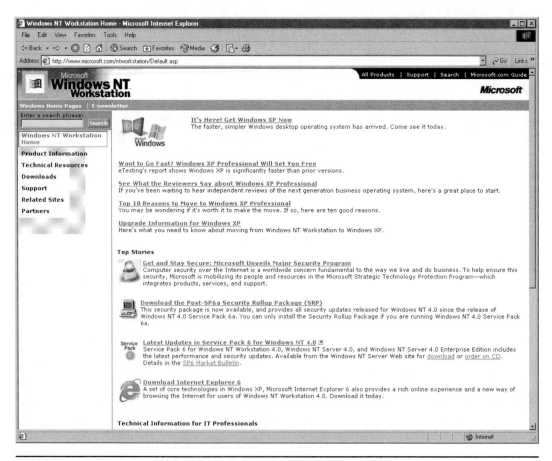

• Windows NT Workstation home page

Introduction to Client/Server Networking

The service pack level in NT 4.0 is critical; you should never install and use Windows NT 4.0 without planning to add a service pack immediately after the installation.

Although service packs that fix problems are a fact of life with today's very complex OSs, Windows NT 4.0 service packs are also renowned not for just fixing problems with the OS, but for adding new features as well. However, sometimes the fixes and/or new features actually cause new problems. Therefore, most organizations that exercise any standards and control over their desktop computers mandate that a new service pack can't be installed until it has been thoroughly tested on non-production PCs in a test lab.

Determine the Method of Installation

To install Windows NT (without using a third-party product), you can choose a manual installation or an automated installation, both of which have variations.

Manual Installation

A manual installation is high maintenance, requiring your attention throughout the entire process to provide information and to respond to messages. You will perform a manual installation in Step-by-Step 4.21. This is the method you would choose for a unique installation, or if the number of computers is too few to warrant the time, effort, and expense that an automated installation requires.

After deciding on a manual installation, you still have choices to make:

- Will the source files (those in the i386 directory on the Windows NT 4.0 CD-ROM) be located on the local computer or the network server? If you don't have a CD-ROM drive in the computer, but it is connected to a network, you'll have to boot up the computer with an operating system that has the network components installed so you can connect to the server where the source files are stored.

- If the computer does have a CD-ROM drive, will it work for the installation—that is, will the Windows NT 4.0 setup program recognize it and will the computer boot from the CD-ROM drive? If you can boot from the CD-ROM drive, your manual installation can be completed as shown in Step-by-Step 4.21.

- If a CD-ROM drive is present and is recognized by Windows NT Setup (which you may be able to determine only by trying), but you can't boot from it, you will need the three Windows NT 4.0 Workstation setup disks, as well as the CD-ROM disk. Place the first disk in the drive, restart, and follow the on-screen instructions.

Step-by-Step 4.20

Creating the Windows NT 4.0 Setup Disks from Windows or DOS

To create the Windows NT 4.0 setup disks, you can use any version of Windows or DOS, as long as it recognizes the installed CD-ROM drive. For example, from DOS you can use a Windows 98 startup disk with CD-ROM support, as described here. You will need the following:

- A computer running MS-DOS or Windows 3.*x* or greater

- The Windows NT CD-ROM
- Three formatted, blank high-density 3.5-inch diskettes

Step 1

Place the Windows NT CD in the drive. If your computer supports AutoPlay for CDs, the Windows NT CD window will appear. Close the window.

In Windows 95 or greater, select Start | Run. In the Open box, type the following:

```
d:\i386\winnt32 /ox
```

Replace *d* with the drive letter of your CD-ROM drive; i386 is the directory where the installation program is located, winnt32 is the 32-bit NT installation program used by Windows 95 or greater, and /ox is a switch used to create a set of installation floppy disks.

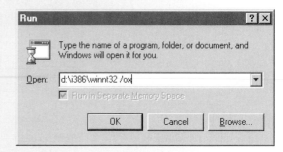

In MS-DOS or Windows 3.*x*, enter the following from a command prompt and click OK:

```
d:\i386\winnt /ox
```

Replace *d* with the drive letter of your CD-ROM drive; i386 is the directory where the installation program is located, winnt is the 16-bit NT installation program used by DOS and Windows 3.*x*, and /ox is a switch used to create a set of installation floppy disks.

Step 2

On the Windows NT 4.00 Upgrade/Installation page, verify that the location of the Windows NT 4.0 files includes the drive letter for your CD-ROM drive and also the i386 directory; then click Continue.

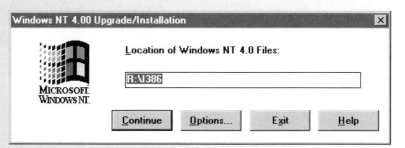

Step 3

Follow the instructions in the Installation/Upgrade Information box and label three formatted, blank high-density 3.5-inch diskettes. Insert the one labeled Windows NT Workstation Setup Disk #3 in the floppy drive and click OK or press ENTER.

Step 4

Follow the instructions on the screen; when Disk #3 has been prepared, you'll be prompted to replace it with Disk #2. When Disk #2 has been prepared, you will be prompted to replace it with the disk labeled Windows NT Workstation Setup Boot Disk. When this disk has been prepared, you have your entire set.

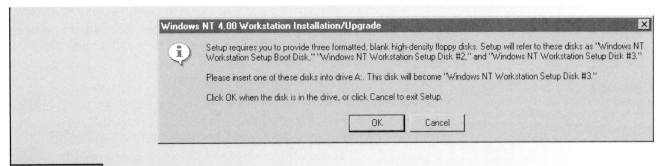

Windows NT 4.00 Workstation Installation/Upgrade

Setup requires you to provide three formatted, blank high-density floppy disks. Setup will refer to these disks as "Windows NT Workstation Setup Boot Disk," "Windows NT Workstation Setup Disk #2," and "Windows NT Workstation Setup Disk #3."

Please insert one of these disks into drive A:. This disk will become "Windows NT Workstation Setup Disk #3."

Click OK when the disk is in the drive, or click Cancel to exit Setup.

[OK] [Cancel]

Step 5

If you are installing NT on the same computer, leave the diskette in the drive and restart the computer. However, if you want to install NT on a different computer, remove the diskette and keep all three diskettes together until you are ready to use them in Step-by-Step 4.21.

Automated Installation

You perform an automated installation of Windows NT 4.0 using scripts that someone (often a team of people) has prepared ahead of time. This method is used by organizations with large numbers of desktop computers that need identical applications and desktop configurations. This method requires training and planning by one or more people.

The WINNT and WINNT32 Setup Programs

Automated installations and some manual installations may require the use of the WINNT.EXE or WINNT32.EXE program.

- An automated installation using the scripting method for Windows NT 4.0 provided by Microsoft uses either of these programs with appropriate command-line switches to select the scripts.

- A manual installation in which you don't boot from the CD or the setup boot disks requires the use of one of these programs; which one depends on the operating system in control at the time. Did you boot from a DOS disk to install from source files over the network? Then you need to use WINNT.EXE, the version for DOS or Windows 3.*x*. Are you upgrading from Windows 95 to Windows NT? Then you need to boot into Windows 95 and run WINNT32.EXE.

A Windows NT Installation Strategy

Regardless of the method you choose to use for your installation, we strongly suggest a strategy commonly used with Windows NT 4.0—install Windows NT 4.0 using the generic drivers provided with the OS, especially for your video adapter. You will not be able to access all of the capabilities of the adapter right away, but hang in there—we have a reason for this strategy. After you have the OS installed and running with basic drivers, you should apply service packs. It turns out that some newer drivers do install, but they do not work until you apply service packs.

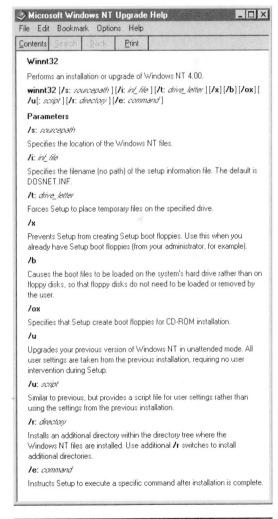

Microsoft Windows NT Upgrade Help

File Edit Bookmark Options Help

[Contents] [Search] [Back] [Print]

Winnt32

Performs an installation or upgrade of Windows NT 4.00.

winnt32 [**/s**: *sourcepath*] [**/i**: *inf_file*] [**/t**: *drive_letter*] [**/x**] [**/b**] [**/ox**] [**/u**[: *script*] [**/r**: *directory*] [**/e**: *command*]

Parameters

/s: *sourcepath*

Specifies the location of the Windows NT files.

/i: *inf_file*

Specifies the filename (no path) of the setup information file. The default is DOSNET.INF.

/t: *drive_letter*

Forces Setup to place temporary files on the specified drive.

/x

Prevents Setup from creating Setup boot floppies. Use this when you already have Setup boot floppies (from your administrator, for example).

/b

Causes the boot files to be loaded on the system's hard drive rather than on floppy disks, so that floppy disks do not need to be loaded or removed by the user.

/ox

Specifies that Setup create boot floppies for CD-ROM installation.

/u

Upgrades your previous version of Windows NT in unattended mode. All user settings are taken from the previous installation, requiring no user intervention during Setup.

/u: *script*

Similar to previous, but provides a script file for user settings rather than using the settings from the previous installation.

/r: *directory*

Installs an additional directory within the directory tree where the Windows NT files are installed. Use additional **/r** switches to install additional directories.

/e: *command*

Instructs Setup to execute a specific command after installation is complete.

• WINNT32.EXE syntax

This is because support for such newer technology as the AGP video adapters wasn't included in Windows NT 4.0, but was added in service packs. After applying the appropriate service pack, install the new drivers.

Gather the Materials Needed for Installation

If your computer and its components are newer than 1996 (and we hope they are!), Windows NT 4.0 will not have all of the correct drivers for your system. A `driver` is a special file containing program code that allows an OS to interact with and control a hardware device. You will need the device drivers for your installed hardware. Driver files are supplied by the manufacturer of the device, so if you can't locate the driver disk that came with the device, contact the manufacturer. Today that's as easy as connecting to the manufacturer's web site and downloading the driver.

If you'll be installing Windows NT 4.0 from source files on a network server, you won't need the CD, but you will need to be able to start your computer with an OS configured with the correct drivers and network client software to access the network and the server.

If your computer will boot from a CD-ROM, you need only the Windows NT 4.0 Workstation CD; if your computer has a CD-ROM drive but can't boot from it, you'll also need the three Windows NT Workstation setup disks. If that's the case, and if you don't have the diskettes, you can create a new set. Refer back to Step-by-Step 4.20 for instructions to do this.

You should also have a 3.5-inch diskette ready so that you can create a recovery disk during the installation.

Begin Installation

If you have selected and prepared the hardware, determined your strategy for installation, checked out the service pack level approved for use at your school or at work, then you are nearly ready to install.

Whenever possible, do a clean installation of a new operating system. What is a clean installation? With Windows, it means installing the OS on a perfectly clean hard disk. We even prefer to start with an unpartitioned hard disk. Unless it is a brand-new hard disk, we remove the old partition and allow the setup program to create a new partition and format it during the installation process.

Step-by-Step 4.21

Installing Windows NT 4.0 Workstation

The steps in this exercise assume a clean install on an unpartitioned hard drive. You will need the following:

- A Microsoft/Intel standard personal computer (desktop or laptop) configured to boot from CD-ROM

- An unpartitioned hard disk (disk 0, the first hard disk)

- The Windows NT 4.0 Workstation CD

- Three Windows NT setup disks, if your computer doesn't boot from CD-ROM

- One 3.5-inch diskette to use as an emergency repair disk

- The CD key code from the envelope of your NT CD

- A 15-character (or less) name for your computer, unique on your network
- The name of the workgroup to be used in the class lab
- A 14-character (or less) password for the Administrator account on your computer

- The TCP/IP configuration information for your computer, or confirmation from your instructor that you should configure Windows NT to get an IP address automatically

Step 1

Insert the Windows NT 4.0 Workstation CD and restart the computer. After the computer restarts, you'll briefly see a black screen with a message at the top left: "Setup is inspecting your computer's hardware configuration …" Then a nearly empty blue screen appears, labeled simply Windows NT Workstation Setup. This is the preparation for text mode of the setup program. When all of the NT Setup files are loaded into memory, the setup program's version of the NT kernel will be loaded and initialized (made active).

```
Windows NT Workstation Setup

  Welcome to Setup.

  The Setup program for the Microsoft(R) Windows NT(TM) operating system
  version 4.0 prepares Windows NT to run on your computer.

      • To learn more about Windows NT Setup before continuing, press F1.

      • To set up Windows NT now, press ENTER.

      • To repair a damaged Windows NT version 4.0 installation, press R.

      • To quit Setup without installing Windows NT, press F3.










  ENTER=Continue   R=Repair   F1=Help   F3=Exit
```

Step 2

For the next several screens, follow the instructions, responding based on the list at the beginning of this step-by-step. In addition, if your hard disk is unpartitioned, have NT Setup create a partition that is greater than 500MB and that leaves unpartitioned space available for use later. Select NTFS as the file system for the new partition. Accept the default location for the setup program to install the OS. At the conclusion of the text-mode setup, your computer will reboot.

Step 3

After the reboot, NT Setup starts in GUI mode, and the words "Windows NT Setup" appear over blue and black wallpaper. This will be the background for NT Setup until the next reboot. The first message box on this background shows the progress while files are copied. Reinsert your Windows NT 4.0 CD now.

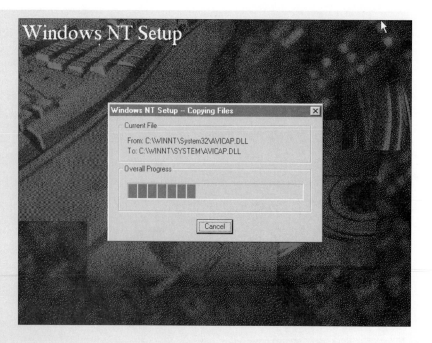

Step 4

The Welcome to the Windows NT Setup wizard message appears, informing you that it will perform three parts: gathering information about the computer, installing Windows NT networking, and finishing setup. Notice that the first step is highlighted. This message will reappear at the beginning of the next two parts of the setup. To continue, press ENTER or click the Next button.

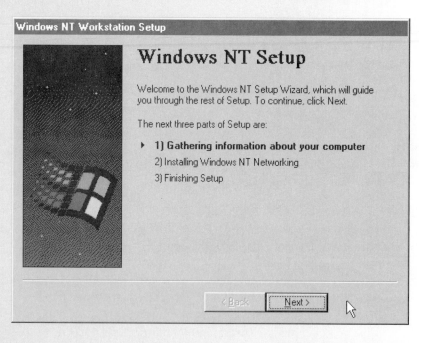

Step 5

The wizard will guide you through the information gathering steps. You will have to make choices and provide more information. Select Typical on the Setup Options page, fill in the Name and Organization page, and have NT Setup install the most common components. Provide the setup program with the information from the list at the beginning of this step-by-step.

Step 6	During the steps for installing Windows NT networking, use the information about your network settings that you prepared at the beginning of this step-by-step.
Step 7	During the steps for finishing setup, select your time zone and test your display settings; then NT Setup will copy the files necessary to complete the installation and configure the components. When it is finished, you will be prompted to restart the computer. A test of a successful installation is a successful reboot, so remove any floppy disks and CDs and then click the Restart Computer button. Log on with the Administrator account, using the password you provided during setup.

Verify Network Access

You have successfully installed Windows NT Workstation on a user's desktop. If the user requires access to a LAN and the computer was connected to the LAN during installation, it should have all the right stuff to work on the LAN, but you must verify that the computer can connect to the other computers on the network. Right now we'll have you do a simple test of network connectivity because this is a task normally done immediately after installing an OS.

The simplest test, although it is not entirely reliable, is to use Network Neighborhood to see other computers on your network. In the illustration, the list includes an NT Server named HTC1, a Windows XP computer named LAGUNA, and the computer on which we installed Windows NT 4.0 Workstation, SEDONA-NT. If you encounter problems with your network connection in the class lab, ask your instructor to help you solve the problem.

• Network Neighborhood

Windows NT 4.0 Service Packs

When you install any software, it is important always to check for the latest updates to the software.

There are several ways to find the version and service pack information, but using WINVER from Start | Run is our favorite because it's fast. This option displays the About Windows NT message box that contains version

Try This!

Verify Network Access Using Network Neighborhood

Your instructor will tell you what computers should be visible on your network. Try this:

1. On the desktop, locate and double-click the Network Neighborhood icon.

2. When the Network Neighborhood window opens, you will see a listing of the computers visible on your network. If other computers are visible to you, then you are connected to the network, even if you cannot see your own computer.

and licensing information, as well as the amount of memory available. It also shows the service pack level, right after the version information, if a service pack has been installed. This is the same message box you see if you select Help | About from the menu in Windows NT Explorer or My Computer.

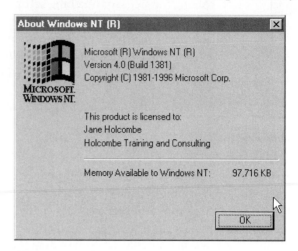

• About Windows NT

Installing Service Packs

In this exercise, you will install the latest service pack. You will need the following:

■ The computer on which you successfully installed Windows NT in Step-by-Step 4.21, connected to a LAN, with the correct drivers and protocols for your network

■ A username and password for an account that is a member of the Administrators group

■ Internet access from your lab computer, or a location on the local network or on your hard drive where the instructor has placed the service pack for you to download

Step 1

Log on as an administrator. Point your Internet browser to `www.Microsoft.com/ntworkstation`. On the Windows NT Workstation page, look for a link to the latest service pack. Click the link and follow the directions. Select the Intel X86. But wait—we're not done. You also must choose between the standard encryption version and the high-encryption version. Read the restriction on this at `www.Microsoft.com/exporting`. When you have decided on the version to use, select the link to download it.

Step 2

You will have to specify a language. After you initiate the download, you should see a Confirm File Open box. You do not want to open (run) the service pack program during the download, but click Save As and save the file to your desktop (or another location, if desired).

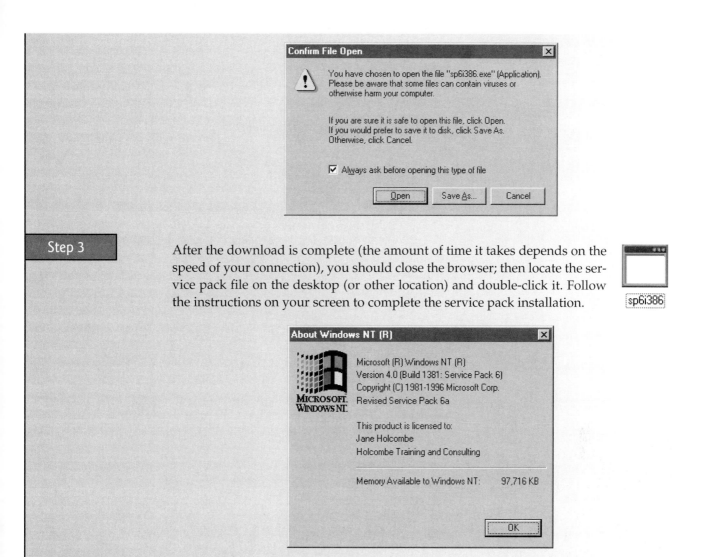

Step 3

After the download is complete (the amount of time it takes depends on the speed of your connection), you should close the browser; then locate the service pack file on the desktop (or other location) and double-click it. Follow the instructions on your screen to complete the service pack installation.

Step 4

When the service pack is installed, run WINVER.

◼ Customizing and Managing Windows NT 4.0 Workstation

After you've installed an OS, you need to configure and manage it for the person who will use it. This can involve a variety of tasks, including creating a new hard disk partition, installing or removing programs, and customizing the desktop. Take some time now to learn about these tasks.

Creating a New Hard Disk Partition

Creation of a disk partition may seem like an advanced task for a survey class, but if you install Windows NT 4.0 Workstation on a new computer, the probability that you will have unpartitioned disk space after the installation is very high. Therefore, creating a new hard disk partition once in a lab situation is a valuable experience for you.

Inside Information

Create Versus Create Extended

Selecting Create in Disk Admin-istrator will create a new primary partition (of which you may have no more than four per physical disk), and selecting Create Ex-tended will create a new extended partition, of which you can have no more than one per physical disk. Without going into the bor-ing details of what is wrong with extended partitions, simply re-member that an extended parti-tion is not a good thing unless you are dual-booting between Windows NT 4.0 and an OS that cannot use more than one primary partition per physical disk.

A partition defines the boundaries on a hard disk that can be used as if it were a separate physical disk. The two standard partition types are primary and extended. A **primary partition** can have a single drive letter assigned to the entire partition. An **extended partition** can have multiple logical drive letters. Each area that is defined as a drive letter is a volume, so a primary partition has a single volume, and an extended partition can contain one or more volumes. A PC will start an OS from a primary partition that is also marked as Active. An extended partition cannot be marked as active and therefore cannot be used to start an OS.

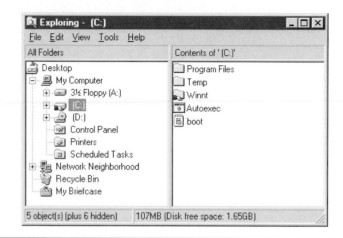

• Drive letters

A hard disk can have a total of four partitions, but never more than one extended partition. Extended partitions came about to get past limits of the DOS, Windows 3.*x*, and Windows 9*x* OSs. You don't need or want an ex-tended partition if you are not using one of these OSs.

When you create a new primary partition, it is automatically assigned a logical drive letter, but you will have to format it before it can be used to store files and folders. When you create a new extended partition, you must define the size and number of logical drives. The tool you use to manage disks in Windows NT is Disk Administrator, which you will use in Step-by-Step 4.23.

Step-by-Step 4.23

Creating a New Partition

In this exercise, you will create a new partition on your hard disk. You will need the following:

■ The computer on which you successfully installed Windows NT in Step-by-Step 4.21

■ Unpartitioned hard disk space

■ A username and password for an account that is a member of the Administrators group

■ A blank diskette

Step 1

Log on as an administrator and launch Disk Administrator by selecting Start | Programs | Administrative Tools | Disk Administrator. The first time you run Disk Administrator, you will see a message box stating that it will update system configuration information.

Click OK to close the message box, and Disk Administrator will start. On the first startup screen, you'll also see a message stating that "Disk Administrator needs to write information (the signature) on the disk." Click OK to allow it to do this and then click Yes in the Confirm box. You don't have any choice, but you won't see this message again.

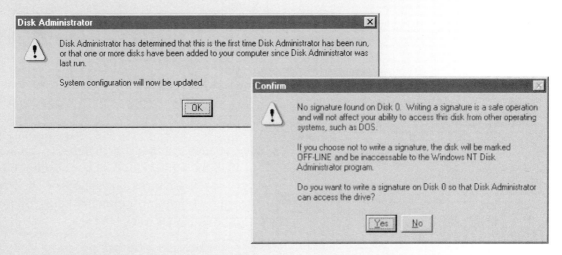

Step 3

In Disk Administrator, each physical disk is numbered, beginning with zero. The partitions are defined and labeled in boxes with color-coded bars at the top. The key is in the bottom of the window. If you installed NT according to the instructions in Step-by-Step 4.21, drive C: is a primary partition with the NTFS file system. Drive letters are assigned to hard disk volumes first and then to laser disk drives.

Step 4

To create a new partition in the unpartitioned space, click the area labeled Free Space and then go to the menu bar and select Partition | Create. Read the resulting message in the Confirm box and click Yes to confirm and continue.

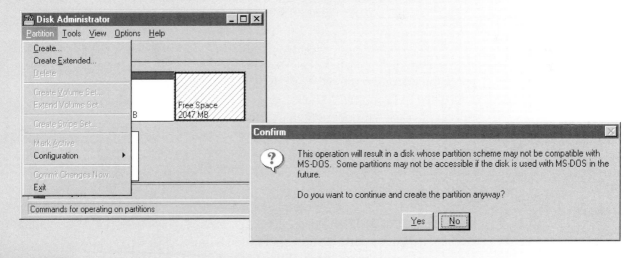

Step 5

In the Create Primary Partition dialog box, enter a size for the new partition in the entry box or accept the maximum size; then click OK. Ask your instructor for guidance if you are not sure what size to create.

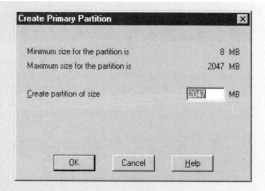

Step 6

The new drive will show a drive letter (if you created a new primary partition). Before you can format the new drive, you must commit the changes, which saves the changes in the registry—a huge listing of all the settings for the OS. To commit the changes, right-click the new partition, select Commit Changes Now, and then click Yes in the Confirm box. An information box labeled Disk Administrator reminding you to update the emergency repair configuration will follow this. Click OK.

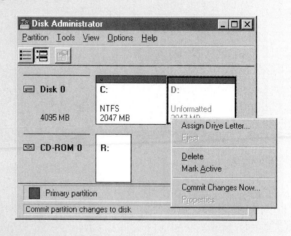

Step 7

To format the drive, right-click it and select Format. In the Format box, select the NTFS file system, leave the allocation unit size at the default value, and type **DATA** in the Volume Label box. Do not select either format option; then click Start. In the warning box, click OK. A progress bar will appear in the Formatting box. Click OK when the box pops up with the Format Complete message; then click Close in the Format dialog box.

Step 8

Confirm that you now have drive C: and D:, each of which is a primary partition on your hard disk, and then close Disk Administrator.

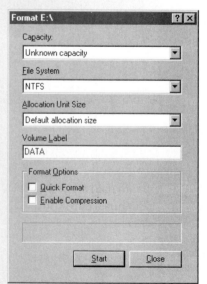

Step 9

Update the emergency repair configuration information in the registry and create a new emergency repair disk. Select Start | Run. In the Run box, type **RDISK** and press ENTER. Click Update Repair Info. This updates the Repair folder (C:\WINNT\REPAIR if NT is installed in WINNT) with a copy of portions of the registry, including the system portion, which now contains information about the new drive.

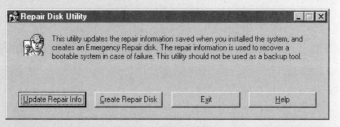

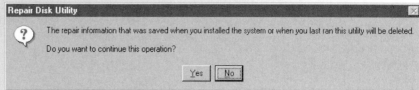

<table>
<tr><td>Step 10</td><td>When the repair information has been updated, you will be prompted to create an emergency repair disk. Click Yes and follow the instructions. Disk Administrator will format the disk and then copy the contents of the Repair folder to the disk. When this process is complete, remove the disk and place it in a safe location.</td></tr>
</table>

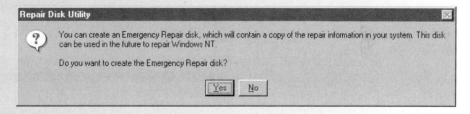

Installing and Removing Applications and Windows Components

After you have installed the OS, you need to install the applications required by the user. Many applications have their own installation programs. In addition, Windows NT has a special Control Panel applet, Add/Remove Programs, that you can use to install and uninstall applications and Windows components.

Step-by-Step 4.24

Using Add/Remove Programs to Install Applications

In this exercise, you will use Add/Remove Programs to verify which programs and Windows components have been installed and to uninstall one of those components. You will need the following:

- The computer on which you successfully installed Windows

- A username and password for an account that is a member of the Administrators group

Step 1

Log on as an administrator and select Start | Settings | Control Panel | Add/Remove Programs. Note the programs listed on the Install/Uninstall page.

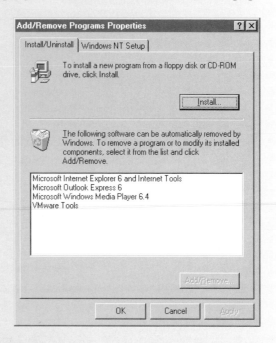

Step 2

Click the Windows NT Setup tab and note the Windows components listed on that page. Be very careful not to click a check box unless you really want to check or uncheck that component. Click each name (not the check box) and note the Details button. This button becomes active when the listed item includes more than one component. Select Accessories; then click the Details button to see all of the Accessories.

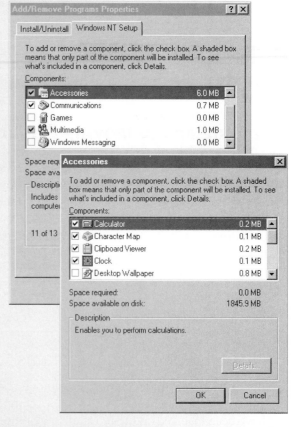

Step 3

Click Cancel to close the Accessories details box. Back on the Windows NT Setup page, notice that no Games components have been installed. Install a game now. Click Games and then click Details. Click the check box by FreeCell and then click OK to close the Games box; click OK to close Add/Remove Programs.

Step 4

Verify that the FreeCell Game was installed by locating it on the Start menu and starting it. You will find it at Start | Programs | Accessories | Games | FreeCell. Exit FreeCell when you are done.

Preparing the Desktop for Users

After you have installed Windows and tested any required network connectivity, added required service packs, and installed applications, you are ready to customize the desktop. Your goal should be to make the desktop visually pleasant for the user and to make any necessary changes that make using the OS easier.

Novice Users Will Customize the Desktop

One observation many professionals have related to us is that they continue to encounter client users who are new to working with computers and need to be guided through the procedures for turning on the computer, logging on, and performing new tasks. Revisiting the same novice user within a week, they find a customized desktop with a picture of their children or pet poodle as wallpaper. This tells us that they were given a good introduction. Some organizations don't allow such personalization for a variety of reasons, such as corporate image, propriety, and security when computers are in a public area. However, when it is allowed, this type of customization can make the user feel more comfortable with the computer.

Inside Information

When to Click Apply
Countless times, when an instructor demonstrates Windows to a class, students have pointed out that dialog boxes are sometimes closed without clicking Apply and, therefore, that the changes won't take effect. This isn't true. The Apply button appears in dialog boxes that have multiple tabbed sheets. If you make changes on one tabbed sheet and want to move to another within the same dialog box, click Apply. This applies the changes from that tabbed sheet without closing the dialog box. When you are done working in a dialog box, you don't have to click both Apply and OK to have changes take effect—OK applies all changes and closes the dialog box.

Step-by-Step 4.25

Customizing the Desktop

Experience will teach you the best methods for customizing the desktop. In this exercise, you will customize the settings for My Computer and Windows NT Explorer and use the Display applet to modify the desktop. Although the particular changes you make in this exercise may not be appropriate for most users, you will have an opportunity to view

many of the settings available to you. You will need the following:

■ The computer on which you successfully installed Windows

■ A username and password for an account that is a member of the Administrators group

| Step 1 | Log on as an administrator and right-click My Computer. This brings up the context menu. Notice that one of the options, Open, is in bold. The bold item in a context menu is the default action that occurs when you double-click an object. You are going to change this default behavior. But first, click an empty portion of the desktop to close the context menu without making a choice (the ESC key also closes open menus and dialog boxes). |

| Step 2 | Double-click My Computer. This brings up Folder view. This is what Open means for this object. Leave this window open and go back to the desktop. Right-click My Computer and select Explore to start My Computer in Explorer view. Compare the two views |

and see which you prefer. Do you like the one-dimensional, single-pane window of Folder view or the double-pane window of Explorer view, with a hierarchy of objects in the left Folder pane and the contents on the right?

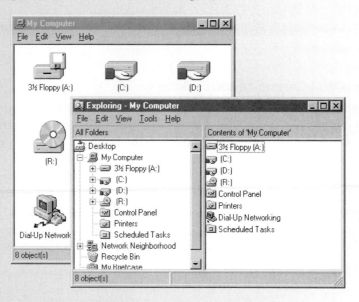

Step 3

We prefer Explorer view. Therefore, one of the first things we do for our own desktops is to make Explorer view the default, as you will do next. (Let's pretend that this is your preference, too!) Click one of the open My Computer windows and select View | Options. In the Options dialog box, click the File Types tab. In the list of registered file types, scroll down and select Folder (*not* File Folder).

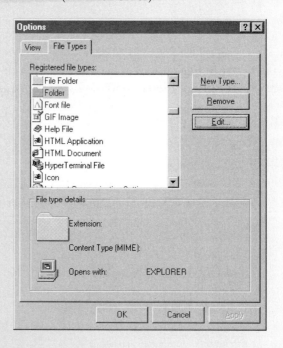

Step 4

Notice under File Type Details that Folder opens with Explorer, which opens a folder, whether it is opened in Folder view or Explorer view. With Folder selected, click the Edit button. In the Edit File Type dialog box, the word *Open* in the Actions list is bold. That

indicates that it is the default action. To change the default, click Explore and then click the Set Default button.

Step 5

Click OK to close the Edit File Type dialog box. Click the Close button to close the Options dialog box and to make the change take effect. Test the change by right-clicking on My Computer. Explore should now be in bold. Test it further by double-clicking the My Computer icon. It should now open in Explorer view.

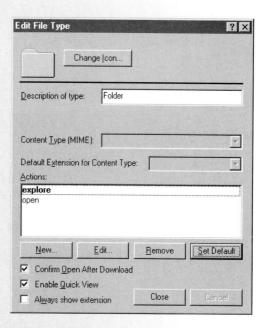

Step 6

Right-click the desktop to open the Display Properties dialog box and click the Appearance tab. Select each of the schemes in the drop-down list box and use the preview box at the top to choose a new scheme. When you find one that suits you, select it; then click OK to close the Display Properties dialog box and to apply the change you made.

■ Managing Windows NT Workstation Security

After you have completed the basic configuration tasks, you have more work to do. Windows NT was the first Microsoft desktop operating system to offer both a local security database for authentication of users and the ability to set permissions on local printers and on local files and folders, provided they are on NTFS volumes. Windows 9x provided no real security on the desktop. Logon rules could be enforced only at the network level. Someone who had access to the local computer had full access to every file, folder, and local printer.

In this section, you will first create local accounts so you can authenticate users and assign permissions to resources, such as files, folders, and printers. Then you will practice file and folder management, including assigning permissions to users. You will also create and manage a local printer.

Managing Users, Groups, Rights, and Permissions

Each Windows NT (all versions), Windows 2000, and Windows XP computer has a local account database in which an administrator can create security accounts. Security accounts include individual user accounts and group accounts that can contain multiple users. A skillful administrator can use these accounts to protect sensitive information on a computer. Users and groups can be assigned permissions to printers and to files and folders on an NTFS volume.

In a Microsoft workgroup, the only security accounts are on the individual Windows desktop computers (using Windows NT, Windows 2000, and Windows XP). In a Microsoft domain, security accounts are contained in a centralized accounts database on special servers called domain controllers. A special relationship then exists between the domain security accounts database and the security accounts on individual desktops.

Join us for a brief overview of user and group objects and of how permissions and rights are assigned in Windows NT 4.0.

Users and Groups

Windows NT requires an authenticated logon with a valid username and password. The username you use may be from an account that exists either in the local security database on that computer or in the security database on a special network server. When your Windows NT Workstation computer is a stand-alone system (not on a network), or is on a network but is a member of a peer-to-peer group called a workgroup, you can log on only with a local user account. For this chapter, assume that you are logging on using a local account.

In addition to individual user security accounts, NT uses security groups so that administrators can group user accounts to make the granting of permissions and rights easier.

Built-In User Accounts   Windows NT 4.0 Workstation has two built-in user accounts. When you installed Windows NT Workstation on your lab computer, you had to provide the password for the only active user account NT creates automatically: Administrator. The Administrator account is an all-powerful account. If a malicious person gets access to it, that person has full control of your computer. This account cannot be deleted, but it can be renamed, which is a good practice, as long as you remember the new name when you need to log on as a powerful user.

Another user account, Guest, is created, but disabled, by default. It is very rare to enable this account on a Windows NT Workstation computer, so we won't waste your time with an explanation.

Built-In Group Accounts   In addition to the built-in user accounts, NT Workstation has several built-in group accounts. They include Administrators, Backup Operators, Guests, Power Users, Replicator, and Users. By default, Administrator is the only member of the Administrators group, Guest is the only member of the Guests group, and all local user accounts are members of the Users group. The other groups are empty until an administrator creates additional local user accounts. All local user accounts automatically become members of the Users group. In other cases, an administrator adds users to the groups.

An administrator creates and manages users and groups with the User Manager program, which you can start from Start | Programs | Administrative Tools | User Manager.

In addition to the groups an administrator can create and administer in User Manager, there are special default groups that you cannot create or modify. Their membership is predefined, and they are available to you only when you assign permissions or rights. The most important of these is the **Everyone group**, which includes all users on a network, even those who haven't been authenticated.

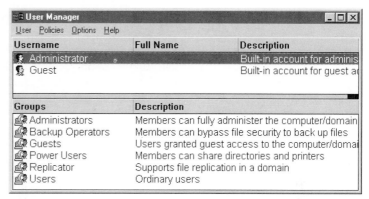

• User Manager

User Rights

In addition to permissions, Windows NT has user rights. A right is the privilege to perform a system-wide function, such as access the computer from the network, back up files, change the system time, or load and unload device drivers. You can view the user rights of an NT computer by opening User Manager and selecting User Rights from the Policies menu. NT makes a distinction between basic rights and advanced rights, normally hiding the advanced user rights in the User Rights Policy dialog box. Table 4.2 shows the built-in groups with their default rights. As you can see, rights are what make the Administrators group so powerful.

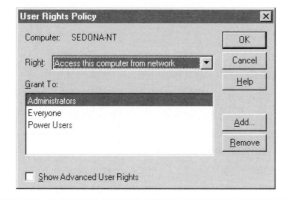

• User Rights

Table 4.2	Windows NT 4.0 Workstation Default Basic User Rights	
Group Name	**User Rights**	
Administrators	Access this computer from network	
	Back up files and directories	
	Change the system time	
	Force shutdown from a remote system	
	Load and unload device drivers	
	Log on locally	
	Manage auditing and security log	
	Restore files and directories	
	Shut down the system	
	Take ownership of files or other objects	
Power Users	Access this computer from network	
	Change the system time	
	Force shutdown from a remote system	
	Log on locally	
	Shut down the system	
Backup Operators	Back up files and directories	
	Log on locally	
	Restore files and directories	
	Shut down the system	
Users	Log on locally	
	Shut down the system	
Guests	Log on locally	
Everyone	Access this computer from network	
	Log on locally	
	Shut down the system	

Permissions

In the NTFS file system, each folder and file has a set of security permissions associated with it. Permissions define what a user or group can do to an object. Table 4.3 lists the standard folder permissions.

Do you have a folder that contains payroll information? You can assign permissions to certain users and groups, and you can keep others out, implicitly or explicitly. You keep users out implicitly simply by not including them in a file or folders list of permissions. You keep users out explicitly by granting them the No Access permission—which is as clear as you can get.

Table 4.3	Standard NT Folder Permissions
Permission	**Description**
No Access	Prevents a user from accessing a folder
List	Allows a user to see the contents of a folder and change to another folder
Read	Permits a user to read and execute a file
Add	Allows a user to add new files or folders to a folder without reading or changing existing files or folders
Add and Read	Allows a combination of the Add and Read permissions
Change	Permits a user to read and add to a folder and to change the contents of existing files and folders.
Full Control	Allows a user to read and change a folder, add new files, change permissions on the folder and its contents, and take ownership of the folder

Because permissions are set on individual objects, you view permissions through the Properties dialog box of a file, folder, or printer.

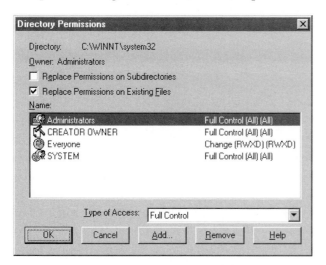

- Directory Permissions

Planning for Users, Groups, and Permissions

If a computer is used by only a single user, you need to create only one additional user account. If an NT Workstation computer is used by more than one local user, you should create additional local accounts. If the computer is a member of a Windows NT or Active Directory domain, you can give access to files, folders, and printers on that computer to the users and groups in the domain. If the computer is a member of a workgroup, it must have local accounts for granting access to network users.

You must be logged on as a member of the Administrators group to create users or groups, and you must provide certain information for each user you create. To complete the New User dialog box, have this information at hand. We like using planning forms as we prepare to create accounts.

A completed planning form for new users might look like Table 4.4. An asterisk indicates a required field in User Manager's New User dialog box. All users are automatically members of the Users group, but we included it in the planning form. Full Name and Description are optional, but it is good practice to complete these fields. You can add users to groups in the New User dialog box, in the New Group dialog box, or in the properties of the user account. If User Must Change Password at Next Logon is turned on by default, users log on with the password assigned in the New User dialog, but will be prompted to immediately change the password. The default groups are normally sufficient on an NT Workstation computer; therefore, no new groups are included.

Table 4.4	User and Group Planning Form			
User Name*	**Full Name**	**Description**	**Password***	**Groups**
Ssmith	Sue Smith	Manager	Ssmith	Users Power Users
Rjones	Ron Jones	Clerk	Rjones	Users

Managing Users and Groups

To complete this exercise, you will need the following:

- The computer on which you successfully installed Windows

- A username and password for an account that is a member of the Administrators group

Step 1

Log on to your lab computer as Administrator. Select Start | Programs | Administrative Tools | User Manager. On the menu bar, select New User.

Step 2

Complete the New User form for Sue Smith, filling in the correct fields from Table 4.4. You must enter the password two times, first in the Password field and again in the Confirm Password field. Leave the check by User Must Change Password at Next Logon; then click Groups.

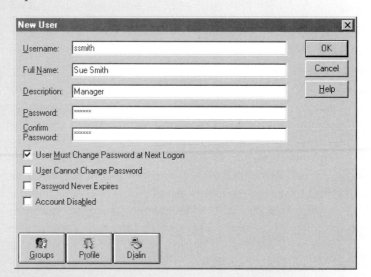

Step 3

In the Group Memberships dialog box, notice that Sue Smith is automatically a member of the Users group. To add her to the Power Users group, click Power Users in the Not Member Of list; then click the Add button. Click OK to add Sue to the Power Users group. Confirm that the information is correct in the New User dialog box; then click OK in the New User dialog box to create the new account.

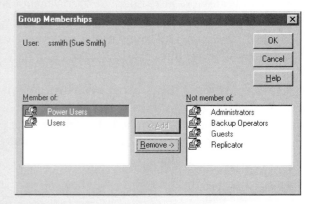

Step 4

Repeat Steps 2 and 3 to create a user account for Ron Jones. Do not add him to the Power Users group.

Test the new accounts by logging off as Administrator and logging on as a new account. To log off, press CTRL-ALT-DELETE, which brings up the Windows NT Security dialog box. Select Log Off and click OK in the Log Off Windows NT box. When you log on as each user, you will have to change the password.

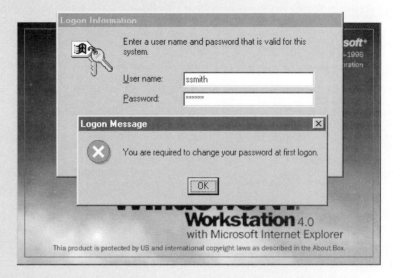

Mapping to Shared Folders

In Windows NT Workstation 4, you can browse shared network folders using Network Neighborhood, and thereby access files and subfolders located in those shared folders. However, there are a number of situations in which you will instead want to have a shared folder accessible as a drive letter from your local computer. For example, if you frequently need to access the contents of a shared folder, it's usually faster to access it as though it was a disk drive attached to your computer. Another reason for doing this is to access a shared folder's contents through the command prompt.

You do all this by creating *drive letter mappings* in which your local computer attaches to a remote shared folder and makes it appear to your computer (through, for example, File Manager) as a drive letter. Step-by-Step 4.27 shows you two different ways to map remote shared folders to drive letters in NT Workstation 4.

Mapping a Drive Letter to a Shared Folder on a Network

For this exercise, imagine that there are two remote folders that you frequently access that you would like to have appear as a drive letter on your local computer. The first one is your personal home directory on a server called SERVER01. Your home directory is shared with the share name DARLA. You will map this shared folder to drive letter H: (a mnemonic for "Home directory"). The second one is a shared folder, also on SERVER01, that files that everyone in your workgroup uses. The group folder uses the share name IT. You will map the IT share to drive letter G: (mnemonic for Group). In this exercise, you'll learn two different ways of mapping these remote folders to drive letters.

Step 1

Open Network Neighborhood by double-clicking it, and then navigate to open the remote server SERVER01 by double-clicking on the server. In the resulting window, you'll see all of the shared folders and printers of the server.

Step 2

Right-click on the share called DARLA. From the pop-up menu, choose Map Network Drive. You will see the Map Network Drive dialog box.

Step 3

In the top field of the dialog box, you can choose the drive letter to which to map this folder. From the drop-down field, choose H:. If you wish the drive mapping to automatically be re-created every time you log into your computer, check the Reconnect and Login check box. Then click OK to close the Map Network Drive dialog box and create the mapped drive. If you open My Computer after doing this, you should see a new Drive H, and opening it will open the shared folder on the remote server.

Step 4

To create the next drive mapping, you will use the command prompt. Open a command prompt, type **NET USE G: \\SERVER01\IT**, and then press ENTER.

After doing this, close the command window and re-open My Computer. You will see that you now have a drive letter mapping to drive G:, and opening it will open the shared folder IT on SERVER01.

After a drive letter mapping is created, you can work with the contents of the drive letter exactly as if it were really a new hard disk volume on your local computer. You can drag and drop files, use the **copy** command, and if your network permissions allow, can even delete or modify files.

Step 5

Removing a drive letter mapping is easy, and can also be done either graphically or through the command line. To remove a drive letter graphically, simply right-click on the drive as it appears in My computer, and choose Disconnect from the pop-up menu. To remove a drive letter mapping from a command prompt, you use the **NET USE** command with the /DELETE parameter. For example, to remove the G: drive letter mapping, you would type **NET USE G: /DELETE** and then press ENTER.

Chapter 4 Review

■ Chapter Summary

After reading this chapter and completing the exercises, you should understand the following.

Planning the Hard Disk Configuration

- It is necessary to have a minimum amount of free space available on the partition to install Windows NT Server.

- Windows NT Server supports three protocol standards, namely, TCP/IP, NWLink, and NetBEUI.

- Windows NT Server can be installed on multiple platforms.

- Two types of partitions in Windows NT 4.0 installation are system partition and the boot partition.

File System Considerations

- Windows NT Server can be installed either using the FAT file system or the NTFS file system, which has been specifically developed for Windows NT.

- Using NTFS allows the systems administrator the benefit of security features inherent in Windows NT. The FAT file system is not very ideal in this respect.

- When using NTFS for system partition, it is important that the FAT file system is kept intact until the installation is completed.

- The CONVERT utility included with NT 4.0 Server provides the option of converting a FAT partition into NTFS.

- FAT is the ideal file system choice when information needs to be shared between operating systems on a multiboot computer.

- Operating systems such as Windows 95 and DOS cannot access NTFS drives.

- In case Windows NT is installed as an NTFS partition, the system partition needs to be set up as FAT to enable other systems to boot correctly.

- If you install Windows NT Server in the same subdirectory as Windows 3.1 or Windows for Workgroups, the original operating system will no longer be available.

- Per-server licensing is ideal for networks that have only one server with multiple workstations connected to it. The number of client access licenses required depends on the number of workstations connected to the server.

- Per-seat licensing enables each client to access any number of servers with only one license. The number of logons is not controlled.

- It is safer to select the Per Server option because the administrator can make a one-time switch to the Per Seat option. The reverse is not possible.

Naming Conventions

- Windows NT converts the friendly name given to each computer into any identifiable means of routing the information.

- The NetBIOS name of a computer can be 15 characters in length; the share name can be 255 characters in length.

- The server name in Windows Networking should be preceded by two backslashes, with one backslash separating the server (computer) name and share name.

Preparing for Installation

- During the pre-installation process, the FDISK and FORMAT utilities from a DOS boot disk are used to partition and format the hard disk.

Network Installation

- In a network installation, files are made available (shared) from another network computer, such as another server or workstation. Files are then transferred across the network to the local hard disk during the installation process.

Configuring Microsoft Network Client Administrator

- The installation startup disk is a single bootable disk that contains the network client software and allows you to access the network share and proceed with the installation.

- Installation disk set is a complete set of disks used to install the network client software on a personal computer.

Creating a Network Boot Disk Using the Windows NT Client Administrator

- While creating a network boot disk using the Windows NT Client Administrator, the Client Administrator configures the disk as a boot disk. A boot disk loads the network drivers, connects to the server, enables logon to the domain, and provides access to shared resources.

Starting a Network Share Installation Process

- When running the setup program for network share installation process, it is better to copy the files to the local directory. This makes the process faster and reduces the strain on the file server.

Re-creating Windows NT Boot Floppy Disks

- The setup program for this creates the disks in reverse order, with the third disk being created first and the first disk last. Hence, it is important to check if the disks are labeled correctly.

Network Installation Switches

- The /b switch is used in a network installation. This switch determines whether or not floppy disks are needed during the installation.

Installing Windows NT Networking

- Start Search option aids the program to look for an adapter card to be used during installation.

CD-ROM Installation

- The option to boot from the CD-ROM drive is configured from within the computer's BIOS. Make sure that the CD-ROM drive is compatible with Windows NT.

- If your CD is unsupported under Windows NT Server 4.0, copy the contents of the appropriate subdirectory to the hard disk prior to installation and run the setup program from this location.

Installing NT on RISC-based Computers

- Windows NT cannot set up and configure RISC partitions. Hence, it is necessary to previously set up the partitions.

- If you are installing a primary domain controller, it will suffice to specify the computer name and the domain name. If the installation is a backup domain controller or a stand-alone server, the Computer Name, Domain Name, Administrator User Name, and Administrator Password fields need to be completed.

Upgrade Installation

- Windows NT 3.51 and Windows NT 4.0 do not use the same default directory.

- When upgrading from Windows 95, make sure that it is not in the FAT32 format. Windows NT 4.0 cannot access the FAT32 file system.

Unattended Installation

- SETUPMGR is a GUI program that enables the setting up of answer files for unattended installation.

- There are three groups of options in the SETUPMGR utility: General Setup, Network Setup, and Advanced Setup.

- The General tab includes basic information about how setup will run in unattended mode.

- The Computer Role tab gives the option of choosing the role of the computer, the workgroup name, and the account name.

- The License Mode lets you specify the license mode if the Computer Role tab indicates that the computer is being set up as a server or domain controller.

- The Time Zone tab lets you select the time zone where the computer is located.

- The Display Settings tab configures display properties during installation.

- The Install Directory tab aids in specifying the location of installation files.

Networking Options

- The Networking Options area provides information on network adapter card configuration, bindings, protocols, the Internet, and modems.

- The Adapters tab allows specifying the network adapters to install.

- The Protocols tab helps in defining what protocols to load and install. The TCP/IP, NetBEUI, and NWLink (IPX/SPX-Compatible Transport) protocols are available in this tab.

- The Services tab allows the identification of the network services to install. By default, SNMP

(Simple Network Management Protocol), Client Services for NetWare, and RAS (Remote Access Service) are available.

- The Internet tab is accessible only if the computer role in the General Setup section is set up as a server. This tab tells the setup program to install Internet Information Server (IIS) and presents configuration information for it.

- The Modem tab must be completed only if the RAS is selected in the Services tab. This tab aids in specifying the COM port, modem type, manufacturer, and provider, as well as the driver to install.

Advanced Options

- The Advanced Options window allows advanced users to specify additional information for the unattended installation process.

- The File System tab gives the options of whether to leave the current file system intact or convert the file system to NTFS. If the Convert to NTFS option is chosen, it becomes possible to extend the partition beyond two gigabytes (a FAT limitation).

- The Mass Storage tab specifies additional mass storage devices that need drivers to be installed.

- The Display tab, Pointing Device tab, and the Keyboard tab together help in specifying display drivers for the installation process.

- The Advertisement tab enables the customization of the banner text, logo, and background information pertaining to the installation.

- The Boot Files tab allows you to specify a list of boot files.

Unattended Setup and the Uniqueness Database File

- A UDF allows an administrator to specify information for each individual workstation or server that is being installed.

- A domain is a group of computers containing domain controllers that share account information and have one centralized accounts database. A server can belong to only one domain.

Server Roles

- A primary domain controller is the central server in the network. There must be only one PDC per domain.

- Member servers, also called stand-alone servers, have no responsibility in the accounts database and security information.

- The BDC is responsible for helping maintain user account database information. Administrative privileges in the domain are required to install the BDC.

- In the Server Manager, the Promote option on the Computer menu changes to a Demote option if the original PDC is highlighted on the list of computers in the domain. This step is necessary if the original PDC has been substituted by a BDC by the administrator.

Server Promotion Rules

- Stand-alone servers cannot be promoted or demoted. To change the role of a member server, it is necessary to re-install Windows NT Server.

Removing Windows NT

- The FDISK utility from DOS or Windows 95 can be used to delete a FAT partition.

- The FDISK utility cannot be used to delete NTFS partitions because DOS and Window 95 do not recognize NTFS partitions.

- The DELPART utility found in the Windows NT Resource Kit CD can be used to delete NTFS partitions. Another method to perform this task is to use OS/2 version of FDISK. Deletion of NTFS partitions is also possible by initiating a new Windows NT Server installation and choosing Delete partition in the text portion of the setup process.

Changing the Boot Loader in an Existing FAT Partition to MS-DOS

- The master boot record changes when Windows NT Server installs. Hence, in case a server needs to be set up with a different operating system, the master boot record is rewritten for the new operating system.

- To change the default operating system as MS-DOS without removing the Windows NT Server, change the startup process using the Control Panel. Select the Startup tab in the system properties window and choose MS-DOS as the default operating system.

Preparing for Windows NT 4.0 Workstation Installation

■ Before installing Windows NT on a computer hard disk, ensure that the computer is a complete system comprising hardware that is compatible with Windows NT 4.0. The hardware should match minimal hardware recommendations.

■ Patches are the software fixes that programmers create based on the feedback received from clients.

■ The service pack level in NT 4.0 is critical. After installation, ensure that a service pack is added immediately.

■ The NT 4.0 service packs were numbered through 6a (a post–Service Pack 6 release), which was followed by the Post–SP6a Security Rollup Package (SRP).

■ The manual installation method is chosen when there are not many computers to be installed with Windows NT.

■ The automated installation method is deployed by large organizations that have numerous desktop computers requiring identical applications and desktop configurations.

■ Whatever the manner of installation, it is better to install Windows NT 4.0 using the generic drivers that are available with the operating system. This can be done after applying the appropriate service packs.

■ A driver is a special file containing program codes that allow an OS to interact with and control a hardware device.

■ A clean installation implies that the operating system is installed on a perfectly clean hard disk.

■ To get information about the version and service pack, use WINVER from Start | Run. The About Windows NT message box in this option contains license and version information as well as other details.

Creating a New Hard Disk Partition

■ A partition defines the boundaries on a hard disk. After partitioning, the hard disk can be used as if it were a separate physical disk. Two standard partition types are primary and extended.

■ A primary partition can have only a single drive letter assigned to the entire partition. On the other hand, an extended partition can have multiple logical drive letters.

■ A hard disk can have a total of four partitions. However, it cannot have more than one extended partition.

Managing Users, Groups, Rights, and Permissions

■ Security accounts contain individual user accounts and group accounts. An administrator can use these accounts to protect sensitive information on a computer. The group accounts include Administrators, Backup Operators, Guests, Power Users, Replicator, and Users.

■ The Everyone group contains all users on a network, including those who have not been authenticated. This is a special default group that cannot be created or modified.

Using and Managing a Local Printer

■ To use a local printer, the printer driver needs to be installed by the administrator. The printer driver can be installed either by using the Windows NT CD or by installing a printer driver that comes with the printer.

Mapping to Shared Folders

■ In Windows NT Workstation 4, the files and subfolders contained in the shared network folders can be accessed using Network Neighborhood.

■ On entering Network Neighborhood and right-clicking on the shared folder of your choice, choose Map Network Drive. In the dialog box, choose the drive letter to which you want to map this folder. Click OK to close the Map Network Drive dialog box and create the mapped drive.

■ To remove a drive letter graphically, simply right-click on the drive as it appears in My Computer and choose Disconnect from the pop-up menu. To remove a drive letter mapping from a command prompt, type the **NET USE** command with the /DELETE parameter.

◼ Key Terms

Advanced Setup (151)

backup domain controllers (BDCs) (155)

boot disk (139)

boot partition (131)

client access licenses (132)

CONVERT utility (131)

discovery (155)

Disk Administrator (131)

domain (154)

driver (166)

Everyone group (181)

extended partition (172)

FAT (file allocation table) (131)

FDISK (133)

file system (131)

FORMAT (133)

General Setup (151)

installation disk set (138)

installation startup disk (138)

member server (156)

mirroring (133)

multiboot configuration (131)

naming conventions (133)

NetBEUI (130)

NetBIOS (130)

Network Setup (151)

New Technology File System (NTFS) (131)

NWLink (130)

partitioning scheme (131)

patches (131)

per-seat licensing (162)

per-server licensing (132)

primary domain controllers (PDCs) (155)

primary partition (172)

protocol standards (172)

protocols (130)

RDISK utility (146)

scripts (165)

switches (143)

system partition (131)

TCP/IP (130)

Uniqueness Database File (UDF) (154)

Universal Naming Convention (UNC) (133)

updates (162)

Windows NT Server (130)

◼ Key Term Quiz

Use the Key Terms list to complete the sentences that follow. (Not all terms will be used.)

1. Two licensing options that come as part of Windows NT are _____ and _____.

2. _____ is the process of by which data on one disk is duplicated on a separate disk.

3. Windows NT Server supports three protocol standards, namely, _____, _____, and _____.

4. Two types of partitions involved in Windows NT 4.0 installations are the _____ partition and the _____ partition.

5. The _____ available with the NT 4.0 Server aids in converting a FAT file partition into NTFS from the DOS session prompt.

6. Microsoft uses the _____ form of Universal Naming Convention.

7. _____ and _____ are used before installing Windows NT 4.0 Server to partition and format the hard disk.

8. A _____ loads the network drivers, connects to the server, enables logon to the domain, and provides access to shared resources.

9. There are three groups of options, _____, _____, and _____, with the SETUPMGR utility.

10. A _____ allows an administrator to specify information for each individual workstation or server that is being installed.

◼ Multiple-Choice Quiz

1. The NETBIOS name of a computer should not be more than how long?

   a. 20 characters

   b. 30 characters

   c. 225 characters

   d. 15 characters

2. What is the minimum free partition space mandated by Microsoft for Intel *x*86-type computers?

   a. 112MB

   b. 130MB

   c. 124MB

   d. 210MB

3. What is the name for a single bootable disk that contains the network client software and allows you to access the network share and proceed with the installation?

   a. Installation startup disk

   b. Installation disk set

   c. Network boot disk

   d. Installation setup disk

4. What utility helps to create or update a repair disk?

   a. SETUPMGR

   b. RDISK

   c. FDISK

   d. Server Manager

5. What are TCP/IP, NWLink (IPX/SPX-compatible), and NetBEUI?

   a. Protocols

   b. Network services

   c. Network components

   d. Utilities

6. Which of the following helps in setting up answer files for unattended installation?

   a. SYS utility

   b. SETUPMGR

   c. Server Manager

   d. FDISK

7. Which tab enables you to configure display properties during installation?

   a. Display Setting

   b. General

   c. Computer Role

   d. Install Directory

8. Which tab lets you customize the banner text, logo, and background information for your installation?

   a. Advertisement

   b. Mass Storage

   c. File System

   d. Boot Files

9. What is a group of computers containing domain controllers that share account information and have one centralized accounts database?

   a. Network

   b. Domain

   c. Cluster

   d. Sector

10. How many primary partitions can a hard disk have?

    a. Two

    b. One

    c. Four

    d. Three

11. What is the name of the process of copying the security information (accounts and permissions) to the BDCs and performing periodic updates to keep the information up-to-date?

    a. Synchronization

    b. Configuration

    c. Discovery

    d. Authentication

12. What is dedicated to process high-end searches and nonsecurity type functions?

    a. PDC

    b. BDC

    c. Member server

    d. Server Manager

13. Where is the CD key on most Microsoft software located?

    a. On the CD sleeve

    b. On the CD cover

    c. On the CD itself

    d. On the CD jacket

14. What is also referred to as a stand-alone server?

    a. PDC

    b. BDC

    c. Member server

    d. SQL server

15. What is the name for a special file containing the program code that allows an OS to interact with and control a hardware device?

    a. Driver

    b. Adapter

    c. Diskette

    d. Floppy disk

■ Essay Quiz

1. Give a brief description of the functions of the backup domain controller.

2. List the tasks that the text mode of the installation setup program performs.

3. Write down the steps to be undertaken to change the boot loader in an existing FAT partition.

4. Before installing Windows NT 4.0 Workstation, what are the preparatory steps to be kept in mind?

Lab Projects

• Lab Project 4.1

Install Windows NT 4.0 Server on your hard disk. Attempt to partition the hard disk during the Windows NT 4.0 Server installation process using the FAT partitioning format.

• Lab Project 4.2

Delete the system files to remove Windows NT 4.0 Server from a FAT partition.

Networking with Windows 2000

In this chapter, you will learn how to

- **Prepare for a Windows 2000 Server installation**
- **Install and configure Windows 2000 Server**
- **Create and administer user accounts, shares, and printers on a Windows 2000 Server**
- **Use Windows Backup to back up a Windows 2000 Server**

In this chapter, you learn how to install Windows 2000 Server, and then how to perform basic Windows 2000 Server administration. Before you install Windows 2000 Server, however, you first must conduct a variety of preinstallation checks that prepare the system for the process. Next, you perform the actual installation, providing necessary information that the installation program needs. Finally, you test the installation by having a client computer log in to the server properly and perform some basic network duties. All these steps are described in detail in this chapter.

Distinguish Windows 2000 Versions

Windows 2000 is an entire family of products, all built on essentially the same programming code, but with significant feature and tuning differences. Windows 2000 is an upgrade from the Windows NT line of products, which ended with Windows NT 4.

The desktop version of the product family is called *Windows 2000 Professional.* Windows 2000 Professional is made to run on business desktop computers and is not an upgrade for Windows 9*x*/Windows ME. Windows 2000 Professional supports the following broad features:

- Runs on systems with a minimum of 64MB of RAM (Microsoft claims that Windows 2000 Professional runs faster overall than Windows 9*x*/ME on systems with 64MB of RAM—an impressive claim that you should verify for yourself)

- Supports up to 4GB of physical RAM

- Supports one or two processors

- Works with Windows 2000 Server to take advantage of Active Directory and Intellimirror

- Includes support for plug and play (PnP) devices (PnP was not really supported in Windows NT)

- Includes all Windows NT's features, including a preemptive, protected, multiprocessing operating system

- Fully supports mobile computer features, including power management

Windows 2000 Server Standard Edition is the mainstream server version of Windows 2000. It includes all the power of Active Directory, as well as the following features:

- New management tools (compared to those provided with Windows NT) based on the Microsoft Management Console (MMC)

- Windows Terminal Services, which allows Windows 2000 Server to host graphical applications, much like a mainframe hosts applications for dumb terminals

- Internet and web services (DHCP, DNS, Internet Information Server, and Index Server)

- RAS and VPN services

- Transaction and messaging services

- Support for up to four processors

- Support for the latest versions of the standard network protocols

Windows 2000 Advanced Server is the mid-range offering of Windows 2000 Server products. It enhances the features of Windows 2000 Server by adding the following:

- Support for up to 8GB of installed RAM

- Network load balancing (for example, Advanced Server can share a heavy TCP/IP load among a number of servers and balance their loads)
- Windows 2000 clustering
- Support for up to 8 processors
- Support for 2-node clusters

The most powerful version of Windows 2000 Server is the Datacenter Server version. This version is used when extremely large databases need to be hosted for thousands of users or when other extremely heavy demands need to be placed on Windows 2000 Server. Datacenter Server includes all the features of the other versions of Windows 2000 Server, plus the following:

- Support for up to 64GB of installed RAM
- Support for up to 32 processors
- Support for 4-node clusters

Prepare for Installation

Before installing Windows 2000 Server, you first must prepare the server computer that you will use and make important decisions about the installation. This preparation stage consists of a number of tasks, including the following:

- Make sure the server hardware is certified for use with Windows 2000 Server.
- Make sure the server is properly configured to support Windows 2000 Server.
- Carry out any needed preinstallation testing on the server hardware.
- Survey the hardware prior to performing the installation.
- Decide how you will install Windows 2000 Server, after gathering all the configuration information you will need during the installation.
- Back up the system prior to an upgrade.

These tasks are discussed in the following sections.

Check Hardware Compatibility

Microsoft maintains an extensive Hardware Compatibility List (HCL) that lists different hardware components and their testing status on various Microsoft products, such as Windows 2000 Server. To avoid problems with your server, it is important you make sure that the server itself and any installed peripherals have been tested with Windows 2000 Server and work properly. The latest version of the HCL can be found at www .microsoft.com/hcl. You can also find a text-based copy on the Windows 2000 Server CD-ROM. Using the web HCL is preferred, however, because it might have more current data than the file included on the installation CD-ROM.

Check the Hardware Configuration

Purchasing a computer for use as a server can be a complex task. You have to contend with the myriad details of installed RAM, processor configuration, disk configuration, and so forth, as well as factor in your anticipated needs to come up with a reasonable server configuration.

Windows 2000 Server requires the following *minimum* hardware configuration:

- One 133-MHz Pentium class processor or greater
- 256MB of RAM
- About 1GB of free disk space for the installation process
- A CD-ROM or network connection from which Windows 2000 Server is installed; if you are using a CD-ROM drive, Microsoft recommends one that is 12x speed or faster

The preceding are the minimum requirements specified by Microsoft. You should carefully consider using more capable hardware than that specified, particularly for any kind of server (even one that will support only a few users).

Instead, follow this advice when configuring a server for Windows 2000:

- Start with at least a single fast Pentium IV processor running at 1,000 MHz or greater. Pentium 4 Xeon processors are a benefit in a server and you should carefully consider the price of such systems relative to the expected performance improvement (all else being equal, a Pentium 4 Xeon family processor will perform about 15 to 20 percent faster than an equivalent Pentium 4 processor). Also, consider using a system that has either two or more processors or the capability to add additional processors later if your needs grow faster than expected.

- Windows 2000 Server runs best on systems that have plenty of RAM. For a server, make sure you have at least 384MB of RAM. If you plan on supporting all the different services available with Windows 2000 Server (such as Terminal Services, RAS, DHCP, DNS, and so forth), 512MB of RAM might be a better choice than 384MB of RAM. One gigabyte of RAM is not an unreasonable amount, particularly for servers that will experience heavy loads. (Don't forget, you can start with 384MB of RAM and install more if needed, and possibly at a less expensive price than when you first purchase the server.) Do *not* attempt to run Windows 2000 Server on a system with less than 256MB.

- A fast SCSI-based disk subsystem is important, particularly for servers that will store a lot of data.

- Windows 2000 Server requires a lot of disk space for its initial setup. The formula to determine the amount of disk space is 850MB + (RAM in MB $\times$ 2). In other words, you need 850MB, plus another 2MB of disk space for each megabyte of installed RAM in the server.

This is a minimum amount required for installation. Installing the server onto a system that will use FAT32 (File Allocation Table) formatted disks requires an additional 150MB or so because FAT32 stores files less efficiently than NTFS. Installing Windows 2000 Server from a network installation point also requires more disk space: estimate about 150MB of additional disk space if you will be installing over a network connection rather than from CD-ROM.

When sizing a server, remember this rule of thumb: get the most capable server you can afford and make sure it is expandable to meet your future needs, through the addition of more RAM, more processors, and more disk space. Even with all of that, it is common for servers to be replaced three to four years from the date they were placed into service.

Test the Server Hardware

You found all your server hardware in the Windows 2000 Server HCL, you made sure your server is adequately sized, you purchased it, and you have your shiny new Windows 2000 Server CD-ROMs sitting there, all ready to be installed. Is it time to start the installation yet? Well, not quite. Before installing any NOS, particularly on a server that will be used for production, make sure you carry out hardware testing (also called burn-in) on the server before installing Windows 2000 Server. Computer hardware tends to be most reliable after it has been running for a while. In other words, failures tend to happen when equipment is new, and the chance of hardware failure decreases rapidly after the hardware has been up and running for 30 to 90 days. Because of this, it's a good idea to test new servers for at least a week (testing for two weeks is even better) before proceeding to install the NOS. Doing this can help provoke any early failures in the equipment, during a time when they're easy to fix and they won't affect any users or the network. Moreover, many servers have a 30-day return or exchange policy from their manufacturer, so if you discover problems, you'll have a chance to return the system and perhaps start over with a different model.

You test the hardware using diagnostic software that should have come with the server or is available from the maker of the server. Most such diagnostic software enables you to choose which components of the system are tested and enables you to test them in an endless loop, logging any discovered errors to a floppy disk or to the screen. You should focus the tests on the following components:

Server-testing software often enables you to choose between nondestructive and destructive testing of the disks. (Destructive means that any data on the disks is erased during the testing.) Destructive testing is best for discovering any errors on the disks. This is one reason that you want to carry out this testing before you install your NOS.

- Processor(s)
- System board components (interrupt controllers, direct memory access [DMA] controllers, and other motherboard support circuitry)
- RAM
- Disk surfaces

If the diagnostic software allows you to do so, you can usually safely skip testing components such as the keyboard or the display. Your primary concern is that the unit continues running properly when it is under load for an extended period of time. You also want to make sure that the RAM is working properly and that no bad sectors show up on the disks during testing. It's also a good idea during testing to power the unit on and shut it down a number of times, since the impact to the unit of initially powering on often can provoke a failure in any marginal components.

Survey the Server Prior to an In-Place Upgrade

The Windows 2000 family of products takes advantage of PnP (plug and play) hardware, and can detect and automatically configure any PnP devices to work with Windows 2000 Server during the installation. PnP is not perfect, though. For one thing, you might have installed components that are not PnP devices, and Windows 2000 will be unable to configure those devices. Also, sometimes PnP devices can conflict with other devices, or the drivers for a specific device might not allow proper configuration for some reason. Because of these imperfections, it's important to survey the components installed in the server before installing Windows 2000 Server as an upgrade. Performing a survey is not really important when setting up a new server.

For the survey, write down all the installed devices, along with the resources that each one uses in the server. The resources include the IRQ channel, DMA channel, and memory I/O addresses used by each device. Then, if a device isn't working properly after you install Windows 2000 Server, you might be able to configure the device manually to known settings that work.

 Some server computers come with utilities such as Compaq's SmartStart. Such utilities handle the server at a hardware level and keep the information in a space separate from the NOS. Server utilities such as Compaq's make life much easier when you are trying to troubleshoot a hardware problem with the server.

Make Preinstallation Decisions

After configuring, checking, preparing, and testing your hardware, you can actually begin installing Windows 2000 Server. During this process, you first spend time making a number of important preinstallation decisions that you must be prepared to specify during the installation. The following sections discuss these choices.

Upgrade or Install?

You can upgrade a server running Windows NT Server 3.51 or 4.0 to Windows 2000 Server and maintain all your existing settings, user accounts, file permissions, and so forth. You can also perform a full installation where you wipe out any existing NOS on the server. You must perform a full installation to a new server or to one running any NOS other than Windows NT Server. If you are running an upgradeable version of Windows NT Server, however, pros and cons exist to both approaches.

 If you are running Windows NT Server 4 Enterprise Edition, you can upgrade only to Windows 2000 Advanced Server.

The main benefit to upgrading is that all your existing settings under Windows NT Server will be maintained and automatically carried forward into your Windows 2000 Server installation. These include networking details, such as TCP/IP configuration information, as well as security settings that you might have tediously set up over time. In fact, if the server can be upgraded, you should plan on doing so, unless you need to change something fundamental in the server, such as changing from FAT to NTFS.

FAT or NTFS?

Windows 2000 Server supports hard disks formatted using either File Allocation Table (FAT16 and FAT32) or **NT File System (NTFS)**. Important advantages exist to using NTFS under Windows 2000 and, in some cases, it is required. You would want to install Windows 2000 Server onto a disk that

If you are installing Windows 2000 Server onto a system that has only a single FAT partition and you want to dual-boot Windows 2000 Server with that other operating system, but you want to establish a new NTFS partition for Windows 2000 without having to destroy the existing FAT partition, you can use ServerMagic from PowerQuest to accomplish this. ServerMagic enables you to resize an existing FAT partition without losing any of its data and it also fully supports FAT and NTFS partitions. Without a product such as ServerMagic, you instead have to back up the FAT partition, destroy it as you repartition the hard disk, and then restore the other operating system (and all applications and files) to the new, smaller FAT partition.

uses the FAT file system only when the system must be used in a **dual-boot setup**, where it retains the capability to boot another operating system, such as Windows 98. Even in cases where you need to maintain dual-boot capability, though, you're better off maintaining a primary FAT partition for the other operating system and setting up an extended partition with NTFS to hold Windows 2000 Server. In such cases, Windows 2000 automatically installs dual-boot support that enables you to choose which operating system to use when the system is started.

NTFS is required for any Windows 2000 Servers that will function as domain controllers and also is the only file system that enables you to take full advantage of Windows 2000's security features. Moreover, NTFS is optimized for server performance and performs better than FAT under almost all circumstances.

Domain Controller, Member Server, or Stand-Alone Server?

Before deciding this question, you need to understand two important concepts in Windows 2000 networks: domains and workgroups. A **domain** is a sophisticated administrative grouping of computers on a Windows 2000 network that makes it possible to administer the network's resources from a single point and to implement strong security. Domains enable you to manage multiple Windows 2000 or Windows NT servers more easily. A **workgroup** is a simple collection of computers on a network and is suited only to pure peer-to-peer networks.

You can configure Windows 2000 Servers in one of three modes to support either domains or workgroups, as follows:

- Domain controllers hold the domain's Active Directory information and authenticate users and access to resources. Most Windows 2000 networks have at least one domain and therefore need at least one domain controller.

- Member servers are part of a domain, but do not hold a copy of the Active Directory information.

- Stand-alone servers do not participate in a domain but instead participate in a workgroup.

Except in the smallest of networks, it's a very good idea to have two domain controllers. This way, all of your domain information is preserved and available to the network should one of the domain controllers crash. Domain information is automatically synchronized between the available domain controllers.

Prior to Windows 2000, Windows NT servers that were domain controllers had to be designated as either primary domain controllers (PDCs) or backup domain controllers (BDCs). Windows 2000 with Active Directory simplifies matters significantly so that all Windows 2000 domain controllers are simply that: domain controllers. Each domain controller holds a copy of the Active Directory data and can perform all the functions of the other domain controllers. Previously, the PDC performed all administrative tasks, whereas the BDCs simply kept read-only copies of the domain information to continue authenticating security on the network in case the PDC failed. Windows 2000 Server, on the other hand, uses the concept of **multimaster domain controllers**, which all seamlessly operate the same way as the other domain controllers.

Per Seat or Per Server?

Another important choice to make when installing Windows 2000 Server is how the server will manage its Client Access Licenses (CALs). Windows

2000 Server supports two different ways of managing CALs: per server and per seat. Per-server licensing assigns the CALs to the server, which will allow only as many connections from computers as there are installed CALs on that server. Per-seat licensing requires purchasing a CAL for each of your client computers, which gives them the right to access as many Windows 2000 servers as they wish; the servers will not monitor the number of connections. Generally, Microsoft recommends that you use Per-server licensing when running a single server and per-seat licensing when running multiple servers. If you are unsure of which mode to use, Microsoft recommends that you choose Per Server because Microsoft lets you change to Per Seat mode once at no cost (whereas changing from Per Seat to Per Server has a price). Carefully review licensing options with your Windows 2000 reseller to determine the most economical way to license your network servers properly.

Wait! Back Up Before Upgrading!

If you are installing Windows 2000 Server as an upgrade to another NOS, such as Windows NT Server, it's vital that you fully back up the server prior to installing Windows 2000 Server. (It's a good idea to make two identical backups, just in case.) You should use whatever backup software you normally use for your existing NOS, making sure the software can properly restore the previous NOS in case you need to "unwind" the upgrade process and revert to your starting point. Even when you are performing an upgrade to Windows NT and will not be reformatting any of the disks, making a preinstall backup is good insurance in case of trouble.

Install Windows 2000 Server

There are a number of ways to begin the installation of Windows 2000 Server. You can

- Configure the server computer to boot from the Windows 2000 Server CD-ROM

- Begin the installation while running Windows NT Server

- Begin the installation while running Windows 95 or 98

- Prepare boot diskettes and use them to begin the installation process

- Install from a network installation point that has been previously set up

When setting up a new server, you have only two real choices to begin the installation: boot from the Windows 2000 Server CD-ROM or prepare boot diskettes. Most servers can boot from their CD-ROM drives, which is the best way to perform the installation. If you find that you instead need to prepare boot diskettes, you can do so by running the MAKEBOOT.EXE program found on the Windows 2000 Server CD-ROM. The example installation in this chapter assumes that you are booting the installation process from the Windows 2000 Server CD-ROM.

Run the Windows 2000 Server Setup Program

The following sections describe the process of running the installation program for Windows 2000 Server and installing it onto a server. If you are learning about Windows 2000 Server and have a suitable computer to use, you should take the time to install Windows 2000 Server so that you understand how the process works. Or, if you like, you can read along through the following descriptions in order to familiarize yourself with the installation process. (We recommend actually performing an installation such as the one described here, and then "playing with" the resulting server as a way of more quickly and completely learning about Windows 2000 Server.)

When you boot from the Windows 2000 Server CD-ROM, the program first presents a text-based screen that walks you through the early installation choices you will make. You first press ENTER to confirm that you wish to install Windows 2000 Server, or press F3 to exit the installation program.

The program then prompts you to choose whether you wish to install Windows 2000 Server or to repair an existing Windows 2000 Server installation. You press ENTER to choose to install Windows 2000 Server.

Next, the program requires that you agree to the Windows 2000 Server license agreement. Press F8 to agree to the license and proceed.

The next screen begins the meat of the installation process. You see a screen listing all available disk partitions to which you can install Windows 2000 Server. You can perform the following actions at this point:

- Use the arrow keys and press ENTER to select an existing disk partition.

- Press the letter C on the keyboard to create a new disk partition from unpartitioned disk space (a new server installation usually requires that you create a partition).

- Press the letter D on the keyboard to delete an existing partition (you usually must do this only when removing all vestiges of a previous operating system, after which you will create the installation partition you need).

When you press the letter C to create a partition, the program prompts you for the size of the partition you wish to create. By default, the program offers the maximum size partition. To accept this choice, simply press ENTER, at which point the program creates the new partition. You then return to the screen listing all partitions, and the program displays the new partition that you created as "New (Unformatted)." Choose this partition and press ENTER to proceed.

A brief discussion about choosing between FAT and NTFS appears earlier in this chapter, in the section "FAT or NTFS?"

After you select the new partition, the program prompts you to choose a disk format: either FAT or NTFS. For most servers, you use only NTFS partitions, so choose NTFS and press ENTER to continue. The installation program then formats the partition for you.

After the format completes, files necessary to continue the installation of Windows 2000 Server are automatically copied to the new partition. After copying the files, the program automatically restarts the system, and the graphical portion of the installation starts automatically.

The graphical setup program walks you through various installation choices you must make during the setup process. Although you can modify most of these choices later, it's best if you can make the correct choices the first time during the initial installation of Windows 2000 Server. The remainder of this section continues the installation process and discusses the choices that the program presents.

The graphical setup program first attempts to detect and set up all the basic devices installed in the computer. This process takes five to ten minutes.

Once the basic devices are installed and set up, you are prompted to choose the locale and keyboard settings you wish. These choices default to English (United States) and U.S. Keyboard Layout (if you're using a copy of Windows 2000 Server purchased for the United States), so you can usually just click the Next button to continue.

Next, the program prompts you to enter your name and organization name. Most companies prefer that you *not* personalize the operating system to a particular individual. Instead, use a name such as "IT Department" and then enter your company's name in the field provided. Click Next to continue.

The program then prompts you to choose either Per Server or Per Seat licensing. Refer to the discussion earlier in this chapter, in the section "Per Seat or Per Server?" which discusses this choice. Then choose the appropriate option button. If you choose Per Server, select the number of licenses you own. Then click Next to continue.

The next dialog box is important. You enter the name of the computer to which you are installing Windows 2000 Server; you also enter the initial Administrator password. The computer name that you choose will be the name of the server and the name seen by users when they browse the servers on the network. If possible, you should choose a name that you won't need to change later. For the Administrator password, choose a good, strong password that could not easily be guessed. The Administrator password is the key to doing anything you need to do with the server, so you need to choose a password that will be secure. As a rule of thumb, choose an Administrator password with eight or more characters, including both letters and numbers. Make sure it's also a password you will remember! After completing the fields, click Next to continue.

Next, the program displays a dialog box that lists all the different components you can optionally install with Windows 2000 Server. If you are following along and performing a sample installation of Windows 2000 Server to learn about the installation process, only basic choices related to setting up a file and print server should be selected. However, the following is a list of all the choices (you can choose to add these components after the main installation is complete):

- **Certificate Services (1.5MB)** `Certificate Services` are used to enable public-key applications. You do not need to install this option unless you have an application that requires these services.

- **Cluster Services (2.2MB)** Windows 2000 `Cluster Services` enable two or more servers to share a common workload and to provide fail-over support in case one of the servers experiences a hardware failure. You do not need to install this option unless you are building a high-availability server cluster.

- **Internet Information Server (ISS) (28.7MB)** **Internet Information Server (IIS)** allows a Windows 2000 Server to operate as a web and FTP server. Choosing this option installs IIS along with a number of support features related to IIS. You do not need to install IIS for a file and print server.

- **Management and Monitoring Tools (15.7MB)** Choosing this option installs supplemental management tools, including the following:

  - Connection Manager components for managing RAS and dial-up connections

  - Directory Service Migration Tool for migrating from NetWare Directory Services (NDS) to Windows 2000 Active Directory

  - Network Monitor Tools, which you can use to perform rudimentary network packet analysis and decoding

  - Simple Network Management Protocol, which lets the Windows 2000 Server report management information to an SNMP management computer on the network

- **Message Queuing Services (2.4MB)** **Message Queuing Services** queue network messages used with certain client/server applications. Unless such an application requires you to do so, you needn't install this tool.

- **Microsoft Script Debugger (1.6MB)** This option adds tools that enable you to debug scripts written in VBScript and Jscript. Because you might occasionally need to access the Internet through a web browser on the server (to download driver updates, for example) and because you might develop server-based scripts written in VBScript or Jscript, you should choose to install this tool.

- **Networking Services (3.6MB)** This installation choice is a catch-all for a wide variety of network services that you might choose to install on your server. In particular, you should consider selecting several of these options for a file server or print server. First, consider installing Dynamic Host Configuration Protocol (DHCP), which allows the server to manage a range of IP addresses and to assign addresses automatically to client computers. Second, consider installing Windows Internet Name Service (WINS), which provides name resolution and browsing support to client computers that are running pre-Windows 2000 operating systems (such as Windows NT and Windows 9x) and are using only the TCP/IP protocol. Neither of these options is required for a basic file server or print server, however.

- **Other Network File and Print Services** This option enables you to install the additional support required to share the server's files and printers with Macintosh computers and Unix-based computers. You

For a basic file server or print server, it's a good idea to choose to install the Network Monitor Tools, which you can select as part of the Management and Monitoring Tools installation option. First, select Management and Monitoring Tools in the dialog box, and then click on the Details button and choose Network Monitor Tools.

needn't select this option if all your client computers are running some version of Windows.

- **Remote Installation Services (RIS) (1.4MB)** With RIS, you can remotely install Windows 2000 Professional onto network computers that support a feature called *remote boot.* You need a dedicated partition on the server to host the Windows 2000 Professional disk images. You do not need this tool for a basic file and print server.

- **Remote Storage (3.5MB)** The `Remote Storage` feature enables you to configure a Windows 2000 Server disk to move rarely accessed files automatically onto an available tape drive or writeable CD. The operating system can automatically recall these files if they are needed. Most servers do not need this tool.

- **Terminal Services (14.3MB) and Terminal Services Licensing (0.4MB)** These two options enable a Windows 2000 Server host multiple Windows sessions for remote computers, in which the applications execute on the server and the client computer handles only the display and keyboard/mouse input for the application. Windows Terminal Services works somewhat the same as mainframes, where all the work is performed on the mainframe and the client acts only as a terminal to the mainframe. You do not need these options for file servers or print servers.

> Understanding and administering Terminal Services can be complicated and requires some techniques not readily apparent at first glance. Taking a course or purchasing a book on Terminal Services is probably a good suggestion, especially if using Terminal Services as an exclusive remote control or remote access solution.

After choosing from the preceding options, click Next to continue. The program then prompts you for information about a modem attached to the server, if one exists. You can provide your area code and any number you need to dial to get an outside line, and indicate whether the phone line supports tone dialing or pulse dialing. Complete the requested fields and click Next to continue.

Next, the program prompts you to enter the correct date and time, as well as the time zone in which the server resides. Update these fields if necessary and click Next to continue.

The program next prompts you to select your network settings. You can choose between Typical settings or Custom settings. For a small network, you can usually safely choose the Typical settings option. Choosing Custom settings enables you to define details, such as exactly what networking components will be installed and how each is configured. For this example of a basic installation of Windows 2000 Server, Typical settings is chosen.

Next, the program prompts you to choose between setting up Windows 2000 Server as a member of a workgroup or a domain. A discussion about the differences between these two choices appeared earlier in this chapter, in the section "Domain Controller, Member Server, or Stand-Alone Server?" You cannot join the new server to a domain, however, unless the domain already exists and a domain controller is available to authenticate (allow) the new server into the domain. For a new server, even one that will be a domain controller, therefore, choose Workgroup and click Next to proceed.

The setup program then completes its portion of the installation of Windows 2000 Server, using the information you provided.

Installing Windows 2000 Server

In this project, you will install Windows 2000 Standard Server onto a computer running Windows ME. This is a good way to start to learn about Windows 2000 Server without having to dedicate a computer to running it. When complete, you will be able to dual-boot to either Windows 98 (or other Win9x operating systems, like Windows ME) or Windows 2000 Standard Server.

To complete this exercise, you will need the following:

- A computer that meets the minimum requirements for Windows 2000 Server
- A CD-ROM drive that supports bootable CDs
- A Windows 2000 Server CD-ROM

Step 1

On the computer that already has an earlier version of Windows installed, make sure that it has adequate capacity to install and run Windows 2000 Server. This topic is discussed earlier in this chapter, but basically the computer should have a Pentium 133MHz or faster processor, 256MB of RAM, and about 1GB of free disk space.

Step 2

Insert the Windows 2000 Server CD-ROM and boot the computer to the CD-ROM drive. (On some computers, you may have to change your BIOS settings to enable booting from CD-ROM.)

Step 3

Follow through the text-based portion of the installation process. When you are prompted for a disk partition on which to install Windows 2000 Server, you can choose any available disk partition that has adequate space, including the partition that already contains Windows. Do not choose to format the disk if you are installing to the partition that contains Windows; Windows 2000 Server will install and run on a FAT- or FAT32-formatted partition. If, however, you have an available partition that you don't mind erasing, you can choose to format that partition with NTFS and to install Windows 2000 Server to that partition. Provided the main partition is unchanged, dual-boot will still work in this configuration.

Step 4

Restart the computer at the end of the text-based installation portion to begin the graphical portion of the installation.

Step 5

Follow through and complete the basic questions asked during the beginning of the graphical installation, such as choosing a locale and keyboard and entering your name.

Step 6

When prompted, choose Per Seat licensing for a stand-alone learning server.

Step 7

When prompted, enter in a name for this server (this is the name by which the server will be seen on the network) and assign an Administrator password (make sure it's one you won't forget).

Step 8

When prompted, make appropriate choices about what Windows 2000 Server services to install. For a good all-around server on which to begin learning about Windows 2000 Server, choose Internet Information Server, Management and Monitoring Tools, and Networking Services.

Step 9	Complete the remainder of the installation, choosing Typical when prompted for the networking portion of the server setup, and either Domain Controller or Stand-Alone Server when prompted for the server type. Do NOT choose Domain Controller if you are performing this installation in a functioning company network without checking first with the network administrator (and probably not even then to avoid causing problems on the network). If you are using a small home network, however, you can experiment with working with a domain controller by choosing that option.

After the graphical portion of the installation completes, you are prompted to restart the computer. When the computer restarts, you will see a menu that lets you choose to boot to either Windows 2000 Server (this will be the default choice) or the existing version of Windows.

Complete Windows 2000 Server Setup

After the main setup program completes, the system restarts to the Windows 2000 Server login prompt. To log in to the server, press CTRL-ALT-DEL. You log in as Administrator, using the password you defined as part of the setup process in the preceding section. The Windows 2000 Server desktop then appears, along with the Windows 2000 Configure Your Server program (called the Server Configuration program for the remainder of this section), which walks you through the remaining steps required to get the server operational. Figure 5.1 shows the Server Configuration program running on the Windows 2000 desktop.

If you are setting up a single server for a small network—the assumption made for the example in this chapter—you can choose the option marked "This is the only server in my network," as shown in Figure 5.1. For more

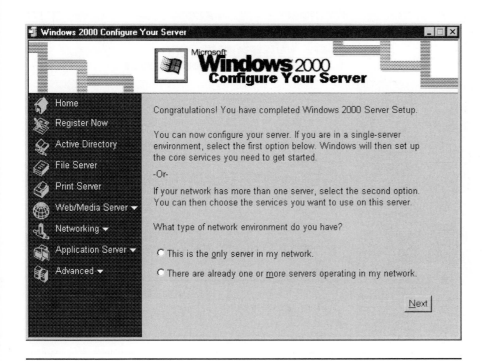

• **Figure 5.1**   The Windows 2000 Server Configuration program

complicated Windows 2000 installations, choose "There are already one or more servers operating in my network," which requires more detailed setup knowledge.

You then see a confirmation screen (shown in Figure 5.2) that confirms you want to set up the server with Active Directory, DHCP, and DNS services, which are standard for a single server in a network. If you like, you can read more about these services by clicking the links shown in the Server Configuration dialog box. Once you are done, click Next to proceed.

Next, the program prompts you for the name of the domain you will create and any Internet domain of which the server needs to be aware. The domain name cannot have spaces and you should choose a simple name, one you can work with easily. Many companies choose the name of their company, or some abbreviation thereof, for their domain name. You also enter any Internet domain name that exists for your network. The Internet domain name is one owned by your company. For example, if you work for a company called Acme Corporation, you can call your Windows 2000 domain ACME, and your Internet domain would probably be acme.com. (If your company doesn't have an Internet domain name registered, enter **local** in the field instead.) For this example, the Windows 2000 domain name will be OMH and the Internet domain name will be **local**. Enter your information and click Next to continue. After a pause, the program warns you that the choices you have made will now be installed and the server will be restarted. Click Next a second time to do this. Note that the program might prompt you for a Windows 2000 Server CD-ROM during this process.

After the system installs the components needed and restarts, you need to complete some final steps in the Server Configuration program (shown in Step-by-Step 5.2), after which you will be done installing the server.

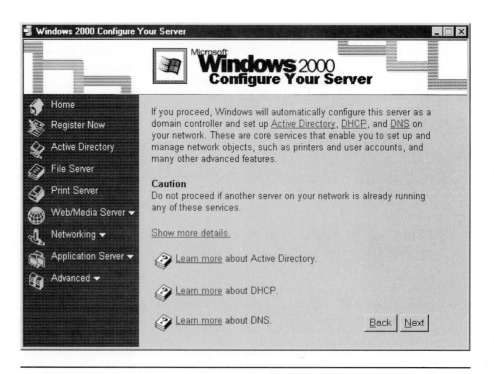

• **Figure 5.2** Confirming the installation of core network services

Completing a Network Server Configuration

This step-by-step shows you how to complete the configuration of a network server. This is distinct from the installation of Windows 2000 Server, and involves making choices about the network that the server will service, as well as enabling some important services. In this example, you are configuring a server that is acting as a domain controller. The configuration is something that you run whenever you want, although typically it immediately follows installation.

To complete this exercise, you will need the following:

- A computer that has Windows 2000 Server installed (preferably from just after completing Step-by-Step 5.1)
- A working Ethernet card connected to a LAN
- A Windows 2000 Server CD-ROM

Step 1   Right-click the desktop object My Network Places and choose Properties from the pop-up menu.

Step 2   Right-click the Local Area Connection object and choose Properties from the pop-up menu. This opens the Local Area Connection Properties dialog box.

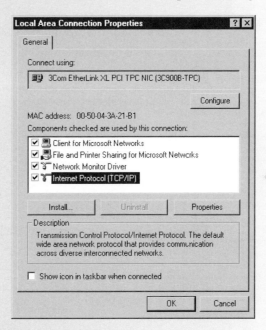

• The Local Area Connection Properties dialog box

Step 3   Choose the Internet Protocol entry and click the Properties button.

Step 4   Click the Use the Following IP Address option button.

Step 5   Enter the correct IP number for this server to use as its IP address. If you don't have an existing range of numbers and your network isn't directly connected to the Internet, use 10.10.1.1.

Enter the correct subnet mask. If your network hasn't used subnet masks before, choose 255.0.0.0.

Step 7

In the Preferred DNS Server field, enter the IP address that you just assigned to the server. In this example, 10.10.1.1 is used. At this point, the Internet Protocol (TCP/IP) Properties dialog box should look like that shown in the illustration. Click OK to close the various Properties dialog boxes already opened.

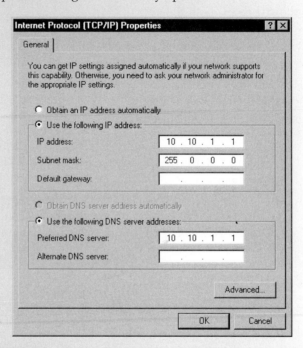

- The Internet Protocol (TCP/IP) Properties dialog box with sample choices

Step 8

You now need to authorize DHCP services. Open the Start menu and choose Programs, Administrative Tools, and DHCP. You then see the DHCP Manager program.

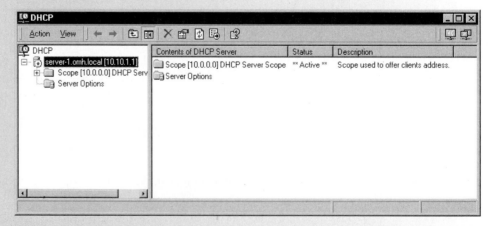

- The DHCP Manager program

Step 9	Expand the tree in the left pane. Then, right-click the server shown in the pane, choose All Tasks, and then Authorize. This authorizes the server to fulfill DHCP requests and enables the server to parcel out IP addresses to client computers on the network.
Step 10	Shut down and restart the server for the preceding changes to take effect.

Configure a Server Client

Before you can *really* finish setting up a new server, you need to test its ability to allow a client computer to connect to it. To do this, you need to perform the following steps:

1. Create a test user account.
2. Create a shared resource on the server for the client computer to access.
3. Configure a Windows 9*x* client to connect to the server.
4. Actually log in to the server with the client computer and verify that everything is working properly.

The following sections explain how to carry out these tasks.

Create a User Account

The first order of business to confirm server functionality is to create a test user account, with which you can log in to the server from a network computer. You can use the Administrator account for this if you wish to skip this step, but using a sample user account is better.

Start by opening the Start menu, choosing Programs, and then choosing Administrative Tools. Then, finally, select the entry called Active Directory Users and Computers. This opens the Windows Management Console application with the Active Directory Users and Computers settings, as shown in Figure 5.3.

As with most Windows programs, the left pane enables you to navigate a tree (in this case, the tree of user and computer objects) and the right pane shows the details for the selected branch of the tree. To add a user, right-click the server in the left pane, choose New, and then choose User from the pop-up menu. You then see the Create New Object (User) dialog box shown in Figure 5.4.

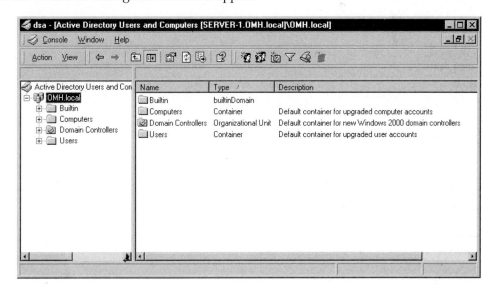

• Figure 5.3   Active Directory Users and Computers

Enter the first and last name for the user you wish to create and then enter a logon name in the User Logon Name field. The program generates the remaining fields automatically based on the information you just entered, although you can change their settings if you want. In the example shown in Figure 5.4, the user FredF will log in to Active Directory using the user account **fredfomh.local**. After entering in the information, click Next to continue.

Now enter a starting password for the account you just created. For this example, simply use the password **password**. (Remember to remove this test user account after you finish with your testing. You don't ever want to leave a user account active on the system with a password that others can easily guess.) Click Next to continue and then click Finish to complete creating the user account.

Create a Shared Folder

The next step is to create a resource—in this case a folder—that the test user should be able to access from a computer on the network. Windows 2000 Server shares folders through a mechanism called a `share`. A share is a browseable resource that remote users can access, provided they have sufficient privileges to do so.

To set a folder so it can be accessed over the network, create a normal folder on one of the server's disk drives. Right-click the folder and choose Sharing from the pop-up menu. This displays the Sharing tab of the folder's Properties dialog box, as shown in Figure 5.5.

To make the folder shared, first click the Share This Folder option button. Next, review the share name (which is automatically assigned based on the folder name) and modify it if you like. Then click OK to finish sharing the folder.

> By default, new shares created on the server allow everyone full control of their contents. To change this default setting, you need to click the Permissions button and then modify the permissions.

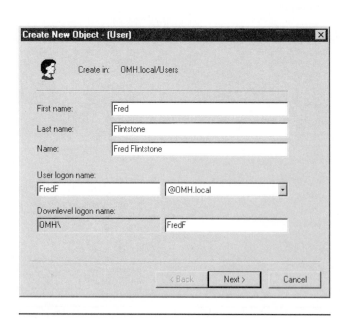

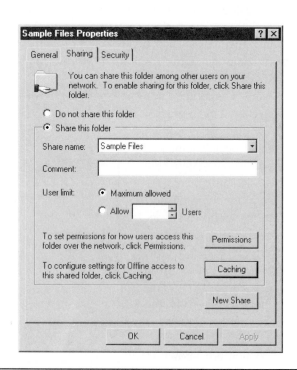

• **Figure 5.4**   Create New Object (User) dialog box

• **Figure 5.5**   The Sharing tab of a folder's Properties dialog box

Setting Up a Windows 9x Client to Access the Server

In this exercise, you set up a Windows 95 or Windows 98 client to access the new server. To complete this exercise, you will need the following:

- A client computer with Windows 95 or Windows 98 installed onto it

- The installation media for the client operating system (you may be prompted for it by Windows 95 or 98 during this exercise)

- A server computer with Windows 2000 installed onto it, with a working network configuration

- A network LAN connection between the client and the server

Step 1

In the Control Panel, open the Network object. This activates the Network dialog box.

Step 2

Click the Add button, choose Client in the Select Network Component Type dialog box, and then click Add to bring up the Select Network Client dialog box.

Step 3

In the Select Network Client dialog box, choose Microsoft from the list of manufacturers, and then choose Client for Microsoft Networks in the right pane. Click OK to continue.

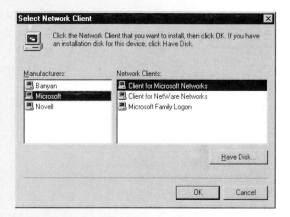

- Choosing to install Client for Microsoft Networks

Step 4

After a short while, the Network dialog box reappears in the foreground, with both the Client for Microsoft Networks and the TCP/IP protocol installed.

Step 5

Select Client for Microsoft Networks and click the Properties button.

Step 6

In the Client for Microsoft Networks Properties dialog box, select the check box Log Onto Windows NT Domain, and then type the name of the domain in the field provided. For the example used in this chapter, the domain name is simply OMH.

Step 7

Click OK to close the Network dialog box.

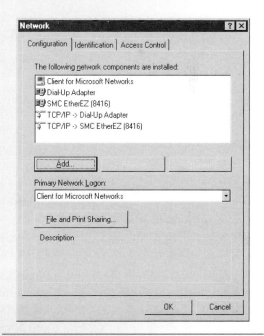

- The Network Properties dialog box with installed components

Once you close the Network dialog box, you might be prompted for your Windows 9x CD-ROM so that the necessary components can be installed. After the installation of the network components is complete, the program prompts you to restart the computer, which you must do before the network settings are made active.

Test the Client Connection

After completing the preceding steps, you can now log on to the domain being administered by Windows 2000 Server and browse the files that you placed into the shared folder.

When the computer restarts after you complete the steps in the preceding section, the program prompts you to log in to the domain before displaying the Windows 9x desktop. Enter the test user account name (FredF), the domain name (OMH), and the password that you assigned (password) to log in to the domain. If you have entered the information correctly, you will log in to the domain. If any problems occur, such as an unrecognized username, password, or domain name, the program warns you and gives you a chance to correct them.

Sometimes a server might not appear automatically in Network Neighborhood, particularly if it has recently been installed. If you encounter this problem, open the Start menu, choose Find, and then choose Computer. Type the name of the server that you set up in the Find dialog box and click Find Now. After a moment, the server should appear in the Find dialog box and you can double-click to open it.

Once Windows 9x starts, you should be able to open Network Neighborhood and see the server that you installed included in the list of servers. When you open the server, you can see any shares on the server to which you have access. Among those folders, you will see netlogin and sysvol, as well as the folder that you created and shared. You should be able to open the sample share and see the files that you placed in the folder. You should also be able to manipulate those files, delete them, rename them, open them, and so forth just as if you were working with files on a local hard disk.

Administering Windows 2000 Server

Installing and setting up Windows 2000 Server is only the tip of the iceberg. Far more important and time-consuming is the process of administering the server. This process includes regular and common duties such as adding new users, deleting old users, assigning permissions to users, performing backups, and so forth. These topics are the subject of this section. Learning how to do all these things and to do them well will ensure that the network and the server remain productive and secure.

Review Network Security

Before delving into the administrative activities discussed in this chapter, you should spend some time thinking about network security and how it relates to your specific company. Network security is an important subject, and administering a server must be predicated on maintaining appropriate security for your network.

The key here is to remember that every network has an appropriate level of security. The security requirements for a Department of Defense (DoD) contractor who designs military equipment will be different from the security requirements for a company that operates restaurants. The important thing, therefore, is first to determine the appropriate security needs of your network. Many beginning network administrators forget this important fact and set up their networks to follow the strongest security measures available. The problem with this approach is that these measures almost always reduce the productivity of people using the network. You need to strike a balance between productivity and security, and the answer will be different for every company.

For example, Windows 2000 Server enables you to set various security policies that apply to users. These include forcing password changes at intervals you specify, requiring that passwords be of a certain minimum length, causing new passwords always to be unique and not reuses of old passwords, and so on. You could set up these policies to require passwords that are at least 20 characters long and that must be changed weekly. If users don't resort to writing down their passwords so they can remember them from week to week, these settings would be more secure than shorter, less-frequently changed passwords. A 20-character password is virtually impossible to crack using standard methods, and weekly password changes reduce the chance that someone else will discover a user's password and be free to use it for an extended period of time. The problem with policies this strict, however, is that users will frequently forget their passwords, be locked out of the system for periods of time, and require a lot of help from the network administrator (you!) to clear up these problems each time they occur. For a DoD contractor, these trade-offs might be worthwhile. For the restaurant operator, however, they would be inappropriate and would end up hurting the company more than they help. So, the point to remember is that network security should always be appropriate to the company and its specific network, and that it is important to define appropriate security levels early on and to get the necessary support from management for the trade-offs you think appropriate.

A related point is this: Sometimes security that is too strong results in reduced security over the long run, at least for certain things. For example, in the preceding example with the frequently changing, 20-character passwords, you can be assured that a large percentage of users will have to write down their passwords so they can remember them and gain access to the system. The problem here, of course, is that a written password is far less secure than one that is remembered, because someone else can find the written password and bypass security easily after doing so.

The final point—and the reason you should pay attention to this subject before learning about administration—is that you should determine the appropriate network security early so that you can allow for it as you administer the network on a daily basis. Network security doesn't have to take up much of your time, provided you set up your administrative procedures so they presuppose the level of security you require. For example, if you know what your password policies will be on the network, it takes only a few seconds to ensure that each new user has those policies set for their account. If you know you maintain a paper-based log of changes to security groups in the network, then it takes only a second to follow this procedure as you

Every account created for a Windows 2000 Server domain is assigned a special number, called a Security ID (SID). The server actually recognizes the user by this number. SIDs are said to be "unique across space and time." This means that no two users will ever have the same SID, even if they have the same username or even the same password. This is because the SID is made up of a unique number assigned to the domain and then a sequential number assigned to each created account (with billions of unique user-specific numbers available). If you have a user called Frank, delete that account, and then create another account called Frank. Both accounts will have different SIDs. This ensures that no user account will accidentally receive permissions originally assigned to another user of the same name.

change group membership occasionally. Failing to determine these security practices and policies early on will result in having to undertake much larger projects as part of a security review or audit. Security is an area where you're much better off doing things right the first time!

Administer User Accounts

For anyone—including the administrator—to gain access to a Windows 2000 Server, he or she must have an account established on the server or in the domain (a *domain* is essentially a collection of security information shared among Windows 2000 servers). The account defines the *username* (the name by which the user is known to the system) and the user's password, along with a host of other information specific to each user. Creating, maintaining, and deleting user accounts is easy with Windows 2000 Server.

To maintain user accounts, you use the Active Directory (AD) Users and Computers management console. You can open this console by clicking the Start menu, choosing Programs, and then selecting Administrative Tools. Once the console is open, open the tree for the domain you are administering and then click the Users folder. Your screen should look similar to Figure 5.6 at this point.

To accomplish activities in the console, you first select either a container in the left pane or an object in the right pane, and then either right-click the container or object or open the Action pull-down menu and choose from the available options. Because the available options change based on the selected container or object, first selecting an object with which to work is important.

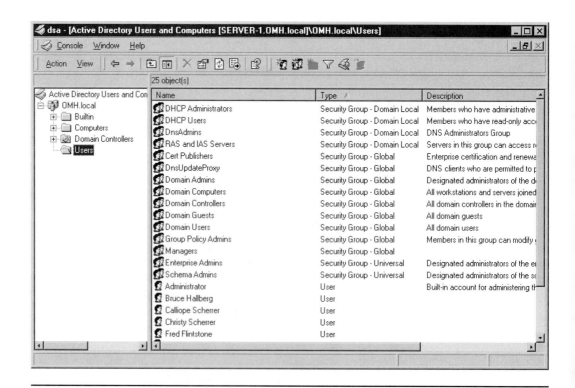

• Figure 5.6   The Active Directory Users and Computers console

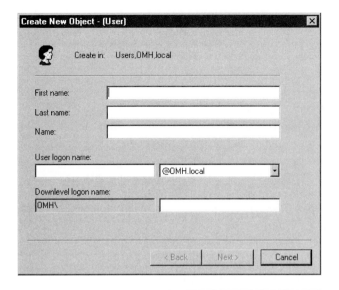

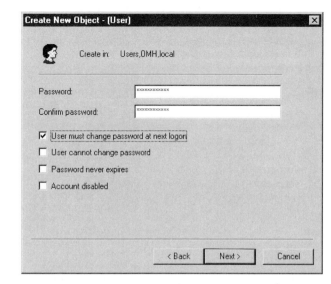

● **Figure 5.7**   Use the Create New Object (User) dialog box to add a new user

● **Figure 5.8**   The second dialog box for adding a new user

Add a User

To add a user with the AD Users and Computers console, start by selecting the Users container in the left pane (with the tree open to the domain you are administering). Then, right-click the Users container, choose New from the pop-up menu, and then choose User from the submenu. You see the Create New Object (User) dialog box shown in Figure 5.7.

Fill in the First Name, Last Name, and User Logon Name fields. Then, click the Next button to move to the next dialog box, which is shown in Figure 5.8.

In the second dialog box, which has no name, you enter the initial password that the account will use. You also select several options that will apply to the account, as follows:

- **User Must Change Password at Next Logon**   Selecting this check box forces users to choose their own password when they first log in to the system.

- **User Cannot Change Password**   You might select this option for resource accounts if you do not want to enable the user to change their password. Generally, however, you should not select this option; most sites allow users to change their own password, and you want to enable them to do so if you've also set passwords to automatically expire.

- **Password Never Expires**   Choose this option to allow the password to remain viable for as long as the user chooses to use it. Activating this option for most users is generally considered a poor security practice, so consider carefully whether you should enable this option.

- **Account Disabled**   Selecting this option disables the new account. The administrator can enable the account when needed by clearing the check box.

> You should establish standards by which you assign logon names on your network. Small networks (those with fewer than 50 users) often just use people's first names, followed by the first initial of their last names when conflicts arise. A more commonly used convention is to use the user's last name followed by the first initial of their first name. This latter standard allows far more combinations before conflicts arise, and you can then resolve any conflicts that arise by adding the person's middle initial, a number, or some other change so that all usernames at any given time on the system are unique.

After entering the password and selecting the options you want, click Next to continue. You will then see a confirmation screen. Click Next a final time to create the account or click Back to return to make any needed changes.

Modify a User Account

The dialog boxes you see when creating a user account are much simpler than the one you see when modifying a user account. The dialog box in which you modify the information about a user contains many other fields that you can use to document the account and to set some other security options.

To modify an existing user account, right-click the user object you wish to modify and choose Properties from the pop-up menu. You then see the tabbed dialog box shown in Figure 5.9.

In the first two tabs, General and Address, you can enter some additional information about the user, such as his or her title, mailing address, telephone number, e-mail account, and so forth. Because Active Directory also integrates with new versions of Exchange Server, this information might be important to enter for your network.

The third tab, Account, is where you can set some important user account options. Figure 5.10 shows the Account tab.

The first line of the dialog box defines the user's Windows 2000 logon name, as well as the Windows 2000 domain in which the user has primary membership. The second line defines the user's Windows NT logon name, which the user can optionally use if he or she needs to log in to the domain from a Windows NT computer or use an application that doesn't yet support Active Directory logins. (Although you can set these two logon names to be different, doing so rarely is a good idea.)

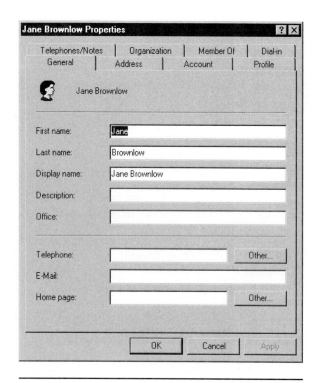

• **Figure 5.9**   A user's Properties dialog box

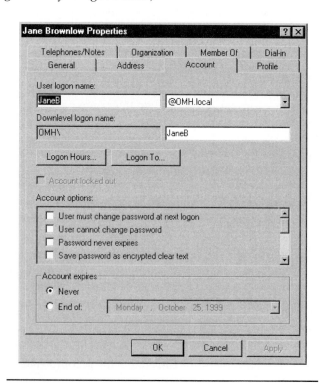

• **Figure 5.10**   The Account tab of a user's Properties dialog box

Clicking the Logon Hours button displays the dialog box shown in Figure 5.11. In this dialog box, you select different blocks of time within a standard week and then click the appropriate option button to permit or deny access to the network for that time period. In Figure 5.11, the settings permit logon times only for normal work hours, with some cushion before and after those times to allow for slightly different work hours. By default, users are permitted to log on to the network at any time, any day of the week. For most networks, particularly smaller networks, permitting users to log on at any time is generally acceptable.

Another button on the Account tab of the user's Properties dialog box (refer to Figure 5.10) is the Logon To button, which opens the Logon Workstations dialog box shown in Figure 5.12. By default, users can log on to any workstation in the domain, and the domain authenticates them. In some cases, a system might require stricter security, where you specify the computers to which a user account can log on. For example, you might set up a network backup account that you use to back up the network and then leave this account logged on all the time in your locked computer room. Because the backup account has access to all files on the network (or it couldn't do its job), a good idea is to limit that account to log on only to the computer designated for this purpose in the computer room. You use the Logon To button to set up this type of restriction.

You should be aware that allowing a user named George (for example) to log on to another user's computer does not mean that George can log on with the other user's permissions or access anything that only the other user can access. This simply means George can use the listed physical computer to log on to his own account from that computer.

The Account Options section of the Account tab enables you to select various binary (On/Off) account options. Some of the options, such as requiring a user to change his or her password at the next logon, you set as you add the account. Some options listed are unique to the user's Properties dialog box. The two most important of these additional options are Account Is Disabled and Account Is Trusted for Delegation. Account Is Disabled, if selected, disables the user account while leaving it set up within Active Directory. This option is useful if you need to deny access to the network, but might need to reenable the account in the future. (Also, Account Is Disabled is handled as a high-priority change within the domain, and it takes effect immediately, even across large numbers of domain controllers.) Because deleting an account also deletes any permissions the user might have, you should always disable an account if you might need to grant access to the network again to that user. (For example, if someone is on vacation, you could disable the user's account while he or she is gone and then clear the Account Is Disabled check box

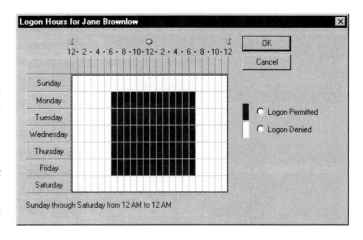

• **Figure 5.11**   Setting logon time restrictions for a user

The Logon To feature works only if the network uses the NetBIOS or NetBEUI protocols. This feature will not work with TCP/IP-only networks.

• **Figure 5.12**   Restricting the computers to which a user can log on

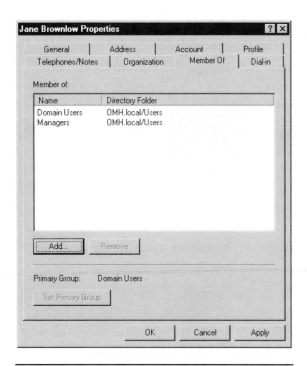

Jane Brownlow Properties

General | Address | Account | Profile |
Telephones/Notes | Organization | Member Of | Dial-in |

Member of:

Name	Directory Folder
Domain Users	OMH.local/Users
Managers	OMH.local/Users

[Add...]   Remove

Primary Group: Domain Users

[Set Primary Group]

OK   Cancel   Apply

• **Figure 5.13**   Controlling a user's membership in groups

If you need to delete a large number of accounts, you can save time by selecting them all before choosing the Delete or Disable Account commands. Just be sure you haven't selected accounts that you don't want to delete or disable!

when the user returns.) You must select the second option, Account Is Trusted for Delegation, if you want to designate the user account to administer some part of the domain. Windows 2000 Server enables you to grant administrative rights to portions of the Active Directory tree without having to give administrative rights to the entire domain.

The last option on the Account tab of the user Properties dialog box is the expiration date setting, Account Expires. By default, it is set to Never. If you wish to define an expiration date, you may do so in the End Of field. When the date indicated is reached, the account is automatically disabled (but not deleted, so you can reenable it if you wish).

Another tab that you will use often in the user's Properties dialog box is the Member Of tab, in which you define the security groups for a user. Figure 5.13 shows this tab. Security groups are discussed later in this chapter.

Delete or Disable a User Account

Deleting a user account is easy using the Active Directory Users and Groups Management console. Use the left pane to select the Users folder and then select the user in the right pane. Either right-click the user and choose Delete, or open the Action pull-down menu and choose Delete.

Disabling an account is just as easy. As before, first select the user account. Then, right-click it and choose Disable Account, or open the Action pull-down menu and choose Disable Account.

Work with Windows 2000 Security Groups

On any network, you usually have to administer permissions to many different folders and files. If you were able to grant access only by user account, you'd quickly go crazy trying to keep track of all the necessary information. For example, suppose that a group of people, such as an accounting department, has different permissions to access 20 different folders on the server. When a new accountant is hired, do you have to remember or look up what all those 20 folders are so you can give the accountant the same permissions as the rest of his or her department? Or, suppose that a user who has many different permissions changes departments. Do you have to find each permission that the user has so you can make sure that the user has only the appropriate permissions for his or her new department?

To address such problems, all network operating systems support the concept of security groups (or just *groups*). You first create such a group and then assign all the appropriate users to it so you can administer their permissions more easily. When you grant permission to a folder on the server, you do so by giving the group the network permission. All the members of the group automatically *inherit* those permissions. This inheritance makes maintaining network permissions over time much easier. In fact, you shouldn't try to manage network permissions without using groups this way. You might quickly become overwhelmed trying to keep track of everything, and you're almost certain to make mistakes over time.

Not only can users be members of groups, but groups can be members of other groups. This way, you can build a hierarchy of groups that makes administration even easier. For instance, suppose that you define a group for each department in your company. Half those departments are part of a larger division called Research and Development (R&D) and half are part of Sales, General, and Administration (SG&A). On your network, some folders are specific to each department, some are specific to all of R&D or SG&A, and some can be accessed by every user on the network. In such a situation, you would first create the departmental groups and then create the R&D and SG&A groups. Each departmental group would then become a member in either R&D or SG&A. Finally, you would use the built-in Domain Users group, or another one you created that represents everyone, and then assign R&D and SG&A to that top-level group for every user.

Once you've done this, you can then grant permissions in the most logical way. If a resource is just for a specific department, you assign that departmental group to the resource. If a resource is for R&D or SG&A, you assign those divisions to the resource; then all the individual departmental groups within that division will inherit permission to access the resource. If a resource is for everyone, you would assign the master, top-level group to the resource. Using such hierarchical group levels makes administering permissions even easier, and is practically necessary for larger networks with hundreds of users.

Create Groups

You create groups using the same console as you use for users: the Active Directory Users and Computers. Groups appear in two of the domain's containers: Builtin and Users. The Builtin groups are fixed and cannot be deleted, and cannot be made members of other groups. The Builtin groups have certain important permissions already assigned to them, and other groups you create can be given membership in the Builtin groups. Similarly, if you want to disable a particular Builtin group, you would do so simply by removing all its member groups. Figure 5.14 shows the list of Builtin groups for Windows 2000 Server.

 Be careful changing the membership of the Builtin groups. For most networks, while it's important to understand what these groups are and how they work, you generally want to leave them alone.

Generally, you work only with groups defined in the Users container. Figure 5.15 shows the default groups in the Users container, which you can distinguish from user accounts by both the two-person icon and the Type designation.

To add a new group, first select the Users container in the left pane. Then, open the Action pull-down menu, choose New, and then choose Group. You see the Create New Object (Group) dialog box shown in Figure 5.16.

First, enter the name of the group in the field provided. You'll see the name you enter echoed in the Downlevel Group field. The Downlevel Group field enables you to specify a different group name for Windows NT computers. However, using different group names is usually not a good idea because it can quickly make your system confusing.

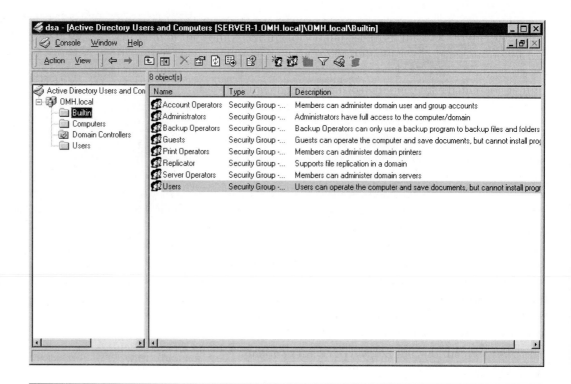

● **Figure 5.14**   Viewing the list of Builtin groups

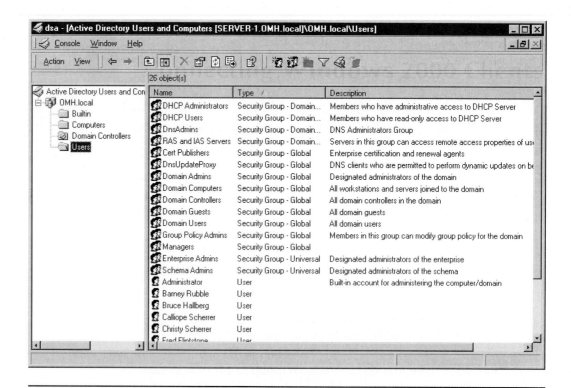

● **Figure 5.15**   Default groups in the Users container

After naming the group, you need to select from the available option buttons in the lower half of the dialog box. Group Scope refers to how widely the group is populated throughout a domain. A *Universal group* exists throughout an organization, even when the organization's network is made up of many individual domains. Universal groups can also contain members from any domain in an organization's network. A *Global group*, on the other hand, can contain members only from the domain in which they exist. However, you can assign Global groups permissions to any domain within the network, even across multiple domains. Finally, *Domain Local groups* exist only within a single domain and can contain members only from that domain.

After you set the group's scope, you can also select whether it will be a Security group or a Distribution group. *Distribution groups* are used only to maintain e-mail distribution lists and have no security impact in Windows 2000 Server. They are used only for e-mail applications such as Microsoft Exchange Server 2000.

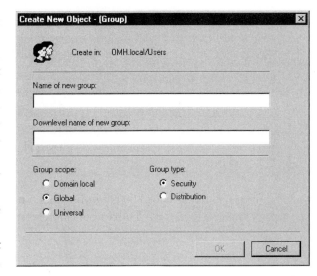

● **Figure 5.16**   The Create New Object (Group) dialog box

Maintain Group Membership

After you complete the Create New Object (Group) dialog box entries and click OK, the program creates the group, but it starts out with no membership. To set the membership for a group, follow these steps:

1. Select the group and open its Properties dialog box (right-click and then choose Properties from the pop-up menu).

2. Click the Members tab. You see the group properties dialog box shown in Figure 5.17.

Don't worry if you create a group with the wrong scope. You can easily change the group's scope, provided its membership doesn't violate the new scope's rules for membership. To change a domain scope, select the group and open its Properties dialog box (right-click and then choose Properties from the pop-up menu). If the group membership allows the change, you can select a different Group Scope option button.

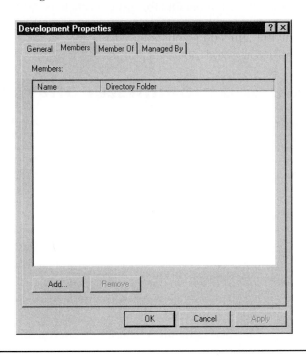

● **Figure 5.17**   The Members tab of the group Properties dialog box

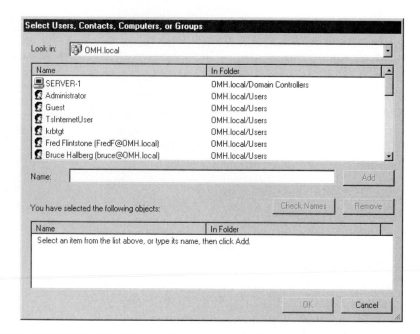

• **Figure 5.18** The Users, Contacts, Computers, or Groups dialog box

3. Click the Add button. You see the Select Users, Contacts, Computers, or Groups dialog box shown in Figure 5.18.

4. Scroll through the list to select each member you want to add to the group, and then click the Add button to add your selected members to the list of members. The list displays only objects that can be made members of the group.

If you want the group to be a member of another group, click the group properties dialog box's Member Of tab, and then click its Add button, similar to how you added members to the group.

Create and Administer Shares

Drives and folders under Windows 2000 Server are made available to users over the network as shared resources, simply called *shares* in Windows networking parlance. You select a drive or folder, enable it to be shared, and then set the permissions for the share.

Review Share Security

You can set both drives and folders as distinct shared resources (or *shares*), whether they are located on a FAT-formatted drive or on an NTFS-formatted drive. In the case of an NTFS-formatted drive (but not on a FAT-formatted drive), however, you can also set permissions on folders and files within the share that are separate from the permissions on the share itself. Understanding how Windows 2000 Server handles security for shares, folders, and files on NTFS drives is important.

Suppose that you created a share called RESEARCH and you gave the R&D security group read-only access to the share. Within the share, you set the permissions on a folder called PROJECTS to allow full read and write access (called *Change permission*) for the R&D security group. The question is, will the R&D group have read-only permission to that folder or Change permission? The answer is that the group will have read-only permission because when security permissions differ between folders within a share and the share itself, the most restrictive permissions apply. A better way to set up share permissions is to allow everyone Change permission to the share and then control the actual permissions by setting them on the folders within the share itself. This way, you can assign any combination of permissions you want; then the users will receive the permissions that you set on those folders, even though the share is set to Change permission.

Also, remember that users receive permissions based on the groups of which they are members, and these permissions are cumulative. So, if you are a member of the Everyone group who has read-only permission for a particular file, but you're also a member of the Admins group who has Full Control permission for that file, you'll have Full Control permission in practice. This is an important rule: Permissions set on folders and files are always cumulative and take into account permissions set for the user individually as well as any security groups of which the user is a member.

The next thing to remember is that you can set permissions within a share (sometimes called *NTFS permissions*) on both folders and files, and these permissions are also cumulative. So, for instance, you can set read-only permission on a folder for a user, but Change permission for some specific files. The user then has the ability to read, modify, and even delete those files without having that ability with other files in the same folder.

The last thing to remember is that there's a special permission called No Access. *No Access* overrides all other permissions, no matter what. If you set No Access permission for a user on a file or folder, then that's it; the user will have no access to that file or folder. An extremely important corollary to this rule is that No Access permission is also cumulative and overriding. So, if the Everyone security group has Change permission for a file, but you set a particular user to No Access for that file, that user will receive No Access permission. If you set No Access permission for the Everyone group, however, then all members of that group will also receive No Access because it overrides any other permissions they have. Be careful about using No Access with security groups! There are many other fine points to setting and maintaining permissions that go beyond the scope of this book, but you can resolve most permission problems if you remember the rules discussed here:

- When share permissions conflict with file or folder permissions, the *most restrictive* one always wins.

- Aside from the preceding rule, permissions are cumulative, taking into account permissions assigned to users and groups as well as files and folders.

- When a permission conflict occurs, the No Access permission always wins.

Creating Shares

As a network administrator, you will have to frequently create and manage the shares on the network. This exercise walks you through creating a new share. You will need the following:

- A computer onto which Windows 2000 Server has been installed

- A properly configured and working network connection

- A client computer running Windows that can log on to the server

Step 1

To create a new share, use either My Computer or Windows Explorer on the server.

Step 2

Right-click the folder or drive you want to share, and then choose Sharing from the pop-up menu. You will see the Sharing tab of the folder or drive's Properties dialog box.

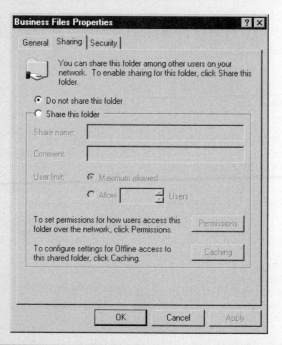

- The Sharing tab of a folder's Properties dialog box

Step 3

Click the Share This Folder option button, assign a share name, and then, if you like, a comment for the share. (Users will be able to see the comment you enter.) After naming the share, you can select a limit to how many users can simultaneously access the share. (Normally, leave User Limit set to Maximum Allowed.)

Step 4

The last step you should take is to check the permissions for the share.

Step 5

Click the Permissions button, which reveals the Permissions dialog box. As you can see, the default setting for a share is for the group Everyone to have the fullest possible access to the share. Normally, this setting is what you want. (See the discussion in the preceding section about share permissions for more information about this setting.) Still, if you need to restrict access to the share in some fashion, the Permissions dialog box enables you to accomplish this. Clicking Add brings up the Select Users, Contacts, Computers, or Groups dialog box, from which you can choose those entities and assign them permissions to the share.

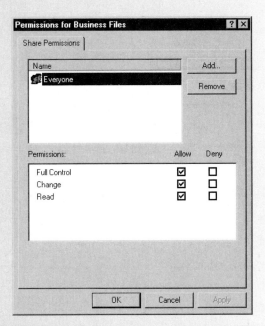

- Setting a share's permissions

Step 6

After adding an entity, you can use the check boxes in the Permissions window of the Permissions dialog box to set the exact permissions you want.

Step 7

Close all of the active dialog boxes using the OK buttons on each one.

Tip: When you click an entity and some of its Permission dialog box's check boxes are grayed, this means that the permissions were inherited from a higher level, usually from permissions set on a containing folder somewhere up the directory tree.

Once a share is created and the share information has propagated through the domain (usually within several minutes), users can browse it through either Network Neighborhood (Windows 9x and NT) or My Network Places (Windows 2000). Double-clicking the share will open it, depending on the permissions.

You can hide a share but still keep it available for users who know the share name. To do so, create the share normally, but append the dollar sign ($) to the end of its name. For example, FILES$ might be a share that users cannot see when browsing available network shares.

Map Drives

You can use shares by opening them in Network Neighborhood or My Network Places, and they function just like the folders in My Computer. However, you might frequently want to simulate a connected hard disk on your computer with a share from the network. For example, many applications that store files on the network require that the network folders be accessible as normal drive letters. The process of simulating a disk drive with a network share is called **mapping**, where you create a map (link) between the drive letter you want to use and the actual network share to remain attached to that drive letter.

You can create a drive mapping in many ways. The easiest way is to open Network Neighborhood from the client computer and then locate the share you want to map. Right-click it and choose Map Network Drive. In the dialog box that appears, the name of the domain and share will appear already typed in for you; simply select an appropriate drive letter for the mapping and click OK. From then on, the share will appear to your computer as that drive letter, and users will see this share's letter in My Computer.

To connect to a hidden share, right-click Network Neighborhood (or My Network Places for Windows 2000) and choose Map Network Drive. Choose a drive letter for the mapping, enter in the complete share name (with the appended dollar sign), and click OK. Provided you have permission to access that share, the mapping will otherwise work normally.

You can also map drives using a command-line utility called NET. The **NET command** takes many different forms and can fulfill many different needs, depending on what parameters you give it. To map a drive, you use the **NET USE** command. Typing **NET USE** by itself and pressing ENTER will list all currently mapped drives. To add a new drive mapping, you would type the following:

NET USE *drive_letter*: *UNC_for_share*

Most network resources in a Windows network use a naming system called the **Universal Naming Convention (UNC)**. To supply a UNC, you start with two backslashes, then the name of the server, another backslash, and the name of the share (additional backslashes and names can refer to folders and files within the share). So, if you want to map drive G: to a share called EMPLOYEES located on the server SERVER, the command would be as follows:

NET USE G: \\SERVER\EMPLOYEES

> You can use the **NET** command from any Windows client for any Windows network. Type **NET** by itself to list all of the different forms of the command. Type **NET command HELP** to see detailed help on the different **NET** commands.

■ Administer Printer Shares

Before setting and working with printers on a network, you need to understand the components involved in network printing and how they interact, as follows:

- A **print job** is a set of binary data sent from a network workstation to a network printer. A print job is the same data as a computer would send to a locally connected printer—it's just redirected to the network for printing.

- The network workstation that sends the print job to the print queue is responsible for formatting the print data properly for the printer. This is done through software installed on the workstation—called a **print driver**—that is specific to each type of printer. Printer drivers are also specific to each operating system that uses them. In other words, a Hewlett-Packard LaserJet 5si driver for a Windows 95 computer is different from an Hewlett-Packard LaserJet 5si driver for a Windows NT Workstation computer. More troublesome, different versions of the same operating system usually use different drivers, so a driver for a Windows 95 computer might not work with a Windows 98 computer and vice versa.

- Print jobs are often sent to the network through a captured printer port. The network client software redirects to the network one of the printer ports on a networked workstation, such as LPT1. The process of redirecting a printer port to a network printer is called **capturing**. Usually, captured ports are persistent and continue through multiple logins until they are turned off.

- Print jobs sent to the network go to a place called a **printer queue**. The print job sits in the queue until the network can service the print job and send it to the printer. Printer queues can hold many jobs from many different users and typically are managed in a first-in, first-out fashion.

- Print jobs are removed from print queues and sent to actual printers by **print servers**. After sending the complete job to the printer, the print server removes the job from the queue. You can accomplish print serving in many different ways. If the printer you are using is connected to a server or workstation on the network, then that server or workstation handles the print server duty. If the printer is directly connected to the network (if it has its own network port), then the printer usually has a built-in print server as part of its network hardware. This built-in print server has the intelligence to log in to the network and to service a particular printer queue.

Print jobs start at the printing application, which sends its printer output to the local operating system. The local operating system uses the printer driver requested by the application to format the actual print job for the printer in question. Then, the local operating system works with the installed network client software to send the formatted print job to the print queue, where the job sits until the printer is available. Then, the print server sends the print job from the queue to the actual printer. Many steps are involved, but once everything is set up, it works smoothly, as you will see in the next section. Figure 5.19 shows an overview of how network printing works.

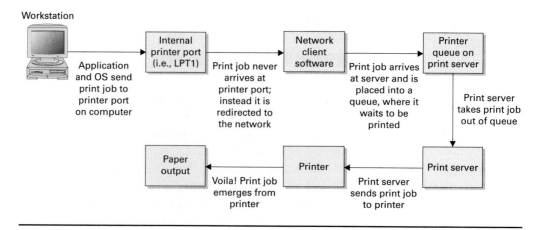

Workstation

Application and OS send print job to printer port on computer

Internal printer port (i.e., LPT1)

Print job never arrives at printer port; instead it is redirected to the network

Network client software

Print job arrives at server and is placed into a queue, where it waits to be printed

Printer queue on print server

Print server takes print job out of queue

Print server

Print server sends print job to printer

Printer

Voila! Print job emerges from printer

Paper output

• **Figure 5.19**   Overview of the network printing process

Step-by-Step 5.5, which follows, shows you how to set up a printer connected directly to a Windows 2000 Server that you will make available to network users. In this case, the printer and its Windows 2000 driver are already installed properly, as they would normally be during the installation of Windows 2000 Server. If they are not properly installed, open the Printers folder and use the Add Printers icon to set up the printer on the server itself.

You can easily set up a printer connected to a server (or workstation) so other network users can access it. However, for networks with more than about 20 users, you're better off either buying printers with network interfaces and built-in print servers or using dedicated print server boxes that interface between a printer and the network. For most laser printers, adding a dedicated network interface and server increases the cost of the printer by about $300. This is money well spent because sending a print job to a printer requires the print server to do a lot of processing. If that print server is also your main file server, its overall performance will decrease significantly while it is printing (and particularly while it services large print jobs). Also, printers with built-in print servers are far easier to relocate on the network. They can go anywhere a network connection exists and where power is available. Once connected to the network at a new location, the printer logs in to the network and starts doing its work immediately.

Step-by-Step 5.5

Setting Up a Network Printer

To complete this exercise, you will need the following:

- A computer onto which Windows 2000 Server has been installed connected to a LAN

- A printer connected directly to the server
- A client computer running Windows connected to the LAN

Step 1

To share a printer connected to a Windows 2000 Server, first open the server's Printers folder. (Open the Start menu, choose Settings, and then choose Printers.) You will see all the installed printers in the Printers folder.

Step 2

Right-click the one you want to share and choose Sharing from the pop-up menu. The Properties dialog box for the printer will appear, with the Sharing tab activated.

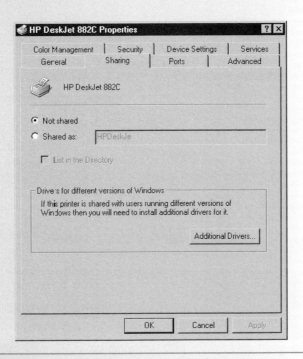

• Enabling printer sharing

Step 3

Click the Shared As option button and then assign the printer a share name, by which the client computers will recognize the printer. At this point, you can click the OK button because the default permissions for a shared printer are for the Everyone group to be able to print to it. Usually, though, you need to check at least two other available settings, as follows:

■ For high-throughput requirements, you might want to use a feature called **printer pooling**, which enables you to set up a number of identical printers, all connected to a single printer queue, that appear to the network as one printer. Users print to the listed printer, and the first available real printer services the job. Using printer pooling, you could have a whole bank of printers appear as one printer to the users and dramatically increase the number of print requests you can handle.

- Remember, however, that pooled printers must be identical, because they will all use the same print driver. The illustration shows the tab on which printer pooling is enabled.

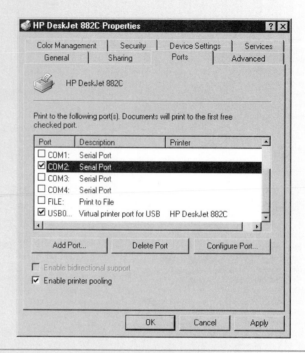

• Enabling printer pooling

- To set the permissions for a shared printer, use the Security tab of the printer's properties dialog box. The groups you see assigned in the illustration are the default assignments for a shared printer, with the Administrators permissions shown. As you can see, three main permissions are assigned to each entity: Print, Manage Printers, and Manage Documents. The Everyone group has permission to print, but not to manage documents in the queue. However, a special group called Creator Owner has permission to manage documents. This means that the user who sent the print job automatically has permission to modify or delete his or her own print job, but not others waiting in the queue.

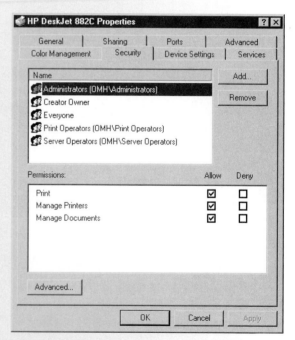

• Setting a shared printer's permissions

Introduction to Client/Server Networking

- Windows 2000 Server can store the appropriate printer drivers for a number of different Windows-based clients that might connect to the server and use its printers. For example, the printer drivers for a particular printer will be different depending on whether the client computer is running Windows 95, Windows 98, Windows NT 4, Windows 2000, or some other version of Windows. When a client computer opens a shared printer on the network, the printer driver is automatically installed for the client computer. You control this setting on the Sharing tab by clicking the Additional Drivers button, which reveals the Additional Drivers dialog box. To add new drivers, click the appropriate client types that may use the shared printer on the network and then click OK. The program then prompts you for the appropriate disks or CD-ROMs to install those drivers. Then Windows 2000 Server distributes those printer drivers to the client computers when they first use the printer.

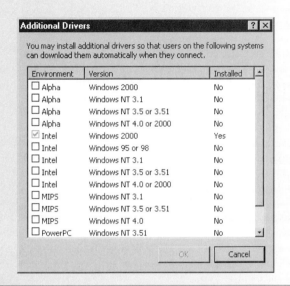

- Loading additional print drivers for a shared printer

Work with Windows 2000 Backup

One single task is more important than any other for a network administrator. This task doesn't have to do with making a network secure from hackers, maintaining users, designing new network segments, or solving server or workstation problems. What is it? Making regular and reliable backups of data on the system.

Taking care to make regular and reliable backups is often a thankless job—*until something happens and the backups are needed,* at which point it becomes the most thank*ful* job in the company! And make no mistake about this: although computers are far more reliable than ever, there are still a myriad of ways in which they can fail and lose or corrupt important data. Remember, there are only two types of network administrators: those who have *had* system crashes and those who *will*. Hardware failures aren't the only culprits, either; applications or users often make mistakes that lose important data. So having good copies of that data on multiple backup tapes can save the day.

Before delving into the details of how Windows 2000 Server's backup software works, you should review some key terms and concepts important in backups.

Every file and folder object on a server has a number of attribute bits attached to it. Some designate the files as being read-only, as system files, or even as hidden files. One is called *archive* (often referred to as the *archive bit),* which marks whether a file has been backed up. Windows 2000 Server keeps track of files that have been modified. Any time a file is modified on the disk, the archive bit is set to "on." (Such bits are usually referred to as being *set,* which means they are on and are set to the value 1, or as being *clear,* which means they are off and are set to the value 0.) When you back up the system, the backed-up files have the archive bit cleared again. This is how the system knows which files need to be backed up and which ones have been backed up.

Treating the archive bit in different ways results in different types of backups, as follows:

- **Normal backups** Back up everything selected for the backup regardless of whether the archive bits are set. All archive bits are set to off as each file is backed up.

- **Copy backups** Back up everything selected for the backup, regardless of whether the archive bits are set. Copy backups do not change the state of the archive bits, however; they remain untouched. Copy backups are used to make a backup without disturbing a sequence of Normal, Incremental, and Differential backups.

- **Incremental backups** Back up only those files that have their archive bits set within the selection set. The backup clears the archive bits.

- **Differential backups** Also back up only those files that have their archive bits set, but the backup leaves the archive bits unchanged.

- **Daily backups** Are a special type of backup in Windows 2000 Server that is like a Differential backup, except it backs up only files modified on a given day.

Now that you understand the different types of backups available, you can consider different tape rotation schemes that make use of these different types of backups.

The simplest backup scheme is just to run Normal backups every night and rotate tapes. In this model, there are many good ways to rotate tapes. One of the best ways that doesn't consume too many tapes is to label four tapes as "Monday" through "Thursday" and to use them on those days. Then, label four tapes as "Friday 1," "Friday 2," up to "Friday 4," and rotate those each week. Then, make a month-end tape on the last day of the month and keep it forever. This scheme is a good trade-off between using tapes and being able to go back in time to restore files. This scheme will use 20 tapes in a year, at which point you should probably replace the rotating tapes.

Another tape rotation scheme involves using the same tapes as listed in the preceding scheme, making full (Normal) backups of the system every Friday night, but then making Incremental backups on Monday through Thursday nights. Because only changed files are backed up during the week, backups during the week happen quickly. The big drawback to this scheme is that if the system crashes on Friday morning, you must restore a lot of tapes to get the system to its most recent backup state. First, you must restore the previous Friday's Normal backup and then restore each of the incremental tapes, in sequence, up to the day when the system crashed. The risk inherent with this scheme is as follows: What do you do if one of those tapes goes bad? Your entire scheme can get messed up if one of the tapes doesn't work. Although bad tapes can be costly in any scheme, they are especially costly in this scheme.

One way around the limitations of the preceding scheme is to use Differential backups during the week, instead of Incremental backups. So, you make a Normal backup Friday night and then a Differential on each day of the week. If you had to restore the system after a crash on Friday morning, all you would need to restore is two tapes: one from the previous Friday and the one from Thursday night. This is because Differential backups back up all changed files since the last Normal backup. Monday's Differential backs up the files changed on Monday, Tuesday's Differential backs up the files changed on Monday and Tuesday, and so on.

Use Windows 2000 Server's Backup Software

Windows 2000 Server includes a reliable, easy-to-use backup software program. While it doesn't have all the bells and whistles of some of the third-party backup software programs available (such as ArcServe or Backup Exec), it does a good job and will meet most needs. To access the Backup program, open the Start menu and choose Programs, Accessories, System Tools, and then Backup. When you start the program, you will first see its welcome screen, as shown in Figure 5.20.

Backup does three important things: it backs up files, restores those files, and helps you prepare for a total system rebuild in case of catastrophic failure. The wizards accessed from the Welcome tab work well and enable you to access all the features of the Backup program easily.

To set up a backup, click the Backup Wizard button on the Welcome tab and then click Next once the opening screen of the Backup Wizard appears. You then see the screen shown in Figure 5.21.

Choose the appropriate option, such as "Back up selected files, drives, or network data," then click Next to continue. You then have a chance to select what you want to back up with the Items to Back Up screen shown in Figure 5-22.

Use the tree views in the left pane to select the drives, files, or other computer contents you want to back up. You can also select a special category

No matter what tape rotation scheme you set up, a good idea is to set up a tape called "Employee Archive." Whenever an employee leaves the company, append his or her files to that tape before you remove those files from the system and keep a list of what employees are on the tape. This gives you a ready reference and quickly available restoration source if a particular person's files are needed at some future time (which happens often).

Although the Backup program included in Windows 2000 Server doesn't offer such a feature, most third-party backup solutions include automatic tape rotation schemes. Such schemes keep track of what tapes you need, how long you've been using them, and what tapes you need in order to restore any given set of files. Using the built-in rotation scheme of any third-party backup software is generally easy, and such schemes usually work well.

A good idea is to keep a recent set of tapes offsite, in case a fire or some other catastrophe destroys your computer room. I recommend sending the next-to-most-recent full backup of your system offsite and keeping the most recent tape available for use. This is because situations frequently occur when you must quickly restore files from a recent backup, so you always want to have the most recent backups available for this purpose. But you also need to keep a rotating tape offsite that doesn't lose too much data, in case the worst happens.

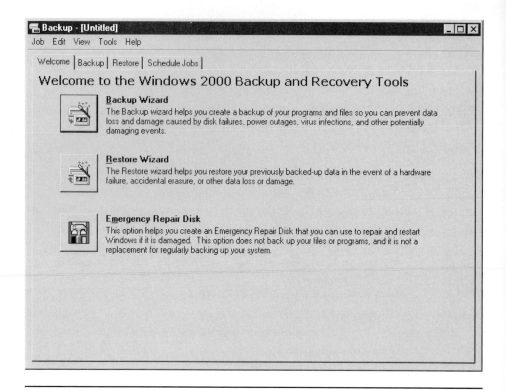

● **Figure 5.20**   Windows 2000 Server's Backup program

called *System State,* which includes all the information necessary to rebuild a Windows 2000 Server from scratch, such as key system files, registry data, and so forth. (Including System State in most backups is usually a good idea.) After selecting what you want to back up, click Next to continue. You see the Where to Store the Backup dialog box shown in Figure 5.23.

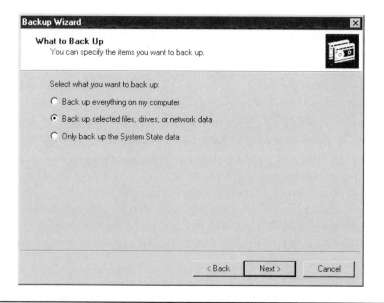

● **Figure 5.21**   Choosing what you want to back up with the Backup Wizard

One nice feature of the Backup program is that you can store a backup on any kind of media attached to the computer, including another disk drive, removable media such as tapes, writeable CDs (CD-R or CD-RW), or JAZ or ZIP drives. In the Where to Store the Backup screen, choose the destination type. Then, if you are performing a file-based backup, assign a name to the backup set. After clicking Next another time, you will see a confirmation screen showing all the pertinent details about the backup you are preparing. An important button on the confirmation screen is labeled Advanced. Clicking the Advanced button takes you through another sequence of dialog boxes in which you can set the following properties:

- Backup type, where you can choose between Normal, Copy, Incremental, Differential, and Daily backup types

- Whether to verify the backup data by having the program read it after it is written and compare its contents to the source contents to ensure that the backup is correct

- Whether to append or overwrite any existing backup data on the media target you chose

- A label for the backup set and media, if you wish to change the default names

- Scheduling information for the backup, which can be used to schedule a backup to take place later, and can also be used to set up automatically recurring backup jobs, which will be managed by the Windows 2000 Server Scheduler service

After completing the Advanced settings, you can click Next on the final Backup Wizard screen either to start the backup or to set it to run at the time that you've scheduled.

Restoring files is easier than backing them up. You can either use the Restore tab or the Restore Wizard. Both methods first prompt you to select either the media or the file you used for the backup from which you want to restore. The methods then enable you to browse the list of backed up files and select the ones that you want to restore. You will have an opportunity to choose whether to overwrite files or to restore the backup to another location on the disk.

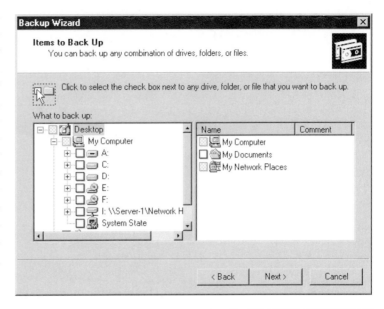

● **Figure 5.22**   Selecting backup material

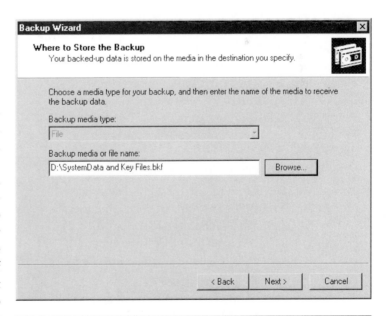

● **Figure 5.23**   Selecting a backup destination

Chapter 5 Review

■ Chapter Summary

After reading this chapter and completing the exercises, you should understand the following.

Networking with Windows 2000

■ Windows 2000 is an upgrade from the Windows NT line of products, which ended with Windows NT 4.

■ The desktop version of the product family is called *Windows 2000 Professional*.

■ Windows 2000 Professional is made to run on business desktop computers and is not an upgrade for Windows 9*x*/Windows ME.

■ Windows 2000 Advanced Server is the mid-range offering of Windows 2000 Server products.

■ The most powerful version of Windows 2000 Server is the Datacenter Server version.

■ This version is used when extremely large databases need to be hosted for thousands of users or when other extremely heavy demands need to be placed on Windows 2000 Server.

■ Before installing Windows 2000 Server, you first must prepare the server computer that you will use and make important decisions about the installation.

■ To avoid problems with your server, it is important you make sure that the server itself and any installed peripherals have been tested with Windows 2000 Server and work properly. Windows 2000 Server runs best on systems that have plenty of RAM. For a server, make sure you have at least 384MB of RAM. If you plan on supporting all the different services available with Windows 2000 Server (such as Terminal Services, RAS, DHCP, DNS, and so forth), 512MB of RAM might be a better choice than 384MB of RAM.

■ Windows 2000 Server requires a lot of disk space for its initial setup. The formula to determine the amount of disk space is 850MB + (RAM in MB × 2). In other words, you need 850MB, plus another 2MB of disk space for each megabyte of installed RAM in the server.

■ Failures tend to happen when equipment is new, and the chance of hardware failure decreases rapidly after the hardware has been up and running for 30 to 90 days.

■ You must perform a full installation to a new server or to one running any NOS other than Windows NT Server.

■ If you are running Windows NT Server 4 Enterprise Edition, you can upgrade only to Windows 2000 Advanced Server.

■ The main benefit to upgrading is that all your existing settings under Windows NT Server will be maintained and automatically carried forward into your Windows 2000 Server installation.

■ Windows 2000 Server supports hard disks formatted using either File Allocation Table (FAT16 and FAT32) or NT File System (NTFS).

■ ServerMagic enables you to resize an existing FAT partition without losing any of its data and it also fully supports FAT and NTFS partitions.

■ NTFS is required for any Windows 2000 Servers that will function as domain controllers and also is the only file system that enables you to take full advantage of Windows 2000's security features.

■ Domains enable you to manage multiple Windows 2000 or Windows NT servers more easily.

■ Except in the smallest of networks, it is a very good idea to have two domain controllers.

■ Windows 2000 Server supports two different ways of managing CALs: Per Server and Per Seat.

■ Microsoft recommends that you use Per Server licensing when running a single server and Per Seat licensing when running multiple servers.

■ When setting up a new server, you have only two real choices to begin the installation: boot from the Windows 2000 Server CD-ROM or prepare boot diskettes.

■ Certificate Services are used to enable public-key applications.

■ Windows 2000 Cluster Services enable two or more servers to share a common workload and to provide fail-over support in case one of the servers experiences a hardware failure.

Administering Windows 2000 Server

■ Network security should always be appropriate to the company and its specific network.

- Sometimes security that is too strong results in reduced security over the long run.

- A domain is essentially a collection of security information shared among Windows 2000 servers.

- The dialog boxes you see when creating a user account are much simpler than the one you see when modifying a user account.

- The Downlevel Group field enables you to specify a different group name for Windows NT computers.

- Using different group names is usually not a good idea because it can quickly make your system confusing.

- Group Scope refers to how widely the group is populated throughout a domain.

- Domain Local groups exist only within a single domain and can contain members only from that domain.

- Distribution groups are used only to maintain e-mail distribution lists and have no security impact in Windows 2000 Server.

- Drives and folders under Windows 2000 Server are made available to users over the network as shared resources, simply called shares in Windows networking parlance.

- Permissions set on folders and files are always cumulative and take into account permissions set for the user individually as well as any security groups of which the user is a member.

- No Access permission is also cumulative and overriding.

- You can use the **NET** command from any Windows client for any Windows network.

- A print job is a set of binary data sent from a network workstation to a network printer.

- The process of redirecting a printer port to a network printer is called capturing.

- The simplest backup scheme is just to run Normal backups every night and rotate tapes.

- Backup does three important things: it backs up files, restores those files, and helps you prepare for a total system rebuild in case of catastrophic failure.

- Restoring files is easier than backing them up.

■ Key Terms

burn-in (198)	**mapping** (228)	**print servers** (229)
capturing (229)	**Message Queuing Services** (204)	**printer pooling** (231)
Certificate Services (203)	**multimaster domain controllers** (200)	**printer queue** (229)
Cluster Services (203)	**NET command** (228)	**Remote Storage** (205)
destructive testing (198)	**NTFS** (199)	**security groups** (220)
domain (200)	**per-seat licensing** (201)	**share** (212)
dual-boot setup (200)	**per-server licensing** (201)	**Universal Naming**
Internet Information Server	**print driver** (229)	**Convention (UNC)** (228)
(IIS) (204)	**print job** (229)	**workgroup** (200)

■ Key Term Quiz

Use the Key Terms list to complete the sentences that follow. (Not all terms will be used.)

1. Hardware testing that is carried out before installing any NOS, particularly on a server that will be used for production is called _____.

2. Data on the disks is erased during _____.

3. You will install Windows 2000 Server onto a disk that uses the FAT file system only when the system must be used in a _____.

4. _____ is required for Windows 2000 Servers that will function as domain controllers.

5. _____ assigns the CALs to the server, which will allow only as many connections from computers as there are installed CALs on that server.

6. _____ requires purchasing a CAL for each of your client computers, which gives them the right to access as many Windows 2000 servers as they wish.

7. A new server installation usually requires that you create a _____.

8. _____ enable two or more servers to share a common workload and to provide fail-over support in case one of the servers experiences a hardware failure.

9. _____ allows a Windows 2000 Server to operate as a web and FTP server.

10. _____ enables you to configure a Windows 2000 Server disk to move rarely accessed files automatically onto an available tape drive or writeable CD.

■ Multiple-Choice Quiz

1. Which of the following describes a simple collection of computers on a network and is suited only to pure peer-to-peer networks?
   a. Cluster group
   b. Network group
   c. Workgroup
   d. Peer group

2. What naming system do most network resources in a Windows network use?
   a. Universal Naming Convention
   b. Windows Naming Convention
   c. Network Naming Convention
   d. The **NET** command

3. Where do print jobs sent to the network go?
   a. Queue
   b. Port queue
   c. Job queue
   d. Printer queue

4. What enables you to set up a number of identical printers, all connected to a single printer queue that appear to the network as one printer?
   a. LAN
   b. Printer pooling
   c. Hub
   d. Printer queue

5. What type of backup is used to avoid disturbing a sequence of Normal, Incremental, and Differential backups?
   a. Normal backup
   b. Copy backup
   c. Incremental backup
   d. Differential backup

6. What is the process of simulating a disk drive with a network share called?
   a. Mapping
   b. Booting

   c. Simulation
   d. Configuration

7. Which of the following is a browseable resource that remote users can access provided they have sufficient privileges to do so?
   a. Hyperlink
   b. Internet
   c. Web link
   d. Share

8. What enables you to resize an existing FAT partition without losing any of its data and fully supports FAT and NTFS partitions?
   a. Compaq's SmartStart
   b. ServerMagic
   c. PowerQuest
   d. Multimaster domain controller

9. What type of software often enables you to choose between nondestructive and destructive testing of the disks?
   a. Server-testing
   b. Partition
   c. Debugging
   d. Anti-virus

10. What is important to do to the components installed in the server before installing Windows 2000 Server as an upgrade?
    a. Disable
    b. Enable
    c. Survey
    d. Scan

11. What program first attempts to detect and set up all the basic devices installed in the computer?
    a. Device setup
    b. Setup.exe
    c. Graphical setup
    d. Win setup

12. What do users find when they browse the servers on the network?
    a. The name of the server
    b. The IP address of the server
    c. An pop-up indicating access is denied
    d. The server code

13. As a rule of thumb, what should an administrator password include?
    a. Four or more symbols
    b. Six or more numbers
    c. Six letters
    d. Eight or more characters

14. Which of the following are used to enable public-key applications?

    a. Certificate Services
    b. Networking Services
    c. Terminal Services
    d. Remote Installation Services

15. What settings enable you to define details, such as exactly what networking components will be installed and how each is configured?
    a. Hardware settings
    b. Custom settings
    c. Typical settings
    d. Standard settings

■ Essay Quiz

1. List the steps you need to follow to configure Windows 2000 Servers in any of Domain Controller, Member Server, or Stand-Alone Server modes to support either domains or workgroups.

2. You want to install Windows 2000 Server, mention several ways, which you can adopt for installation.

3. How do you comprehend the terms domain and workgroup?

4. What do you do if you are to install Windows 2000 Server onto a system that has only a single FAT partition and you want to dual-boot Windows 2000 Server with that other operating system, but you want to establish a new NTFS partition for Windows 2000 without having to destroy the existing FAT partition?

Lab Projects

• Lab Project 5.1

You might frequently want to simulate a connected hard disk on your computer with a share from the network. You can create a drive mapping in many ways. The easiest way is

❶ Open Network Neighborhood from the client computer, and then locate the share you want to map.

❷ Right-click it and choose Map Network Drive.

❸ In the dialog box that appears, the name of the domain and share will appear already typed in for you; simply select an appropriate drive letter for the mapping and click OK.

• Lab Project 5.2

Windows 2000 Server includes a reliable, easy-to-use backup software program. While it doesn't have all the bells and whistles of some of the third-party backup software programs available, it does a good job and will meet most needs. To access the Backup program, open the Start menu. Choose Programs, Accessories, System Tools, and then Backup.

Connecting Client Workstations

In this chapter, you will learn how to

- **Connect client computers to Windows servers**

- **Install Macintosh support on a Windows 2000 server**

- **Network Macintosh clients with Windows and Netware servers**

- **Set up a networking gateway between NetWare and Windows servers**

- **Access Unix-based files from Windows network clients**

- **Install and access Windows Terminal Services**

Windows NT and 2000 networks support many types of client connections. Although this increases the options for interaction, it also increases the overall complexity of a network. Proper selection and implementation of the various client packages can ensure that your network is reliable and easy to use. Management of clients in the enterprise is creating the demand for tools that improve the efficiency of setup and maintenance of client computers. Unfortunately, none of these powerful remote management tools can be implemented until clients have been connected to the network. Inevitably, that task requires some hands-on contact with client workstations.

This chapter discusses several client packages including: client support for NT, Windows 2000, Win 95, Win 3.11, Macintosh, and Gateway Services for Novell servers. The mechanisms NT uses to support file and print sharing will be explained, including the NetLogon service. We will also take a look at Unix file sharing using NFS. The first part of this chapter contains considerations for both Windows 2000 and NT clients. The rest of the chapter has specific information about your particular platform, be it Windows 2000 or NT.

■ Client Considerations

Connecting client computers to Windows networks requires two steps: installing and configuring client software on the machine and establishing accounts for accessing resources on the NT network. While Microsoft and many other vendors provide client software for a wide variety of operating systems and network packages, the bidirectional sharing of resources in terms of security and efficiency is not equivalent across all platforms.

The integration of multiple platforms in an enterprise environment is certain to occur given new networks are rarely built *in toto*, but evolve from existing systems. The "drawbacks" in having to integrate Windows for Workgroups, NetWare, Windows 95, and Macintosh users on the network can be minimized with careful planning. However, you should keep an eye on utilization and, if affordable, upgrade hardware and software to reduce the diversity of platforms in the enterprise.

While all the above clients can be connected to the network, maintaining or achieving the required level of functionality for these clients may be impossible, because client performance or security is insufficient. For example, a small DOS or Windows 3.11 workgroup with 486-based clients that need to access NT, NetWare, and Unix resources could be configured with the entire collection of standard client protocols to provide these services. Unfortunately, the memory demands of the network drivers would leave the clients without enough memory to run applications. The commonsense approach suggests implementing upgraded hardware and operating systems whenever financial constraints permit.

Thin Clients

Full consideration of the best choices for system upgrades is beyond the scope of this chapter, but the classic concept of bringing newer, more powerful machines online is no longer the sole path when replacing antiquated workstations. Although Windows NT and 2000 have special advantages for security and integration in the enterprise, they also require considerable system resources that increase the cost per seat. System management is a separate cost factor to consider when choosing what kind of clients to connect. The "thin client" concept has been receiving significant attention as a means of reducing the total cost of ownership, at the level of both hardware and the system-management expense.

In many ways the thin client is a return to the idea of terminals running server-based applications. The rationale is to present users with applications that they have become familiar with on their PCs and allow them to have these applications "run" on inexpensive desktop workstations. The application displays its results on the thin client, but the CPU and RAM are located on a server. This permits administrators to easily manage the software and keep a close eye on hardware requirements. In addition, the reduction in overall maintenance through consolidation can save time and money. The clients themselves can also be quite inexpensive. However, the demands on the server increase compared to servers providing predominantly file and print services, so the cost for servers will increase as well as the negative consequences of having the servers go offline.

Microsoft has made a clear commitment to provide thin-client technology in its Terminal Server product introduced in beta release at the 1997 Comdex show. This commitment is evident in Windows 2000's Terminal Services applications. The product relies on licensed technologies from Citrix Systems, Inc. (WinFrame), which Citrix has also licensed to a variety of firms who market "Windows terminals" such as Insignia, Tektronix, and Wyse Technology. There are many other companies seeking different thin-client solutions. As with all the issues of enterprise solutions, careful evaluation of the goals of the network must drive the decision process. If many of the client management tools become more sophisticated, the cost of managing workstations that can function without a server will continue to decline toward the costs *predicted* for thin clients. The best answer is certain to depend on the complex economics of hardware pricing, client licensing, and client support in the enterprise.

■ NT Connection Services

Creating client connections that work efficiently in the enterprise requires numerous decisions regarding user accounts. If a goal is to have all resources in the network available for a user under a single account and password, NT may accommodate this, but you still have to coordinate account information for other non-NT servers. This may not impose equal security for all resources attached to all client workstations. The NT Server process that handles requests for access to resources is the NetLogon Service.

For some non-NT users, the connection to an NT network may be a transparent process, but for others, if increased security is implemented, there may be login changes. Currently, it is not possible to have a single username and account managed solely within NT if the enterprise incorporates all possible clients. For example, NetWare network servers can be made available to NT network clients, and a single logon username and password at the NT network client will access both resources once the NetWare account data are entered. The single login has the appearance of a global user account; however, if the user wants to change their password, they will have to change it on both the NT and Novell systems or keep track of two passwords.

Client Access Licenses

When connecting new clients to NT Servers, remember that Client Access Licenses (CALs) are required for the legal use of file, print, and RAS services on the server.

The License Manager

The **License Manager** in NT Server is used to maintain the database of licenses, and it can also track the use of licenses for each user (later in this chapter we will discuss licensing for Windows 2000). This tool tracks licenses for all of Microsoft's networked products (Back Office, SQL Server, Exchange Server, and so on) as well as NT Server CALs. Access to resources of the Server requires that there are available user licenses registered in the

License Manager. For example, if you have a per-server license for ten licenses, and an eleventh user with a valid account attempts to log on to the system, they will receive a message that a Domain Controller could not be located, that they are being logged on from cached data, and that any changes to their profile may not be available. The user will have access to local resources at their workstation, but network drives and printers that are accessed through an NT Server will not be available.

Opening the Licensing icon in the Control Panel allows you to quickly determine which license mode is in effect and how many licenses are present. Figure 6.1 shows the Licensing window. Although this appears to be the same information that is available through the License Manager, it is not. The number of licenses is entered in the License Manager, and that information is then replicated to the Domain Controller. The default replication frequency is every 24 hours, and this means that updates to the License Manager would not be seen immediately in the Choose License Mode dialog box. In Figure 6.1 you can see that there are licenses for ten concurrent connections. If an administrator wanted to add an eleventh account to a domain where all the users were connected to the server all the time, an eleventh license would have to be added in the License Manager. The administrator would also have to be sure to replicate the change to the Domain Controller before the new user would be able to gain access to the server's file, print, and RAS services.

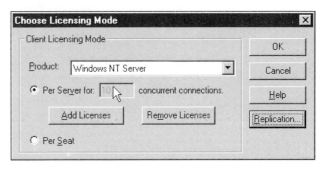

• **Figure 6.1**   Selecting a license mode

Replication

Replication can be forced to occur at a specific time from the Control Panel or the License Manager. Figure 6.2 shows the Replication Configuration window opened from clicking the Replication button in the Licensing tool on the Control Panel. The same window can be accessed from the License Manager if you click the Server Browser tab, select the server, and right-click to obtain the properties for that machine.

You can see that there is a choice to replicate to either the Domain Controller or an Enterprise Server. You should select Domain Controller if the server is not a PDC or if you do not wish the license information to be replicated to a central server. Select and specify the name of the Enterprise Server if the server is a stand-alone server in a domain that is within a larger enterprise. If the server is a PDC and a central management of licenses is called for, selecting the Enterprise Server will forward the domain licensing information on to that machine. The default replication frequency is every 24 hours and when multiple NT Servers are replicating, there will be an automatic delay in the start times for each server to avoid congestion due to simultaneous replication.

NT Server has a License Logging Service that is automatically started upon installation. If this service fails, the License Manager cannot access the license information or replicate it to the Enterprise Server. While this is analogous to a failure to synchronize directory database information or information on resources from browsing, the replication of license information does not make use of server replication/synchronization processes.

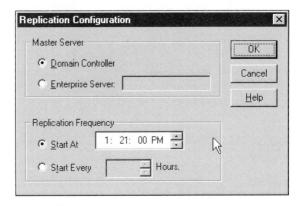

Network Browsing Service

You can see resources available on the network because of the Browser Service. The basic principles underlying browsing

• **Figure 6.2**   Configuring the replication for licenses

are the same across Microsoft's products from DOS through Windows 3.11 to Win 95 and NT. The Browser service was developed in the context of LANs and not WANs, and this is reflected in the distributed nature of the service and the problems it poses when considering its implementation in the enterprise. Windows 2000 uses DNS and Active Directory to locate resources. This section pertains to Windows NT.

Browser Basics

The concept of browsing was that clients would announce their existence on the network when they started up, and their absence would be noted if they were off the network. Achieving this involved having each client broadcasting its presence at some interval. If this were a general broadcast message, it would create a lot of network traffic with the overhead becoming more debilitating as the number of clients increased.

The solution was to have the clients direct their announcement to a Master Browser that would maintain a list of the resources on the network. When clients wished to browse the available resources, they queried the Master Browser, and when clients shut down normally, they announced their departure from the network. The default setting for the browser service in all Microsoft operating systems is AUTO, which means that every client can potentially become a Master Browser in its network segment. It is intuitively obvious that under these conditions all the clients in a network segment would have to negotiate to determine the client designated as the Master Browser, and when the total number of clients increases, the network traffic associated with resolving this will be undesirably large. The rationale behind such a system grew out of the issue of what would happen to browsing if the Master Browser fails. If administrator intervention were required to restore users' ability to see resources on the network, the system would be too brittle.

To avoid overloading the performance of the Master Browser, Microsoft implemented the strategy in which clients that need to browse for resources query a designated Master Browser, which replies with the name or names of other machines designated **Backup Browsers**. These Backup Browsers have a copy of the Master Browser's resource list, and they provide that information to the clients. The Master Browser's task is to create the list, designate backup machines (including recruiting new backups if the total number of clients on the network increases), and forward copies of the browse list to the backups and to higher-level browse masters.

NT provides the extra control (compared to Win 95 and Windows 3.11) of defining characteristics of the roles specific machines will play in the browsing service. This makes NT-only networks easier to manage and requires fewer compromises in performance. In mixed client environments, which are the most commonly encountered, judicious control of which clients participate in browsing may permit a more satisfactory compromise between minimal network traffic overhead and a resilient browsing environment.

At the level of implementation, the Browser service relies on two components:

- **The Browser** Part of the server service. It maintains the browse list, manages the client's participation in browse functions, and responds to the GetBackupList datagram calls that are central to clients' requests for information on shared resources on the network.

- **The Datagram Receiver**   Sends and receives the datagrams regarding browser elections.

It is important to remember that, in the enterprise, successful browsing requires that all clients and servers be configured to support WINS and/or LMHOSTS name resolution and have a TCP/IP protocol configured. Without these steps, browsing cannot take place outside of a network segment (that is, across a router).

Multiple-Client Browsing Environments

Client workstation contributions to browsing within a network can fall into one of four categories (it should be noted that all categories would be considered browser *servers*).

- Non-Browsers
- Potential Browsers
- Backup Browser
- Master Browser

Windows 3.11, Win 95, NT Workstation, and NT Server clients can assume any of these roles. The default setting is that of Potential Browser for Windows 3.11, Win 95, and NT machines.

Client Commonalties   Non-Browsers cannot maintain a list of machines on the network, but they do signal their presence on the network with a periodic broadcast to the Master Browser. The announcement frequency begins at once per minute and progressively declines to once every 2, 4, 8, and finally 12 minutes. If the Master Browser is offline, a Non-Browser computer will not attempt to become a browser. In the enterprise, this might be the preferred setting for most clients, because it will minimize network traffic and streamline browsing. An exception would be in those networks in which clients are turned on and off regularly, because the availability of Master Browsers and backups will be less predictable. Distributing the ability to browse throughout clients will yield the most robust browse capabilities to whatever mix of clients are on at any given time.

Potential Browsers act as Non-Browsers except when a Master Browser specifies that it should become a Backup Browser or if no Master Browser is available; it can join in the process called "election" that occurs to select a new Master Browser server. Potential Browsers are capable of maintaining the browse list needed by clients.

Backup Browsers actively maintain a copy of the Master Browser browse list of the servers and domains. These machines receive directed broadcast requests (the NetServerEnum API calls) from clients that are seeking to obtain a list of shared resources on the network. The backups will periodically query the Master Browser to update its copy of the browse list.

Master Browsers are the recipients of the directed broadcasts of clients announcing their existence, which the Master Browsers use to create the browse list for their part of the network. They generate announcements to the Domain Master Browser (DMB) of their own domain as well as Master Browsers of other domains. Finally, they monitor the total number of clients in their browse list and the number of Backup Browsers. If the ratio of clients to Backup Browsers is too small, the Master Browsers will elevate Potential Browsers to Backup Browsers. This prevents any single backup from being overwhelmed with a workload of responding to client browse requests. The Master Browser will assign a backup for every 32 clients on the network segment (that is, if there are 1–31 clients, there will be 1 backup, 32–63 clients, 2 backups, and so on).

NT Issues   Thus far we have examined some of the similarities among the different browser clients. Now we will focus on differences among NT, Win 95, and Win 3.11 clients.

The Browser server status for NT Servers is determined by whether or not the machine is a PDC. When the NT Server machine is designated as a PDC, its Browser service is set to a fifth category, unique to NT, that of a *Domain Master Browser*. Any other NT Server machines in the domain can be set to one of the four categories previously described.

To manually configure the browser service in NT, there are several values in the Registry for the key \HKEY_LOCAL_MACHINE\SYSTEM\ CurrentControlSet\Services\Browser\Parameters.

For the Value \MaintainServerList, the possible entries are

- **No**   Specifies that the client be a Non-Browser.

- **Yes**   Specifies that the client be a Browser Server. When booted, the client will announce itself and broadcast to determine if there is a Master Browser in its network segment. If there is, the client requests a copy of the browse list and becomes a Backup Browser. If there is no Master Browser, the client forces an election among all clients to choose a Master Browser. This is the default for NT servers when installed as a PDC.

- **Auto**   Specifies that the client be a Potential Browser. This is the default for all non-PDC NT Server and NT Workstation machines.

For the Value \IsDomainMaster, the possible entries are

- **No**   The default value for non PDC machines.
- **Yes**   The default for PDC machines.

 If this value is changed, the machine must be rebooted for the change to take effect.

For the Value \BackupPeriodicity (Range 300–4204967 seconds), the default value is 720. This is the frequency with which the Backup Browser will contact the Master Browser to update its browse list. When the value is set for the NT server that is the DMB, it determines the frequency with which the DMB will update its list from WINS.

Win 95 Issues   In Win 95, the equivalent settings for determining browser server status can be set from the user interface or via the Registry. The settings for Non-Browser, Browser, or Potential Browser can be chosen from the Control Panel | Network menu by clicking on the File & Print Sharing button and choosing the Advanced tab. The choices for Browse Master are Disabled (Non-Browser), Enabled (Browser), and Auto (the default setting, for Potential Browser). The settings can also be found in the Registry under the key:

HKEY_LOCAL_MACHINE\System\CurrentControlSet\VxNETSUP\
Ndi\params

There is only one subkey of interest in \MaintainServerList where entries of No, Yes, and Auto are allowable. There are no equivalents of the subkeys that allow adjustment of the timing of Backup or Master Browser requests for updates in Win 95.

Windows for Workgroups Issues While there is a Registry for Windows 3.11, it has a very different function than the Registry found in NT or 95, and the Browser service is not configured there. Instead, entries need to be made in the SYSTEM.INI file and the [network] subsection. The MaintainServerList= value can be entered in this section and can have the three entries applicable to Win 95 and NT. As for Win 95, the frequency of Backup or Master Browser requests for updates of the browse list cannot be configured in Windows 3.11.

The original browsing service in Windows 3.11 existed prior to NT and, as a result, that original service did not accommodate the concept of DMBs that might exist on a different network segment. To solve this problem, Microsoft includes updated browser services for Windows 3.11 with the NT Server installation CD-ROM in the \Clients\Update.wfw directory. These files must be installed in WFW if those machines are to be able to browse successfully in the enterprise environment. The TCP/IP-32 3.11b protocol located in the \Clients\TCP32WFW directory is also required for correct WFW browsing behavior.

Browser Elections Because of the different Browser statuses that clients can be assigned, you need to consider the reasons for these categories and the impact on network performance. For distributed browsing services to function without direct administrative intervention, it is necessary to accommodate the addition or loss of browser servers on the network. This is accomplished by having a Browser Election held whenever one of three situations occurs:

- A PDC starts up
- A machine designated as a Preferred Master Browser starts up
- A new client starts up and cannot locate a Master Browser

Under these conditions, the computer that has started will generate a special datagram called the election datagram. This is a directed frame that will go to all clients on the network except Non-Browsers. The contents of the datagram are the request for an election and the *election criterion* of the sending computer. You can see when an election has been called because there is an entry in the Event Viewer.

The specific rules for winning elections can be found in the NT Server Resource Kit by searching for "Browser Elections" or reading the MS Knowledge Base article ID # Q102878. Briefly, NT machines are preferred over older operating systems, the PDC has the highest priority, and, other things being equal, machines that have been running longer are given preference.

Both Win 9*x* and Windows 3.11 can fully participate in domain browsing, even to the extent of being Master Browsers. This is valuable if the enterprise contains a network segment on which there are no NT machines. However, for Win 95 or Windows 3.11 clients to be able to fill this role, the Workgroup name assigned to these machines must be the same as the Domain name that they will be participating in.

Browsing on the WAN

Browsing in NT networks evolved from the method developed by Microsoft in its first network products. The concept of browsing across routers was not incorporated into those earlier systems designed for browsing among workgroups. For enterprise implementation, browsing must be extended so shared resources anywhere in the organization can be accessed by users.

To gain cross-router browsing capability, NT takes advantage of the properties of WINS to be able to localize all necessary information for routing the NetServerEnum API calls and browsing datagrams (GetServerList, election, and so on) in one place. To avoid enterprise-wide broadcast messages, the browse process employs directed messages and to achieve this, clients must have a way to have specific IP numbers that they associate with the various browse servers—Backup, Master, and Domain Master Browser servers. WINS accommodates this need by having the different types of Browser servers associated with specific NetBIOS names. The last step is to have the clients associate their IP number with their NetBIOS name via a broadcast when they announce themselves on the network, when their status changes (a Potential Browser is told to become a Backup Browser by the Master Browser), or a browser election has been held.

If WINS services are, for any reason, unavailable, it is possible to create an entry in the LMHOSTS file so you can browse across routers. This method has several drawbacks that make it an unattractive method for the enterprise. For instance, default routers won't forward broadcast messages, and if users find themselves in this situation, they will only be able to browse their local network segment.

The display of resources available across domains does not appear in the File Manager, Explorer, or Network Neighborhood when WINS is not functioning. Users can still browse resources, but they must know the domain name, machine name, and be comfortable entering this information from the command prompt using the **net view** command. Using LMHOSTS requires being able to place an LMHOSTS file on all machines, and each file will require entries for every client and server on the WAN. A single, large LMHOST file copied to every computer might not pose too great a problem, but if that file must be changed every time that a new machine is added or an old one removed, the workload seems unreasonable.

Enhancing Enterprise Browsing

There are many things to keep in mind when evaluating browsing in the enterprise, and we will enumerate several of the most salient. Keep in mind that you will need to make any decisions on browsing based on the specifics of your particular network configuration. This is not a trivial consideration, because it is estimated that approximately 30 percent of daily network traffic can be Browser service announcements, elections, and requests for information. Following are some specific considerations.

When resources go offline, there is a delay before this information is reflected in browse lists. Depending on where the client is relative to the enterprise and the exact configuration of the timing of browse-list updates, it can take many tens of minutes before the loss of resource is reflected in the browse lists. How important this is may depend on how users react to seeing a resource on the browse list in the Explorer or File Manager when they

> In a Windows 2000-only network, there is no need for WINS because all names are DNS names, so searching for network resources will be carried out through a DNS server and the Active Directory.

are unable to connect or access that resource. If the lists are updated more frequently, this places a substantial load on network traffic.

The size of the browse list in NT 4 can be changed, but for NT 3.51 and earlier as well as Win 95 and Windows 3.11, the browse list is limited to 64KB in size. This limits the maximum number of workstations that can be in a single workgroup or domain browse list to less than 3,000. The exact number will depend on the size of the comments associated with machine names. For a large enterprise, this means that mixed platform environments will be unable to have automatic browsing of every available resource if the total number of computers exceeds this.

Browsing is specific to each protocol that is operating on the network. This means, for example, that an announcement will be generated repetitively until all protocols have been alerted. Substantial savings can accrue for each protocol that can be eliminated.

If a configuration is chosen to limit the total number of machines that can become browsers, this will reduce network traffic associated with elections. For network segments that do not have a substantial change in the number of clients each day, administrators could configure only the optimal number of Backup Browsers and have a small (optimal) number of Potential Browsers as a hedge in case of Backup Browser failure.

For clients that will not share any of their own resources, the Server service can be turned off. Since users elsewhere in the network do not need to browse that machine, turning off the Server service means that machine will never announce itself to the Master Domain browser and will not generate periodic announcements either.

Administrators can gain some insight into the existing traffic generated by the Browser service. The browser will generate a record in the system log when errors and elections occur, and these can be viewed with the Event Viewer. Of greater use are two utilities that are available with the NT Server Resource Kit:

- **BROWSTAT.EXE** A command-line program that can be used to gain insight into the network traffic generated to browser events. You can force an election to occur and, by monitoring the traffic, determine if you want to change the configuration of Browser services to minimize the occurrence of elections.

- **BROWMON.EXE** A graphical tool that allows viewing of many browsing statistics. An example of this information is shown in Figure 6.3.

Configuring systems for best performance will be labor intensive without enterprise-wide management tools. You will almost certainly need to change the Microsoft defaults for many implementations since all machines are initially configured by default as Potential Browsers.

NetLogon Service

For Windows NT, the NetLogon service is used by clients to establish a connection with NT Servers. This service is necessary for you to log onto a domain. In the next section, we'll look at how Windows 2000 clients log onto a Windows 2000 Domain.

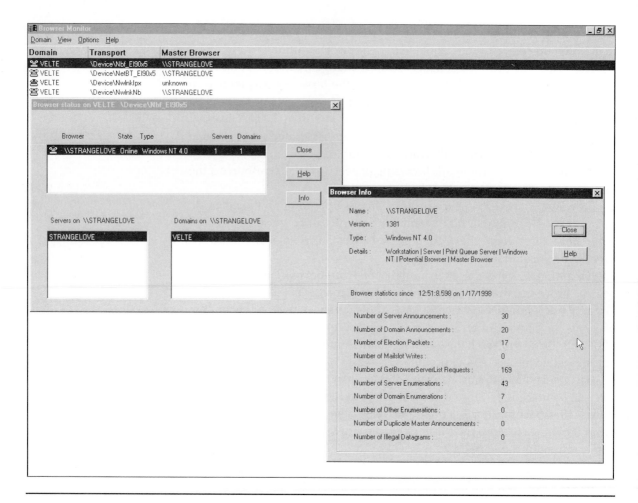

• **Figure 6.3**   The Browser Monitor can provide detailed information about browser traffic.

NT Clients

On NT client machines, user login requests are processed by the Local Security Authority (LSA); if there is no match to an entry in the local user account database, the LSA passes the request to the NetLogon service, which forwards the request to a Domain Controller. The NetLogon service on NT Servers passes these requests to the secure domain directory database or passes requests through to a controller in another domain if the resources requested are located in that domain.

The NetLogon service requires the Workstation and Server services. When connecting NT Workstation clients that have been configured in stand-alone or workgroup mode, be certain these services have been set for automatic startup. This can be verified and set in the Services window of the Control Panel. It also requires enabling the Access This Computer From Network right, which is set in the User Manager. Note that the default settings for this right include permission for everyone to have access to the computer. This means that all users in the domain can sit at the client and log into the domain. This follows the Microsoft practice of having the least restrictive default settings on rights and permissions.

Before the NetLogon service can perform these operations, it must first locate the relevant machine (or machines in the case of NT server NetLogon service). This process is called **discovery**, and it begins as soon as the service is started on bootup. A client NetLogon service will try to "discover" the NetLogon service of the NT Server. If the received username and password information is in the security database, the machines establish a *secure communications channel*. If the discovery fails, the NetLogon service on the client will use cached information for the user created from the last login. This means that the user will be logged into the client and will have the local privileges that existed at the time of the last login.

If the discovery is successful, but no user account is found on the server, there are two possibilities:

- If Guest accounts are enabled and no Guest password is set, the user will be logged on as a Guest; otherwise, the login fails.

- If the client is attempting to log in to a Backup Domain Controller (BDC), the BDC NetLogon service will pass authentication through to the PDC if that machine is available. This can occur in cases where a user password has been changed at the PDC, but that change has not yet been replicated to the BDC (see more on this in the next section). In this case, the PDC would allow the login.

NT Domain Controllers

The NetLogon service on Domain Controllers responds to domain client authentication requests and also establishes secure communication channels with all Domain Controllers with which it has trust relationships. On startup, the domain NetLogon service will attempt discovery with all trusted domains. If necessary, each domain is polled three times within five seconds of bootup. If the discovery fails in this period, the Domain Controller will repeat the attempt any time that a request for authentication is received from a client that requires access to resources outside the domain. If no requests are received, the controller will attempt discovery every 15 minutes.

In NT Server, this service receives requests for authentication from clients and passes requests through to trusted servers in other domains when necessary. This includes both logon authentication as well as requests to access resources (files or printers). If a logged-on user seeks to map a network drive outside the domain, the PDC NetLogon service will pass the request to the PDC of a trusted domain, and if the username and password match the security database in that domain, the request will be honored. If there is a failure, the NT Server will prompt the user to enter a username and password, thus allowing access if the user has two accounts in different domains, or knows the username and password of a valid account in that domain.

The NetLogon service is also responsible for synchronizing the security database between the PDC and the BDCs. Modifications to user or group accounts (passwords, group membership, or user or group rights) are stored in a change log (kept in both memory and on disk \%Systemroot%\ Netlogon.chg). Replicating these changes to the BDC is the responsibility of the PDC's NetLogon service. This is accomplished by the PDC NetLogon service generating a pulse message to which the BDC NetLogon service responds by requesting an update to the directory database. The PDC responds to these requests by sending the contents of the change log to the BDC. This update is termed **partial synchronization**, since only changes

 Clients not running NT Workstation or Server have their access to network resources authenticated by the NetLogon service on the appropriate Domain Controllers. However, users on these clients have no restrictions on their access to local resources.

have been replicated between the PDC and BDC. `Full synchronization` is the copying of the complete directory database from the PDC to the BDC. It is required when the BDC is first set up or if the BDC has been offline for too long a time.

The default size of the change log is 64KB; once the change log is full, new changes bump the oldest changes out of the log file. If the BDC is offline long enough, there will be old changes that will not have been replicated that have been removed from the change log, resulting in a mismatch in the account information for the domain between the PDC and the BDC. Full synchronization is required under these conditions. Since no system alert is normally generated by a failure for correct partial synchronization, you may only be aware of the problem if the PDC is offline and client connections fail when the BDC authenticates login or resource requests.

Table 6.1 contains the group of Registry values under the HKEY_ LOCAL_MACHINE\CurrentControlSet\Services\Netlogon\Parameters key that determine the size of the change log and the timing of requests for replication. The default values are satisfactory unless a PDC must synchronize many BDCs in a domain with heavy network traffic. Increasing partial synchronization frequency increases traffic on the network, but reducing the frequency increases the chance of a loss of synchronization. Increasing the change-log size can provide a false sense of security unless you monitor the contents. You may think the changes in the security database are few and infrequent so the change log never fills. As long as this is true, partial synchronization will always succeed. However, if the log *does* fill up and you are not prepared for it, problems will arise. Furthermore, the larger the change log, the larger the information needed to be sent to the BDCs, and this again increases network traffic.

■ Connecting Windows 2000 Clients

One of Windows 2000's key features is its ability to interconnect and function with a variety of other operating systems. Naturally, the best pairing will come from a Windows 2000 Server and Client. Though connecting a Windows 2000 client to an NT or even AppleTalk network is possible, some

Table 6.1	Registry Settings for the NetLogon Change Log		
Value Name	**Data Type**	**Range**	**Default**
ChangeLogSize	REG_DWORD	64KB to 4MB	64KB
Pulse	REG_DWORD	60 to 172,800 seconds (48 hours)	300 (5 minutes)
PulseConcurrency	REG_DWORD	1 to 500 pulses	20
PulseMaximum	REG_DWORD	60 to 172,800 seconds (48 hours)	7,200 (2 hours)
PulseTimeout1	REG_DWORD	1 to 120 seconds	5
PulseTimeout2	REG_DWORD	60 to 3,600 seconds	300 (5 minutes)
Randomize	REG_DWORD	0 to 120 seconds	1
ReplicationGovernor	REG_DWORD	0 to 100 percent	100
Scripts	REG_SZ	Pathname	NULL
Update	REG_SZ	Yes or No	No

of Windows 2000's features will not be usable. Connecting Windows 2000 Professional to a Windows 2000 Server will yield the best results from this operating system.

Step-by-Step 6.1

Adding a Windows 2000 Workstation to a Domain and Checking the Connection

To complete this exercise, you will need the following:

- A Windows 2000 Server computer configured as a working domain controller, connected to a LAN

- A Windows 2000 Professional computer connected to the LAN

Step 1	Open Windows 2000's Control Panel (to get there, follow Start | Settings | Control Panel) and double-click the System icon.
Step 2	Select the Network Identification tab and click Properties.
Step 3	In the resulting dialog box, shown here, your computer's name will be shown.
Step 4	Click the Domain button and type the name of the domain you wish to join, and then click OK.
Step 5	Next, the Domain Username and Password dialog box pops up. Fill in the Name and Password boxes, accordingly.
Step 6	You should get the message Welcome to the *domain name* domain, which means you have successfully connected to the domain.
Step 7	Click OK to restart the computer, and then click OK again to close the System Properties window.

Identification Changes ? X

You can change the name and the membership of this computer. Changes may affect access to network resources.

Computer name:
`vsi-pdh9je9dowo`

Full computer name:
`vsi-pdh9je9dowo.`

More...

Member of
- ○ Domain:
- ● Workgroup:
  `VELTE.COM`

OK   Cancel

• Adding a Windows 2000 client to a domain

Step 8	Windows 2000 will ask you if you want to reboot the computer now or later. Click Yes and the computer will restart.

To check your connection to the network, follow these steps:

Step 1	Once the computer restarts, log in with your username and password.

<table>
<tr><td>

Step 2
</td><td>

On the desktop, double-click My Network Places, and then double-click the Entire Network icon.
</td></tr>
<tr><td>

Step 3
</td><td>

Select the Entire Contents link, and then double-click the Microsoft Windows Network icon. If you are properly connected, it will look similar to the illustration shown here.
</td></tr>
</table>

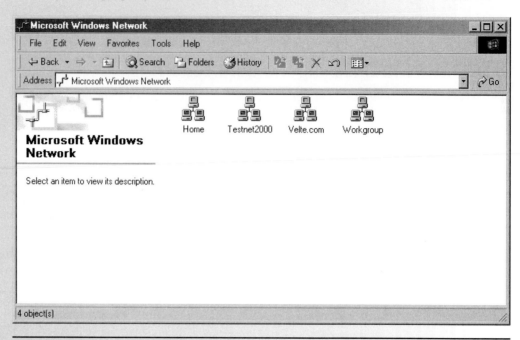

- If you are properly connected to the domain, you will see all the computers in your network.

Step 4

Double-click your domain icon and you will see all the computers in your network.

Logging On

After you add a Windows 2000 Professional workstation to your domain and check your connection, when it comes time to log onto the network, Windows 2000 proceeds through three steps.

1. *The user requests admission to the ticket-granting service for the domain.* To accomplish this, an Authentication Service (AS) Exchange occurs between the Kerberos Security Support Provider (SSP) on the computer and the Kerberos Key Distribution Center (KDC) for the user's account domain. If the process is successful, the user will receive a ticket-granting ticket (TGT) that can be used for future logons.

2. *The user requests a ticket for the computer.* A Ticket Granting Service (TGS) Exchange occurs between the Kerberos SSP on the computer and the KDC for the user's account domain. The result is a ticket the user can present when requesting permission to access the network.

3. *The user requests permission to local system services on the computer.* In this step, the Kerberos SSP on the computer presents a session ticket

to the Local Security Authority (LSA) on the computer. If the computer and the user are on different domains, an additional step is necessary. Before requesting a ticket for the computer, the Kerberos SSP must first ask the user's domain account KDC for a TGT good for admission to the KDC in the computer's account domain. Next, it presents the TGT to that KDC for a session ticket for the computer.

Mixed vs. Native Mode

Windows 2000 can function under one of two modes: **native mode** and **mixed mode**. Native mode is the environment created when both server and client are running Windows 2000. Mixed mode is an environment where client and server are running on different operating systems. As you might expect, mixed mode does not provide the extras and enhanced operability that you get in native mode. For example:

- **Security** While in mixed mode, the Kerberos security feature cannot be used. Rather, the network must revert to Windows NT's SAM security features.

- **Computer naming** Windows NT does not support DDNS for naming computers on a network. In mixed mode, computers must follow NetBIOS naming conventions of 16 characters or less.

Licensing in Windows 2000

In Windows 2000, licenses are maintained on a license server, which is a computer on which Terminal Services Licensing is enabled. Licenses are stored and tracked on the license server. Before any licenses can be issued, a terminal server must be able to connect to a license server. The license server is administered with two tools, the Terminal Services Licensing tool and the License Reporting tool.

The principal tool is the Terminal Services Licensing tool, which can be accessed by opening Terminal Services Licensing in Administrative Tools. Figure 6.4 shows what this application looks like.

This tool is used to manage the following attributes:

- Activating the license server

- Installing licenses

- Viewing licenses, both issued and available

- Advanced options such as deactivating a license server

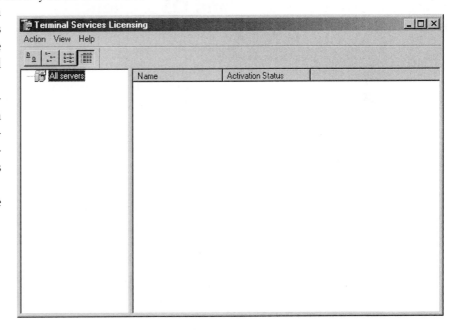

• **Figure 6.4**   Windows 2000 Terminal Services Licensing tool

The license server manages a multitude of licenses necessary under Windows 2000. Some of the licenses include

- **Terminal Services client access licenses (CALs)**   For non-Windows 2000 devices connecting to a Terminal server.

- **Terminal Services Internet connector licenses**   For anonymous use of a Terminal server by nonemployees across the Internet.

- **Built-in licenses**   Clients running Windows 2000 are automatically licensed as Terminal Services Clients.

- **Temporary licenses**   For terminal servers that request a license, but if the license server has none to give, it will issue a temporary license.

The second tool is the License Reporting tool, which is available on the Windows 2000 Resource Kit. The License Reporting tool translates the license server database information into a text file for reporting and analysis.

■ Non-NT Client Connections

For non-Windows NT or 2000 clients, there are different processes that take place to allow these workstations to participate in a Windows domain. Windows 2000 uses its Terminal Services feature (we discuss this later in the chapter) to enable connections to a multitude of non-Windows machines to a Windows 2000 network. Below is a brief description of the steps other clients take to get connected and use resources on a Windows network.

MS-DOS, LAN Manager 2.2c, and OS 2 Clients

NT Server includes the Network Client Administrator program in its Administrative Tools. This program can be used to take the client software that is supplied on the NT Server installation CD-ROM and share it from the CD or from a hard drive on the server. It can also create floppy disks that can be used for a hands-on installation of the client software on DOS, Windows 3.1, or LAN Manager v 2.2c Servers and Workstations. Adding the 32-bit TCP/IP protocol to Windows 3.11 is also supported by the Network Client Administrator. One further feature is that the function of Network Client Administrator can be loaded to non-NT Server machines, including Windows 3.11 and Win 95 computers. This can keep from burdening a server with the task of making sets of startup and installation floppy disks for configuring clients. You need to make system-startup floppy disks in the same format and the same operating system as the one that will be used on the client machine. One can always have a multiple-boot DOS/Windows 3.11/Win 95 machine that can be used for generating the correctly formatted disks and then also run the Network Client Administrator to load the data to the floppies.

When you open the Network Client Administrator, you have four actions you can take:

- Make a startup disk for DOS or Windows clients.

- Make a startup disk that will place software on the local hard drive.

- Copy client-administration tools to another computer.

- View Remoteboot information from clients.

Windows 2000's Terminal Services contains a similar service for linking non-2000 clients. Terminal Services is discussed in greater depth later in this chapter.

DOS or Windows Startup Disk

Make an installation startup disk for a DOS or Windows client. This should be a system disk (that is, formatted with the /s argument). You must be ready to provide the client configuration information and have an appropriately formatted bootable floppy to complete this operation. The first dialog box after choosing to make a startup disk determines the location of the appropriate files to be used, as illustrated in Figure 6.5. The first time the Network Client Administrator is run, the default location is the NT Server CD-ROM, and you can choose to always get the files from there, or place them on and access them from a hard drive. Once a choice has been made about where the installation files will be kept, the dialog box remembers the location that was last used.

The next dialog box is the Target Workstation Configuration dialog box that allows choice of floppy size, the network client startup to install onto the floppy, and what adapter card is in the client.

Next, you will see the Network Startup Disk Configuration dialog box (Figure 6.6). It requires you to enter the computer name that has been assigned or has already been in use, the user name, the domain name that the client will be a part of, and the network protocol that will be the primary protocol. The choices are the IPX protocol, TCP/IP, and NetBEUI. If the client needs to be able to browse outside its network segment, TCP/IP should be chosen. When TCP/IP is chosen, you also can then choose to enable DHCP configuration or directly enter the IP number, subnet mask, and gateway address for the machine.

After this information is accepted, you will be prompted to place the disk into the drive. The necessary files will then be copied to the floppy. Be aware that the information on the disk assumes default settings exist on whatever adapter card was specified. If the card has other settings (for example, a different base address or IRQ), you can change the values by editing the appropriate section of the PROTOCOL.INI file. The title of the specific section containing that information will vary from adapter to adapter, so you need to be familiar with the hardware in each client to easily make the necessary changes. Booting the client with this disk in the boot floppy drive will configure the client and connect to the network. It does not, however, install the client software on the local hard drive.

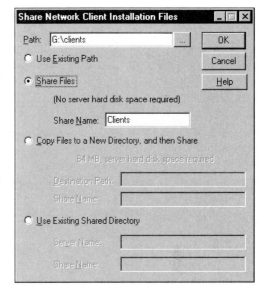

• **Figure 6.5**   Selecting the share network client installation files

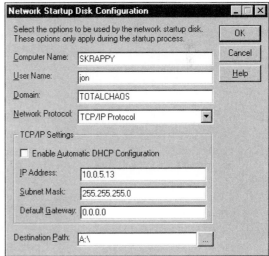

• **Figure 6.6**   The Network Startup Disk configuration settings

Network Installation Disks

The second task of the Network Client Administrator is to produce disks that can permanently set up the client software on the local hard drive.

When you select the Make Installation Disk Set option, you will see the same screen to choose the location of the files needed as you do when making a startup disk. Once that decision has been made, you select the client that you want to have install disks made for. The options on that dialog box include the TCP/IP-32 3.11b protocol for Windows 3.11. The number of disks required for different clients varies, but there is a prompt in the dialog box that tells you how many disks you will need (one for TCP/IP, two for the MS-DOS Client, and four for LAN Manager 2.2c for DOS or OS/2).

Copy Administration Client Tools

The third option in the Network Client Administrator is to copy the client tools to another computer.

Selecting this option takes you to a dialog box that is very similar to the dialog that is seen for the prior two options. For this function, the purpose is to specify where the NT tools will be copied. The location is presumed to be an existing network resource, and it will require 16MB of hard-disk space. The contents of the \Clients folder and subfolders from the NT Server installation CD-ROM will be copied to the target directory, and the \Srvtools folder will be set up as a shared resource. This permits an administrator to run the Win 95 and NT tools contained in those directories from a non-NT Server machine to avoid using server CPU resources. The folders containing the files necessary to create the startup or installation disks are contained in the shared directory. Unfortunately, the Network Client Administrator tool is not transferred to the target client machine. However, the program can be run via its share on the server if needed.

Remoteboot Clients

The final option in the Network Client Administrator concerns clients that have been set up to boot their operating system off a server, thus the term Remoteboot clients. You can view information about the Remoteboot client from this menu. You cannot configure Remoteboot clients from this dialog box; that is done via the Remoteboot Manager on the server.

The use of the Network Client Administrator to configure LAN Manager and DOS clients makes the job easier if you have never done this before. It is always good to have a source of configuration disks in case of system problems, and this makes creation of these tools easy. With the startup disks one can boot a machine, make a network connection, and then continue the installation from a network drive rather than floppies. Still, the system requires a trip to the machine, and that is not as appealing as being able to install or upgrade machines remotely, which is the direction things must go for the enterprise to function in the most cost-effective manner.

Windows 3.11

Connecting existing Windows 3.11 workstations is fairly easy since Windows 3.11 uses the Server Message Block protocol used in NT. NetBEUI is also the default protocol in Microsoft Networking in Windows 3.11. This discussion assumes that Windows 3.11 workstations have Microsoft Networking installed. If there are other protocols in place, such as NetWare or Sun PC-NFS, you will have to determine if maintaining those protocols and their drivers is worthwhile after implementing the connection to the NT network. In most cases, access to resources on these other platforms can be provided to the Windows 3.11 workstations via NT Server, and this can free memory in the application-critical 640KB space on these machines. As always, it is recommended that you verify the functionality of this change before making permanent changes to a large number of workstations.

Step-by-Step 6.2

Logging on from Windows 3.11 to Windows NT

For this exercise, you will need to have the user accounts, profiles, and rights in place before you configure the Windows 3.11 workstations. You will need the following:

- A functioning Windows NT Server computer connected to the LAN

- A client computer with Windows 3.11 installed, connected to the LAN

- Windows 3.11 installation media

Step 1   In the Program Manager, open the Network Group and double-click Network Setup.

Step 2   If the dialog box does not indicate that the Microsoft Windows Network (version 3.11) is present, click the Networks button and select support for Microsoft Networking. If you have made the decision to eliminate support for other networking platforms, you can remove these at this time.

Step 3   When you are finished, click OK to return to the main Setup menu.

Step 4   If there are disk drives or printers that you intend to share on the network, be sure that the main menu dialog box states "You Can Share Your Files And Printers With Others." If it doesn't, click the Sharing button and then click the check boxes indicating that you want to share those resources. Clear these check boxes if you do not want to share Windows 3.11 resources on the network. Click OK to return.

Step 5   Check in the drivers window to be sure that the TCP/IP-32 3.11b driver is installed. If it is not, it is available on the NT Server CD-ROM in the \Clients\Tcp32wfw\Netsetup folder. The Network Client Administrator tool can create a floppy disk for installing this or can share the installation files over the network.

Step 6   Finally, click OK from the main Setup menu to begin the install process for any changes that have been made. You will be prompted to reboot the computer after this. If the Microsoft Network has not been installed before, you will need to reboot now. Otherwise, click the Continue button.

Step 7   After rebooting or clicking Continue, you continue the configuration by selecting Network Group | Control Panel.

Double-click Network to open the Microsoft Windows Network dialog box, shown here.

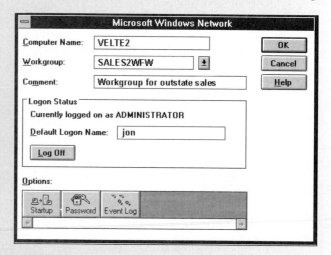

Verify the computer name. Remember, for Windows 3.11 workstations that are being added to an NT network, the network administrator should verify this name so that it does not conflict with any other computer names in use on the network.

In the Workgroup box, select or enter the name of the NT domain that the workstation will become a part of. You can also add a 48-character comment.

For the default logon name, enter the username for the account (or one of the accounts) that has been set up on the NT server for this computer.

Under Options, click the Startup button. This will bring up the Startup Settings window.

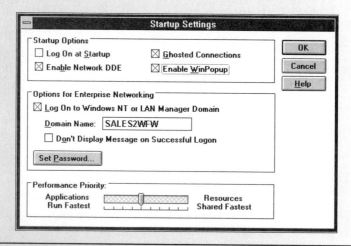

• Setting the startup parameters

Uncheck the Log On At Startup box. Check the box for Log On To Windows NT under the Options for Enterprise Networking and enter the NT domain name (and be sure it is the same as the Workgroup name from the prior screen. Click Set Password.

Step 14	The window shown next contains the Domain authentication information, where you set the Windows 3.11 password. The username and password entered here must match that of the account setup in the NT domain specified, or logon will fail.

This method establishes a domain login for Windows 3.11 users and is the most restrictive method for connecting, but also the most secure. The restrictions require that users go to the Change Domain Password screen to change their password, but this does keep their logon and network resource account information synchronized. This also allows the users to have their profiles and rights managed at the domain level. Windows 3.11 users will be able to connect to network drives and even mount them for reconnection at startup. These connections are made through the File Manager.

Note: You can also make network connections from within an application's File Open dialog box. If the File Manager is open when you make such a connection, this new resource will not appear in the File Manager. Closing File Manager and reopening it will display the information created outside the File Manager.

File Shares

Once you have connected the Windows 3.11 workstation to the network, sharing files can be accomplished from the File Manager. Selecting Disk | Share As or clicking on the icon of the familiar hand holding a folder will bring up the Share Directory dialog box. From that window you can share entire drives or directories within drives. As indicated earlier, you cannot have file ownership for Windows 3.11 files as you can for NTFS.

The security for access to shared resources on the Windows 3.11 machine is minimal. A failed login does not deny the user access to local resources on the Windows 3.11 machine. Furthermore, anyone with direct access to the machine can boot off a floppy disk and have complete access to files. If this is a concern, there are password-protection products offered, such as the Norton Utilities or Central Point Software Utilities. These methods will prevent easy access to sensitive files, but cannot prevent a malicious user from reformatting a hard drive. Don't be lulled into a false sense of security when using the Domain Logon method with Windows 3.11. The usual rule applies: If a resource is sensitive or vital, the machine needs to be physically locked away from unwanted users.

Win 95

Since Windows 95 represents Microsoft's improved Windows 3.11 product, the same functionality (and unfortunately many of the limitations) applies to Win 95 that applied to Windows 3.11. Since the Win 95 GUI was added to NT 4.0, many elements of configuring Win 95 will be very familiar.

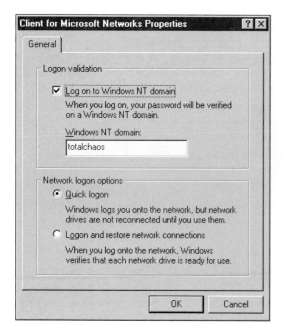

● **Figure 6.7**   Setting the Win 95 client for NT domains

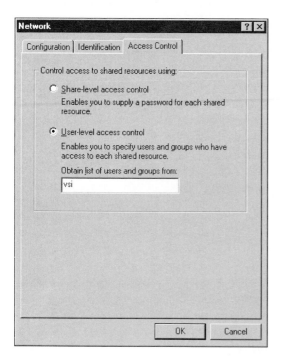

● **Figure 6.8**   Setting the access control

Logon

Clicking on the Network icon in the Control Panel will display the Network Properties window. To connect a Win 95 workstation to the NT network and set up for domain logon as we did for Windows 3.11, the Client for Microsoft Networks must be installed and selected as the Primary Network Logon. Select the Client for Microsoft Networks and click the Properties button. Then you will see a window similar to Figure 6.7. Check the Log On To Windows NT domain box and type in the name of the NT domain where the user accounts have been created for those users who will log on from this machine.

TCP/IP protocol must also be installed and configured correctly for the network. If you intend to share files and/or printers connected to the Win 95 machine, you must have the File and Printer Sharing for Microsoft Networks Service installed. After you verify the correct TCP/IP, DNS, WINS, and bindings settings, click OK to return to the Network dialog box and click the Identification tab. Verify that the computer name is the correct one. As with Windows 3.11 workstations, an administrator should verify that the pre-existing Win 95 machine name does not conflict with existing names on the network. Finally, return to the Network dialog window and click the Access Control tab. If you want to have users log on using NT Server domain authentication, select User-Level Access Control and enter the name of the domain that will authenticate the user accounts, as illustrated in Figure 6.8.

Caution is again urged regarding the image of security created by having the Network Logon authentication. If a user simply hits the Cancel button at the network logon, logon is *not* aborted. The Win 95 client cannot browse resources that depend on a successful login to an NT domain, but the shares for local resources and nondomain resources (Win 95 or Windows 3.11, for example) are still available on the network. Changes made to those shares are also propagated to the network. This means that an unauthorized person can sit at a Win 95 machine and take its shares offline (of course they can simply reformat an entire hard disk if they want also).

File Shares

Windows 95 shares are functionally identical to Windows 3.11 shares in terms of security. There are, however, some differences in terms of the access given to users who connect to the shares over the network. From the File Manager or Explorer, right-click the drive or directory to be shared and select Sharing. The next window allows you to select the users that will be given access to the share and what level of access they will be granted. If you have set up the Win 95 client for network login, then the list of possible users is provided from the Server that the user logs in to. The Read-Only and Full Access options are self-explanatory, but the Custom user rights are a new feature in Windows 95. With the Custom rights method you can allow a network user to read and write to a directory and, in the example shown in Figure 6.9, create a new file or folder. These users would not be permitted to delete files or directories, however.

■ Services for Macintosh

Windows NT and 2000 Server includes well-developed services for giving Mac clients access to Windows network resources and even allows Mac user accounts to be authenticated and managed by Windows Domain Controllers. Many existing Mac networks utilize the AppleTalk network protocol and hardware. Connecting AppleTalk hardware to NT can be accomplished by placing Ethernet cards into the Mac clients. This will improve the network speed over AppleTalk, although many older Macs cannot add Ethernet cards. There are AppleTalk cards available for machines running NT (be sure to verify the hardware compatibility before buying). Another method would be to place an AppleTalk network onto the Ethernet via a LocalTalk/Ethernet router. If this hardware is already in place, then no additional hardware or software is required to connect the Mac clients.

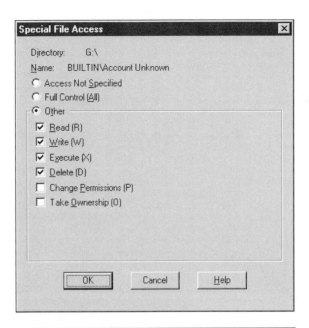

● **Figure 6.9**   Setting custom rights on files

Installing the Service for the Macintosh (SfM)

You can install SfM by clicking on the Network icon in the Control Panel. Click the Services tab and click the Add button. Select Services for Mac from the Service list and click OK. Provide the information on the location of the source files and continue. Once the files have been installed on the server, click the Close button. The bindings will be reevaluated, and then the dialog box for Microsoft AppleTalk Protocol Properties will open and you can specify the network card, AppleTalk zone, and routing settings, as shown in Figure 6.10. Once these settings are as desired, click OK. When you close the Network window, you see the typical NT prompt to reboot the machine; however, apparently the SfM does not require this. The reboot is not damaging, of course, just time consuming.

On leaving the Network window or after a restart, you will find two new tools available. In the Control Panel there is a MacFile icon, and in the Administrative Tools folder on the Start Menu there is now a File Manager entry. The MacFile icon is the Mac Server service, which will have been started if you performed a reboot. If you skipped the boot, clicking on the MacFile icon will generate a message indicating the service has not started. Answer Yes to the request to start it, and once the service is operating you will see the MacFile server window, which is similar to the familiar Server window for NT, shown here.

In Windows 2000 networks, Win 95 clients must upgrade via a service pack to be compatible with the new Active Directory namespace. NT 4.0 clients should upgrade to Windows 2000 to take full advantage of the Windows 2000 features.

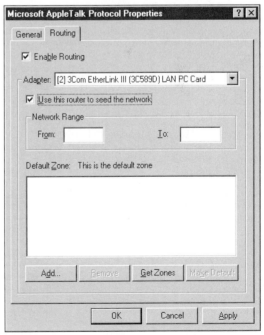

Logon

Macintosh users must log on to be able to

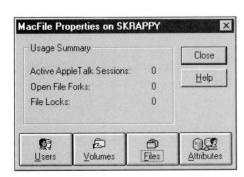

● **Figure 6.10**   Configuring the AppleTalk protocol

gain access to the volumes created using MacFile (described in the next section) or printers shared on the Windows network. If the Mac users have existing accounts within the Windows network, these Windows accounts can be applied to the Macintosh logon. Mac logon can be configured for three levels. These can be selected from the MacFile Server icon in the Control Panel by pressing the Attributes button (see Figure 6.11):

- **Guest**   Check the Allow Guests To Logon box and clear the Require Microsoft Authentication box. Valid Macintosh users that do not have NT network accounts could access SfM-created volumes. Guest accounts would have to be enabled on the NT Server that was being logged onto, but a nice feature is that Guest accounts can be enabled for the NT network and disabled for Mac users by clearing the Allow Guests To Logon box. You should be sure your organization's security policies allow for guest accounts before considering this option.

- **Standard AppleShare Authentication**   Be sure the Require Microsoft Authentication box is cleared. Mac authentication occurs via the AppleShare client software, which is located in the Chooser in MacOS. This system employs clear-text passwords of a maximum of eight characters.

- **NT-Based Authentication**   Do not check the Require Microsoft Authentication box (see illustration) until after the needed files have been copied to the Mac client. After configuration, users will have to use the User Authentication Module (UAM) that Microsoft has included with SfM. Mac users will now provide their NT username and password when connecting to the NT server. This is the standard NT encrypted password that can be up to 14 characters. The Microsoft UAM must be configured on the Macintosh client to implement this option. On the Mac, select the Chooser and from the dialog box select AppleShare (see Figure 6.12).

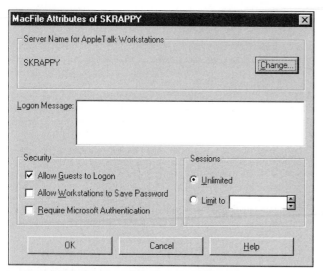

● **Figure 6.11**   The MacFile Attributes window

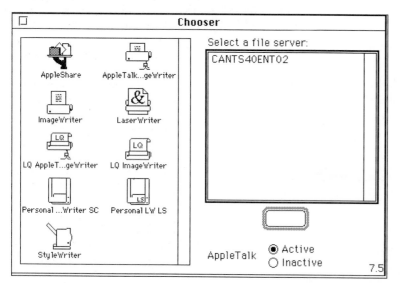

● **Figure 6.12**   Selecting AppleShare within the Mac's Chooser

Pick the AppleTalk zone that was chosen when the SfM was installed on the Windows Server. This will produce a list of servers in that zone, and you can select the Windows server. Clicking on OK will take you to the logon box, where logon is based on either of the first two methods detailed above. Clicking OK will open the server dialog displaying available Mac volumes located on the Windows Server.

When SfM creates a Mac volume, a Microsoft UAM Volume is created, and that will appear in the server list. Select that volume, click OK, and exit the Chooser. Open the Microsoft UAM Volume that should now be on the Mac Desktop. Also open the System Folder for the Mac and locate the AppleShare folder within it. If there is no AppleShare folder, drag and drop the AppleShare folder from the UAM Volume into the System folder. If there is an existing AppleShare folder on the Mac, open the UAM AppleShare folder, select the MS UAM file, and copy it (drag and drop it) into the AppleShare folder on the Mac.

This installation will produce a change in the logon dialog box that Mac users will see when they select to log on to the NT Server. The NT-encrypted username and password authentication based on their NT account are now used to log on to volumes on the NT Server.

Volumes

To create the Macintosh-accessible volumes, open the File Manager from the Administrative Tools. Select the folder that will become a volume, and either select MacFile/Create Volume or click the MacFile—Create Volume icon on the toolbar. You then can provide the Volume Name that Mac users will see. The path is filled in with the resource that you selected. The Password is a security measure *solely* for Mac users. It is not the password associated with the logon account for the user, and it is not relevant for NT clients accessing the same directory. You can also specify Volume Security and the number of users who can connect to the resource.

The volume created contains all elements of the directory tree below the topmost level. You cannot create a separate volume for a subdirectory within the directory tree. If you require separate volume names and access privileges, you must place the desired folders in independent directory trees. Furthermore, if you create a volume for a folder, no new volume can be created that would include that volume. You can see an example of this if you try and create a volume for the entire drive that contains the *%systemroot%* path—you will find that you are told you can't create a volume within another volume. This occurs because the installation of the SfM creates a volume, Microsoft UAM Volume, in that drive. Shown here is a section of a directory tree.

In this tree, the folder labeled MacShare is a volume. The only folder in the figure that could also be created as a volume is the folder MacVolumes. All the other folders are excluded from becoming volumes because MacShare is in their directory tree.

All the information generated in this process is irrelevant for NT clients on the network. The NTFS resources are unaffected by having the access for Mac clients added. Furthermore, if access to Macintosh clients is no longer desired, removal of SfM can be implemented. In this situation, the volumes disappear from Macintosh users, but the files remain as directories on the NTFS drives and are accessible to the NT network as usual.

■ Gateway Services for Novell Networks

Given the large installed base of Novell networks, it is unavoidable that the integration of NetWare resources would be an important consideration

The exact appearance of this dialog box depends on the version of MacOS running on the client and how the options for logon are set for the Mac server level. Users may or may not see options for Guest and clear-text logons. Even if these are visible, once the Use Microsoft Authentication box is checked from the MacFile Server Attributes window, however, only the NT Server will accept the Microsoft UAM logon.

If you create a volume from any folder located on a hard drive larger than 2GB, you will be warned that MacOS limitations may make Mac clients malfunction.

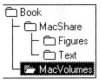

Remember that these volumes cannot be created in FAT-formatted resources. When DOS and Windows 3.11 users view the shared volume, NTFS will create a standard DOS 8+3 filename for longer Mac filenames (which can be up to 31 characters). If Mac users will share extensively with clients using the shorter DOS filename limits, it is wise to have the Mac users restrict their filenames to avoid problems with filename recognition. The advantage of this is that Mac users cannot see the 8+3 names that NTFS will create to pass along to DOS clients. A Mac user that sometimes uses both long and 8+3 filenames could be prevented from saving a file because a file already exists with the 8+3 name. These names created by NTFS from long names are not visible to the Mac user.

when implementing Windows into the enterprise. Realistically, Microsoft would like to take over Novell's customers, and Novell would like to counter Microsoft's surge into their markets. The devotion expressed for one system over the other often has more to do with opinion than experience based on comparative testing of both products in their suitability for the tasks demanded. It is not the purpose of this section to determine which product is the more appropriate for general or specific environments or tasks. A description of the integration tools available from Microsoft will follow. If you have existing Novell installations, you are likely to be aware of Novell's recent efforts at providing their own Windows integration tools.

You must test for yourself which methods are the most beneficial for your situation. A recommended strategy would be to consider what operating system would be the backbone OS for your network. Whether it is Novell or Windows, the client software should be whatever best fits with the overall architecture.

The following sections discuss the NetWare integration tools based in NT Server and Windows 2000. NT Workstation has some similar components. Specifically, the NWLINK IPX/SPX protocol is installed by default, and there is a Client Service for NetWare (CSNW) that parallels the Gateway Service for NetWare (GSNW) provided by Windows NT and 2000 Server. These Workstation elements would not likely be selected for implementation in the enterprise environment where the more elaborate Server tools are available.

A final caveat is that care should be taken to stay abreast of patches released by both Microsoft and Novell for all relevant products. Technical-support departments must face the realities of keeping their customers functional. This means that solutions to problems are generated in response to known problems, but the complexity of the enterprise means that new, unforeseen problems are likely, especially with the continued roll-out of new versions of the operating systems and the existence of the varied legacy client systems.

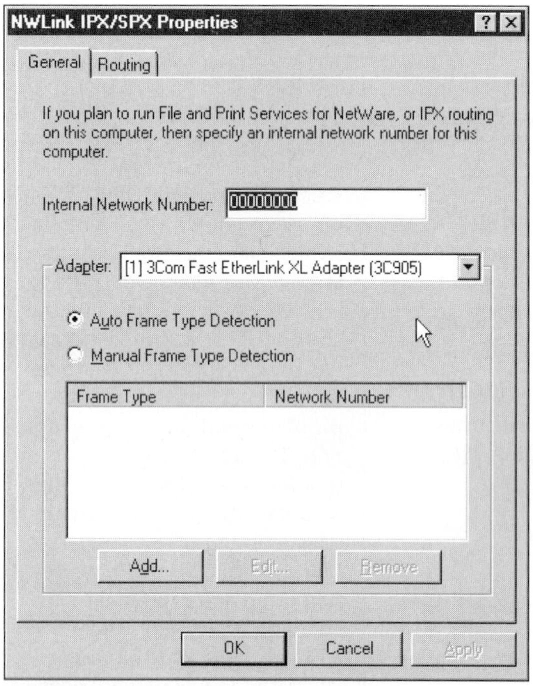

NWLink Protocol

We will just briefly describe the NWLink IPX/SPX protocol, which underlies all of Windows' NetWare integration tools. This stack is installed by default with Windows NT and 2000 Server or Workstation, and it provides the means for NetWare clients using IPX/SPX to access Windows NT and 2000 Servers. To set up the protocol, click the Network icon in the Control Panel, or right-click the Network Neighborhood and choose Properties. In Figure 6.13 you see the NT Server Properties window. This displays the Internal Network Number associated with the network adapter card. This value will be 0 unless the server has more than one Ethernet card installed. If there are multiple adapters, each one can be selected, and the Internal Network Number that you want to associate with each adapter can be set. Finally, the frame type can be specified. The default setting is Auto, which makes the NT machine examine the network at power-up so that it can determine the type or types of frames that are being used. For

• **Figure 6.13**   Configuring NWLink IPX/SPX protocol properties example, NetWare 2.2 and 3.1 have a default of Ethernet 802.3, but NetWare 4.0 uses 802.2.

To select manual frame type, you press the Add button, and this brings up the window shown in Figure 6.14. Making this selection will have a faster response since there is no time taken to examine the frames present on the network. If you specify the frame type, you can have multiple manual selections, and these can each have their own Network Number assigned. This arrangement can be used in combination with multiple network cards in a server to permit selective routing of different frame types, which can improve the throughput of servers. To make this possible, select the Routing tab from the NWLINK Properties window and check the Enable Routing box. You also have to install the Router Information Protocol (RIP) service.

There are a substantial number of parameters underlying NWLink behavior that can be set by editing the Registry. A full description of these can be found in Microsoft article PSS ID#:Q99745, available on the TechNet CD or the Microsoft Support web site (`support.microsoft.com/support/`). Remember that the Performance Monitor can look at NWLink relevant counters for IPX, NetBIOS, and SPX traffic that may be combined with changes to the Registry to achieve specific performance goals.

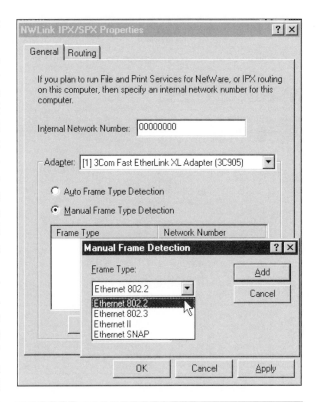

• Figure 6.14 Selecting manual frame types for NWLink

Gateway Services for NT

Installation of the Gateway Services for NetWare (GSNW) on an NT Server provides the integration tool that can offer access to NetWare resources for clients on the NT network. As mentioned earlier, network drivers do exist for Windows 3.11, Win 95, and NT Workstation machines, but providing the service through the NT Server removes the need to maintain the protocols on every client. The administrative load to maintain such functions would be too great in the enterprise, which is why we are not considering those platforms. Another consideration is that GSNW does not work with Novell's IntranetWare.

GSNW has the attraction that clients of NT networks no longer need to have a NetWare-compatible protocol stack running along with the NDIS stack. All requests for NetWare resources are sent through the gateway using standard NT protocols, and the gateway handles the communication with the Novell Server. This obviously places the workload squarely on the Server and GSNW, and a user familiar with NetWare performance that is migrated to NT may notice the difference.

Double-clicking the GSNW icon in the Control Panel will bring up the initial Gateway dialog box, as shown in Figure 6.15. To begin the setup, select the NetWare server that will be the preferred server for the gateway. You can also select Tree and Context information, determine print options, and have Novell logon scripts run if desired. The latter plan can cause problems in NT with drive-letter assignments if the Novell use of drive letters in the logon conflicts with NT. Users can still connect to all desired resources,

This is another place to remind you that multiple-client environments must involve compromises, and that means time. However, a less diverse client environment may restore the performance losses incurred by the multiple-client situation.

As you can see, the gateway concept means that all NT clients will access the NetWare resources that will be specified for this gateway through a single username and password. There may be many enterprise environments that will not accept such an arrangement. At this time, there is no way to avoid this since GSNW accomplishes its task by creating a single share, and all client access from the NT side goes through that point.

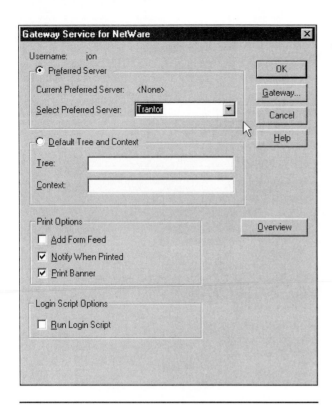

● **Figure 6.15**   Selecting the preferred NetWare server in GSNW

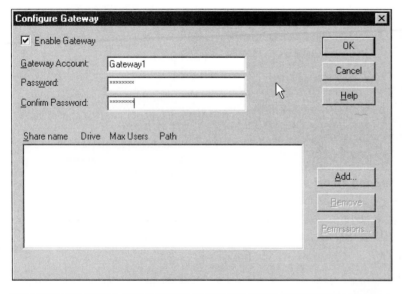

● **Figure 6.16**   Configuring the GSNW gateway

map connections, and have those connections restored at bootup by using the File Manager or Explorer instead of the logon script.

Once you have made the server selection, press the Gateway button to bring up the Configure Gateway dialog box, as shown in Figure 6.16. Check the Enable Gateway box and enter the gateway account name and password. This gateway name is what NT clients will see, so you need to employ a naming strategy that will be familiar to users that are also NetWare clients some of the time. Now you hit the Add button to designate the NetWare resources that will be mapped to the gateway that has been created.

The final step is to specify the resources to share through the gateway, as shown in Figure 6.17. Here you enter the share name (which will be visible to NT clients), the Novell network path to map to that share name (which will not be visible to NT clients), a comment (which can be used to help NT clients recognize NetWare resources that they may know by their NetWare path), and finally a drive letter that the share will be mapped to. Clicking OK will return to the prior menu, and you can repeat the process to make more resources available through the gateway, with the obvious limitation of how many drive letters are free on the server.

NT Server includes an Administrative tool and the Migration tool for NetWare. The tools functions in concert with GSNW when you are both the NT Administrator and NetWare supervisor. The program is designed to allow bringing NetWare user accounts (minus passwords) to NT. While this is an appealing concept, it is limited by the failure of user rights to map perfectly from Novell to NT. For example, the NetWare rights of Grace logins, restrictions on user space, the number of connections, and requiring login from specific workstations does not exist for NT users. Nevertheless, the Migration tool may offer some attractions, and an administrator can perform a test migration that creates log files that will allow evaluation of the success or failure of the process.

Microsoft has introduced two more products that further enhance the chances of migration. The File and Print Services for NetWare (FPNW) and Directory Services Manager for NetWare (DSMN) do not ship with NT Server and must be purchased separately from Microsoft. FPNW, as the name suggests, helps to provide support migration by providing access to applications and files for both NT and NetWare clients. In the context of the Migration tool, when this tool is used with an NT server that is running the

FPNW Server, several of the NetWare user properties that do not normally migrate are now accommodated. DSMN does not require FPNW, but certainly would be valuable in cases where migration was implemented using FPNW. The DSMN is designed to synchronize dual user information (as well as group information) that will exist during the migration process. This means that the SAM database in NT would be linked to the NetWare bindery security database.

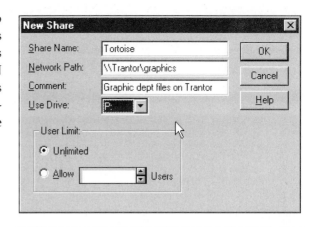

• **Figure 6.17**   Defining a new share for use through GSNW

Windows 2000 Gateway Services for NetWare

Like Windows NT, Gateway Services for NetWare is included with Windows 2000 Server and enables a Windows 2000 Server to connect with computers running NetWare 3.*x* and 4.*x*. Logon script support is also included. Administrators can use Gateway Services to provide gateways for client computer access to files and printers. These features are all on Windows 2000, and no changes are needed to the NetWare client software.

Windows 2000 Professional also includes client services for NetWare. This tool allows Windows 2000 workstations to connect to NetWare servers running NetWare 2.*x*, 3.*x* and 4.*x*. Like Windows 2000 Server, logon script support is also included.

Creating a Gateway

Creating a gateway on Windows 2000 requires a few steps. First, your NetWare server must have a group named NTGATEWAY. Then, you must have a user account on both the NetWare network and the NTGATEWAY group, along with the necessary rights to access it.

The first step is to install a NetWare Gateway. This puts the necessary applications into your Windows 2000 Server, which will serve as the foundation for your gateway efforts.

Step-by-Step 6.3

Installing Gateway Service for NetWare

To complete this exercise, you will need the following:

- A server with Windows 2000 Server installed
- The Windows 2000 Server installation CD-ROM

- A working LAN card and connection on the server

Step 1   Open Network and Dial-up Connections by following Start | Settings | Network and Dial-up Connections.

Step 2	Right-click a local area connection, and then click Properties.
Step 3	On the General tab, click Install.

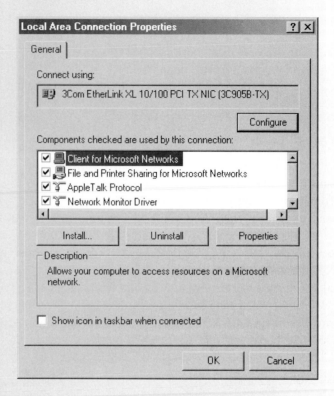

Step 4	In the Select Network Component Type dialog box, click Client and then click Add.
Step 5	In the Select Network Client dialog box, click Gateway (and Client) Services for NetWare, and then click OK.

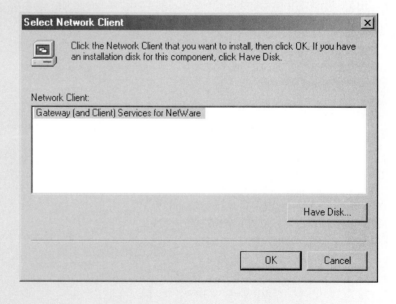

Enabling Gateway Services

Just installing Gateway Services was not enough. Now it is necessary to *enable* Gateway Services. Enabling makes the software link between the Windows 2000 Server and the NetWare server, completing the link. This is accomplished by following Step-by-Step 6.4.

Step-by-Step 6.4

Enabling Gateway Service for NetWare

To complete this exercise, you will need the following:

- A computer with Windows 2000 Server installed

- Gateway Service for NetWare installed onto the server (see Step-by-Step 6.3)

Step 1   Open Gateway Service for NetWare by following Start | Settings | Control Panel | and double-clicking GSNW.

Step 2   Click Gateway, and then select the Enable Gateway box.

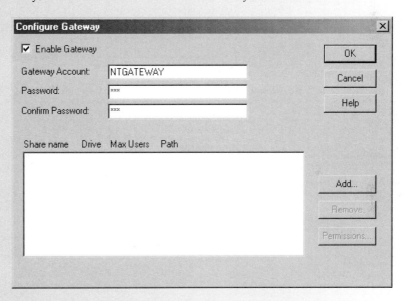

Step 3   In Gateway Account, type the name of your gateway account.

Step 4   In Password and Confirm Password, enter the gateway account password.

Step 5   Click OK and you're finished.

Activating Printer and File Gateways

Now that the Windows 2000 and NetWare servers have been linked through the install and enable process, you must now activate a gateway to each specific volume or printer to allow access to NetWare files and printers. By activating the gateway, you're establishing the resource and share for Windows 2000 clients' use. Step-by-Step 6.5 shows you how to activate a gateway to files:

Step-by-Step 6.5

Activating a File Gateway

To complete this exercise, you will need the following:

- A Windows 2000 Server computer on a LAN with Gateway Service for NetWare installed and activated (see preceding step-by-steps)

- A NetWare server on the LAN with an accessible shared folder or volume and printer queue

Step 1   Open Gateway Service for NetWare by following Start | Settings | Control Panel | and double-clicking GSNW.

Step 2   Select Gateway, and then choose the Enable Gateway box.

Step 3   Click Add to bring up the dialog box shown here. In Share Name, enter the share name clients will use to access the resource.

New Share		
Share Name:		OK
Network Path:		Cancel
Comment:		Help
Use Drive:	Z:	
User Limit:		
● Unlimited		
○ Allow [ ] Users		

Step 4   In Network Path enter the network path of the NetWare directory you want to share.

Step 5   In Use Drive, enter the drive your want to use as a default.

Step 6   Click Unlimited and then click OK.

To activate a gateway to printers:

Step 1   Open Printers by following Start | Settings | Printers.

Step 2   Select Add Printer, and then click Next.

Step 3   Select Network Printer, and then click Next.

Step 4   Under Name, enter the name of the printer in this format:

*servername**sharename*

Step 5

If you need to find the NetWare printer in Shared Printers, click Next.

Step 6

Follow the resulting instructions in the wizard to complete the process, as shown here.

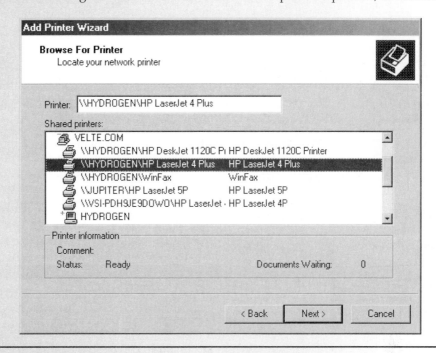

- The Add Printer Wizard will help configure a gateway to NetWare printers.

Step 7

Select the printer you just created and, under the File menu, click Properties.

Step 8

On the Sharing tab, select Shared. In the Shared As text box, enter a name for the printer.

Setting Permissions for NetWare Resources

Once Gateway Services for NetWare is installed, you can regulate how NetWare resources are available over the network. To set permissions for your NetWare resources, follow Step-by-Step 6.6.

> When connecting to NetWare resources, use Client Service for NetWare for frequent access or Gateway Service for NetWare for less frequent access. If you use Gateway Service for NetWare to provide a gateway to NetWare resources, you do not have to install NWLink IPX/SPX/NetBIOS Compatible Transport Protocol on clients.

Step-by-Step 6.6

Setting Gateway Permissions

To complete this exercise, you will need the following:

- A Windows 2000 Server on the LAN with Gateway Service for NetWare installed and functioning (see preceding step-by-steps)

- A NetWare server on the LAN
- Defined users (or groups of users) to which to assign to the Gateway Services resources

Step 1

Open Gateway Service for NetWare by following Start | Settings | Control Panel | and double-clicking GSNW.

Step 2

Select Gateway.

Step 3

Click the share on which you want to set permissions, and then click Permissions.

Step 4

To add users or groups, click Add. In Names, select the user or group, and then select Add. In Type of Access, click the permission for this user or group.

Step 5

To remove users or groups, select the user or group in the list of allowed users, and then click Remove.

Step 6

To change permissions for users or groups, select the user or group, and then select the level of access in Type of Access.

Microsoft Directory Synchronization Services

While Microsoft and Novell bicker over whose directory feature is better, Windows 2000 users can use the Microsoft Directory Synchronization Services to synch their Novell Directory Services (NDS) and Windows 2000 Active Directory, thereby ensuring remote changes to either directory are accurately reflected on the other. MSDSS uses three principles in directory synchronization: sessions, object-level synchronization, and directional synchronization.

Sessions   Sessions is the regular process of synchronizing NDS and Active Directory. To keep the directories in harmony, synchronization sessions are started on a regular basis. During each session, MSDSS queries each directory for changes and then swaps directory changes back and forth. MSDSS uses a map to compare an object's properties and location in one directory to its properties and location in the other, thus ensuring that the two directories are in synch.

Sessions are required for each pair of organizational units (OU) that are synchronized in Active Directory and NDS. Sessions must be established for each OU, and MSDSS supports up to 50 simultaneous sessions. Situations requiring more than 50 simultaneous sessions necessitate another MSDSS server.

Object-Level Synchronization   While in a synchronization session, MSDSS makes changes only to those objects in each directory that changed since the last time the directories were synchronized. No other information is altered. Object-level synchronization reduces network traffic and allows objects to be located differently in each directory.

Directional Synchronization   MSDSS allows flexibility in synchronization configurations, depending on the network's needs.

- **One-way synchronization**   Moves changes made in Active Directory to NDS, but does not reflect changes to Active Directory that were made in NDS. This is also known as `forward synchronization`. One-way synchronization is useful when an administrator want to centralize directory administration in Active Directory.

- **Two-way synchronization**   Looks at changes made in both Active Directory and NDS, and then makes the necessary updates on the other directory. This is also known as both *forward* and *reverse synchronization*. Reverse synchronization looks at changes made on an object on NDS and then changes Active Directory accordingly. Two-way synchronization is useful in situations where there is a need to manage both directories independently, but where common information is maintained on both.

Though directional synchronization requires administrators to decide which type of synchronization they prefer, they are not locked into it. MSDSS allows switching between one- and two-way synchronization.

MSDSS is configured with a wizard that is installed as a Microsoft Management Console snap-in. It allows administrators to view both the Active Directory and NDS trees, allowing a friendly user interface.

MSDSS supports synchronization between Active Directory and NetWare versions 4.0, 4.1, 4.11, 4.2, 5.0, and 5.1. It also allows synchronization between Active Directory and NetWare Binderies for version 3.1, 3.11, 3.12, and 3.2.

Enterprise Considerations in Novell Integration

While Microsoft has provided a means to have NetWare resources in the enterprise made accessible to Windows clients, this does not mean the enterprise network performance will be made satisfactory by implementing these tools. We will just mention several points that create difficulties for network administration and speed with both NetWare and NT systems present.

Using GSNW may provide user access to NetWare servers, but the work associated with dual sets of user accounts for Windows and Novell remains.

In addition, there are considerations that need to be made regarding the number of protocols your network can support. If your goal is to reduce the number of protocols (TCP/IP, IPX/SPX, NetBEUI) on your network, you will want to drive the technology in the direction of a single protocol. With NetWare 4.0, Novell moved into a TCP/IP environment. However, previous versions of NetWare are still found in many environments. Many networks support IPX/SPX on the local- and wide-area networks. The overhead of supporting the protocol is well known. Service Advertisement Protocol, commonly called SAP, is "broadcasted" throughout the network, consuming router and network resources much like NetBIOS broadcasts do. Additionally, IPX/SPX is not transportable over the Internet; it is tunneled in TCP/IP.

▪ Unix Connections

The long existence of Unix in networked environments has resulted in a growing number of products that permit the cross-platform sharing of resources between Windows and Unix systems. Sharing files across systems is now easily accomplished and includes the choice of sharing Unix drives to Windows clients using either the SMB or NFS protocols. We will give a specific example of sharing Unix via an SMB server and via an NFS server and then provide a listing of other products that are available. No special endorsement of the products used in the examples is intended. They were chosen due to their popularity and presence in a number of diverse organization types. As always, given the rapid changes in software capabilities, you must evaluate which offering is the best product given your specific needs.

File Servers

This section will consider the case of making Unix resources visible and "browseable" by NT network clients. The usefulness is straightforward—users who have Unix accounts and frequently work on Unix systems can gain access to their files without having to be sitting at a Unix workstation. Likewise, non-Unix users can easily place or retrieve files on the Unix system to exchange information. However, Unix applications cannot be run from a Windows client using the types of software described in this section. That requires the use of a different type of program such as X-Windows servers, which will be discussed in the next section.

SMB Server

One very popular means of providing Windows clients with access to Unix drives is the SAMBA server package. SAMBA is freeware that runs on Unix servers and provides NT clients access to Unix mounts. Before you turn away from the concept of using a noncommercial product in the enterprise, you need to know that SAMBA has been in existence for a considerable period and has been widely used in both academic environments (where it was developed) and several large corporate sites. SAMBA is a robust, well-tested, and well-documented software package that is definitely worth considering if your goal is to allow clients on a Windows network to read and save files that exist on Unix systems. Complete information and download of SAMBA source code can be obtained from the SAMBA web site (samba.anu.edu.au/samba/).

SAMBA is based on the Server Message Block (SMB) protocol that NT uses for sharing files. SAMBA works by the creation of Unix support for the SMB protocol. The SAMBA daemon responds to SMB requests from Windows network clients and becomes a server to respond to those requests.

Since SAMBA is a process that is installed entirely on Unix systems, a Unix systems administrator will need to install the SAMBA server. The Windows systems administrator has almost nothing to do when connecting network clients to a SAMBA server. If you are aware of the many various versions of Unix that may be in use, rest easy, because SAMBA is compatible with all major versions of Unix (such as products from Apollo, HP, DEC,

NeXT, SCO, Sun, and SGI among others). This section will include a brief description of the requirements for using SAMBA with Windows.

 If DNS is unavailable, the Unix machine DNS names and IP numbers can be placed in the HOSTS file located in the %*Systemroot*%\System32\ drivers\etc directory.

Windows Network Client Requirements   While there are no SAMBA client files that must be installed in Windows 3.11, Win 95, 2000, or NT machines, these computers must have appropriate network protocols and services running to be able to connect to the Unix machines that they will gain access to. These required elements are the TCP/IP protocol and DNS services.

Unix Configuration   The SAMBA server configuration is set in the `SMB.CONF` file. This text file has a section structure that would feel familiar to anyone who has edited the SYSTEM.INI file in Windows 3.11. There are separate sections for each share that will be created that permit setting valid users, read-write privileges, and public access.

There are also two sections that are very important for use in the enterprise environment with large numbers of clients. The [homes] section will automatically permit users that already have accounts on the Unix system to connect to their home directories without having to create individual shares for every account. The [global] section sets several comprehensive properties of the server. Of greatest importance are the security options that determine the method of authenticating users. There are three security modes that can be specified in the [global] section under the security= entries:

- **Security=share**   The *valid users* entry in each share section can specify specific users and their privileges within that share. This is a relatively insecure method and is limited to users who already have Unix accounts, so it is a poor method for general access for Windows network users within the enterprise.

- **Security=user**   In this mode, all authentication occurs via the Unix user accounts. In those cases where all Windows network clients also have accounts on the Unix system, this is a secure and efficient system. For those enterprises that already have Unix accounts for every user of the network, this is a viable option.

- **Security=server**   This mode is the clear choice when all users do not have or should not have Unix accounts. In this mode, user access is authenticated through a server other than the Unix SAMBA server, for example, an NT PDC. This could allow a single NT machine to grant access to both NT and SAMBA resources using a single database of usernames and passwords. It also has the great advantage of not requiring users to change their passwords on two different systems. When this entry is made in the [global] section, the name of the server that will perform the authentication must be added in the *password server=* entry.

This name will be the NetBIOS name of the server. For that machine to be found, it will have to be added to the /ETC/ HOSTS file on the Unix system.

A drawback to SAMBA is that it is only useful if your clients use SMB protocols. This will include Windows 3.11, Win 95, Windows 2000, and NT, but not NetWare or Macintosh clients.

NFS Servers

NFS represents a different approach to providing cross-platform file access between Unix and NT developed by Sun Microsystems, Inc. NFS does not

SAMBA does not yet support encrypted passwords, and NT 4 Service Pack 3 requires this. As a result, for SAMBA installations, Windows 3.11 and Win 95 clients can see the Unix resources, but NT clients cannot. The NT Registry can be edited to permit transmission of unencrypted passwords. In REGEDIT32 select the HKEY_LOCAL_MACHINE tree and go to the \system\currentcontrolset\services\rdr\parameters subkey. Add the new value EnablePlainTextPassword and specify the Data Type as REG_DWORD. Set the data value to 1 and exit the Registry Editor.

use the SMB protocols and instead relies on two means to provide the file access across PC-based and Unix systems. The communication between the server machines and clients employs Remote Procedure Calls (RPC) functioning at the session level. The actual data transfers are achieved via External Data Representation (XD) protocols that handle the translation across operating systems and computer hardware platforms. However, to the NT network user, there is little functional difference between NFS and SAMBA. Unix resources are browseable, and data can be read or written to Unix resources if the permissions are set to allow this.

Windows Network Client Configuration   Unlike SAMBA, NFS client software must be installed to provide the file-sharing services. This is because the RPC and XDR protocols are not built into the Microsoft network platform as is SMB. While this may seem to be a disadvantage, the only complication arises at the level of Windows 3.11 machines because of the need to use memory resources to load the network drivers for NFS. If Windows 3.11 machines must also load protocols for other networks, such as NT and NetWare, the computer may not have enough memory left over to run applications. Otherwise, the third-party NFS software client packages for PCs typically provide for easy installation.

This requirement for installing NFS client software also has the advantage that NFS for the Macintosh exists, and there is even an NFS Gateway for NetWare, although that has some drawbacks in terms of performance compared to full NFS client installations. The bottom line is that more platforms have NFS support than SAMBA.

User authentication is typically handled by the NFS client on the PC via a login window that will accept a username and password that is used to check against the Unix accounts database. If the logon is authenticated, there can be series of "mounts" of Unix resources that can be preconfigured by the user. This is similar to the Reconnect At Logon option for network drives in Microsoft networking. Any requests for connecting to new resources will invoke a comparison of the username and password that were entered at logon with the user permissions for the shared resource. The "mounted" NFS resource will appear as a new drive letter in the File Manager or Explorer just as with Windows shares, NetWare server resources, or SAMBA shares.

It is possible for only the NFS daemon on a Unix system to stop operating. When this occurs, a client will be unable to view files on the Unix system, but it is not always clear that the failure to connect is due to a problem at the client or the server. It used to be that a failure of the NFS daemon would hang the client if it requested resources, but this is not always the case in recent versions of the NFS client software. When connections cannot be made, you need to be sure that the NFS daemon is running and that the resources have been exported by the server.

Unix Configuration   NFS can be considered the mirror image of SAMBA in that there is less work to be done by the system administrator since NFS is the standard method of file transfer used on Unix systems. The Unix administrator must configure the resources to be shared, and this process is one that should be given considerable thought because it is easy to produce a rather haphazard NFS organization that will be subject to more frequent failures. Most Unix systems are designed to have the NFS server come online when the Unix machine is booted if the server has been set up to provide what are termed "exports." These are the resources that are physically located on one or more computers that are placed into the /ETC/EXPORTS file.

The general steps to make a Unix resource available involve creating the correct entries in the /ETC/EXPORTS file. Once that is done, the resources are made available by invoking the command (whose exact form will vary across Unix systems) that activates the exports. The contents of the /ETC/ EXPORTS file include the path name of the resource to be shared and can also include information regarding access privileges (such as read-only or which workstations are permitted access).

Applications Servers

We will just briefly mention methods that can allow applications sharing across platforms. You can get more information by contacting the vendors listed in Table 6.2 (only a representative listing of vendors). The X-Windows packages were developed in the Unix environment to provide a common graphical interface for applications and had nothing to do with the Windows family of products from Microsoft. X-Windows programs have been ported to run under Microsoft Windows and with these programs, any Unix application that will run under X-Windows can now be run from an NT network client.

The ability to run Microsoft Windows applications on Unix workstations is now gaining more attention as the power of PC-based machines has increased to challenge that of RISC workstations. Many Unix users frequently use PCs for many things, and they are beginning to want to stay at their Unix machines and run the same programs for word processing and so on. Unix systems have achieved this using either hardware or software.

Table 6.2	Unix Utility Vendors		
Company	**Product Name**	**Product Type**	**Web Site**
Digital Equipment Corp.	Excursion	X-Windows Server	www.digital.com
Distinct Corp.	Distinct NFS X/32	NFS	www.distinct.com
Frontier Technologies Corp.	X Server Suite	NFS and X-Windows	www.frontiertech.com
FTP Software, Inc.	InterDrive	NFS	www.ftp.com
Hummingbird Communications, Ltd.	eXceed/NT	X-Windows and NFS	www.hummingbird.com
Insignia Solutions	SoftWindows	PC Emulation for Unix	www.insignia.com
Intergraph Corp.	DiskShare and Disk Access	NFS Server and Client	www.intergraph.com
NetManage, Inc.	XoftWare/32, Chameleon32/NFS	X-Windows Server and NFS	www.netmanage.com
Sun Microsystems, Inc.	SunPC	PC emulation for Unix	www.sun.com/desktop/ products/PCCP/sunpc
Vmware, Inc.	VMware	Linux emulation for Windows 2000 and NT	www.vmware.com

PC emulation software running on Unix workstations was the first method used to provide a hardware-independent way to bring Intel-based applications to the Unix world. Two well-known packages are Sun-PC from Sun Microsystems, Inc. and SoftWindows from Insignia Solutions, Inc. Both systems achieve their goal, and they have improved as newer versions have been produced. However, all such methods impose a substantial CPU overhead on whatever Unix hardware is running the emulator. If users are used to running their spreadsheet on a fast PC, they will find the performance of the Unix emulation to be noticeably slower.

One hardware solution offered by some Unix hardware vendors involves having an Intel processor board that can be added to provide support for Microsoft Windows. In the real world, you will most often find a Unix box sitting next to a PC as the most cost-effective solution.

Terminal Services

Terminal Services is a Windows 2000 tool that bestows the Windows 2000 desktop and Windows applications to non-Windows 2000 or Windows 2000 clients through terminal emulation. When a client runs an application via Terminal Services, the application and its resulting processes are run on the server.

Improvements over NT

Windows 2000 Terminal Services has several improvements over Windows NT Server 4.0 Terminal Server Edition:

- Terminal Services is an integrated component of Windows 2000 and can be installed or removed at will. Unlike NT, there is no need for separate Terminal Services Service Packs.

- Under Windows 2000, Terminal Services can be set up for remote administration, or it can be set up as an application server, providing enhanced operability as well as flexibility for its operation.

- Scalability is built into Terminal Services for Windows 2000 Advanced Server, improving and streamlining operations when setting up terminal server farms. High volumes of traffic can be split between several servers, reducing the burden on any one device.

- The Terminal Services Configuration utility has been upgraded and includes a Server Settings section, where you can check the current mode and manage configuration attributes.

- Terminal Services allows remote control or shadowing of another desktop using Remote Desktop Protocol (RDP) client.

- 16- and 32-bit RDP clients included with Windows 2000 Server are improved with the addition of faster input response and persistent caching; automatic driver detection and installation for printers; faster encryption between client and server; cut-and-paste support between local and remote desktops; and multilanguage support.

Terminal Services Modes

There are two modes in which Terminal Services can be operated. Each provides a different level of functionality for administrators.

- **Application Server** In this mode, applications are managed from the server and executed at the client level. Application Server mode saves administrators time by only installing applications on the server, rather than to each client. Client computers then access the applications remotely, with the processes running on the server. Client computers can be either Windows-based or non-Windows-based.

- **Remote Administration** This mode allows any Windows 2000 Server to be remotely administered—complete with functional desktop—from any client computer. Remote Administration is possible on clients running MS-DOS, Windows 9x, Windows NT, and non-Windows-based clients. You must be in this mode to remotely install applications while using an actual terminal session.

Step-by-Step 6.7

Adding Terminal Services

Terminal services can be added to your Windows 2000 computer during installation, or can be added later with the Add/Remove tool. To install Terminal Services after the Windows 2000 operating system has been installed, reinsert the Windows 2000 CD-ROM and use the Add/Remove Tool.

Step 1

Select the Terminal Services box and click Next. A dialog box will ask for the Terminal Services mode.

Step 2

Select Remote Administration Mode or Application Server Mode, as shown in the illustration.

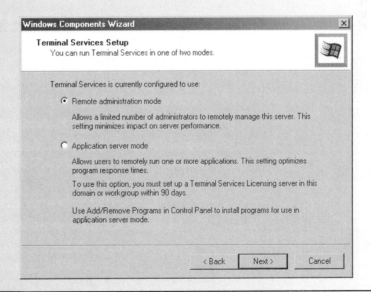

- Windows 2000 Terminal Services allows two modes of functionality.

Connecting New Clients

Windows 2000 Server includes new Terminal Services clients for a number of operating systems. Support includes Windows 3.11, Windows 9x, NT 3.51, NT 4.0, and Windows 2000. Older NT Terminal Server Edition clients will still function while connecting to Windows 2000 running terminal services, but some of the remote desktop features will not work. For best results while operating in mixed mode, use the supplied Windows 2000 Terminal Services clients.

Step-by-Step 6.8

Making Client Floppies

In order to connect client computers to a Windows 2000 Server, client disks must be made for terminals. The disks can be made by following these steps:

Step 1

Open Terminal Services Client Creator by selecting Start | Programs | Administrative Tools | Terminal Services Client Creator.

Step 2

In the Network Client or Service box, select the Terminal Services Client you want to create, as shown here. You will be prompted to select a 16- or 32-bit client.

Create Installation Disk(s)

Network client or service:
Terminal Services for 16-bit windows
Terminal Services for 32-bit x86 windows

OK
Cancel
Help

Destination drive: A: ☐ Format disk(s)

2 disks required

Step 3

Select the location of your floppy drive, insert the first disk, and click OK.

Step-by-Step 6.9

Installing the Client Floppies

Once client disks have been made, they must be installed on terminals through the following steps:

Step 1

At a command-line prompt, type *drive*:**setup** (where *drive* is the letter of the floppy drive containing your install disks). Read the information in the resulting dialog box and click Continue.

Step 2

Enter your name and organization in the appropriate boxes.

Step 3

In the Terminal Services Client Setup dialog box, note the product ID number and click OK.

Step 4	In the License Agreement box, read the agreement and click I Agree.
Step 5	In the Terminal Services Client Setup dialog box, as shown here, begin installation, and then click the large button.

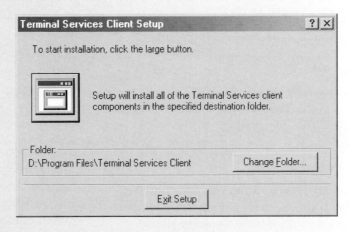

Step 6	If you want to install the client software for all users, click Yes. If you only want to install it for the current user, click OK.
Step 7	In the Terminal Services Client Setup box, click OK to complete the installation.

Installing Applications Under Application Server Mode

Installing applications is a different process when using Terminal Services with Windows 2000 Server. To enable many users to run the same application on the server, Registry and .ini file-mapping support allows applications that were not originally designed to run in a multiuser environment to run correctly.

Not only will users be able to execute these programs at the same time, but they will also be able to save their user preferences for each application. For this to work properly, each user must have a unique home directory. If no home directory is specified, the user's home directory defaults to the user's profile directory, \Wtsrv\Profiles*Username*.

Each user must have a unique copy of the applicable Registry entries or .ini files. Terminal Services copies the Registry entries and .ini files from a common system location to each user. This means that .ini files in the system directory (%*systemroot*%) will be copied to each user's Windows directory. For Registry entries, they will be copied from HKEY_LOCAL_MACHINE\ SOFTWARE\Microsoft\Windows NT\CurrentVersion\Terminal Server\ Install\Software to HKEY_CURRENT_USER\Software.

For Terminal Services to replicate the necessary Registry entries and .ini files for each user, the application must be installed in the Install mode. To do this, use Add/Remove Programs in Control Panel.

 There are limitations to what can be run via Terminal Services. Because many applications share DLLs, only one application can be run at a time. For example, both Microsoft Internet Explorer 3.*x* and Microsoft Internet Explorer 4.*x* share DLLs and will fail to work if they are installed on the same server.

Chapter 6 Review

■ Chapter Summary

After reading this chapter and completing the exercises, you should understand the following.

NT Connection Services

- The Client Access Licenses (CALs) are required to access file, print, and RAS services on the NT Server.

- The License Manager in NT Server is used to maintain the database of licenses and track the use of licenses by each user.

- The Replication Configuration Window from the Control Panel or the License Manager can be used to force replication to occur at a specific time.

- The Domain Controller is used to perform replication if the server is not a PDC or if the user does not wish to replicate the license information on a central server.

- The Enterprise Server is used to perform replication if the server is a standalone server in a domain.

- Windows 2000 uses DNS and Active Directory to locate resources.

- The default setting for the browser service in Microsoft operating system is AUTO.

- The Backup Browser maintains a copy of the Master Browser's resource list and provides this information to the clients.

- The Browser service relies on two components: the Browser and the Datagram Receiver.

- In an enterprise setup, all clients and servers are configured to support WINS and/or LMHOSTS name resolution and have TCP/IP protocol configuration.

- Client workstation browsing within a network belongs to Non-Browsers, Potential Browsers, Backup Browser, or the Master Browser category.

- Non-Browsers do not maintain a list of machines on the network, but signal their presence on the network by sending periodic broadcast to the Master Browser.

- The print processor is a software component that works with the printer driver to translate print jobs into instructions comprehensible to the particular model of a print device.

- The Browser service of a NT Server machine is set to Domain Master Browser, when it is designated as a PDC.

- The Registry for the key \HKEY_LOCAL_MACHINE\SYSTEM\CurrentControlSet\Services\Browser\ Parameters contains entries No, Yes, and Auto for the value \MaintainServerList to manually configure the browser service in NT.

- The Browser services entries for Windows 3.11 are made in the SYSTEM.INI file and the [network] subsection.

- NT uses the properties of WINS to localize information for routing the NetServerEnum API calls and browsing datagrams, to gain cross-router browsing capability.

- The LMHOSTS file can be used to browse across the router if WINS services are unavailable.

- The browse list size for NT 4 can be changed, while the browse list for NT 3.51, Win 95, and Windows 3.11 is limited to 64KB in size.

- The two utilities available with NT Server Resource Kit are: the BROWSTAT.EXE and the BROWMON.EXE.

- The NetLogon service requires the Workstation and Server services and is used by clients to establish connection with NT Servers.

- The Local Security Authority (LSA) processes the user login request on the NT client machine.

- The NetLogon service, on Domain Controllers, responds to domain client authentication requests and establishes secure communication channels with all Domain Controllers with which it has a trust relationship.

- The NetLogon service is also responsible for synchronizing the security databases between the PDC and the BDCs.

- The group of Registry values under the HKEY_LOCAL_MACHINE\CurrentControlSet\Services\Netlogon\Parameters key determines the size of the change log and the time of requests for replication.

Connecting Windows 2000 Clients

- Windows 2000 can function under native mode or mixed mode. Native mode is the environment created when both the server and the client are running Windows 2000. Mixed mode is an environment where the client and the server are running on different operating systems.

- In Windows 2000, licenses are maintained on a server that has Terminal Services Licensing enabled.

- The Terminal Services Licensing tool can be accessed by opening Terminal Services Licensing in Administrative Tools.

Connecting Non-NT Clients

- Windows 2000 uses Terminal Service feature to enable non-Windows machines to connect to a Windows 2000 network.

- NT Server includes the Network Client Administrator program in its Administrative tools.

- An installation startup disk for DOS or Windows client is required to run the Network Client Administrator.

- The Network Client Administrator is used to configure LAN Manager and DOS clients.

- Microsoft Windows 3.11 uses the Server Message Block protocol or the NetBEUI protocol for networking.

- Windows 3.11 does not support file ownership.

- The Client for Microsoft Networks must be installed and selected as the Primary Network Logon to connect a Win 95 workstation to the NT network.

- The File and Printer Sharing for Microsoft Networks Service should be installed to share files and/or printers connected to the Win 95 machine.

- The Read-Only, Full Access, and Custom user rights provide file share security in Windows 95.

Services for Macintosh

- Windows NT and 2000 Server include well-developed services for Mac clients to access Windows network resources.

- Mac networks utilize the AppleTalk network protocol and hardware to access Windows network resources.

- Mac logon can be configured for three levels: Guest, Standard AppleShare Authentication, and NT-Based Authentication.

- A Microsoft UAM Volume is created when Service for the Macintosh (SfM) creates a Mac volume.

- The NT-encrypted username and password authentication based on the NT account is used to log on volumes on the NT Server.

- The File Manager from the Administrative Tools is used to create the Macintosh-accessible volumes.

- Mac does not allow a user to create a separate volume for a subdirectory within the directory tree.

Gateway Services for Novell Networks

- The NWLINK IPX/SPX protocol provides the means for NetWare clients using IPX/SPX to access Windows NT and 2000 Servers.

- The Gateway Service for NetWare (GSNW) on an NT Server provides access to NetWare resources for clients on the NT and Windows 2000 Server networks.

- NT Server includes an Administrative tool and a Migration tool for NetWare to import a NetWare user account to NT.

- The File and Print Services for NetWare (FPNW) helps to support migration by providing access to application and files for NT and NetWare clients.

- Directory Services Manager for NetWare (DSMN) is designed to synchronize existing dual user information during the migration process.

- NetWare server must have a group named NTGATEWAY to create a gateway on Windows 2000.

- The Microsoft Directory Synchronization Service (MSDSS) is used by Windows 2000 users to synchronize the Novell Directory Services (NDS) and Windows 2000 Active Directory.

- MSDSS uses three principles in directory synchronization: sessions, object-level synchronization, and directional synchronization.

- MSDSS is configured using the wizard that is installed as a Microsoft Management Console snap-in.

- Service Advertisement Protocol (SAP) uses router and consumes network resources like the NetBIOS broadcast.

Unix Connections

- SAMBA is a server package based on the Server Message Block (SMB) protocol that is used by NT for sharing files.

- The SAMBA daemon responds to SMB requests from Windows network clients.

- The SAMBA server configuration is set in the SMB.CONF file.

- The [home] section and the [global] section in the SMB.CONF file are configured for the enterprise environment with large numbers of clients.

- The three security modes that are specified in the [global] section under the security=entries are: security=share, security=user, and security=server.

- NFS provides cross-platform file access between Unix and NT.

- The NFS client software must be installed to provide file-sharing services.

- The X-Windows packages are developed in the Unix environment to provide a common graphical interface for applications.

Terminal Services

- Terminal Services is a Windows 2000 tool that enables non-Windows 2000 clients and Windows 2000 clients to access Windows application through terminal emulation.

- When a client runs an application via Terminal Services, the application and its resulting processes are run on the server.

- Terminal Service allows shadowing of another desktop using Remote Desktop Protocol (RDP) client.

- The two modes in which Terminal Services can be operated are: Application Server and Remote Administration.

- Terminal Service can be added to Windows 2000 computer during installation, or later using the Add/Remove tool.

- Windows 2000 server includes new Terminal Services clients for Windows 3.11, Windows 9x, NT 3.51, NT 4.0, and Windows 2000.

- Registry and .ini file-mapping support allows execution of applications in a multiuser environment.

- Terminal Services copies the Registry entries and .ini files from a common system location to each user.

- The application must be installed in the Install mode for Terminal Services to replicate the necessary Registry entries and .ini files for each user.

■ Key Terms

Backup Browsers (246)	**License Manager** (244)	**SAMBA** (278)
discovery (252)	**mixed mode** (257)	**sessions** (276)
election datagram (249)	**native mode** (257)	**SMB.CONF** (279)
forward synchronization (277)	**NetLogon** (251)	
full synchronization (254)	**partial synchronization** (253)	

■ Key Term Quiz

Use the Key Terms list to complete the sentences that follow. (Not all terms will be used.)

1. The _____ tool tracks licenses for all of Microsoft's networked products and NT Server CALs.

2. _____ Browsers maintain a copy of the Master Browser browse list of servers and domains.

3. A _____ is a command-line program that is used to gain insight into the network traffic generated to browser events.

4. Clients use the _____ service to establish a connection with NT Servers.

5. _____ is the process of copying the complete directory database from the PDC to the BDC.

6. AppleTalk hardware can be connected to NT by placing _____ cards into the Mac clients.

7. A _____ contains all elements of the directory tree below the topmost level.

8. _____ are required for each pair of organizational units (OU) that are synchronized in Active Directory and NDS.

9. The _____ server package enables Windows clients to access Unix drives.

10. The SAMBA server configuration is set in the _____ file.

■ Multiple-Choice Quiz

1. What option is used to perform replication if the server is NOT a PDC?
   a. Domain Controller
   b. Workstation Controller
   c. Enterprise Server
   d. Professional Server

2. What is the default setting for the browser service in all Microsoft operating systems?
   a. Yes
   b. No
   c. Disabled
   d. Auto

3. Which of the following cannot maintain a list of machines on the network?
   a. Backup Browsers
   b. Master Browsers
   c. Non-Browsers
   d. Potential Browsers

4. The group of Registry values under which key determines the size of the change log and the request time for replication?
   a. HKEY_LOCAL_MACHINE\ CurrentControlSet\Services\Netlogon\ Replication
   b. HKEY_LOCAL_MACHINE\ CurrentControlSet\Services\Netlogon\ Parameters

   c. HKEY_LOCAL_MACHINE\SYSTEM\ CurrentControlSet\VxNETSUP\Ndi\params
   d. KEY_LOCAL_MACHINE\SYSTEM\ CurrentControlSet\Services\Browser\ Parameters

5. Which of the following is *not* a browser server?
   a. Backup
   b. Domain Master
   c. Master
   d. Slave

6. Which right in Windows 95 enables a network user to read and write to a directory and create a new file or folder?
   a. Read-Only
   b. Write
   c. Full Access
   d. Custom

7. What command-line program can be used to monitor the network traffic generated to browser events?
   a. BROWSTAT.EXE
   b. BROWMON.EXE
   c. BROWSE.EXE
   d. BROWNET.EXE

8. What service is also responsible for synchronizing the security database between the PDC and the BDCs?

   a. Logon

   b. NetLogon

   c. Synchronization

   d. TicketLog

9. What is the copying of the complete directory database from the PDC to the BDC called?

   a. Backup synchronization

   b. Domain synchronization

   c. Full synchronization

   d. Partial synchronization

10. Which mode is an environment where the client and the server run on different operating systems?

    a. Mixed

    b. Native

    c. Partial

    d. Remote

11. To what drives does the SAMBA server package provide Windows clients access?

    a. NetWare

    b. OS/2

    c. Unix

    d. Windows 3.11

12. What protocol enables NT clients to use SAMBA for sharing files?

    a. File Transfer Protocol (FTP)

    b. External Data Representation (XD)

    c. NetBEUI

    d. Server Message Block (SMB)

13. What service enables clients to access Windows applications through terminal emulation?

    a. GSNW

    b. NetLogon

    c. Terminal

    d. X-Windows

14. What type of synchronization reduces network traffic and allows objects to be located differently in each directory?

    a. Directional

    b. Forward

    c. Object-level

    d. Reverse

15. What protocol is not transportable over the Internet but is tunneled in TCP/IP?

    a. AppleTalk

    b. IPX/SPX

    c. NetBEUI

    d. SAP

■ Essay Quiz

1. List the three levels for configuring a Mac logon.

2. List the three Microsoft Directory Synchronization Services (MSDSS) principles in directory synchronization.

3. Describe the [homes] section in the enterprise environment, while configuring the SAMBA server.

4. List the three modes of security that can be specified in the [global] section under the security options.

Lab Projects

• Lab Project 6.1

Mary wants to perform a replication on the stand-alone server in the domain. She does not wish to replicate the license information to the central server.

Which option will enable her to perform this task?

• Lab Project 6.2

John is working on Windows 2000 Server and wants to access data on the NetWare server. Which service will provide him with a logon script support and

enable him to connect to computers running NetWare 3.*x*?

TCP/IP

In this chapter, you will learn how to

- Configure TCP/IP on servers and clients
- Determine valid TCP/IP addresses and subnets
- Configure and manage network routing
- Use Unix TCP/IP-related commands

The goal of this chapter is to teach you about implementing, managing, and troubleshooting TCP/IP in an existing Windows 2000 or Unix network environment. It's a very broad chapter, covering skills and concepts "from the ground up," so to speak. As such, it helps to understand how certain features are dependent on other features working properly. For example, a successful deployment of an application across multiple computers requires that Active Directory be working properly. A successful Active Directory implementation, in turn, requires a successful DNS installation. And DNS is part of a valid, working network infrastructure.

In this chapter, you'll learn from the ground up, starting with basic TCP/IP addressing. We'll look at the "rhyme and reason" behind TCP/IP, as well as specific techniques for setting up, maintaining, and troubleshooting TCP/IP networks.

Configure TCP/IP on Servers and Clients

Transmission Control Protocol/Internet Protocol (TCP/IP) is a set of protocols that enables computers to communicate with one another. It has been in use for over 20 years and is the set of protocols used by the Internet, as well as countless smaller networks.

The protocols were developed by the Internet Engineering Task Force (IETF) using a system based on Requests for Comments (RFCs). The RFC system allows engineers to post technical papers describing new technologies to an electronic bulletin board for review and comments by peers. Today, there are over 3,000 RFCs published on IETF's web site at www.ietf.org.

A TCP/IP network is composed of **hosts**. A host, in turn, is any device or service that's connected to the network. The hosts use a couple of different addresses to identify and communicate with one another, a *hardware address* and an *IP address*.

Hardware Addresses

To connect to a network, a host must have a network interface card (NIC) installed. Every NIC that's manufactured is given a unique 48-bit hardware address. The hardware address is literally "burned into" the card during the manufacturing process, and as a rule cannot be changed by the user. (Actually, some devices do allow you to change a card's hardware address, though it's unlikely you'd ever want to do this.)

 The terms "Ethernet board" and "Ethernet card" are often used as synonyms for "network interface card."

Before we go any further, we need to point out that the term "hardware address" could probably win some kind of award for having the most synonyms on the planet. While we'll stick to the term "hardware address" in this book, you may come across any of the following terms used as a synonym:

- Media Access Control (MAC) address
- Physical address
- Ethernet address
- Token Ring address
- NIC address

As mentioned, the hardware address is a 48-bit number, something along the lines of 000000001000000010101101011110111110000010110111, although it's far more common to see it expressed as six hexadecimal numbers separated by hyphens or periods, as in 00-80-AD-7B-E0-B7 or 00.80.AD.7B.E0.B7. You can view a machine's hardware address by entering the **ipconfig /all** command at a command prompt. (To get to the command prompt in Windows 2000, click the Start button and choose Programs | Accessories | Command Prompt.) The hardware address is next to Physical Address in the display, as in the example shown in Figure 7.1. (To close the Command Prompt window, type **exit** and press ENTER.)

```
Command Prompt                                                    _ □ ✕
(C) Copyright 1985-1999 Microsoft Corp.

C:\>ipconfig /all

Windows 2000 IP Configuration

        Host Name . . . . . . . . . . . . : server01
        Primary DNS Suffix  . . . . . . . :
        Node Type . . . . . . . . . . . . : Broadcast
        IP Routing Enabled. . . . . . . . : Yes
        WINS Proxy Enabled. . . . . . . . : No

Ethernet adapter Local Area Connection:

        Connection-specific DNS Suffix  . :
        Description . . . . . . . . . . . : CNET PRO200WL PCI Fast Ethernet Adap
ter
        Physical Address. . . . . . . . . : 00-80-AD-7B-E7-18
        DHCP Enabled. . . . . . . . . . . : No
        IP Address. . . . . . . . . . . . : 192.168.0.2
        Subnet Mask . . . . . . . . . . . : 255.255.255.0
        Default Gateway . . . . . . . . . :
        DNS Servers . . . . . . . . . . . :

C:\>
```

● **Figure 7.1**   The hardware address is listed as Physical Address in an ipconfig /all
command's output.

IP Addresses

In addition to the hardware address that's physically burned into each NIC, each host on a TCP/IP network also has an **IP address** (sometimes called an *Internet address*). Unlike the hardware address, the IP address is a *logical address* that's assigned by a network administrator, or by DHCP (Dynamic Host Configuration Protocol), which can automatically assign an IP address when the host first connects to the network. The IP address is flexible in that it can be assigned or changed at any time.

Each TCP/IP address is a 32-bit number, as in 11111111111111111010011 0111001110. You'll rarely see a TCP/IP address expressed in that binary notation. Instead, you'll see them expressed in **dotted quad format** (also called *dotted decimal notation*), where the address is divided into four *octets*. Each octet represents 8 bits of the address, and is expressed as a decimal number in the range of 0 to 255. Dots are used to separate the octets, as in the example 192.168.1.1.

Subnet Masks

Every host that has an IP address also has a **subnet mask**. The name "subnet mask" is a good one, because it "masks" the portion of the IP address that identifies the network to which a host belongs. Like IP addresses, a subnet mask is a 32-bit number. A series of 1's are used to identify the network portion of the address. The 0's are used to represent the host portion of the address. For example, Figure 7.2 shows an IP address expressed in binary format (1's and 0's). Beneath that is a subnet mask, also expressed in binary. The 1's "mask off" those digits in the IP address that identify the network as a whole. The 0's represent the portion of the address that identifies the host.

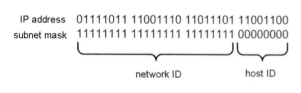

● **Figure 7.2**   An IP address and subnet mask in binary
format, where 1's "mask" the portion of the
address that identifies the network

It's customary to display the subnet mask in dotted quad format, just as we usually do with IP addresses. The binary octet 11111111, when converted to decimal, is 255. The binary octet 00000000 is, of course, just 0 in decimal. Thus, we can display an IP address/subnet mask pair in the following more "human readable" format:

192.168.221.204

255.255.255.0

In English, we can say the preceding IP address/subnet mask combination identifies "host number 204 on network number 192.168.221." However, it would be more correct to say that it identifies host number 204 on the network 192.168.221.0 because host number 0 on a network isn't really a host at all. Rather, a 0 in the host portion of the address is the address of the network as a whole.

Here's another way to view it. Think of the network ID as the area code, and the host ID as the specific phone number. But, unlike telephone numbers, where all area codes are three digits, the number of digits used for the area code can vary. The subnet mask "masks" the bits that represent the area code (network ID). The unmasked bits are the telephone number (host ID).

Getting IP Addresses

Just as a person's Social Security Number uniquely identifies them among all the millions of U.S. citizens, an IP address uniquely identifies each host on the Internet. Which perhaps brings up the question, "With millions of IP addresses already taken, how do I know what IP addresses I can use for my network?" The answer to that question is a resounding "It depends." Every single computer that can *access* the Internet doesn't necessarily have its own unique IP address. However, the hosts that *serve* the Internet—that is, the hosts that can be reached from other computers on the Internet—all do have unique IP addresses. Each of those servers also has a unique *fully qualified domain name (FQDN)*. For example, the FQDN www.microsoft.com uniquely identifies the web site host, www, on the unique domain name microsoft.com.

Class A, B, and C Addresses

There was a time when IP addresses were assigned to organizations based on their size—or roughly the number of computers that would be connected to the network. The largest organizations, such as IBM, General Electric, MIT, and Xerox, were assigned Class A addresses. Slightly smaller organizations received Class B addresses, and the smallest organizations got Class C addresses. Class A IP addresses all start with the number in the range of 1 to 126 and, by default, have a subnet mask of 255.0.0.0. Class B addresses have starting numbers in the range of 128 to 191, and use a standard subnet mask of 255.255.0.0. Class C network addresses all start with a number between 192 and 223, and have a default subnet mask of 255.255.255.0.

Some ranges of IP addresses, such as those starting with 127 and those starting with 224 through 255, aren't classified as A, B, or C. These addresses are reserved as follows:

- 127.*x.y.z* (reserved *loopback* address)
- 224.*x.y.z* through 239.*x.y.z* (Class D reserved *multicast* addresses)
- 240.*x.y.z* through 254.*x.y.z* (Class E reserved experimental addresses)

There are also ranges of *private* IP addresses, which can assigned to hosts that are clients to, but not servers on, the Web, as listed here:

- 10.0.0.0 through 10.255.255.255 (subnet mask 255.0.0.0)
- 172.16.0.0 through 172.31.255.255 (subnet mask 255.255.0.0)
- 192.168.0.0 through 192.168.255.255 (subnet mask 255.255.255.0)

Table 7.1 summarizes what you've just learned about the *classed* (also called *classful*) IP addresses. Each class is defined by a certain range of IP addresses. Each class also has "set aside" some private addresses that can be used on a local network without approval from a governing body that assigns globally unique IP addresses.

While the private IP addresses can't be used for servers on the Internet, they can access the Internet through a proxy server or Network Address Translation (NAT).

Table 7.1	Ranges of Public and Private IP Addresses			
Class	From...	To...	Default Subnet Mask	Private
Class A	1.x.y.z	126.x.y.z	255.0.0.0	10.x.y.z
Loopback	127.x.y.z			
Class B	128.x.y.z	191.x.y.z	255.255.0.0	172.16.y.z through 172.31.y.z
Class C	192.x.y.z	223.x.y.z	255.255.255.0	192.168.y.z
Class D	224.x.y.z	239.x.y.z	N/A	N/A
Class E	240.x.y.z	254.x.y.z	N/A	N/A

Recall that the subnet mask identifies which portion of an IP address represents the address of the network as a whole versus the address of an individual host. In a subnet mask, each 255 value indicates 8 bits. The more bits there are in the host portion of the IP addresses, the more unique hosts you can identify on that network. Table 7.2 illustrates this by comparing Class A, B, and C networks. As you increase the number of bits used to identify the network, you increase the number of networks you can have within the class. But, at the same time, because you're taking away bits for identifying individual hosts, you decrease the maximum number of hosts a given network could contain.

Subnet and Broadcast Addresses

As previously stated in our discussions of the network and host portions of IP addresses, you can use the bits to the right of the network portion of the address to identify individual hosts on the network. While that's true, there are a couple of exceptions. As mentioned, the lowest possible number is reserved as the *network ID* (also called the *subnet address*, the *subnet ID*, or *IP network address*). For example, if the IP address is 169.254.1.x with a subnet mask of 255.255.255.0, you cannot assign the address 169.254.1.0 to any specific host, because 169.254.1.0 is reserved as the network ID.

The highest possible address in the range of available addresses is reserved as the broadcast address. The broadcast address is used when a host needs to send a message to all other hosts on the network. Using the example 169.254.1.x with a subnet mask of 255.255.255.0, the highest possible host ID is 11111111, or 255 in binary. Hence, you cannot assign the address 169.254.1.255 to a host because that address is reserved for broadcasting. (We'll discuss broadcasting in depth a little later in this chapter.) So, when you break it all down, here's what you end up with, given 169.254.1.x with the subnet mask 255.255.255.0:

```
169.254.1.0       subnet address (network ID)
169.254.1.255     broadcast address
```

Table 7.2	Number of Networks and Hosts per Network for Each TCP/IP Address (Classes A–C)				
Class	Subnet	Network Bits	Possible Networks	Host Bits	Hosts per Network
A	255.0.0	8	126	24	16,777,214
B	255.255.0.0	16	16,384	16	65,534
C	255.255.255.0	24	2,097,152	8	254

That leaves the following host addresses remaining, which you can assign to hosts:

```
169.254.1.1 to 169.254.1.254
```

It's not always quite as simple as that because subnetting would allow you to break that network into smaller subnets, as we'll discuss later in the chapter. But before we complicate matters, let's look at another address you're likely to assign to hosts in your network, the default gateway.

The Default Gateway

Every computer in a network is likely to have a default gateway address. This address represents an interface to computers outside the local subnet. The most common example is a NIC that connects the subnet to the Internet, as in the example shown in Figure 7.3. There, the address 192.168.100.2 identifies the NIC that connects the computer to other computers in the local subnet. The IP address 192.168.100.1 identifies the NIC that connects that computer to the Internet (in other words, computers not within the local subnet).

To understand how it works, you first need to be aware that all information sent across the network is divided into *packets* (also called *frames*), each of which contains the data to be sent, as well as the IP address of the destination. When the NIC is handed a packet, it compares the network portion of the destination address to the network portion of its own address. If it determines that the destination address is not the same as its own subnet address, it just sends the packet to the default gateway instead.

In the example shown in Figure 7.3, the server at the top of the subnet is playing the role of a router, in that it accepts messages that are intended for a host that's not in the current subnet and sends them out through the default gateway. Any Windows 2000 Server computer can play the role of a router, as you'll learn later. The important point to remember for now is that the default gateway address represents the place to which all "foreign" packets are sent. If any host in the subnet needs to send a packet to some host that's not in its own subnet, the packet gets shipped straight to the default gateway.

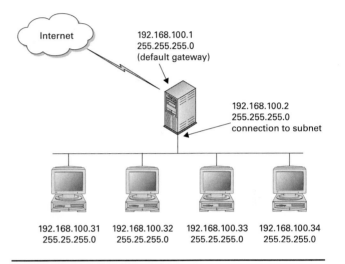

• **Figure 7.3**   The default gateway provides access to computers outside the local subnet.

Step-by-Step 7.1

Configuring TCP/IP on Servers

In this exercise, we'll look at the specific steps required to assign an IP address to a Windows computer on a LAN. We'll use an example of assigning a *static* IP address to a computer running

Windows 2000 Server. A static IP address is one that's assigned by the administrator and never changes. Here are the steps involved:

Step 1

Open the Network and Dial-Up Connections window, either from the Settings menu on the Start menu or by right-clicking My Network Places on the desktop and choosing Properties.

Step 2

Right-click the icon for your Local Area Connection and choose Properties.

Step 3

In the dialog box that opens, click Internet Protocol (TCP/IP) and then click the Properties button.

Step 4

Choose Use the Following IP Address to set a static IP address.

Step 5

Fill in this computer's IP address and subnet mask as in the example shown in the illustration. Of course, you'll want to use an IP address and subnet mask appropriate for your own network.

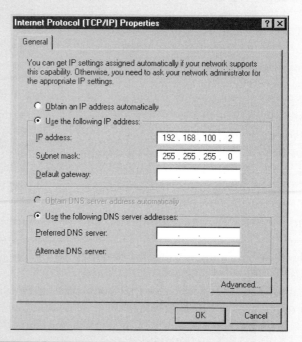

• The TCP/IP Properties dialog box

Step 6

If you already know the IP addresses of the default gateway and DNS servers for this network, you can fill those in as well. Otherwise, you can leave those options blank for now.

Step 7

Click the OK button in the current dialog box, and then click the OK button in the remaining dialog box to close that. You can also close the Network and Dial-Up Connections window if you like.

If you have access to two or more computers, and they're connected right now, you can repeat these steps on any other computers in the network. Generally, Microsoft recommends using dynamic IP addressing in client computers. But until you have a DHCP server set up to assign IP addresses automatically, you can just assign static IP addresses to all of your computers.

Classless Inter-Domain Routing (CIDR)

The classed A, B, and C networks were fine in the early days of the Internet, when there were relatively few networks connected. But, as time went by and the Internet grew, it became clear that the powers that be were going to run out of globally unique IP Class A, B, and C addresses.

To gain some flexibility in doling out ranges of globally unique IP addresses, the registrars came up with Classless Inter-Domain Routing (CIDR, pronounced *cider*) addresses. CIDR addresses don't use traditional subnet masks to identify the network and host portions of an IP address. Rather, they use a /x at the end of the IP address, where x is the number of bits used to indicate the network portion of the address.

For example, the address 199.199.199.123/26 would be called a *slash 26* address. When viewing the address in binary format, the top (leftmost) 26 bits would be the ones assigned by the registrar, leaving the remaining 6 bits for the administrators assigned to hosts. Referring back to our discussion of subnet masks, if we write the address 199.199.199.5 in binary, and then use corresponding 1's and 0's to mask the network portion of the address, we end up with the address and mask shown in Figure 7.4.

You can easily convert a /x to a more traditional subnet mask, though you'll need to covert binary numbers to their decimal equivalents. You just have to jot down the 32-bit mask with x number of 1's, followed by enough 0's to make the number 36 bits in length. Divide that 32-bit number into four octets. Then convert each octet to a decimal number. For example, let's take the /26 designation. We jot down 26 ones, followed by 6 zeros:

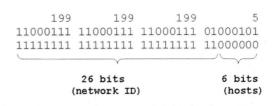

199.199.199.5/26

199	199	199	5
11000111	11000111	11000111	01000101
11111111	11111111	11111111	11000000

26 bits
(network ID)

6 bits
(hosts)

• **Figure 7.4** The address 199.199.199.5/26 in binary with 1's representing the network portion in the lower mask

```
11111111111111111111111111000000
```

Use dots to separate that into four 8-bit octets:

```
11111111.11111111.11111111.11000000
```

Now convert each binary octet to a decimal number, and you get the following:

```
255.255.255.192
```

Thus, 255.255.255.192 and /26 are just two different ways of expressing the same thing—a subnet mask that, in binary, has 26 network bits and 6 host bits. If you take a look at Table 7.3, you'll see conversions of a series of /x designations to binary and to subnet masks, and you'll see the progression. The last number in the subnet mask is just the last octet converted from binary to decimal.

Before we get any deeper into this business of working with binary numbers, let's take a moment to look at some strategies you can use to convert decimal to binary, and vice versa.

Converting Between Binary and Decimal

The easiest way to convert a binary number to decimal, or a decimal number to binary, is to use the Windows Calculator. Click the Start button, choose Programs | Accessories | Calculator. From the Calculator's menu bar,

Table 7.3	Some /x Designations, with Their Corresponding Subnet Masks in Binary and Decimal	
/x Designation	Subnet Mask in Binary Format	Subnet Mask
/24	11111111.11111111.11111111.00000000	255.255.255.0
/25	11111111.11111111.11111111.10000000	255.255.255.128
/26	11111111.11111111.11111111.11000000	255.255.255.192
/27	11111111.11111111.11111111.11100000	255.255.255.224
/28	11111111.11111111.11111111.11110000	255.255.255.240
/29	11111111.11111111.11111111.11111000	255.255.255.248
/30	11111111.11111111.11111111.11111100	255.255.255.252

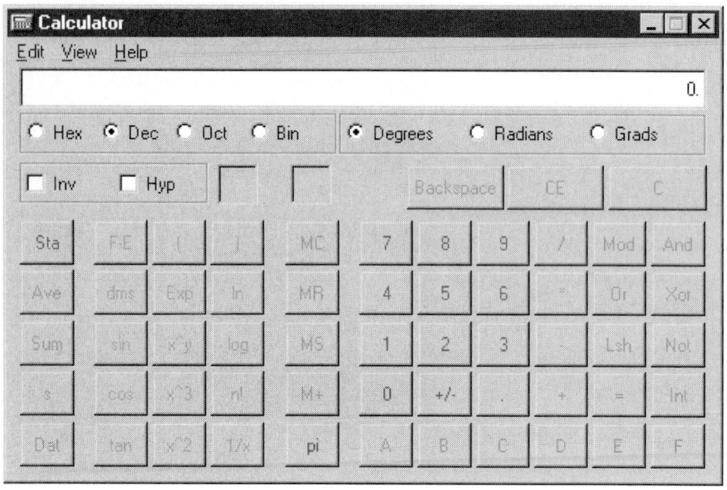

• **Figure 7.5** The Windows Calculator in Scientific view

choose View | Scientific to get to the view shown in Figure 7.5. Notice the Hex (hexadecimal), Dec (decimal), Oct (octal), and Bin (binary) options.

To convert from decimal to binary, first click the Dec option button to let the Calculator know that you're about to enter a decimal number. Then enter your decimal number and click the Bin option button to view that value in binary. For example, if you punch in the number 18 in decimal, and then click the Bin option button, the calculator displays 10010, which is the number 18 in binary. To convert that to the 8-bit chunk typically used in TCP/IP addressing, just pad the left side with leading 0's, such as 00010010.

To convert decimal to binary, start by clicking the Bin option button. Then type in the binary number. Leading 0's will be ignored because they have no value, so just start typing at the first 1. For example, to convert 00110011 to decimal, you'd type or punch in 110011. Then click the Dec option button to see the result, 51.

◼ Determine Valid IP Addresses

When you're working with a standard Class C address, it's easy to figure out the subnet address, broadcast address, and remaining addresses that are available to assign to hosts within the network. Recall that the subnet address is the last octet set to its lowest possible value, 0 in a Class C address; and the broadcast address is the last octet set to its highest possible value, 255 when you're talking about an octet (because 11111111 = 255). You can assign all the addresses between those two extremes to hosts within your network. Thus, we end up with this:

```
Subnet mask: 255.255.255.0
Subnet address: 192.168.0.0
```

```
Broadcast address: 192.168.0.255
Remaining addresses for hosts 192.168.0.1 to 192.168.0.254
```

Working with these same numbers in binary shows why this all makes sense. For example, using those same values, 192.168.1.0 and a subnet mask of 255.255.255.0 in binary, we can use the letter *n* to identify network bits, and *h* to identify host bits:

```
     192       168         0          0   IP Address (decimal)
11000000 10101000 00000000 00000000   IP address (binary)
nnnnnnnn nnnnnnnn nnnnnnnn hhhhhhhh   network or host
11111111 11111111 11111111 00000000   Subnet mask (binary)
     255       255       255        0   Subnet mask (decimal)
```

Subnetting

When we subnet a Class C address (in other words, break it down into two or more subnets), we're "swiping" host bits and making them into subnet bits. Let's see what happens when we change the subnet mask in the preceding example from 255.255.255.0 to 255.255.255.224. The bits that are affected by the change are indicated next by the letter *s*, to indicate that they're "swiped" bits now used to identify the subnet:

```
     192       168         0          0   IP address (decimal)
11000000 10101000 00000001 00000000   IP address (binary)
nnnnnnnn nnnnnnnn nnnnnnnn ssshhhhh   net, sub, or host
11111111 11111111 11111111 11100000   Subnet mask (binary)
     255       255       255      224   Subnet mask (decimal)
```

It's important to keep in mind that the subnet is a *mask,* not a number per se, and as such you must have a series of contiguous 1's for the network/subnet, followed by contiguous 0's for the host portion. Thus, only values that have leading 1's, like 10000000, 11000000, 11100000, and so forth, are valid. There are only nine possibilities, as summarized in Table 7.4.

It wouldn't actually make sense to have a /32 designation (for example, 255.255.255.255 subnet mask), because there wouldn't be any bits left in the host portion of the address. We've only included that in the table to show the progression.

Finding Valid IP Addresses

You can determine how many subnets, and how many hosts per subnet, you'll get from each /x designation as follows:

Number of subnets = 2^n
Number of hosts = $2^h - 2$

where *n* is the number of network bits, and *h* is the number of host bits. Because there are always 32 bits in

Table 7.4	The Full Range of Viable Subnet Octets in Binary and Decimal	
/x	Last Octet (Binary)	Last Octet (Decimal)
/24	00000000	0
/25	10000000	128
/26	11000000	192
/27	11100000	224
/28	11110000	240
/29	11111000	248
/30	11111100	252
/31	11111110	254
/32	11111111	255

the mask, and we're given the number of network bits by the $/x$ designation, we know there will always be $32 - n$ host bits available. (Incidentally, the reason you have to subtract 2 from the hosts calculation is because the highest and lowest addresses are reserved for the subnet address and broadcast address, respectively, so you can't assign those two addresses to hosts.)

With that in mind, Table 7.5 lists some $/x$ designations, the number of subnets each provides, and the number of hosts you'll get per subnet. We've included /31 and /32 in the table just to illustrate the progression. These actually are invalid for practical use, though, because they don't leave a sufficient number of bits for addressing hosts.

Suppose you want to work with the IP address 192.168.0.1/25. You know you have two subnets to work with. But what are the ranges of available IP addresses to work with? Well, we know the network ID of the first subnet is

```
192.168.0.0
```

We know we have 126 host addresses to work with, and the first possible host address is 192.168.0.1. Therefore, the range of available addresses must be

```
192.168.0.1  to 192.168.0.126
```

The broadcast address would be one higher than the last host address, so it must be

```
192.168.0.127
```

That covers the first subnet. The second subnet then starts right after the first subnet's broadcast address. Thus, the subnet address of the second subnet must be

```
192.168.0.128
```

Once again, we have 126 possible host addresses. The first valid host address would be one greater than the subnet address, so the range must be

```
192.168.0.129 to 192.168.0.254
```

Table 7.5	Number of Subnets and Possible Hosts per Subnet per /x Designation				
/x Designation	n Bits in Last Octet (x – 24)	Available Subnets (2^n)	h Bits (32 – n)	Hosts per Subnet ($2^h - 2$)	Subnet Mask (Decimal)
/24	0	1	8	254	255.255.255.0
/25	1	2	7	126	255.255.255.128
/26	2	3	6	62	255.255.255.192
/27	3	8	5	30	255.255.255.224
/28	4	16	4	14	255.255.255.240
/29	5	32	3	6	255.255.255.248
/30	6	64	2	2	255.255.255.252
/31*	7	128	1	0	Not valid
/32*	8	256	0	0	Not valid

*Invalid because they don't leave a sufficient number of host bits.

because that's the range of numbers needed to address 126 hosts. The second subnet's broadcast address would be one greater than the last host address, so that address must be

```
192.168.0.129 to 192.168.0.254
```

Table 7.6 summarizes the preceding information. As you can see, we've actually taken a Class C address and split it right in half, making two equal-sized subnets.

If you use a /26 designation with a class C address of 192.168.9.9, you end up with 2^2 or 4 subnet bits. To determine the remaining host bits, we subtract 26 from 32, which tells us we have 6 host bits to work with. Thus, the maximum number of hosts per subnet would be $2^6 - 2$, or 62. Again, reserving the lowest and highest address within each of the four subnets for the network ID and broadcast address leaves us with the subnets and IP addresses listed in Table 7.7.

In a nutshell, we've taken the Class C address 192.168.0.0 and divided it into four separate, equal-sized chunks. The starting address of each subnet is exactly 64 greater than the previous subnet's starting address, because we have 64 addresses per subnet (60 hosts plus the subnet and broadcast addresses).

Subnetting is simple to do with a good subnet calculator, such as the SolarWinds.Net Advanced Subnet Calculator, available from www.tucows.com. But even without a subnet calculator, you can figure out anything as long as you know the network address and subnet mask. For example, suppose a senior administrator asks you to configure some new network using 192.168.0.160 with a subnet mask 255.255.255.240. What IP addresses can you assign to your host? Right off the bat, we know our network address, because that's a given:

```
192.168.0.160 subnet address (given)
```

So, how many hosts per subnet? First, we need to figure out how many subnet bits are available, so we convert the last octet in the subnet mask, 240, to binary, which yields 11110000. So, we have 4 host bits to work with, and hence $2^4 - 2$, or 14 hosts per subnet. We know that the IP address of the first host will be one greater than the subnet address, thus our range of IP addresses is

```
192.168.0.161 to 192.168.0.174 (14 hosts per subnet)
```

The broadcast address is one more than the last IP address, and thus is the following:

```
192.168.0.175 (broadcast address)
```

Table 7.6	IP Addresses and Subnet Masks for 192.168.0.0/25 (126 Hosts per Subnet)				
Subnet	Subnet Address	First Host	Last Host	Broadcast Address	Subnet Mask
1	192.168.0.0	192.168.0.1	192.168.0.126	192.168.0.127	255.255.255.128
2	192.168.0.128	192.168.0.129	192.168.0.254	192.168.0.255	255.255.255.128

Table 7.7	IP Addresses and Subnet Masks for 192.168.0/26 (62 Hosts per Subnet)				
Subnet	Subnet Address(s)	First Host	Last Host	Broadcast Address	Subnet Mask
1	192.168.0.0	192.168.0.1	192.168.0.62	192.168.0.63	255.255.255.192
2	192.168.0.64	192.168.0.65	192.168.0.126	192.168.0.127	255.255.255.192
3	192.168.0.128	192.168.0.129	192.168.0.190	192.168.0.191	255.255.255.192
4	192.168.0.192	192.168.0.193	192.168.0.254	192.168.0.255	255.255.255.192

Broadcasting

Hosts on small subnets often use *broadcasting* to communicate with one another. Broadcasting is required when a given host doesn't know the address of some host with which it needs to communicate. To illustrate how broadcasting works, let's suppose a host named Igor needs to contact a host named Franz, but doesn't know Franz's hardware address or IP address. How's Igor going to get his message across? Easy. Because he doesn't know of a specific address to send the message to, he sends it to the broadcast address, which, in turn, automatically delivers the message to every host in the subnet. You might think of Igor sending his message to the subnet's broadcast address as being the same as Igor shouting "Igor at 192.168.0.2 here. If there is a Franz out there, please send me your address."

Every host on the network hears the broadcast message and checks to see who the message is intended for. Each host examines the message to see if the name Igor is looking for matches its own name. If the names don't match, the message is just ignored and no reply is sent back to Igor. However, when Franz sees that the message is addressed to him, he replies, "Hey Igor at 192.168.0.2, Franz here, and my address is 192.168.0.5," as illustrated in Figure 7.6. So now Igor and Franz know each other's addresses, and can send messages directly back and forth.

That all works just fine and dandy, but there's one big drawback. Igor has to pester every host in the LAN just to find the one host he's really trying to communicate with. That's not a big deal on a single small subnet. However, if you look at an extremely large network, like the Internet, you can see why broadcasting would create way too much traffic and take way too long. For example, suppose you type **www.GeneralSpecificX.com** into your web browser, which knows nothing about that site's IP address. If your browser had to go to every single host on the Internet asking "Are you www.GeneralSpecificX.com?," it would be pestering literally hundreds of millions of computers with this stupid question. And those other hundreds of millions of hosts would be pestering each other, and your

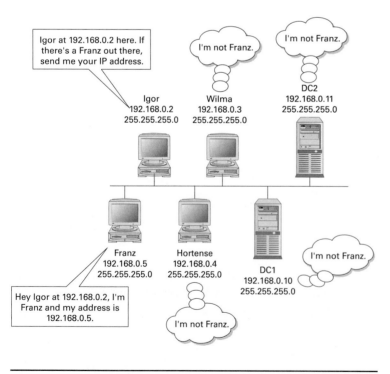

• Figure 7.6   Igor broadcasting a message to everyone, trying to find Franz

computer, with similar stupid questions. There'd be so much bandwidth eaten up by all these broadcasts, it would be impossible to get anything else done.

So what's the solution to the broadcasting problem? In a word, *routing*. As you may recall, a router (or default gateway) connects a subnet to the "outside world." One side of the router has an IP address that makes it a member of the subnet to which it's connected. As such, the router "hears" all the broadcast messages going across the subnet. However, the one thing it won't do is send those broadcast messages through to the outside world. In other words, when

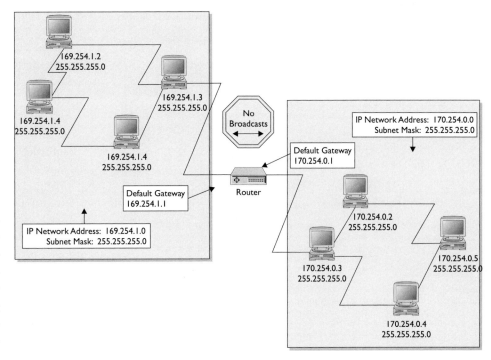

● **Figure 7.7**   An intranet composed of two subnets joined by a router

the router gets a broadcast message, it "shuts down the gateway," in essence saying "Broadcast messages stop here," as illustrated in Figure 7.7.

Configure Routing

So now, armed with this information, let's look at the concept of *routing*, which is central to TCP/IP. The simplest form of routing is the network that's attached to the Internet via a router or modem and an Internet service provider (ISP). Hosts within the local subnet can communicate by broadcasts, and such messages stay within the subnet. Messages that are destined for hosts outside the local subnet are sent to the default gateway, which is the IP address of the device that connects the subnet to the Internet, as illustrated in Figure 7.8. That device then forwards the message to the ISP, who handles it from there.

Small Business Routing Scenario

In a small business, we might find multiple routers connecting multiple departmental subnets, as shown in Figure 7.9. In that scenario, Router1 connects the Marketing and Sales subnets, Router2 connects Sales to Accounting, and Router3 connects Accounting to Marketing. Any host in the company can contact any other host, because all the subnets are connected by routers.

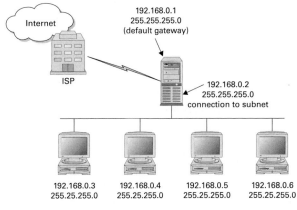

● **Figure 7.8**   A small subnet that uses a default gateway to access the Internet

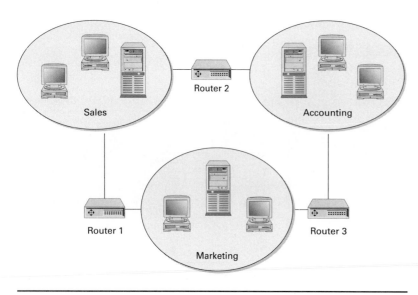

In this scenario, computers within any given department can communicate with one another by broadcasting. But, for a message to reach a *remote network* (some other department's subnet), the message will have to cross one or two routers. For efficiency, we'd prefer messages to take the shortest path through one router. For example, we'd prefer a message being sent from Sales to Marketing to go through Router1. However, if Router1 were unavailable, Sales could still get its message across to Marketing by going through Router2 and Router 3. Hence, we get some *fault tolerance* here in that if one router goes down, messages can still get through.

• **Figure 7.9**   A small business scenario with routers connecting three departmental subnets

Corporate Scenario

We can keep scaling up to larger, more complex scenarios. For example, Figure 7.10 shows a larger corporate or enterprise network with all kinds of networks and protocols joined together with a bunch of routers. In that example, Windows 2000 Server computers are used as routers (as opposed to "dedicated routers"). We'll show you how to make a Windows 2000 Server computer into a router momentarily.

Obviously, we won't get into all of the configuring needed to set up such a complex network right here. The point, though, is that a little bit of routing goes a long way in connecting all kinds of networks together, providing network communications across a wide variety of platforms. The Internet *is* exactly that: a complex of computers, cables, networks, and routers connecting computers and networks around the globe.

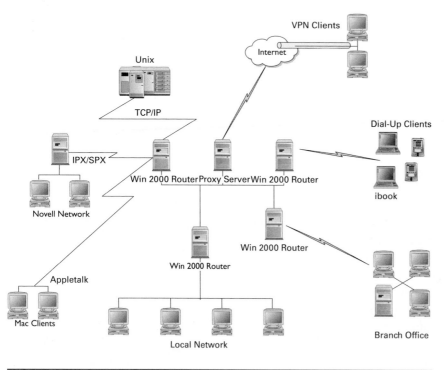

• **Figure 7.10**   A corporate routing scenario involving many routers and protocols

Finally, bear in mind that there are no geographical boundaries here either. Any given subnet or network can be anywhere in the world. A large enterprise with offices in Europe, Asia, Mexico, and the United States would still use the same basic routing mechanisms to connect all these far-flung clients together into a (relatively) seamless network where any host could communicate with any other host, anywhere in the world.

Building a Windows 2000 Router

As you probably know, you can buy "dedicated" routers from manufacturers like Cisco and Lucent. But it's not entirely necessary to do so, as any Windows 2000 Server computer can easily play the role of router. Configuration is easy as well. First, you need to have two separate subnets to connect, of course. On the Windows 2000 Server computer that will be playing the role of router, you need to make sure the Routing and Remote Access Server is configured. Here's how:

Step 1

Click the Start button, choose Programs | Administrative Tools | Routing And Remote Access. The Routing and Remote Access console opens.

Step 2

Click the name of the server that will be acting as router. If you've never configured this service before, you'll see a message prompting you to configure the service now, as shown in the illustration. Click the Action button and choose Configure Routing and Remote Access.

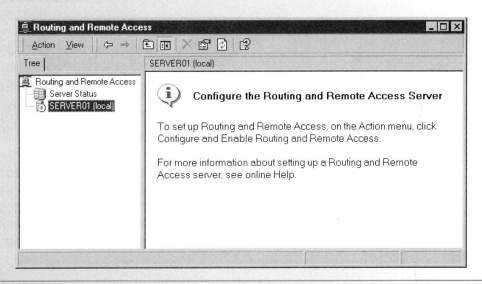

- Routing and Remote Access Services, not yet configured

Step 3

A wizard opens up and takes you through the steps required for the basic configuration. In this scenario, you'd choose Network Router when prompted for the configuration type, and click the Next button.

Step 4

Follow the wizard through until you get to the Finish page.

When you've completed the wizard, you're ready to start the next phase, which involves installing the NICs. You would just go through the usual procedure. When both NICs are installed, each will have its own icon in Network and Dial-Up Connections, as in the example shown in Figure 7.11.

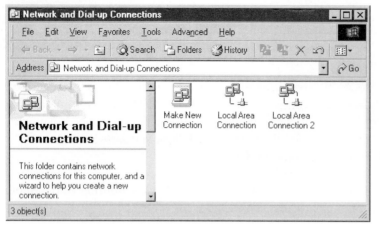

Because each NIC is a separate network interface, each can have its own unique TCP/IP settings. In this situation, you need to configure each NIC with a valid IP address for the subnet to which it connects. For example, take a look at Figure 7.12. The subnet on the left has the address 192.168.0.0 subnet mask 255.255.255.0. The subnet on the right has the address 192.168.100.0 subnet mask 255.255.255.0. These are two separate subnets, because the network portions of their IP addresses clearly don't match.

To get routing to work, each NIC needs to be connected to and configured as a host within its subnet. For example, in the example shown in Figure 7.12, we've given NIC1 the IP address 192.168.0.1, thereby making it a host on the 192.168.0.0 subnet. We gave NIC2 the IP address 192.168.100.1, making it a host on the 192.168.100.0 subnet. By the way, a computer that contains two or more NICs is called a *multihomed computer*. Server01 in this example is, obviously, a multihomed computer at this point.

To use the router, all the hosts on network 192.168.0.0 would need to be configured to use 192.168.0.1 as their default gateway. All the hosts on subnet 192.168.100.0 would use 192.168.0.1 as their default gateway. Thus, broadcasts and other communications within each subnet stay in their respective subnets. Messages intended for "some other subnet" are sent to the interface on the router.

Finally, you'll want to make sure routing is enabled on the server. Typically, the wizard you ran earlier in this section would be sufficient to get that going. But just in case you have any problems with the router connection, you'll want to make sure the service is enabled. Again, open the Routing and Remote Access Services administrative tool, right-click the server's name in the console tree, and choose Properties. On the General tab, make sure routing is enabled. For this scenario, where you have only two subnets connected, you'll also want to make sure the Local Area Network (LAN) Routing Only option is selected, as shown in Figure 7.13.

How Routing Works

To understand the basics of routing, start with a single source host that's trying to get a message to some other destination host. The source host's own IP address is 192.168.100.33 with a subnet mask of 255.255.255.0. The destination host's IP address is 192.168.100.122 with a subnet mask of 255.255.255.0.

• **Figure 7.11**   Each installed NIC has its own icon in Network and Dial-Up Connections.

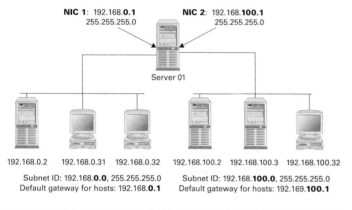

• **Figure 7.12**   Server01 playing the role of router between 192.168.0.0 and 192.168.100.0

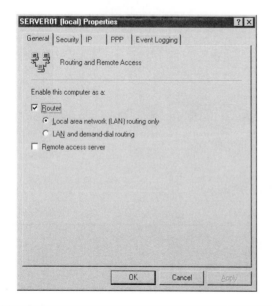

• **Figure 7.13**   Routing must be enabled for a Windows 2000 Server computer to function as a router.

If we stack the IP addresses and subnet mask one atop the other, we can see that the destination host is on the same network (or subnet) as the source host:

```
192.168.100.33    (source)
192.168.100.122 (destination)
255.255.255.0    (subnet mask)
```

The source host can "see" this same relationship. It "knows" that the destination host is on the same subnet. So it need not go through any routers to get to that host.

Viewing the Routing Table

Every computer on a TCP/IP network has a built-in routing table. The routing table is built automatically from known information. You can view the routing table by entering the command `route print` at the command prompt. The results might look something like the example in Figure 7.14.

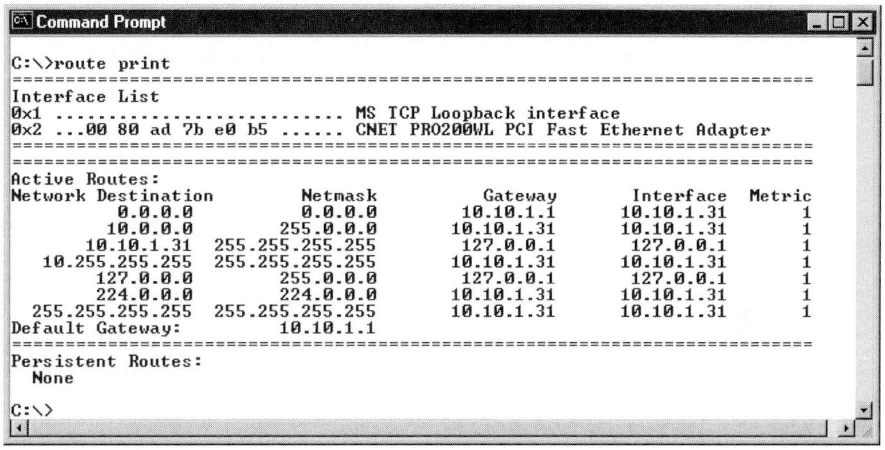

To interpret the command's output in this example, you first need to know some things about the machine on which the command was entered. In this example, we entered the command at a Windows 2000 Professional computer that has the following TCP/IP configuration:

• **Figure 7.14**   Sample output from a route print command

```
TCP/IP Address:     10.10.1.31
Subnet mask:        255.0.0.0
Default gateway:    10.10.1.1
```

The lines under Interface List indicate this computer's network interfaces. The first item, 0x1, is the TCP loopback interface used in conjunction with the loopback address for testing purposes. Every TCP/IP client has the same loopback address of 127.0.0.1; the loopback interface is just the address where loopback messages get sent. Later in this chapter, you'll see how you can use that address for testing and troubleshooting. The second item in this example, 0x2, is this computer's NIC. You can see its hardware address, as well as the make and model of the card. This particular machine has only one NIC installed. If it were a multihomed machine with multiple NICs, those additional NICs would be listed as 0x3, 0x4, and so forth.

The next section of the display, titled Active Routes, lists routes that this machine knows about. Each row is divided into the following columns:

- **Network Destination**   A potential destination IP address, to which messages might be sent.

- **Netmask**   A subnet mask for the network destination, which further defines which addresses will be included in this route.

- **Gateway** The IP address that provides access to the network destination addresses.

- **Interface** The local IP address that leads to the gateway.

- **Metric** The "cost" of a route in terms of "hops" across routers that will be required. The path from a host to its default gateway is also considered a hop, so there is always at least one hop, even when no routers are involved.

Now let's take a look at some of the routes listed in the sample output. The first line looks like this:

```
Network Destination     Netmask     Gateway      Interface      Metric
0.0.0.0                 0.0.0.0     10.10.1.1    10.10.1.31          1
```

The address 0.0.0.0 with the netmask 0.0.0.0 translates roughly to "the place you should go if none of the lines in the routing table apply." In other words, this row defines the default gateway for all packets that aren't within broadcast range, and that don't meet any of the criteria in the other lines in the routing table.

Let's take a look at the next line now:

```
Network Destination     Netmask       Gateway      Interface      Metric
10.0.0.0                255.0.0.0     10.10.1.31   10.10.1.31          1
```

This line says that "To get to any address that starts with 10. (in other words, 10.0.0.0 subnet 255.0.0.0), use your own NIC at 10.10.1.31. There will not be any router hops to make." This makes sense if you think about it for a minute. Recall that this is a machine on a Class A network. We know this because its own IP address and subnet mask are 10.10.1.31 and 255.0.0.0. So it stands to reason that in order to get a message out to another machine on this same network, the machine could use its own NIC (10.10.1.31) as the gateway to the local network, and there wouldn't be any routers involved.

The third route network destination, 10.10.1.31 netmask 255.255.255.255, refers to the local computer. This line essentially says "To get to yourself, use the loopback address 127.0.0.1." The next destination, 10.255.255.255 netmask 255.255.255.255, is the broadcast address. So this line says "To broadcast a message to all hosts on the 10.0.0.0 network, use your own 10.10.1.31 NIC." The next destination address, 127.0.0.0 netmask 255.0.0.0, is the reserved loopback address. Because the netmask uses 255.0.0.0, this line says "Any message sent to 127.*anything.anything.anything* gets sent to the IP address 127.0.0.1."

The network destination 224.0.0.0 netmask 224.0.0.0 is the reserved `multicast address`. For now, it's sufficient to know that multicasting is a means of sending a single stream of data to multiple IP addresses, sort of like a radio station that just sends out its show via an antenna, and any radio that happens to be tuned to that station hears the show. The 255.255.255.255 netmask 255.255.255.255 is the *limited broadcast address*, any alternative route used by some broadcasts to the local subnet.

The last section, titled Persistent Routes (see Figure 7.14), lists static, permanent routes created by an administrator. In the sample output, there are none listed, simply because we haven't created any. We're relying on the default gateway address to handle all messages with destinations outside the local subnet. But you can't always rely on that. We'll discuss why, and how to get around it, in the next section.

Viewing a Computer's Routing Table

As we mentioned, every computer has a built-in routing table. So you can do this simple exercise on virtually any Windows machine. We didn't create an exercise that actually lets you change the routing table, as you wouldn't want to play around with that on a real, production network. Furthermore, you could only create a route to a viable network, and of course we don't know what, if any, networks you're connected to. But, anyway, to perform this simple exercise on a Windows 2000 machine, follow these steps:

Step 1   Click the Start button and choose Programs | Accessories | Command Prompt.

Step 2   Type **route print** and press ENTER.

Step 3   That's it. If you'd like a printed copy, type **route print prn** and press ENTER.

Step 4   Type **exit** and press ENTER if you want to close the Command Prompt window.

The output of your **route print** command may not match the example shown in this chapter, but you should see many of the same default routes.

Configuring Routing Tables

Suppose you work in a company that has an intranet composed of three networks and two routers, as shown in Figure 7.15. Notice some features of this scenario. We have three separate Class C networks here. Network A's network address is 200.50.50.0, Network B's network address is 199.150.150.0, and Network C's address is 197.100.100.0. Networks A, B, and C could all be subnets of one Class C address, in which case you'd need a custom subnet mask. But for our current example, that wouldn't matter. Either way, you'd still need routers to connect the various networks or subnets.

Notice that Network C contains two routers, one at the address 197.100.100.101 and the other at 197.100.100.102. There is no Internet connection in this example, which means there is no default gateway to which Network C can just send all messages intended for hosts outside itself. So how does a host on Network C (say,

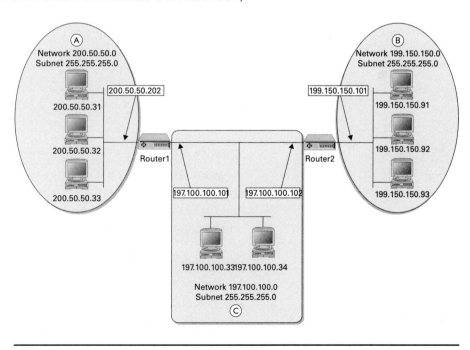

● **Figure 7.15**   Three networks connected by two routers

197.100.100.33) get a message to a host on Network A (say, 200.50.50.31)? The obvious answer is through Router1. But the machine can only know this if its routing table tells it to go through Router1. You can manually add a route to a machine's routing table to handle a situation like this. In this example, in order for a host from Network C to get a message to Network A or B, it would need the following "instructions" placed in its routing table:

- To get a message to Network A (200.50.50.0), send it to Router1 at 197.100.100.101.

- To get a message to Network B (199.150.150.0), send it to Router2 at 197.100.100.102.

These "instructions," which are formally called *static routes*, can be added to the routing table using the **Route** command with the following syntax

```
route [-p] ADD destination MASK subnet gateway METRIC m IF interface
```

where

- **–p** is an optional switch. If included, manually added routes are persistent, in that they exist from one reboot to the next. If omitted, the route exists only during the current session, and will cease to exist after the machine is rebooted.

- *destination* is the address or range of addresses that this routing table applies to.

- *subnet* is the subnet mask for the destination that identifies the network and host portions of the destination address.

- *gateway* is the IP address that provides access to the network.

- *m* is the number of router hops required to get to the destination.

- *interface* is a single-digit number identifying which NIC card interface to use. You can omit this to have the command locate the best interface automatically.

Let's look at an example. Suppose we want to tell one of the workstations in Network C "When you get a message that's addressed to any address starting with 200.50.50, send it to IP address 197.100.100.101." To do that, we get to the command prompt on that computer and enter the following command:

```
route -p ADD 200.50.50.0 MASK 255.255.255.0 197.100.100.101 METRIC 2
```

We'd also want to tell that computer to send all messages destined for any address starting with 199.150.150 to 197.100.100.102, the near-side IP address of the router that connects network C to network B. So we'd also enter this command:

```
route -p ADD 199.150.150.0 MASK 255.255.255.0 197.100.100.102 METRIC 2
```

The command will check the specified route before adding it to the routing table. If for some reason the specified network cannot be reached, the entry will be rejected and you'll see an error message to that effect. The problem could be a simple typo or a connection problem to the remote network.

After you've successfully entered a route, it will appear in the output of the **route print** command. If you included the **–p** switch, the route will be listed under the Persistent Routes heading. Otherwise, the new route just appears in the regular list of routes. In this example, the following lines would be added under Persistent Routes:

```
Network Destination    Netmask        Gateway         Interface       Metric
200.50.50.0            255.255.255.0   197.100.100.101  197.100.100.33    2
199.150.150.0          255.255.255.0   197.100.100.102  197.100.100.33    2
```

Notice that in both **route add** commands, we omitted the IF *interface* parameter. Since this machine has only one NIC, the **route add** command can test the connection and figure this out on its own.

How Routing Conflicts Are Handled

Recall that our small sample network contained no default gateway to the Internet. As such, there's no way for our sample host to communicate with the outside world beyond Networks A and B. But suppose we add another NIC to that machine, or an Internet connection through some other machine on the same subnet. For the sake of example, let's say that the default gateway address to the Internet is at 197.100.100.1. When we do a **route print** command on that machine, the output might include the following routes:

```
Network Destination    Netmask        Gateway         Interface       Metric
0.0.0.0                0.0.0.0         197.100.100.1   197.100.100.1    40
200.50.50.0            255.255.255.0   197.100.100.101  97.100.100.33    2
199.150.150.0          255.255.255.0   197.100.100.102  197.100.100.33    2
```

The large metric, 40, is somewhat typical of an Internet connection where many routers might have to be crossed to get to a specific destination on the Internet. But more importantly, there's also a conflict here. The default gateway address 0.0.0.0 says "Use 197.100.100.1 for all communications outside this subnet." But then, the next two lines say "Use 197.100.100.101 for communications to 200.50.50.0, and 197.100.100.102 for communications to 199.199.150.0." So, which will it be when it comes time to send a message to Network A, the default gateway address or the specified route?

For example, let's say some hypothetical routing table contains these two routes:

```
Network Destination    Netmask          Gateway         Interface       Metric
200.50.50.0            255.255.255.0     197.100.100.101  197.100.100.33    2
200.50.50.200          255.255.255.255   197.100.100.102  197.100.100.34    2
```

The first route tells the machine to send anything destined for the network 200.50.50.0 through 197.100.100.101. The second one tells the machine that a message specifically destined for 200.50.50.200 netmask 255.255.255.255 goes through 197.100.100.102. Since the second entry has the more specific netmask, 255.255.255.255 (in other words, "this particular host"), as opposed to an entire network (255.255.255.0), the second item wins. In the event that two routes have identical subnet masks, the route with the smallest metric will be chosen first.

> You can intentionally add some conflicting, static routes to a routing table for fault tolerance. Give the preferred route a low metric, such as 1; the "backup" route a higher metric, like 2; and so forth.

Managing the Routing Table

The **route** command offers two more options that you can use to manage a routing table. The **route delete** command allows you to delete static routes from the routing table. For example, entering the command

```
route delete 200.50.50 200
```

would delete the route that has the network destination address 200.50.50.200. If you have two routes with the same network destination address but different gateways, you can include the gateway address to specify the record you want to delete.

You can use the * wildcard character in both the **print** and **delete** versions of the command. For example **route print 200*** displays only routes whose network destination starts with 200. The **route delete 200*** command would delete all routes whose network destinations start with 200.

The **route change** command lets you change an existing static route, for example,

```
route change 199.150.150.0 MASK 255.255.255.0 197.100.100.102 METRIC 4
```

The **route** command alone on a line prints help for the command (same as entering the command **route /?**).

Now that we've told you all of this, let us first point out that it's very unlikely that you'll ever have to go from one machine to the next, setting up all these routes. Thanks to dynamic routing and modern routing protocols like RIP (Routing Information Protocol) and OSPF (Open Shortest Path First), routers can keep machines informed of available routes, and individual hosts can compare routing tables to one another and keep each other up to date. For now, the important thing is to understand that all machines have a routing table. And even if you don't specifically need to manually add static routes to a machine's table, it's good to be able to interpret the contents of the table for troubleshooting purposes.

■ Troubleshoot TCP/IP and Routing

As you probably know, there's a lot more to a TCP/IP network than just assigning IP addresses to machines. There are many things that can go wrong after the network is built, and even more things that can go wrong as you're building the network. For the rest of this chapter, we'll take a look at some diagnostic tools and troubleshooting techniques that you can use at any time to solve problems as they arise.

Troubleshooting with ipconfig

As the name implies, **ipconfig** is a command for checking a machine's IP configuration. Checking a host's IP configuration is always the best first step in troubleshooting connectivity problems. Entering just the command **ipconfig** at the command prompt displays basic IP configuration information (IP address, subnet mask, default gateway, and DNS suffix) for each network adapter in the computer. Settings that haven't been configured yet are left blank.

For more detailed information, use the **/all** switch by entering the command **ipconfig /all**. This command will display general information about the current computer's IP configuration, followed by detailed information about each installed NIC. Figure 7.16 shows an example of the display produced by an **ipconfig /all** command. Here's a brief description of what each line is about.

```
Command Prompt                                                          _ □ ✕
<C> Copyright 1985-1999 Microsoft Corp.

C:\>ipconfig /all

Windows 2000 IP Configuration

        Host Name . . . . . . . . . . . . : server01
        Primary DNS Suffix  . . . . . . . :
        Node Type . . . . . . . . . . . . : Broadcast
        IP Routing Enabled. . . . . . . . : Yes
        WINS Proxy Enabled. . . . . . . . : No

Ethernet adapter Local Area Connection:

        Connection-specific DNS Suffix  . :
        Description . . . . . . . . . . . : CNET PRO200WL PCI Fast Ethernet Adap
ter
        Physical Address. . . . . . . . . : 00-80-AD-7B-E7-18
        DHCP Enabled. . . . . . . . . . . : No
        IP Address. . . . . . . . . . . . : 192.168.0.2
        Subnet Mask . . . . . . . . . . . : 255.255.255.0
        Default Gateway . . . . . . . . . :
        DNS Servers . . . . . . . . . . . :

C:\>
```

• **Figure 7.16**   Sample ipconfig /all command display

- **Host Name**   This computer's hostname, which might be a single name like server01 if DNS hasn't been set up yet, or it might be a FQDN like server01.certifiable.net if DNS is set up.

- **Primary DNS Suffix**   If DNS has been set up, the domain portion of the DNS name (for example, certifiable.net) appears here.

- **Node Type**   Describes the method used to resolve NetBIOS-style hostnames, like server01, to IP addresses.

- **IP Routing Enabled**   A simple Yes or No answer describing whether or not this machine is functioning as a router.

- **WINS Proxy Enabled**   Specifies whether WINS name resolution is enabled.

Information that's specific to network adapter cards is listed under the Ethernet Adapter heading. The name of the connection, as it appears in the Network and Dial-Up Connections window is followed by these lines:

- **Connection-Specific DNS Suffix**   If DNS is enabled, shows the DNS domain name that's specific to this network interface card.

- **Description**   The make and model of the network interface card.

- **Physical Address**   The hardware address of the network interface card.

- **DHCP Enabled**   Determines whether or not this card's address can be assigned automatically by a DHCP server (Yes) or was manually entered (No).

- **IP Address**   The IP address of the network interface card.

- **Subnet Mask**   The subnet mask of the network interface card.

- **Default Gateway**   The IP address of the default gateway where messages outside the broadcast range will be sent.

- **DNS Servers**   If DNS is set up, lists the IP address of all available DNS servers.

In terms of what we've discussed so far in this chapter, what you're mainly looking for in **ipconfig**'s output is to ensure that the computer has a valid IP address and subnet mask. If there is a gateway of some sort on the network, whether it be a dedicated router or just a computer that provides access to the Internet, the default gateway address for that router must be correct as well. If you find an error that needs correcting, you can make changes through the TCP/IP Properties dialog box, described previously in Step-by-Step 7.1.

The **ipconfig** command works only on systems that have the TCP/IP networking protocols installed. If entering the **ipconfig /all** command returns an error message like "TCP/IP is not running on this system," there's a problem with the NIC or with the TCP/IP installation. To check to see if the NIC is working properly, open the Control Panel, open the System icon, and click the Hardware tab. Then click the Device Manager button and expand the Network Adapters category. Double-click the icon for your NIC to view its properties. If the dialog box doesn't indicate any problems, you know the problem lies outside the NIC.

> Windows 2000 doesn't automatically install drivers for every NIC on the market, so it's a good idea to check the card and TCP/IP right after you install Windows or install a new card.

If the Properties dialog box indicates, instead, that there is a problem with the card, first check to make sure the card is on the Windows 2000 Hardware Compatibility List. Optionally, you can search for updated drivers via the Internet, and use the Update Driver button on the Drivers tab of the Properties dialog box to install the updated driver.

Step-by-Step 7.4

Checking an IP Configuration

If you support computers or networks professionally, you'll be using the **ipconfig /all** command pretty frequently. So, in this exercise, we'll go through the simple steps necessary to use the command:

Step 1   Click the Windows Start button and choose Programs | Accessories | Command Prompt.

Step 2   Type **ipconfig /all** and press ENTER. You should see output similar to the example shown previously in Figure 7.16, but with the data from the current machine.

Step 3   After viewing the output, type **exit** and press ENTER to close the Command Prompt window.

*Note: Just about all versions of Windows support the **ipconfig** command. However, Windows 95 and 98 use the command WINIPCFG instead.*

Troubleshooting with ping

Whereas **ipconfig** is a good tool for checking a machine's IP configuration, the ping (Packet Internet Groper) utility is the preferred tool for checking to see if a NIC is working, and for checking connectivity between two machines. Basically, **ping** sends an *echo request* message that basically asks "Are you there?" If the machine being pinged can be reached from the current machine, **ping** displays that machine's reply. Otherwise, it displays a list of "Request timed out" error messages.

A good strategy for troubleshooting TCP/IP problems with **ping** is to start with the local host, and then gradually work your way out to hosts that are increasingly distant from the local host, as discussed in the sections that follow.

Ping the Loopback Address

For testing and debugging purposes, you can start by pinging the loopback address, 127.0.0.1. That is, at the command prompt, type **ping 127.0.0.1** and press ENTER. You should get a reply, as in the example shown in Figure 7.17.

If pinging the loopback address results in an error message, there's likely a communication problem between Windows 2000 and your NIC. In that case, Microsoft recommends that you remove and reinstall TCP/IP.

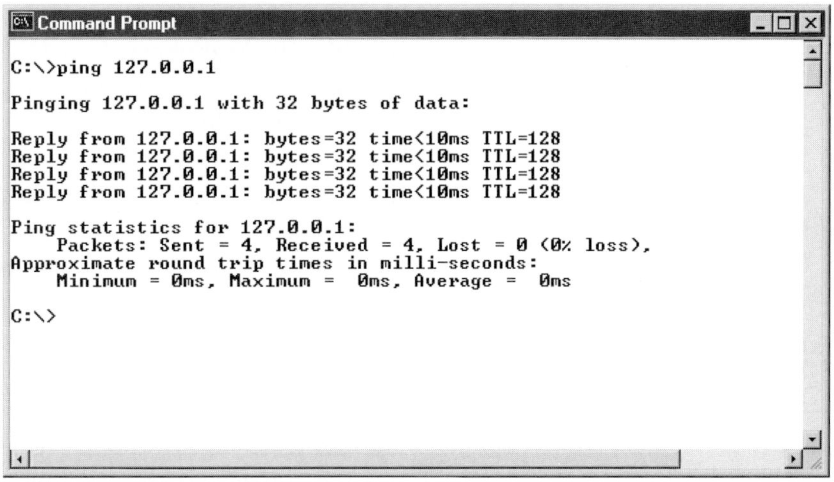

```
Command Prompt                              _ □ ✕

C:\>ping 127.0.0.1

Pinging 127.0.0.1 with 32 bytes of data:

Reply from 127.0.0.1: bytes=32 time<10ms TTL=128
Reply from 127.0.0.1: bytes=32 time<10ms TTL=128
Reply from 127.0.0.1: bytes=32 time<10ms TTL=128
Reply from 127.0.0.1: bytes=32 time<10ms TTL=128

Ping statistics for 127.0.0.1:
    Packets: Sent = 4, Received = 4, Lost = 0 (0% loss),
Approximate round trip times in milli-seconds:
    Minimum = 0ms, Maximum =  0ms, Average =  0ms

C:\>
```

• **Figure 7.17**   Results of pinging the loopback address 127.0.0.1

Ping Your Own IP Address

If you can successfully **ping** the loopback address, try pinging the local PC's IP address. Once again, you should see some sort of successful feedback. If you get an error message instead, there's likely a communication problem between your NIC and Windows 2000. In that case, Microsoft recommends that you remove and then reinstall your NIC's driver.

Ping the Default Gateway Address

If your network has a functioning default gateway, you can ping its IP address to verify connectivity to the gateway. For example, if the default gateway address is 192.168.0.1, but pinging that address returns "Request timed out" errors, there's a problem with the address or the connection. If some other administrator already set up the default gateway, verify that you're using the correct default gateway address, and also have that administrator verify that the default gateway is properly connected to the network and functioning correctly.

Ping Nearby IP Addresses

Next, try pinging a host on the near side of the router (a computer on the same subnet) by its IP address. For example, let's say you have a computer named server01 configured as IP 192.168.0.1 and another set up as client01, IP 192.168.0.2. If you're sitting at 192.168.0.1 and want to check connectivity with the other machine, enter the **ping** command followed by that machine's address; for example, **ping 192.169.0.2**. If the connection works, you'll get a successful reply. If instead of a reply you get a "Destination host unreachable" error message, then obviously there's some problem.

If you were able to successfully ping the loopback address, but can't **ping** a separate machine, first check the network cabling. Many connectivity problems are nothing more than faulty cable connections. Another obvious but often overlooked potential cause should be checked—make sure the computer that you're trying to ping is up and running and connected to the network! Finally, if you have basic connectivity but still can't ping the other machine, the reason may lie in faulty ARP cache entries. You can use the **arp** command, discussed in a moment, to view the contents of the cache, as well as to delete faulty entries.

Ping More Distant IP Addresses

If your network contains routers or you have an Internet connection, you can use the **ping** command to test connectivity to hosts on the far side of your router (outside your local subnet). The same basic syntax applies— **ping** *ipaddress*. For example, if you're connected to the Internet, you could try pinging a web site of ours by entering **ping 208.55.30.20**.

Be forewarned that some web sites, including `www.microsoft.com`, are designed not to respond to *ICMP Echo Requests*, which is the official name of the type of packet a **ping** command sends. So, if a first attempt fails, try some other sites. If you can't ping any web sites, try pinging your default gateway address. If you can't ping your default gateway, check to make sure its IP address and subnet mask are set up correctly, and that you're pinging the correct address of the default gateway.

Pinging Hostnames

If you can **ping** a host by its IP address, but not its hostname, you should suspect a problem with your DNS configuration or name resolution.

You can also **ping** another computer by its hostname. For example, if you're sitting at a computer named client01, which has a connection to a computer named server01, you can **ping** the server by entering the command **ping server01**. Once again, if the connection works, you'll get a positive response. If the **ping** fails, it could be a name resolution problem.

Troubleshooting with ARP

The **Address Resolution Protocol (ARP)** maintains a cache of IP address to hardware address mappings. Entering the command **arp –g** or **arp –a** displays the current mappings. Faulty ARP entries can cause **ping echo** requests to other computers in the network to fail. For example, if you can **ping** both the loopback address and your own IP address, but not any other IP addresses, you might be able to fix the problem by clearing out the ARP cache. You can clear individual entries using the syntax **arp –d** *IPaddress*, where *IPaddress* represents the entry you want to remove. You can delete all ARP entries by using the * wildcard with **–d** (for example, **arp –d ***) or by entering the command **netsh interface ip delete arpcache**.

Troubleshooting with Tracert

If you cannot **ping** a host outside your subnet, you can use the **tracert (Trace Route)** command to locate where the problem might lie. **Tracert** provides information about each router or gateway that a message crosses when trying to reach another host. Each router that the message crosses is considered a *hop*.

The basic syntax for the command is **tracert** *IPaddress*, where *IPaddress* is the IP address of the destination you're trying to reach—just as in the **ping** command. For example, entering the command **tracert 208.55.30.20** would return a list of routers crossed on the way to that destination. The basic format of the display will look like this, where *name* represents the hostname of each router (as available) and *xxx.xxx.xxx.xxx* represents each router's IP address:

```
Tracing route to www.coolnerds.com [208.55.30.20]
over a maximum of 30 hops:

1    1 ms     1 ms     1 ms   name xxx.xxx.xxx.xxx
2   12 ms    19 ms    19 ms   name xxx.xxx.xxx.xxx
3    9 ms    15 ms    50 ms   name xxx.xxx.xxx.xxx

Trace complete.
```

By default, **tracert** is limited to testing 30 hops. But you can use the **–h** switch to test more or fewer maximum hops. For example, if 30 hops weren't enough to reach the destination host, you could try something like **tracert –h 40 208.55.30.20** to increase the maximum number of hops to 40.

Step-by-Step 7.5

Tracing a Route

If you have Internet access from your current machine, you can try out the **tracert** command by following these simple steps:

Step 1

Click the Windows Start button and choose Programs | Accessories | Command Prompt.

Step 2

Type **tracert 208.55.30.20** to ping a server over the Internet (or use another IP address provided by the instructor). You should see output similar to the example shown here, though the names and IP addresses of routers crossed will be different.

```
Command Prompt                                                     _ □ ×

C:\Documents and Settings\Alan>tracert 208.55.30.20

Tracing route to www.coolnerds.com [208.55.30.20]
over a maximum of 30 hops:

 1    <1 ms    <1 ms    <1 ms  cn780605-a.mshome.net [192.168.0.1]
 2   443 ms    510 ms   614 ms  10.87.14.1
 3   541 ms    283 ms   340 ms  r1-fe1-0.jamison1.pa.home.net [24.18.63.113]
 4   342 ms    183 ms   107 ms  r1-ge5-0.wyn1.pa.home.net [24.2.5.1]
 5   241 ms    323 ms   561 ms  bb1-srp2-0.rdc2.pa.home.net [216.197.151.81]
 6   380 ms     67 ms   391 ms  c1-pos4-0.phlapa1.home.net [24.7.74.57]
 7   779 ms    274 ms   353 ms  c1-pos6-0.cmdnnj1.home.net [24.7.65.225]
 8   121 ms    341 ms   442 ms  c1-pos2-0.bltmmd1.home.net [24.7.65.222]
 9   328 ms    181 ms   174 ms  c2-pos1-0.washdc1.home.net [24.7.65.89]
10   889 ms    232 ms    57 ms  24.7.71.6
11    41 ms     74 ms    27 ms  p16-0-0-0.r01.mclnva02.us.bb.verio.net [129.250.
5.253]
12   229 ms    695 ms   477 ms  p16-0-0-0.r00.atlnga03.us.bb.verio.net [129.250.
2.49]
13   679 ms    612 ms   494 ms  p4-0-2-0.r01.bcrtfl01.us.bb.verio.net [129.250.4
.54]
14   288 ms    347 ms   594 ms  ge-1-1.r01.border.boca.verio.net [129.250.28.52]

15   685 ms    588 ms   408 ms  ge-8-1.r01.edge.boca.verio.net [208.55.254.9]
16   494 ms    270 ms   105 ms  www.coolnerds.com [208.55.30.20]

Trace complete.
```

• Results of a sample tracert command

Because you're tracing the route to an IP address that's on the Internet, the trace should complete successfully, provided your Internet connection is working.

If there is a problem with a router between your computer and the destination computer, you may receive feedback that looks more like this:

```
Tracing route to www.coolnerds.com [208.55.30.20]
over a maximum of 30 hops:

  1   10 ms   10 ms   10 ms   xxx.xxx.xxx.xxx
  2   50 ms   50 ms   51 ms   xxx.xxx.xxx.xxx
  3   xxx.xxx.xxx.xxx   reports: Destination net unreachable.
```

Or perhaps like this:

```
Tracing route to www.coolnerds.com [208.55.30.20]
over a maximum of 30 hops:

  1   10 ms   10 ms   10 ms   xxx.xxx.xxx.xxx
  2    *       *       *      Request timed out
  3    *       *       *      Request timed out
  4    *       *       *      Request timed out
```

If a router's IP address appears repeatedly in the display, that's called *looping*, and means the router is not forwarding to the next router. This is most often caused by an improper configuration at that specific router. Of course, whenever you encounter a problem tracing the route to an Internet address, it's very likely that the faulty router will be outside your company's internal network. The only thing to do, in that case, is to report the problem to your ISP. If the router is in-house, but outside your area of responsibility, you should report the problem to the administrator of that specific router.

Like **ping, tracert** will accept a hostname as well as an IP address. For example, you could enter the command **tracert www.coolnerds.com** to ping the host at 208.55.30.20. As with **ping**, if you're able to get to the host by its IP address but not by its hostname, then you know you have a name resolution problem on your hands.

Finally, don't forget that when it comes to troubleshooting routing problems, the **route print** command can be an ideal resource for seeing where a machine "thinks" it's supposed to route certain messages. Scan the table for conflicting routes, and remember that a route with a more specific netmask will take precedence over a conflicting route in the table that has a less specific netmask.

Troubleshooting with pathping

The **pathping** command combines features of **ping** and **tracert**, with some additional functionality. Whereas **tracert** can only point out places where these is no connectivity at all, **pathping** can point out routers that are slow or inconsistent in moving data along due to network congestion or dropped packets that need to be re-sent. To do this, **pathping** sends multiple **ping echo** requests to all the routers along a route for 25 seconds. Then it calculates the average time and percentage of lost packets encountered at each router. The resulting display helps you pinpoint which router along a path would be causing slow or inconsistent performance.

For example, suppose users are complaining the connection to a server named EgyptDC01 is slow or inconsistent. You enter the command **pathping EgyptDC01** from the source (any machine that's experiencing problems), and get the following results (The information that's relevant to this example is boldfaced; your **pathping** command won't do that):

```
Tracing route to egyptdc01 [10.10.1.2]
over a maximum of 30 hops:
 0 myServer [172.16.87.35]
 1 aroute1 [180.10.20.22]
 2 aroute2 [192.168.52.1]
 3 aroute3 [192.168.80.1]
 4 aroute4 [10.10.20.22]
 5 egyptdc01 [10.10.1.2]

Computing statistics for 125 seconds...
            Source to Here    This Node/Link
Hop RTT Lost/Sent = Pct Lost/Sent = Pct Address
 0                                       myServer [172.16.87.35]
                              0/ 100 = 0% |
 1 46ms      0/ 100 = 0%      0/100 = 0% aroute1 [180.10.20.22]
                             21/ 100 = 21% |
 2 21ms     16/ 100 = 16%     3/100 = 3% aroute2 [192.168.52.1]
                              0/ 100 = 0% |
 3 20ms     10/ 100 = 10%     0/100 = 0% aroute3 [192.168.80.1]
                              0/ 100 = 0% |
 4 21ms     12/ 100 = 12%     1/100 = 1% aroute4 [10.10.20.22]
                              0/ 100 = 0% |
 5 20ms     12/ 100 = 12%     0/100 = 0% egyptdc01 [10.10.1.2]

Trace complete.
```

The **This Node/Link: Lost/Sent = Pct** and **Address** display the link between two router IP addresses. The value followed by the pipe character (|) is the loss rate for the specific link. In the example output, you can see that the link between 180.10.20.22 and 192.168.52.1 has a 21 percent loss rate. Dropped packets need to be retransmitted. So, with such a high drop rate, you can see that this link is the problem. So **pathping** has helped you locate the source of the problem. You could then go to that router, or contact its administrator, to try to resolve that problem. Most likely, the router is overloaded.

TCP/IP on Unix

Many applications require individuals to access resources on remote machines. To meet this need, more and more computers are linked together via various types of communications facilities into many different types of networks. Nowadays, a large percentage of computers have connections to the Internet, a vast network of computers.

This section will concentrate on the commands built into Unix for TCP/IP networking. The Internet is based on TCP/IP networking and was originally built using Unix to link computers running Unix.

Traditionally, basic communications capabilities in Unix, such as file transfer and remote execution, were provided by the UUCP System (short for Unix-to-Unix Copy). However, UUCP communications are based on point-to-point communications and are relatively slow and unsophisticated. They are not adequate for supporting high-speed networking and do not meet the requirements for distributed computing. Moreover, the UUCP System is not available for many operating systems, so UUCP communications often cannot be used for file transfer or remote execution in heterogeneous environments.

Unix includes networking capabilities that can be used to provide a variety of services over a high-speed network. Using these capabilities, you can carry out such network-based tasks as remote file transfer, execution of a command on a remote host, and remote login. Because these capabilities are available on computers running different operating systems, including Windows, the Mac OS, and all Unix variants, TCP/IP networking can be used in heterogeneous environments. Networking based on TCP/IP is the basis for the Internet, which links together computers running many operating systems into one gigantic network. This chapter describes how to use the basic commands in Unix to carry out networking tasks.

If your computer is not part of a network that is directly connected to the Internet, you can connect your computer to the Internet using a regular telephone connection or an ISDN connection.

■ Unix Commands for TCP/IP Networking

One of the major networking capabilities in Unix comprises the basic commands for TCP/IP networking. These commands are used to establish TCP/IP connections and provide a set of user-level commands for networking tasks. Most versions of Unix include two sets of commands used to supply networking services over the Internet: the *Berkeley Remote Commands,* which were developed at the University of California, Berkeley, and the *DARPA commands.*

The DARPA commands include facilities, independent of the operating system, for such tasks as terminal emulation, file transfer, mail, and obtaining information on users. You can use these commands for networking with computers running operating systems other than Unix.

The Berkeley Remote Commands include Unix computer–to–Unix computer commands for remote copying of files, remote login, remote shell execution, and obtaining information on remote systems and users.

Different versions of Unix also provide additional networking capabilities. In particular, distributed file systems, such as the Network File System (NFS), are an important networking capability of Unix.

The next section describes how to use the user-level Unix TCP/IP commands: the Berkeley Remote Commands and the DARPA commands.

In this section, it is assumed that TCP/IP commands have been installed and configured on your system and that your system is part of a TCP/IP network.

The Remote Commands

Unix incorporates the Berkeley Remote Commands, which were originally developed as part of the BSD System. These are commonly known as the *r* commands*, because their names start with *r*, so that *r** matches all their names when the * is considered to be a shell metacharacter.

You can use the Remote Commands to carry out many different tasks on remote machines linked to your machine via a TCP/IP network. The most commonly used of these commands are **rcp** (remote *copy*), used to transfer files; **rsh** (remote *sh*ell), used to execute a command on a remote host; and **rlogin** (remote *login*), used to log in to a remote host.

The Remote Commands let you use resources on other machines. This allows you to treat a network of computers as if it were a single machine.

Security for Berkeley Remote Commands

When remote users are allowed to access a system, unauthorized users may gain access to restricted resources. Which remote users have access to a system can be controlled in several ways.

Security for the Remote Commands is managed on both the user level and the host level. On the user level, the system administrator of a remote machine can grant you access by adding an entry for you in the system's password files. Also, the system administrator on the remote machine may create a home directory on that machine for you.

Host-Level Security   On the host level, each host on a TCP/IP network contains a file called /etc/host.equiv. This file includes a list of the machines that are trusted by that host. Users on remote machines listed in this file can remotely log in without supplying a password.

For example, if your host, michigan, trusts the remote machines jersey, nevada, and massachusetts, the /etc/host.equiv file on michigan looks like this:

```
$ cat /etc/host.equiv
jersey
nevada
massachusetts
```

If the /etc/host.equiv file contains a line with just a plus sign (+), this machine trusts all remote hosts.

User-Level Security   Another facility is used to enforce security on the user level. A user who has a home directory on a remote machine may have a file called .rhosts in his or her home directory on that machine. This file is used to allow or deny access to this user's login, depending on which machine and which user is trying to gain access. The .rhosts file defines "equivalent" users, who are given the same access privileges.

An entry in .rhosts is either a hostname, indicating that this user is trusted when accessing the system from the specified host, or a hostname followed by a login name, indicating that the login name listed is trusted when accessing the system for the specified host. For example, if khr has the following .rhosts file in /home/khr on the local system,

```
$ cat .rhosts
jersey
nevada
massachusetts rrr
massachusetts jmf
delaware
delaware  rrr
```

then the only trusted users are khr, when logging in from jersey, nevada, or delaware; rrr, when logging in from massachusetts or delaware; and jmf, when logging in from massachusetts.

When security is loose on a system, .rhosts files are owned by remote users, to facilitate access. However, when security is tight, root (on the local machine) will be the owner of all .rhosts files and will deny write permission by remote users.

Remote Login

At times you may need to log in to another Unix computer on a TCP/IP network and carry out some tasks. This can be done using the **rlogin** command. You can use this command to log in to a remote machine and use it as if you were a local user. This is the general form of this command:

```
$ rlogin machine
```

For example, to log in to the remote machine jersey, use the following command:

```
$ rlogin jersey
Password: u2a33t    {not displayed}
UNIX System V Release 5.0 AT&T 3B2
jersey
Copyright (c) 1999 SCO
All Rights Reserved
Last login: Sun May 22 16:29:13 from 192.11.105.32
$
```

In this case, the remote host jersey prompted the user for a password. The remote user correctly entered the password and was logged into jersey. The remote host jersey also supplied the last login time for this user, and the place from which the user last logged in. (In this example, this is specified by the Internet address of a machine on the TCP/IP network, 192.11.105.32.)

The **rlogin** command supplies the remote machine with your user ID. It also tells the remote machine what kind of terminal you are using by sending the value of your *TERM* variable. During an **rlogin** session, characters are passed back and forth between the two systems because during the session you remain connected to your original host.

You can also use **rlogin** to log in to a remote system using a different user ID. To do this, you use the –l option followed by the user ID. For example, to log in to jersey with user ID *ams*, use this command:

```
$ rlogin -l ams jersey
```

Unlike **rlogin**, you can use **telnet** to log in to machines running operating systems other than Unix. However, when you use **telnet** to log in to a Unix computer, **telnet** does not pass information about your environment to the remote machine, whereas **rlogin** does this.

rlogin Access   Under some circumstances, you can use **rlogin** to log in to a remote machine without even entering your password on that machine. At other times you will have to supply a password. Finally, under some circumstances you will not be able to log in at all. You are denied access when you attempt to log in to a remote machine if there is no entry for you in the password database on that machine.

If you do have an entry in the password database, and if the name of your machine is in the /etc/hosts.equiv file on the remote machine, you are logged in to the remote machine without entering a password. This happens because the remote machine trusts your machine.

You are also logged in without entering a password if the name of your local machine is not in the /etc/hosts.equiv database, but a line in .rhosts in the home directory of the login on the remote machine contains either your local machine's name, if the login name is the same as yours, or your local machine's name and your username.

Otherwise, when you do have an entry in the password database of the remote machine, but the name of your machine is not in the /etc/hosts.equiv file on the remote host and there is no appropriate line in the .rhosts file in the home directory of the login on the remote machine, the remote machine prompts you for a password. If you enter the correct password for your account on the remote machine, you are logged in to this remote machine. However, even though you can log in, you will not be able to run remote processes such as **rsh** or **rcp**. This prevents you from using a multihop login to a secure machine.

When you use **rlogin** to attempt to log in to a machine that is not known by your machine, your system will search without success through its host database and then return a message that the remote host is unknown. For example, suppose you attempt to log in to the remote host nevada from your machine, but this machine is not in the host database of your machine. Your machine will return with the message:

```
$ rlogin nevada
nevada: unknown host
```

Logging in to a Succession of Machines   You can successively log in to a series of different machines using **rlogin** commands. For example, starting at your local machine you can log in to jersey using this command:

```
$ rlogin jersey
```

When you are successfully logged in to jersey, you can log in to nevada by issuing the command

```
$ rlogin nevada
```

from your shell on jersey. This would log you in to all three systems simultaneously.

Aborting and Suspending rlogin Connections   To abort an **rlogin** connection, simply enter CTRL-D, **exit**, or **~.** (tilde dot). You will return to your original machine. Note that when you have logged in to a succession of machines using **rlogin**, typing **~.** returns you to your local machine, severing all intermediate connections. To abort only the last connection, type **~~.** (tilde tilde dot).

If you are using a job control shell, such as **jsh**, you can suspend an **rlogin** connection, retaining the ability to return to it later. To do this, type **~** CTRL-Z (tilde CTRL-Z). When you suspend an **rlogin** connection, this connection becomes a stopped process on your local machine and you return to the original machine from which you issued the **rlogin** command. You can reactivate the connection by typing **fg** followed by a RETURN, or % followed by the job number of the stopped process.

When you are logged in to a succession of machines using **rlogin**, typing **~** CTRL-Z returns you to your local machine. Typing **~~** CTRL-Z (tilde tilde CTRL-Z) suspends only your last **rlogin** connection.

You can change the **~** to another character (here noted as *c*) by using the **~e** option followed by the character you want to be the abort sequence, as shown in the following format:

```
$ rlogin ~ec remote_host_name
```

For example, the command

```
$ rlogin  ~e+ jersey
```

begins the remote login process to jersey and sets the abort sequence to +. (plus dot).

Copying Files Using rcp

Suppose that you want to send a letter to everyone on a mailing list, but the file containing the names and addresses is located on a remote machine. You can use the **rcp** command to obtain a copy of this list. The **rcp** command is used to copy files to and from remote machines on a TCP/IP network.

This is the general form of an **rcp** command line:

```
$ rcp source_machine:file destination_machine:file
```

To use **rcp** to transfer files to or from a remote machine, you must have an entry in the password database on that machine, *and* the machine you are using must be in the remote machine's list of trusted hosts (either in the / etc/host.equiv file or in your .rhosts file on the remote machine).

Copying from a Remote Host   To be able to copy a file from a remote machine, you must have read permission on this file. To use **rcp** to copy a file into a specified directory, giving the file the same name it has on the remote system, use a command line of the form:

```
$ rcp host:pathname directory
```

For example, to copy the file named /home/phonelist on the remote machine jersey into your directory /home/data on your local machine, naming the file /home/data/phonelist, use the command

```
$ rcp jersey:/home/phonelist  /home/data
```

You can also change the name of the file when you copy it by specifying a filename. This is the general form of this use of the **rcp** command:

```
$ rcp host:pathname directory/file
```

For example, the command

```
$ rcp jersey:/home/phonelist /home/data/numbers
```

copies the file /home/phonelist on jersey into the file /home/data/numbers on your local machine.

When you copy files using **rcp**, you can use whatever abbreviations for directories are allowed by the shell you are using. For example, with the standard shell, the command line

```
$ rcp jersey:/home/phonelist $HOME/numbers
```

copies the file /home/phonelist on jersey to the file *numbers* in your home directory on your local machine.

Copying from Your Machine to a Remote Machine   You can also use **rcp** to copy a file from your machine to a remote machine. You must have write permission on the directory on the remote machine that you want to copy the file to.

This is the general form of the **rcp** command used to copy a file from your machine to a remote machine:

```
$ rcp file host:directory
```

For example, to copy the file /home/numbers on your machine into the directory /home/data on the remote host jersey, naming it /home/data/numbers, use this command:

```
$ rcp /home/numbers jersey:/home/data
```

To rename the file on the remote machine, use a command line of the following form:

```
$ rcp file host:directory/file
```

For example, the command

```
$ rcp /home/numbers jersey:/home/data/lists
```

renames the copied file /home/data/lists.

Using rcp to Copy Directories   You can copy entire directory subtrees using the **rcp** command with the **–r** option. This is the general form of the command line used to copy a remote directory into a specified directory on your machine:

```
$ rcp -r machine:directory directory
```

For example, you can copy the directory /home/data on the remote machine jersey into the directory /home/info on the local machine using this command:

```
$ rcp -r jersey:/home/data /home/info
```

To copy a local directory into a specified directory on a remote host, you use a command line of the form:

```
$ rcp -r directory machine:directory
```

Thus, to copy the directory /home/info on the local machine into the directory /home/data on the remote machine jersey, use the command line:

```
$ rcp -r /home/info jersey:/home/data
```

Using Shell Metacharacters with rcp   Be careful when you use shell metacharacters with **rcp** commands. Shell metacharacters are interpreted on the local machine instead of on the remote machine unless you use escape characters or quotation marks. For example, suppose you want to copy the files /etc/f1 and /etc/f2 on the remote machine jersey, and that in your current directory on the local machine you have files named *friends* and *fiends*. To attempt to copy the files /etc/f1 and /etc/f2 on jersey into your current directory, you type this:

```
$ rcp jersey:/etc/f*
```

Your local shell expands *f** to match the filenames *friends* and *fiends*. Then it attempts to copy the files /etc/friends and /etc/fiends on jersey, which was not what you intended.

You can avoid this problem using an escape character like this:

```
$ rcp jersey:/etc/f\*
```

You can also use this:

```
$ rcp \'jersey:/etc/f*\'
```

Creating a Remote Shell with rsh

Sometimes you may want to execute a command on a remote machine without logging in to that machine. You can do this using the **rsh** (for *r*emote *sh*ell) command (HP-UX users should note that this command is called **remsh** in HP-UX systems). An **rsh** command executes a single command on a remote Unix System host on a TCP/IP network.

To use **rsh**, you must have an entry in the password database on the remote machine, and the machine you are using must be a trusted machine on this remote host, either by being listed in the /etc/hosts.equiv file or by having an appropriate entry in your .rhosts file in your home directory on the remote machine.

This is the general form of an **rsh** command:

```
$ rsh host command
```

For example, to produce a complete listing of the files in the directory /home/khr on jersey, use this command:

```
$ rsh jersey ls -l /home/khr
```

The output of the **ls –l** command on jersey is your standard output on your local machine.

The command **rsh** does not actually log in to the remote machine. Rather, a daemon on the remote machine generates a shell for you and then executes the command that you specify. The type of shell generated is determined by your entry in the password database on the remote host. Also, the appropriate startup file for your shell (that is, your .profile on the remote host if you use the standard shell) is invoked.

Shell Metacharacters and Redirection with rsh

Shell metacharacters and redirection symbols in an **rsh** command that are not quoted or escaped are expanded at the local level, not on the remote machine. For example, the command

```
$ rsh jersey ls /usr/bin > /home/khr/list
```

lists files in the directory /usr/bin on the machine jersey, redirecting the output to the file /home/khr/list on the local machine. This is the outcome because the redirection symbol > is interpreted at the local level.

To perform the redirection on the remote machine and place the list of files in /usr/bin on jersey into the file /home/khr/list on jersey, use single quotes around the redirection sign >:

```
$ rsh jersey ls /usr/bin '>' /home/khr/list
```

Using a Symbolic Link for rsh Commands

When you find that you often issue **rsh** commands on a particular machine, you can set up a symbolic link that lets you issue an **rsh** command on that host simply by using the name of that host. For example, suppose you run the command

```
$ ln -s /usr/sbin/rsh /usr/hosts/jersey
```

and put the directory /usr/hosts in your search path. Instead of using the command line

```
$ rsh jersey ls /usr/bin
```

you can use the simpler command line:

```
$ jersey ls /usr/bin
```

When you make this symbolic link, you can also remotely log in to jersey by simply issuing the command:

```
$ jersey
```

This is shorthand for this:

```
$ rlogin jersey
```

Using rwall

Another **r*** command that you might find useful is **rwall** (from *remote write all*), available on many versions of Unix. This command is used to send a message to all users on a remote host (as long as this host is running the **rwall** daemon, **rwalld**). (Note that this capability is often restricted to just root by system administrators.) For example, you can send a message to all users on the remote machine saginaw using the following command:

```
$ rwall saginaw
Please send your monthly activity report to
Yvonne at california!ygm by Friday.  Thanks!
CTRL-D
```

You end your message by typing CTRL-D to signify end-of-file. This message will be delivered to all users on saginaw, beginning with the line that looks like this:

```
Broadcast message from ygm on california ...
```

The Secure Shell (ssh)

The Berkeley Remote Commands allow users access to resources on remote computers. Unfortunately, systems that enable these commands are vulnerable to attack by unauthorized parties. For example, an intruder with root access to a computer on the network, or who has tapped into the network itself, can obtain passwords of users. Because of these and other security concerns, on many Unix systems the Berkeley Remote Commands are turned off.

To solve the security problems of the Berkeley Remote Commands while allowing the same functions they perform to be carried out, Tatu Ylönen at the Helsinki University of Technology, Finland, created the *Secure Shell* (ssh). The Secure Shell is a program that allows users to log in to computers over a network, to copy files from one computer to another, and to execute commands on a remote machine, all in secure ways. The Secure Shell provides security by authenticating users and by providing secure communications over connections that may not be secure. That is, the Secure Shell was designed to carry out the same functions as the Berkeley Remote Commands **rlogin**, **rsh**, and **rcp**, without leading to the same security vulnerabilities. The Secure Shell provides security in many ways. For example, when the secure shell is used, both ends of the connection are automatically authenticated and all passwords sent over the network are first encrypted. The Secure Shell uses both private- and public-key cryptography for encryption and authentication functions. The particular algorithms employed vary according to whether you are using a free version or a commercial version of the Secure Shell software.

The particular commands in the Secure Shell program that replace **rlogin**, **rsh**, and **rcp** are called **slogin**, **ssh**, and **scp**, respectively. For example, to use **slogin** to set up a secure login for the user ams on the remote system jersey, you would use the command

```
$ slogin -l ams jersey
```

Note that you can add additional options to these commands to customize their use; check the manual pages for details.

If the Secure Shell is not already installed on the system you use, you can obtain it over the Internet. For noncommercial use you can obtain ssh free of charge from ftp.cs.hut.fi/pub/ssh/. To install this software on your system, first download the file, and then run the command

```
$ gzip -c -d ssh-1.2.26.tar.gz | tar xvf -
```

Next, change to the directory ssh-1.2.26 (replace "1.2.26" in the command line and in the directory name with the latest release of ssh when you carry out this process). Continue by following the directions in the file INSTALL. For commercial use, you will need to purchase the Secure Shell from a company called Data Fellows. Consult their web page at www.datafellows.com for more information.

The Secure Shell is being standardized by the Internet Engineering Task Force (IETF). Besides being available for common Unix platforms, it is also available for Windows, OS/2, and Macintosh systems. There is also a Java implementation.

Obtaining Information About Users and Hosts

Before using remote commands, you may want to obtain some information about machines and users on the network. You can get such information using any of several commands provided for this purpose, including **rwho**, which tells you who is logged in to machines on the network; **finger**, which provides information about specific users on a local or remote host on your network; **ruptime**, which tells you the status of the machines on the network; and **ping**, which tells you whether a machine is up or down.

The rwho Command

You can use the **rwho** command to print information about each user on a machine on your network. The information you get includes the login name, the name of the host, where the user is, and the login time for each user. For example:

```
$ rwho
avi     peg:console     Oct 15 14:53
khr     pikes:console   Oct 15 17:32
jmf     arch:ttya2      Oct 15 12:21
rrr     homx:ttya3      Oct 15 17:06
zeke    xate:ttya0      Oct 15 17:06
```

The finger Command

You can obtain information about a particular user on any machine in your network using the finger command . You obtain the same type of information about a user on a remote machine as you would for a user on your own machine. To obtain information about a user on a remote host, supply the user's address. For example, to obtain information about the user khr on the machine jersey, use this command line:

```
$ finger khrjersey
```

On some machines, **finger** is disabled for remote users for security reasons.

The ruptime Command

You can use the **ruptime** command to obtain information about the status of all machines on the network. The command prints a table containing the name of each host, whether the host is up or down, the amount of time it has been up or down, the number of users on that host, and information on the average load on that machine for the past minute, 5 minutes, and 15 minutes. For example:

```
$ ruptime
aardvark    up 21+02:24,    6 users,    load   0.09,  0.05,  0.02
bosky       up 20+07:58,    5 users,    load   1.23,  2.08,  1.87
fickle      up  6+18:48,    0 users,    load   0.00,  0.00,  0.00
jazzy       up  1+02:31,    8 users,    load   4.29,  4.07,  3.80
kitsch      up 21+02:06,    9 users,    load   1.06,  1.03,  1.00
lucky       up 21+02:06,    4 users,    load   1.09,  1.04,  1.00
olympia     up 21+02:05,    0 users,    load   1.00,  1.00,  1.00
sick      down  2+07:14
xate        up  2+06:39,    1 user,     load   1.09,  1.20,  1.57
```

The preceding shows that the machine aardvark has been up for 21 days, 2 hours, and 24 minutes, has 6 current users logged in, had an average load of 0.09 processes in the last minute, 0.05 processes in the last 5 minutes, and 0.02 processes in the last 15 minutes. The machine *sick* has been down for 2 days, 7 hours, and 14 minutes.

The ping Command

Before using a remote command, you may wish to determine whether the remote machine you wish to contact is up. You can do this with the **ping** command. Issuing this command with the name of the remote machine as an argument determines whether a remote host is up and connected to the network or whether it is down or disconnected from the network.

For example, the command

```
$ ping jersey
jersey is alive
```

tells you that the remote host jersey is up and connected to your network. If jersey is down or is disconnected from the network, you would get this:

```
$ ping jersey
no answer from jersey
```

A remote system may be running and connected to your network, but communication with that system may be slow. You can obtain more information about the connection between your system and the remote system if you are running a variant of Unix that supports options to the **ping** command. For example, you may be able to monitor the response time between your system and the remote system (on Solaris, the **–s** option to **ping** does this). You may even be able to track the actual route that packets between your system and the remote system take in the Internet (on Solaris the –svlR combination of options does this). Consult the manual page for **ping** on your particular system for details on how to obtain similar information for Internet connections from your system.

Chapter 7 Review

■ Chapter Summary

After reading this chapter and completing the exercises, you should understand the following.

Learning About TCP/IP Networking

■ TCP/IP (Transmission Control Protocol/Internet Protocol) is a set of protocols that enable computers to communicate with one another.

■ The protocols were developed by the Internet Engineering Task Force (IETF) using a system based on Requests for Comments (RFCs).

■ A host is a device or service that's connected to the network.

■ To connect to a network, a host must have a network interface card (NIC) installed.

■ The terms "Ethernet board" and "Ethernet card" are often used as synonyms for "network interface card."

■ You can view a machine's hardware address by entering the **ipconfig /all** command at a command prompt.

■ In addition to the hardware address that's physically burned into each NIC, each host on a TCP/IP network also has an IP address (sometimes called an Internet address).

■ The IP address is flexible and can be assigned or changed at any time.

■ You'll rarely see a TCP/IP address expressed in that binary notation. Instead, you'll see them expressed in dotted quad format (also called dotted decimal notation), where the address is divided into four octets. Each octet represents 8 bits of the address, and is expressed as a decimal number in the range of 0 to 255. Dots are used to separate the octets, as in the example 192.168.1.1.

Determining Valid IP Addresses

■ The "subnet mask" "masks" the portion of the IP address that identifies the network to which a host belongs.

■ A series of 1's are used to identify the network portion of the address. The 0's are used to represent the host portion of the address. The 1's "mask off" those digits in the IP address that identify the network as a whole. The 0's represent the portion of the address that identifies the host.

■ The subnet mask "masks" the bits that represent the area code (network ID). The unmasked bits are the telephone number (host ID).

■ While the private IP addresses can't be used for servers on the Internet, they can access the Internet through a proxy server or Network Address Translation (NAT).

■ The lowest possible number is reserved as the network ID (also called the subnet address, the subnet ID, or IP network address).

■ The broadcast address is used when a host needs to send a message to all other hosts on the network.

■ All information sent across the network is divided into packets (also called frames), each of which contains the data to be sent, as well as the IP address of the destination.

■ Any Windows 2000 Server computer can play the role of a router.

■ In case any host in the subnet needs to send a packet to some host that's not in its own subnet, the packet gets shipped straight to the default gateway.

■ A static IP address is one that's assigned by the administrator and never changes.

■ There's no rule that says you must use dynamic addresses on hosts and static IP addresses on servers. But Microsoft recommends that approach; you should keep it in mind when answering any questions about assigning IP addresses to hosts.

■ When viewing the address in binary format, the top (leftmost) 26 bits would be the ones assigned by the registrar, leaving the remaining 6 bits for the administrators assigned to hosts.

■ The easiest way to convert a binary number to decimal, or a decimal number to binary, is to use the Windows calculator.

■ Subnetting is simple to do with a good subnet calculator, like SolarWinds.Net Advanced Subnet Calculator, available from www.tucows.com. Even without a subnet calculator, you can figure out anything as long as you know the network address and subnet mask.

- Broadcasting is required when a given host doesn't know the address of some host with which it needs to communicate.

Configuring Routing

- The simplest form of routing is the network that's attached to the Internet via a router or modem and an Internet service provider (ISP).

- A little bit of routing goes a long way in connecting all kinds of networks together, providing network communications across a wide variety of platforms.

- In the event that two routes have identical subnet masks, the route with the smallest metric will be chosen first.

- You can intentionally add some conflicting, static routes to a routing table for fault tolerance.

- Windows 2000 doesn't automatically install drivers for every NIC on the market, so you need to check the card and TCP/IP right after you install Windows, or install a new card.

Troubleshooting TCP/IP and Routing

- All versions of Windows support the **ipconfig** command. However, Windows 95 and 98 use the command **winipcfg** instead.

- A good strategy for troubleshooting TCP/IP problems with **ping** is to start with the local host, and then gradually work your way out to hosts that are increasingly distant from the local host.

- If you can ping a host by its IP address, but not its hostname, you should suspect a problem with your DNS configuration or name resolution.

Learning Unix Commands for TCP/IP Networking

- Security for the Remote Commands is managed on both the user level and the host level.

- On the host level, each host on a TCP/IP network contains a file called /etc/host.equiv.

- The .rhosts file defines "equivalent" users, who are given the same access privileges.

- Shell metacharacters are interpreted on the local machine instead of the remote machine unless you use escape characters or quotation marks.

- The Berkeley Remote Commands allow users access to resources on remote computers. Unfortunately, systems that enable these commands are vulnerable to attack by unauthorized parties.

Key Terms

Address Resolution Protocol (ARP) *(318)*

broadcast address *(296)*

default gateway address *(297)*

dotted quad format *(294)*

finger command *(331)*

hosts *(293)*

IP address *(294)*

multicast address *(310)*

ping (Packet Internet Groper) *(316)*

route print *(309)*

subnet mask *(294)*

subnetting *(297)*

TCP/IP *(293)*

tracert (Trace Route) *(318)*

Key Term Quiz

Use the Key Terms list to complete the sentences that follow. (Not all terms will be used.)

1. A TCP/IP network is composed of _____.

2. Every host that has an IP address also has a _____.

3. The highest possible address in the range of available addresses is reserved as the _____.

4. _____ represents the place to which all "foreign" packets are sent.

5. The _____ is a complex of computers, cables, networks, and routers connecting computers and networks around the globe.

6. You can view the routing table by entering the _____ command at the command prompt.

7. _____ is a means of sending a single stream of data to multiple IP addresses.

8. The **ipconfig** command works only on systems that have the _____ networking protocols installed.

9. _____ provides information about each router or gateway that a message crosses when trying to reach another host.

10. You can obtain information about a particular user on any machine in your network using the _____.

■ Multiple-Choice Quiz

1. Every NIC that is manufactured is given what type of unique hardware address?

    a. 32-bit

    b. 48-bit

    c. 16-bit

    d. 64-bit

2. What is every computer in a network likely to have?

    a. Default gateway address

    b. Broadcast address

    c. Subnet mask

    d. tracert

3. What do hosts on small subnets often use to communicate with one another?

    a. IP address

    b. Ports

    c. Routers

    d. Broadcasting

4. What is a computer containing two or more NICs called?

    a. Stand-alone computer

    b. Personal computer

    c. Multihomed computer

    d. Server

5. If you cannot ping a host outside your subnet, what command can you use to locate where the problem might lie?

    a. ping

    b. ipconfig

    c. ipconfig /all

    d. tracert

6. What is it called if a router's IP address appears repeatedly in the display?

    a. Protocol error

    b. Multicasting

    c. Messaging

    d. Looping

7. Whenever you encounter a problem tracing the route to an Internet address, where is the faulty router very likely to be?

    a. Outside your company's internal network

    b. Inside your company's internal network

    c. Tracing your company's internal network

    d. Mapping your company's internal network

8. What command combines features of **ping** and **tracert**?

    a. finger

    b. pathping

    c. ruptime

    d. Berkeley Remote

9. How many sets of commands used to supply networking services over the Internet do most versions of Unix include?

    a. Three

    b. Five

    c. Two

    d. Four

10. During what session are characters passed back and forth between the two systems because you remain connected to your original host during the session?

    a. login

    b. rlogin

    c. ping

    d. man

11. What command is used to copy files to and from remote machines on a TCP/IP network?

 a. telnet

 b. jersey

 c. rcp

 d. DARPA

12. What command can you use to obtain information about the status of all machines on the network?

 a. Ipconfig /all

 b. finger

 c. ping jersey

 d. ruptime

13. What uses both private- and public-key cryptography for encryption and authentication functions?

 a. rwho command

 b. Modem

 c. rwall command

 d. Secure Shell

14. Which type of faulty entries can cause **ping echo** requests to other computers in the network to fail?

 a. ARP

 b. Command

 c. IP

 d. TCP/IP

15. If pinging the loopback address results in an error message, there's likely a communication problem between Windows 2000 and your NIC. In that case, what do you need to remove and reinstall?

 a. Windows 2000

 b. TCP/IP

 c. NIC

 d. Internet Explorer

■ Essay Quiz

1. List Active Routes and explain each of them.

2. What are the steps necessary to use the **ipconfig / all** command?

3. Write a note on Berkeley Remote Commands and DARPA commands.

4. What is Secure Shell?

Lab Projects

• Lab Project 7.1

Ensure that you have proper Internet access from your current machine. Try out the **tracert** command by following these simple steps:

❶ Click the Windows Start button and choose Programs | Accessories | Command Prompt.

❷ Type **tracert 208.55.30.20** to ping a web site.

❸ After viewing the output, type **exit** and press ENTER to close the Command Prompt window.

• Lab Project 7.2

The **ipconfig** command works only on systems that have the TCP/IP networking protocols installed. If entering the **ipconfig /all** command returns an error message such as "TCP/IP is not running on this system," there's a problem with the NIC or with the TCP/IP installation. Check to see if the NIC is working properly.

chapter 8

Configuring Hard Drives

In this chapter, you will learn how to

- **Describe how hard drives store data**

- **Physically install a hard drive in a PC**

- **Configure a newly installed hard drive**

- **Maintain and troubleshoot a hard drive**

- **Use PartitionMagic to create and maintain hard drive partitions**

- **Use Norton Ghost to backup and restore complete partitions**

By now you probably appreciate that every PC runs programs—lots of programs—and every PC needs a place to store all of those programs so they are available when you need them. This big storage area on a PC is the hard drive. Hard drives can hold a tremendous amount of information—current drives store over 200GB of data!

You'll begin this chapter by taking a look inside a hard drive to see how it works and to learn some important terms, like EIDE and SCSI. After that, you'll learn how to install a hard drive in a typical system. Finally, you'll find out what it takes to keep your hard drive running at top efficiency and what you can do to fix some of the more common hard drive issues you're likely to encounter.

How Hard Drives Store Data

The hard drive is the great paradox of the PC. Incredibly complex devices, hard drives are also fairly simple to install and use. They store extremely sensitive data, yet they can withstand an amazing amount of punishment. No larger than a small book, a single hard drive can store many thousands of books. Let's begin by examining the insides of these incredible devices to get a sense of how they perform their amazing feats.

If you open a hard drive, you'll see what seems to be a fairly simple apparatus: a number of shiny disks with some read/write armatures at each side of each drive.

If you flip a hard drive over and look at its underside, you'll find that it's covered by a computer circuit board. This board contains most of the logic that controls the movement of the disks and read/write arms inside the drive. This board is called the *hard drive controller* circuit board.

The disks, read/write arms, and controller circuitry work together to do one thing: store ones and zeros—lots and lots of ones and zeros. The data on the drive must be *organized* in some way that enables the PC to *retrieve* all of those stored ones and zeros. That organization is based on an electronic division of the drive, which is called the drive's `geometry`.

Geometry

Have you ever taken a close look at a music CD? No matter how hard you look, you can't tell whether it actually contains any music until you drop it into your CD player. The moment you start playing the CD, however, you know *something* is on that CD. The music on the CD is stored as a series of microscopic pits arranged in distinct, concentric circles on the disc. You can say that the physical placement of those circles of tiny pits is the CD's *geometry*.

Hard drives also have a geometry. Unlike a CD, a hard drive uses microscopic magnetic spots on a `platter` instead of the tiny pits found on a CD, but in both cases the "marks" form concentric circles. Thus, a hard drive's geometry is similar to that of a CD, even though the medium is quite different.

Geometry determines where a hard drive stores data on its stacks of disks. Just as with the music CD, if you opened up a hard drive, you would not see the geometry. Unlike the CD, however, each model of hard drive has a *different* geometry. We describe the geometry of a particular hard drive with a set of numbers that refer to three unique values: the number of heads, the number of cylinders, and the number of sectors per track.

Heads

The heads of a hard drive are its `read/write heads`. Every platter requires two heads: one to read the top side and

• Internal and external views of a typical hard drive

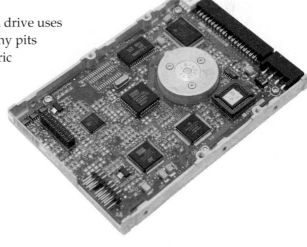

• Controller board on a typical hard drive

> ⚠ Opening a hard drive will destroy it. *Never* open a hard disk unless it's already on the way to the trash heap and you're curious to look inside.

• Four platters = eight heads

Inside Information

Hard Drive Makes and Models

Every hard drive has a make and a model, just like an automobile. Four of the biggest hard drive manufacturers are Seagate Technology, IBM, Western Digital, and Fujitsu. A typical make and model number for a hard drive is Seagate ST3120023A. The make and model number always are displayed on the hard drive. Knowing the make and model of your hard drive is critical for both installing and fixing the drive.

Two tracks—one on top and another underneath.

Every head has many hundreds of tracks on each side.

• Tracks on hard drive platters

• A cylinder is a group of tracks of the same diameter.

one to read the bottom side. If a hard drive has four platters, for example, it needs eight heads.

Because every platter needs two heads, you might assume that hard drives always have an even number of heads, but you'd be mistaken. Most hard drives have an extra head or two for their own use. These extra heads help guide the read/write heads into the correct position, as well as perform other jobs unique to that drive. Therefore, a hard drive can have either an even or an odd number of heads.

Cylinders

The second element of hard drive geometry is the cylinder. To visualize a cylinder, imagine removing both the top and bottom ends of a soup can, washing off the label, and cleaning out the inside. Now imagine sharpening the rim of the soup can so it easily cuts through the hardest metal. Visualize placing the soup can over the hard drive and pushing it down through the drive. The can will cut an identical circular hole through every stacked platter in the drive. Of course, real hard drive platters don't have holes in them—but they do have circles on them where the can would cut the platters: one on the top of the platter, and a matching one on the underside. Each of these circles is called a **track**, and tracks are where you store data on a hard drive.

Each platter has tens of thousands of concentric tracks on each side. Interestingly, the individual tracks themselves are not directly part of the drive geometry. Our interest lies in only the *groups* of tracks of the same diameter (think of the can cutting each platter in the same place). Each group of tracks of the same diameter going vertically completely through the drive is a called a **cylinder**.

A hard drive contains more than one cylinder! Get yourself about a thousand more cans, each a different diameter, and push them through the hard drive. A typical hard drive has thousands of cylinders.

Sectors per Track

Imagine cutting the hard drive like you would a round birthday cake, slicing each track into a number of tiny arcs. Each arc is called a sector, and each sector stores 512 bytes of data.

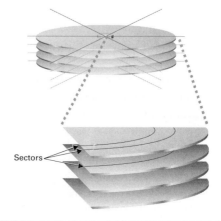

Sectors

• A sector is a section of a track.

Introduction to Client/Server Networking

The sector is the universal atom of all hard drives: you can't divide data into anything smaller than a sector. Although sectors are important, the number of sectors is not a geometry value. The sectors geometry value actually refers to the `sectors per track`, often written sectors/track. The number of sectors in each track is equivalent to the number of "slices" in the hard drive.

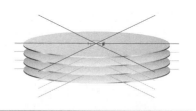

• Six sectors per track (sectors/track)

Working with Geometry

Hard drive geometries are premade at the factory. The only thing you need to do is to make sure that the PC knows the geometry when you install a new hard drive into a computer. You'll learn how to do that in the section "Installing a Hard Drive" later in this chapter.

If a sector is the smallest storage area on your drive, what about a file that is smaller than 512 bytes? It still uses an entire sector. Nobody said computers were completely efficient! On the other hand, how do you store a file that is *larger* than 512 bytes? That's the job of the next two parts of the hard drive system you're going to learn about: partitions and file systems.

Partitions and File Systems

Can you imagine a world where every time you tried to save or retrieve data, you had to point the computer to the exact cylinder, head, and sector you wanted to use? Nobody else could either! Long before any hard drive ever made it into a PC, people realized that most of the details of the storage and retrieval process needed to be hidden from the users if hard drives weren't going to be impossibly difficult to use. One solution to this problem is the `partition`. A partition is a discrete electronic chunk of a hard drive used as an underlying structure for organizing data on the drive. Each partition has, in effect, its own personal card catalog, called a `file allocation table` `(FAT)`. The job of this "card catalog" is to keep track of the location of all files on a given partition.

Windows 9x systems do not allow more than one primary partition per drive. More modern versions of Windows, including NT, 2000, and XP, *do* allow up to four primary partitions on one drive; however, there is rarely any point in actually creating multiple primary partitions. In the Windows world, the overwhelming standard is *one* primary partition per hard drive.

Partitions

Windows PCs use two types of partitions. The type of partition a hard drive uses depends on the operating system. Every hard drive must have at least one partition. The most common type is the `primary partition`. The other type is the `extended partition`. In most cases, a hard drive is configured with one primary partition, which is assigned the drive letter C:, but there are plenty of exceptions.

Primary partitions differ from extended partitions in two very important ways. First, *only* primary partitions are bootable—your computer automatically looks for a primary partition at boot time. If you plan to boot to an operating system on a hard drive, you must install that operating system in a primary partition. Extended partitions are not required and are not bootable. Second, primary partitions are assigned a drive letter, but extended partitions are not, at least not directly. Once created, extended partitions must be divided into one or more `logical drives`, and it is these logical drives that have drive letters associated with them. On your computer, you might have a 100GB hard drive. Instead of having one big primary partition, you could create a 50GB primary partition and a 50GB extended partition.

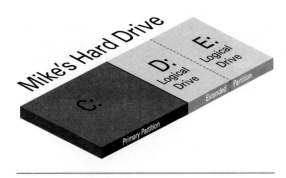

• Partitioning of Mike's hard drive

Then you could divide the extended partition into two logical drives of 25GB each. The primary partition would be drive C:, and the two logical drives D: and E:.

Why not just make the entire hard drive a single 100GB partition? You certainly could, but dividing the drive like this makes backup easier. The operating system lives on the C: drive, so it's good to store all of your critical data on one of the logical drives, which you back up regularly. Keep copies of all of your drivers on the second logical drive for emergency access in case the C: drive fails. On most computers, however, you will find the entire drive formatted as one big primary partition, labeled the C: drive. That's fine for many users, but now you know you have options if you need them!

So where is all this partition information stored? All partition information is stored in a specific place on the hard drive called the boot sector. The boot sector consists of five distinct pieces: the **master boot record (MBR)** and the four partition information areas. The MBR is simply a tiny bit of code that helps the operating system load the correct partition.

When you boot your computer, the PC automatically starts reading the boot sector, looking for a primary partition from which to boot. The boot sector information directs the PC to begin reading the operating system from the primary partition, enabling your system to boot. In theory, you can have up to four primary partitions on a single hard drive, each loaded with a different operating system. In practice, about the only time you'll see more than one primary partition is when someone has loaded multiple operating systems on a single hard drive.

Suppose you were sufficiently geeky to have four different operating systems to choose from on your hard drive; how would the MBR know which partition to boot from? That's where the *active partition* comes into play. The MBR always boots to the active partition. Only one primary partition at a time can be set as the active partition. In most cases, this doesn't matter, though, because in most cases there is only one primary partition, which is automatically set as the active partition.

File Systems

To store files in a partition, your PC needs a filing system that defines the names of the files, as well as a system to track which sector stores which file. Additionally, you want to be able to create folders so that you can organize the contents of the drive. Over the years, Windows has used a number of different file systems, but they all have the same function. Essentially, they work like the card catalogs in libraries, which tell you where a particular book can be found on the shelves: that is, file systems tell the software where to find the data files stored on the hard drive. Let's look at the three generations of "card catalogs" used by Windows PCs.

FAT16   The oldest of the Windows file systems is called FAT16. FAT stands for File Allocation Table, and the number 16 refers to the fact that this file system allocates 16 bits to store the address of each sector. The File Allocation Table of a FAT16 file system is stored at the beginning of the partition, before any other data.

The first versions of FAT16 (going *way* back to the DOS days here) had a limitation: the largest partition that FAT16 could handle was only 32MB.

 A single primary partition or logical drive can use only one file system.

Now keep in mind that at this time, hard drives held only 5 to 10MB, so the first version of FAT worked just fine. However, as hard drives grew, it became obvious that a new and improved version of FAT16 was needed.

When DOS 4.0 came out in the late 1980s, a new version of FAT16 came out as well. This new version grouped sectors together into a new "atom" called a *cluster*. The number of sectors in a cluster depended on the size of the partition. The larger the partition, the more sectors per cluster. This improved FAT16 could support partitions of up to 2GB.

FAT16 was the only choice for later versions of DOS, Windows 3.1 (the version of Windows before Windows 95), and the first versions of Windows 95. However, the constant increases in hard drive size motivated Microsoft to come up with a new file system.

 Even though FAT16 is now considered obsolete, it is still supported by every version of Windows, emphasizing yet again how important backward compatibility is to computer makers!

FAT32   As hard drives began to approach and pass the 2GB limit of FAT16, Microsoft recognized the need for a new file system that could handle larger partitions. Microsoft introduced a new type of file system called FAT32. As its name implies, FAT32 uses 32 bits to address each cluster. This didn't just double the maximum partition size, however, because the math involved is exponential: instead of $2^{16} \times 512$ bytes per sector, a partition could hold $2^{32} \times 512$ bytes per sector, raising the capacity from 32 *mega*bytes to a whopping 2 *tera*bytes (in theory—however, Windows 2000 supports FAT32 partitions of up to only 32 *giga*bytes). FAT32 is the file system of choice for all versions of Windows 9*x* with the exception of the very first version of Windows 95. If you have a system running a later version of Windows 95, any version of Windows 98, or Windows Me, it probably has a FAT32 file system.

NTFS   Windows NT, 2000, and XP all use the vastly more powerful, robust, and flexible `NT File System (NTFS)`. What makes NTFS so great? Well, let's just say that NTFS is virtually indestructible, provides ultrahigh security for files, on-the-fly file and folder compression and encryption, and a wealth of other features. NTFS uses a super-FAT called the `master file table (MFT)` that builds substantially on the FAT concept. Unlike FAT16 and FAT32, NTFS enables users to adjust the cluster sizes, although people rarely do so. NTFS supports partitions of up to 2 terabytes.

So Many File Systems!   With so many file formats, how do you know which one to use? In almost all cases, you want to use the best file format your operating system supports. If you have a Windows 9*x* system that supports FAT32, use it. If you have Windows 2000 or XP, use NTFS. Sometimes you may encounter systems that use NTFS as the primary file system but have an extra FAT32 partition for backward compatibility or dual-boot purposes.

Step-by-Step 8.1

Identifying Your File System

Every version of Windows has some method to enable you to identify the file system used by your hard drives. In this exercise, you will learn how to

identify your file system using both Windows 98 and Windows XP. The Windows 98 procedure works for any Windows 9*x* system, and the XP procedure also works for Windows 2000 systems. Windows 9*x* systems provide two ways to determine the type of file system being used: you can run a program called FDISK, or you can check the properties of the drive in My Computer. Windows 2000 and XP also let you check the properties of the drive in My Computer, and you can use the Disk Administrator tool.

To complete this exercise, you will need the following:

■ A computer system running Windows 98

■ A computer system running Windows 2000 or XP

Step 1

Boot the computer running Windows 98. Choose Start | Run and type **command** to open a command prompt window. Type **FDISK** and press ENTER to run the FDISK program. Select Yes if prompted to choose large disk support. Select option 4, Display Partition Information. Make a note of the partition information that you see.

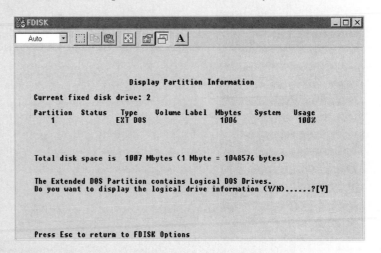

Step 2

Press the ESC key to return to the main FDISK screen. If you have more than one hard drive, select menu option 5 and then select the other hard drive. Again select option 4 to display the partition information and then make a note of it. Close FDISK and then close the command prompt window.

Step 3

Now try the second method. Open My Computer. Select the primary hard drive, right-click the icon, and select Properties. In the Drive Properties dialog box, examine the General tab, which should be displayed by default. Look for the FAT16 or FAT32 file system designation. Make a note of it. Close the dialog box and My Computer.

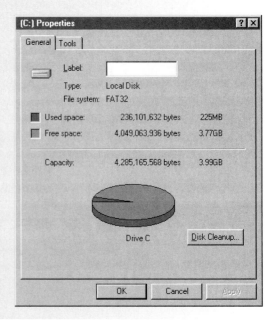

Step 4

Now boot the computer running Windows 2000 or XP. Open My Computer. Select the primary hard drive, right-click the icon, and select Properties. In the Drive Properties dialog box, examine the General tab, which should be displayed by default. Make a note of the file system designation, which in this case should be NTFS. Close the dialog box and My Computer.

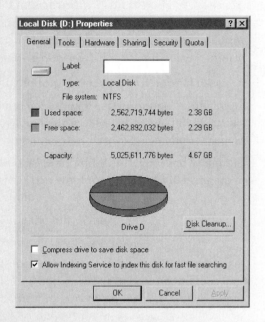

Step 5

Open the Control Panel, double-click to open Administrative Tools, and then open the Computer Management applet. Click Disk Management to display information on all fixed drives, including the file system type of each partition. Note whether your hard drive has one or multiple partitions, and whether you have any FAT32 partitions (probably you don't). Close the applet and the Control Panel.

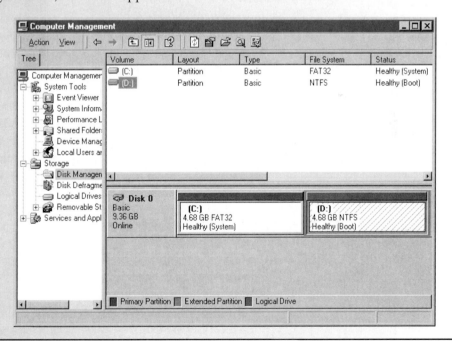

■ Installing a Hard Drive

Now that you know about the physical hard drive, partitions, and file systems, you are ready to install a hard drive. This section presents the issues to

> ⚠ Everything you are about to learn can and will *wipe out all data* on a hard drive. Don't perform any of the steps in this section on a drive that contains data that you want to keep!

consider and steps to follow to install a new hard drive in your system unit and get it ready for work.

EIDE Versus SCSI

Two totally incompatible drive technologies are used in PCs. In this chapter, you will work with the far more common technology, **Enhanced Integrated Drive Electronics (EIDE)**. EIDE drives are used in over 95 percent of all computers and are almost certainly the type of drive you'll want to know how to install. The other type of drive technology is called small computer systems interface (SCSI, pronounced "skuzzy"). It's easy to tell a SCSI drive from an EIDE drive; drive makers learned a long time ago to advertise the drive technology on the drive itself, so all you need to do is read the back of the case.

You can also look at a drive's connections. EIDE drives use a unique 40-pin connector, whereas SCSI drives use either a 50-pin connector or, more often these days, a high-density (a nice way to say that it has tiny pins), 68-pin connector.

Hard Drive Terminology

No one can outdo the hard drive industry in creating confusing acronyms. Here are some of the terms you'll run into:

- **ATA** Advanced Technology Attachment, or ATA, is the real family of standards behind IDE or EIDE. The ATA umbrella includes a number of standards that define everything from the physical connections to the speed of the drives. These standards span ATA-1 through ATA-7.

- **ATAPI** The ATA Programmable Interface, or ATAPI, standard was introduced as part of the ATA-2 standard. The ATA-2 standard was remarkable in that it allowed storage devices other than hard drives (CD-ROMs, Zip drives, tape drives) to use the ATA connections.

- **EIDE** EIDE was a marketing term invented by Western Digital about 12 years ago to reflect their adoption of the ATA-2 standard. It added slightly to the standard by allowing a maximum of four ATA devices. The term EIDE is used universally to describe all drives under the ATA-2 through ATA-5 standards.

- **IDE** More correctly called ATA-1, IDE was the predecessor of EIDE. It uses the same cables but much slower drives. Actual IDE drives are obsolete, and you are unlikely to encounter one, but you will still hear the term used as shorthand for EIDE technology. IDE systems supported a maximum of two hard drives.

- **PIO** Programmable Input/Output, or PIO, was the original method for transferring data between the hard drive and RAM in early versions of ATA. It was replaced by UDMA and is now obsolete.

- **UDMA** Ultra Direct Memory Access, or UDMA, is the current method for transferring data between the hard drive and RAM. The term UDMA is rarely used, however; instead, you will see references to **ATA speed ratings**.

What you'll find interesting in the real world is how badly these terms are used. The knowledge of a computer person is often judged by the use of these terms. For example, a tech who calls an EIDE drive an "ATA drive" shows that he or she is familiar with the terminology. Although ATA is more correct, the term EIDE is used so overwhelmingly that even we will use it in this chapter. You are encouraged to use these terms correctly in the real world—but also realize that these terms are largely interchangeable.

EIDE drives have different UDMA speed ratings. ATA speed ratings measure how fast the hard drive is capable of transferring data to the rest of the system, expressed in MBps. This is a maximum potential speed, which is not achieved under most conditions. The standard speeds are 33, 66, 100, and 133 MBps. The common terms for these speeds are ATA33, ATA66, ATA100, and ATA133.

These speed ratings are important for two reasons besides just performance. First, ATA33 uses an older 40-wire cable, whereas all the newer speed ratings use an 80-wire cable. Second, your motherboard is designed to use a certain speed of hard drive. If you match a slower hard drive controller with a faster hard drive or vice versa, the resulting data transfer speed will be that of the slower device. For best performance, match the speed rating of your hard drive to the speed rating that your motherboard is designed to support, and use the proper cable for that speed.

A final terminology issue you should be aware of (before we dive into a discussion of EIDE cables) concerns the term *controller*. The actual controller for an EIDE drive is located on the drive itself; however, it is common to refer to the 40-pin motherboard connection at the other end of the drive cable (Figure 8.1) as a controller, too. Strictly speaking, this usage of the term is incorrect, but you need to recognize it when you hear it because, like many such errors, it has become a common reference.

• **Figure 8.1**   EIDE connectors on a motherboard

EIDE Cables

Every EIDE controller can support two EIDE drives. EIDE cables have three connections: one for each drive and one for the controller. As mentioned earlier, there are two types of EIDE cables: the older 40-wire version and the newer 80-wire version (Figure 8.2).

Even though one cable has 80 wires and the other has 40 wires, they both have only 40 *pins*—so what happens to the extra 40 wires in the 80-wire cable? Because they're used only to reduce interference, these wires don't have pin connections. Instead, they simply terminate inside the connectors.

Master/Slave

When two devices share a single ribbon cable and both have their own onboard controllers, one device needs to be configured to handle the control work for both devices. The device that is doing the controlling is called the master. The other device's controller needs to be configured so it knows that the first controller is in charge. The device that's not in charge is called the slave. When you install a hard drive,

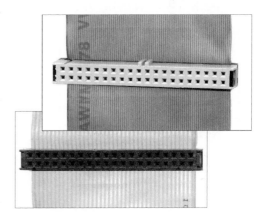

• **Figure 8.2**   Comparison of 40-wire (bottom) and 80-wire (top) EIDE ribbon cables

• **Figure 8.3** Setting a jumper for master or slave operation on a hard drive

Most drives come from the factory preset as master or single.

you must configure these settings. Every EIDE drive has several small jumpers that are designed to let you configure it as a master or a slave.

So how do you know where to place the jumpers to make a drive a master or a slave? Well, all good drives will have this information printed clearly on the drive itself (Figure 8.3). Most EIDE drives have two different master settings. One master setting is for a master with a slave present, and the other setting is for a drive without a slave present. Again, the documentation on the drive itself will show you these settings.

On rare occasions, you may stumble across a drive that does not have these settings printed on it. In these cases, visit the support section of the manufacturer's web site. As a rule, hard drive makers provide excellent documentation for their drives.

Remember that you must configure the master/slave setting properly if you want drives on the same ribbon cable to operate. If you have one drive, it must be set to master or single, depending on the manufacturer's requirement. If you have a second drive on the same ribbon cable, it must be set as a slave, and the first drive must be set as the master with a slave present if such a setting exists.

ATA Speed Ratings

Where you place the master and slave drives on the cable doesn't matter on the older ATA33 drives that use the 40-wire cables. The master can be on the end of the cable or in the middle. However, on drives using more modern ATA speeds (ATA66 and faster), the location of the master and slave on the 80-wire cables is critical. The 80-wire cables have three color-coded connectors (Figure 8.4). The colored connector (usually blue but sometimes red) must attach to the controller on the motherboard. The black connector, on the end, must attach to the master (or single) drive. If you have a slave drive, it must attach to the gray connector, in the middle.

Nearly all motherboards come with two EIDE controllers. One controller is the primary controller, and the other controller is the secondary controller. On most systems, these are clearly marked as IDE0 (primary) and IDE1 (secondary).

On modern systems that use ATA66 or better, usually only the primary controller uses a high-speed connection, and the secondary connection uses

• **Figure 8.4** Colored connectors on an 80-wire cable

the older ATA33 standard. Motherboards that follow this scheme often have one colored controller and one white controller (Figure 8.5). When you see this, you can start with the assumption that the colored controller is the primary one.

The first hard drive in a system should always be the master (or single) on the primary controller. A second hard drive is normally installed as the primary slave, but there's nothing intrinsically wrong with making the second drive a secondary master.

One issue that comes up often concerns the interchangeability of ATA33 and the faster standards. For example, can you install an ATA100 hard drive on an old-style ATA33 controller using the older 40-wire cable? You certainly can! You just won't get the speed enhancement of the faster ATA100 standard, but the drive will work fine. So how about installing an ATA100 drive on an ATA66 controller with an 80-wire cable? That will also work, but the drive will run only at ATA66 speeds. Pretty much everything is interchangeable but will run at the speed of the slowest device.

• **Figure 8.5**   Different-colored connectors on a motherboard

BIOS Limitations

After a drive is physically installed, you must configure its geometry so that the system can work with the drive. Back in the bad old days, that meant that you had to fire up the System Setup utility and manually punch in the geometry—and if you got one of the values wrong, the drive would not function. Fortunately, those days are long gone. Now every System Setup utility includes a special setting called Autodetect (or just Auto) that tells the system to query the drive at bootup to get all the necessary geometry information (Figure 8.6).

Autodetect is a great tool when installing a new hard drive. After you've installed the drive, you can run Autodetect to see whether the system recognizes the drive. If Autodetect doesn't see the drive (Figure 8.7), you know you've made a mistake with the cabling, jumpers, or power.

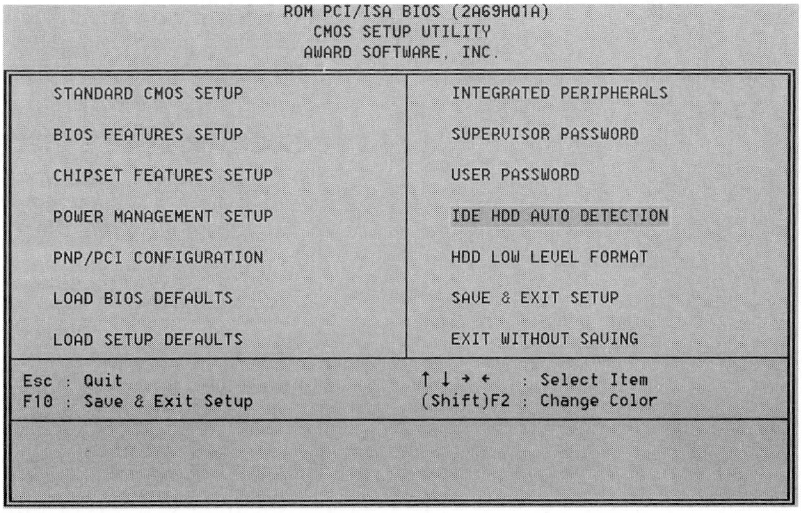

People new to installing hard drives are sometimes confused because most System Setup utilities still provide settings, usually labeled User or Manual, that allow manual configuration of the geometry settings. These settings are there for a few rare situations and can be ignored.

Just as operating systems over the years have evolved to support larger hard drive sizes, so has the BIOS. The earliest BIOS programs could not support drives larger than 504MB. If you installed a new 50GB hard drive and ran

```
                    ROM PCI/ISA BIOS (2A69HQ1A)
                        CMOS SETUP UTILITY
                       AWARD SOFTWARE, INC.

   STANDARD CMOS SETUP              INTEGRATED PERIPHERALS

   BIOS FEATURES SETUP             SUPERVISOR PASSWORD

   CHIPSET FEATURES SETUP          USER PASSWORD

   POWER MANAGEMENT SETUP          IDE HDD AUTO DETECTION

   PNP/PCI CONFIGURATION           HDD LOW LEVEL FORMAT

   LOAD BIOS DEFAULTS              SAVE & EXIT SETUP

   LOAD SETUP DEFAULTS             EXIT WITHOUT SAVING

   Esc : Quit                      ↑ ↓ → ←  : Select Item
   F10 : Save & Exit Setup         (Shift)F2 : Change Color
```

• **Figure 8.6**   Autodetection at system setup

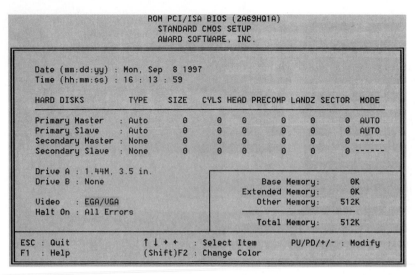

```
                    ROM PCI/ISA BIOS (2A69HQ1A)
                         STANDARD CMOS SETUP
                        AWARD SOFTWARE, INC.

   Date (mm:dd:yy) : Mon, Sep  8 1997
   Time (hh:mm:ss) : 16 : 13 : 59

   HARD DISKS          TYPE   SIZE   CYLS HEAD PRECOMP LANDZ SECTOR  MODE

   Primary Master  : Auto      0      0    0     0      0      0     AUTO
   Primary Slave   : Auto      0      0    0     0      0      0     AUTO
   Secondary Master : None     0      0    0     0      0      0     ------
   Secondary Slave : None      0      0    0     0      0      0     ------

   Drive A : 1.44M, 3.5 in.
   Drive B : None                     ┌────────────────────────────────┐
                                      │   Base Memory:        0K        │
   Video   : EGA/VGA                  │ Extended Memory:      0K        │
   Halt On : All Errors               │   Other Memory:     512K        │
                                      │                                 │
                                      │   Total Memory:     512K        │
                                      └────────────────────────────────┘
   ESC : Quit              ↑ ↓ → ←  : Select Item    PU/PD/+/- : Modify
   F1  : Help             (Shift)F2 : Change Color
```

● **Figure 8.7**   Screen when Autodetect does not find a drive

Many people want to know what capacity of drive they should buy. There's no formula to determine this. In most cases, you should simply purchase the largest-capacity drive you can afford. If you are going to be working with graphics and video, a large capacity is particularly important. You should never consider buying a drive smaller than 30GB, but that's not saying much—it's hard to find a drive smaller than 20GB on a new system nowadays.

Autodetect, it would report a 504MB drive. Back in 1990, a new standard called LBA increased the maximum supported drive size to 8.3GB. Most drives today use a relatively new standard called INT13 Extensions that enables your BIOS to recognize drives of up to 137GB. Unless you have a system that predates 1997, odds are good you have a BIOS with INT13 Extensions.

So what about hard drives bigger than 137GB? There's a new standard called ATA-6 that introduces a new limit: a whopping 144 petabytes (144,000,000GB). This new standard—better known, as peddled by Maxtor Corporation, as Big Drives—should keep us from worrying about maximum drive size for a while.

So what do you do if you install a drive in a system and Autodetect can't see the entire contents of the drive? The best option is to contact your motherboard maker and see if it has a BIOS update that will upgrade your BIOS so your system can recognize the drive. These days, this can be done pretty easily from most manufacturers' web sites.

If your motherboard manufacturer doesn't have a BIOS upgrade, you can still use the drive, although the solution is not pretty. You can install a drive overlay program that, in essence, adds a little extra BIOS to your hard drive and enables your system to recognize the drive. Drive overlay programs usually come on floppy disks with new hard drives. Because, essentially, you're storing a BIOS on your hard drive, drive overlays are inherently risky. When you use an overlay program, file corruption may result in the loss of all data on the drive. However, if a BIOS upgrade isn't available, an overlay is your only option.

Every drive manufacturer makes its own drive overlays, and each has its own installation method. Most require a bootable floppy disk (good thing you know how to make one of those!). Read the instructions carefully before you use a drive overlay!

Physically Installing a Hard Drive

Okay—armed with all of this knowledge, it's time for you to install your EIDE hard drive. The first step is to determine what speed of hard drive your motherboard can handle. A quick check of the motherboard documentation should give you that information.

Next, make sure that you get a drive with at least that speed—remember that faster drives are always backward compatible. It's not uncommon to see an old PC using a fast new hard drive, not because the system can use the speed but because that's all that's available.

The next step is to set the jumpers to single or master. Find those jumpers and set them correctly! Then plug the ribbon cable into the drive and into the controller on the motherboard. Remember that, as with all ribbon cables, you must orient the colored edge of the ribbon cable toward the number one pin (Figure 8.8).

Rounded hard drive cables can save you space inside the computer case, but they can be tricky to orient correctly. Many rounded cables have no colored stripe or other device to tell you where the number one pin is located. Worse, many rounded cables lack an orientation notch. In many cases, you simply have to guess which direction to orient the cable. Don't worry about guessing, though, because if you plug in the cable backward, you won't damage anything—you just won't see the drive when you use Autodetect. If you think you've installed the cable backward, shut down the system and reorient the cable; then restart the system and see if Autodetect works. After you install the ribbon cable, insert a power connector in the drive (Figure 8.9).

A good approach is to avoid permanently mounting a new hard drive until after the drive passes autodetection. It's too easy to make little mistakes that require you to remove and reinsert the drive. Instead, just slide the drive into a mount, or even leave the drive dangling until Autodetect sees the drive.

After the drive is physically installed, it's time to fire up the system and head into the System Setup program to see whether it recognizes the drive. You can sometimes skip this step because most BIOS programs by default set the primary master drive to Auto; if you watch the boot process carefully, you may see the system recognize the hard drive at bootup.

Many BIOS programs report the hard drive by its model number—good thing you know the model number of your hard drive!—but this is not a perfect test because many others don't report this information. Additionally, if a BIOS has a manual User setting, it will repeatedly report the manual settings and ignore the newly installed drive. Unless your BIOS reports the new drive by model number, the safe course of action is to enter the System Setup utility and run the Autodetect feature.

• **Figure 8.8**   Properly oriented ribbon cable connected to an IDE connector

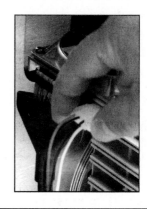

• **Figure 8.9**   Installing power for a drive

Step-by-Step 8.2

Adding a Second Drive

Adding a second hard drive to an existing system is one of the most common system upgrades. This exercise uses a hardware configuration found on most PCs. To complete this exercise, you will need the following:

- A computer system (with any operating system)
- A single hard drive installed in the system and configured with one primary partition (C:)

- A second hard drive compatible with the system
- A 40-wire or 80-wire (depending on the hard drive) ribbon cable to connect the second hard drive when you install it
- A Phillips screwdriver sized for the computer screws
- Motherboard documentation for the system, if available

Step 1   First, power down and unplug the system if you haven't already done so. Take antistatic precautions and set up a neat work area. Open the case, carefully setting aside any screws in a small container. Now inspect the system to see what hard drive *speed* the motherboard can handle. If you see an 80-wire cable on your system, you know that the primary controller will accept at least ATA66, but play it safe anyway and check the motherboard documentation.

Step 2

Determine the maximum hard drive *size* the system can handle. You can make a pretty good guess by noting the size of your existing drive. If the drive in the system is 10GB, you can feel pretty confident that the system is running INT13 Extensions, in which case it can handle a drive of up to 137GB.

Step 3

After you've selected a hard drive to install, you must select the controller on which you will install it. The best place to install a second hard drive is on the primary controller, as a slave. Set the jumpers on both drives. Usually, to change the jumpers on the master drive, you will need to remove the drive from its mount so you can see the jumpers and read the jumper documentation. Remember that many hard drives have separate settings for single master and master with slave. As always, put the screws in a container so they won't fall in the case or roll under the furniture.

Step 4

Reinstall the cable, making sure to orient it correctly to the number one pin and to insert the master and slave at the correct locations on the cable. You'll probably need to install the slave drive at this point because there won't be enough cable to let it dangle as you test. Plug in the power cables to both drives, making sure to get them all the way in.

Step 5

Give your installation efforts a final check and then boot the PC. Run Autodetect to verify that *both* drives are recognized by the system. If there's a problem, recheck each step, remove all the connectors and then plug them all back in, and try again. After the system recognizes the drives, *gently* attach them to the drive bays with the screws you carefully set aside for this purpose; then close the case.

■ Configuring a Hard Drive

After a drive has been physically installed and recognized by the BIOS, you need to partition the drive and to add a file system. The process of creating partitions is called *partitioning,* and the process of adding a file system is called *formatting*. In this section, you will learn the tools and the techniques needed to partition and format hard drives under both Windows 98 and Windows XP. There's a strong motivation for showing you two operating systems here. Windows 95, 98, and Me use one method to partition and format, and Windows NT, 2000, and XP use a completely different method. If you want to work with Windows computers, you need to know both methods.

Partitioning

One of the main differences between Windows 9*x* and Windows NT/2000/XP is their treatment of hard drive partitioning. In the Windows 9*x* world, all partitioning is handled by the command prompt program FDISK. Windows NT/2000/XP do not use FDISK; instead, they rely on a graphical tool called Disk Administrator.

Windows 98 Installation

To install Windows 98 onto a blank hard drive, you need a way to access the installation program, which means that you need an installation program that you can boot from somewhere other than the hard drive. Windows 98 takes care of this by making the Windows 98 installation CD bootable. By going into the System Setup utility and setting the system to boot from the CD-ROM before the hard drive, you can begin the installation of Windows 98 directly from the CD itself.

This book does not cover the Windows 98 installation process in detail, but you should become familiar with a few of the screens that tell you that the installation program is handling the partitioning and formatting job for you.

At some point during the installation process, Windows 98 will notice that you have a blank hard drive and will then begin the partitioning process. By default, it will make the entire hard drive a single primary partition using the FAT32 file system. Windows indicates this by setting the Large Drive Support parameter to Yes. If you change this selection to No, the system will create a FAT16 file system. This brings up an interesting point: you determine the file system at the *partitioning* stage, not the formatting stage. This is true with all partitioning methods.

After you select FAT32 by choosing Large Disk Support, the

```
Microsoft Windows 98 Setup

    You have a drive over 512MB in size. Would
    you like to enable large disk support?

    This allows more efficient use of disk space
    and larger partitions to be defined.

    No, do not use large disk support
    Yes, enable large disk support


    To accept the selection, press ENTER.
    To change the selection, press the UP or DOWN ARROW key,
    and then press ENTER.




ENTER=Continue   F1=Help   F3=Exit
```

• Selecting Large Disk Support during Windows installation

installation program informs you that it is about to restart your computer. Be happy—you just created a primary partition and set it as active! Whenever any changes are made to partitions in Windows 9*x*, you must restart the system, but you don't have to worry about it because the Windows installer handles this task for you. You'll learn how the Windows 98 installation process handles formatting in the next section.

Windows 98 and FDISK   For manual partitioning, FDISK is the tool to use. From the early DOS days through Windows Me, the FDISK program was the only means of partitioning a hard drive. All versions of Windows 9*x* continue to use FDISK. FDISK is text-based, non-intuitive, and easy to misunderstand, but fortunately the most recent versions, the ones that came with Windows 98 and Me, have an automated mode that makes them easier to use.

FDISK is traditionally run from the Windows 98 startup disk. The assumption behind this is that if you are running FDISK, you must not yet have any drive partitioned, so you will need to run FDISK from a floppy disk. You can also run FDISK from Windows using a command prompt, however, and this is the usual way you install a second hard drive. This example will assume that you're running FDISK from a bootable floppy. To start FDISK, simply type **FDISK** at the A:\> prompt and press ENTER.

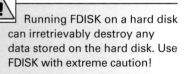
Running FDISK on a hard disk can irretrievably destroy any data stored on the hard disk. Use FDISK with extreme caution!

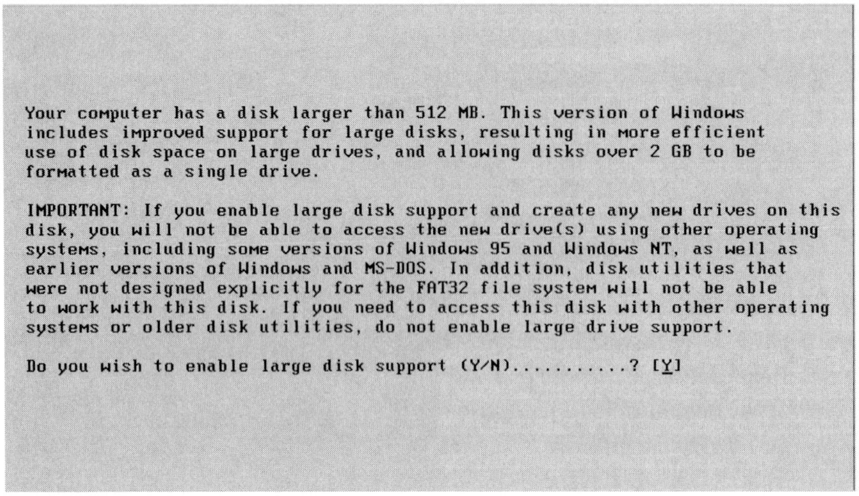

```
Your computer has a disk larger than 512 MB. This version of Windows
includes improved support for large disks, resulting in more efficient
use of disk space on large drives, and allowing disks over 2 GB to be
formatted as a single drive.

IMPORTANT: If you enable large disk support and create any new drives on this
disk, you will not be able to access the new drive(s) using other operating
systems, including some versions of Windows 95 and Windows NT, as well as
earlier versions of Windows and MS-DOS. In addition, disk utilities that
were not designed explicitly for the FAT32 file system will not be able
to work with this disk. If you need to access this disk with other operating
systems or older disk utilities, do not enable large drive support.

Do you wish to enable large disk support (Y/N)..........? [Y]
```

• **Figure 8.10** Prompt for large disk support

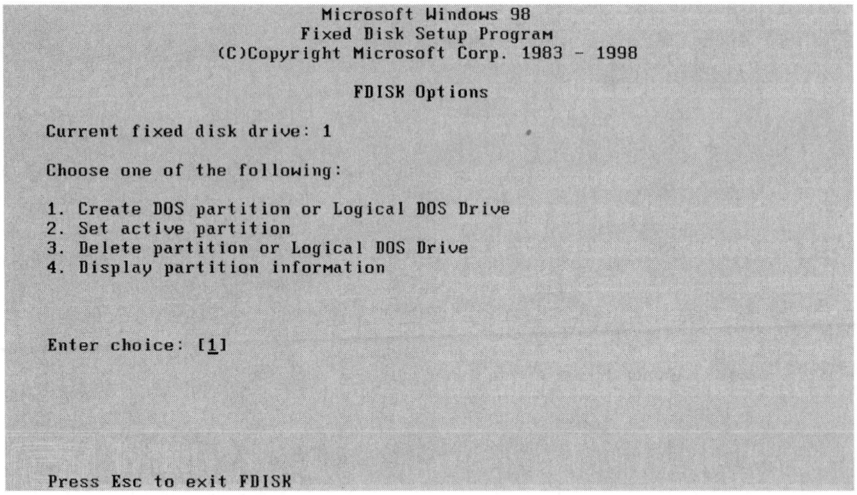

```
                        Microsoft Windows 98
                        Fixed Disk Setup Program
                  (C)Copyright Microsoft Corp. 1983 - 1998

                            FDISK Options

Current fixed disk drive: 1

Choose one of the following:

1. Create DOS partition or Logical DOS Drive
2. Set active partition
3. Delete partition or Logical DOS Drive
4. Display partition information


Enter choice: [1]




Press Esc to exit FDISK
```

• **Figure 8.11** Main FDISK screen

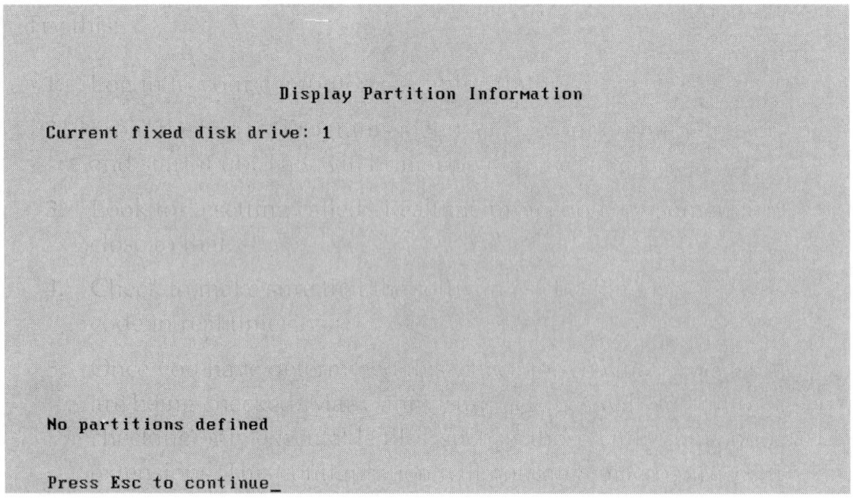

```
                    Display Partition Information

Current fixed disk drive: 1








No partitions defined

Press Esc to continue_
```

• **Figure 8.12** FDISK showing a blank drive

If FDISK detects a hard drive of greater than 504MB, it will prompt you to see if you want large disk support (Figure 8.10). As explained earlier, the program is really asking whether you want to use FAT16 or FAT32. You should respond to this by accepting the default, Y, to use FAT32.

The main FDISK screen provides four menu options: Create DOS Partition or Logical DOS Drive, Set Active Partition, Delete Partition or Logical DOS Drive, and Display Partition Information (Figure 8.11).

In most cases, you have a new, blank drive for which you want to create one large partition. You can see the blank drive in FDISK by selecting option 4, Display Partition Information. To do this, simply press the 4 key and then ENTER. In this example, FDISK reports, "No partitions defined." As shown in Figure 8.12, this is a blank hard drive.

If you want to make just one primary partition, you can use FDISK's automated tool for this purpose. Press ESC to return to the main FDISK screen and then press the 1 key and ENTER to display the Create DOS Partition or Logical DOS Drive screen (Figure 8.13).

At this screen, press 1 to create the primary partition. When you do so, the system asks whether you want to use the maximum available size for a primary DOS partition and make the partition active. If you press ENTER (for Y), FDISK will create a single primary partition on the hard drive (Figure 8.14), and the system will prompt you to restart.

After the drive is partitioned with FDISK and the computer has rebooted to the Windows 98 startup disk, the new drive letter C: appears. Until the drive is actually formatted, however, you won't be able

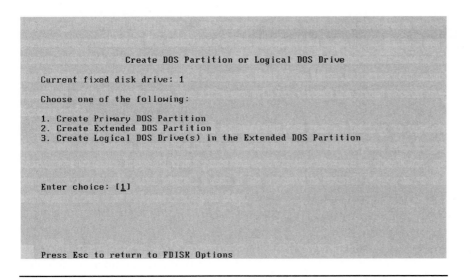

```
                    Create DOS Partition or Logical DOS Drive

Current fixed disk drive: 1

Choose one of the following:

1. Create Primary DOS Partition
2. Create Extended DOS Partition
3. Create Logical DOS Drive(s) in the Extended DOS Partition




Enter choice: [1]




Press Esc to return to FDISK Options
```

• **Figure 8.13**   Create DOS Partition or Logical Drive screen

to access the drive. You'll learn about the formatting process in the next section.

Windows XP Installation

Windows XP also uses a bootable CD-ROM and includes a hard drive setup procedure early in the installation process. The inclusion of NTFS makes the process a bit more complex than the FAT32 process of Windows 98, so it warrants a separate discussion.

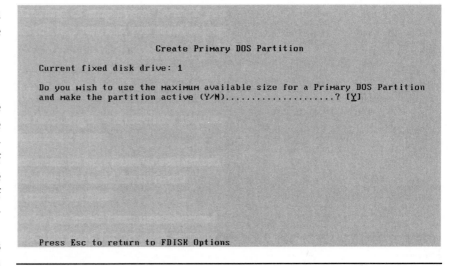

```
                          Create Primary DOS Partition

Current fixed disk drive: 1

Do you wish to use the maximum available size for a Primary DOS Partition
and make the partition active (Y/N).....................? [Y]







Press Esc to return to FDISK Options
```

• **Figure 8.14**   Automated partition creation tool in action

Let's briefly review the process that the Windows XP installation program uses to partition a blank hard drive. When you boot to the installation CD, Windows XP will notice that there are no partitioned hard drives on the system and prompt you to proceed. As instructed, press the letter C. The installation program will search the hard drives and report back. Windows XP then combines completion of the partition with some formatting, prompting you to choose NTFS or FAT.

 The process described here for Windows XP also applies to Windows NT and Windows 2000.

Windows XP and Disk Management   Windows NT, Windows 2000, and Windows XP no longer use FDISK for partitioning, so you must either partition the drive during the initial installation or use the Disk Management utility after you have installed Windows. Of course, you shouldn't change the partition where Windows itself is installed, but Disk Management does a fine job when you need to add a second drive. You will learn to use Disk Management to partition a second drive in Step-by-Step 8.3.

Try This!

Using FDISK

You can run FDISK on any Windows 9x system to inspect the current partitions on any drives on the PC. Try running FDISK on a Windows 9x system to determine the number and size of the partitions on the hard drive. Changing anything using FDISK will destroy data, so you should only tour the existing partitions *without* making any changes. If possible, use a system with *two* installed hard drives.

1. Select Start | Run, type **COMMAND** in the text area, and click OK to open a command prompt window. Type the command **FDISK /STATUS** and press ENTER. A screen appears showing the status information.

2. Now run FDISK without the /STATUS switch, to display the standard FDISK menu screen. If the system has two hard drives, you will see a fifth menu option, which enables you to select the drive to partition.

```
                    Microsoft Windows 98
                   Fixed Disk Setup Program
              (C)Copyright Microsoft Corp. 1983 - 1998

                         FDISK Options

Current fixed disk drive: 1

Choose one of the following:

 1. Create DOS partition or Logical DOS Drive
 2. Set active partition
 3. Delete partition or Logical DOS Drive
 4. Display partition information
 5. Change current fixed disk drive

Enter choice: [1]




Press Esc to exit FDISK
```

- FDISK with five options

3. Select option 4 (Display Partition Information) to see how the first drive is partitioned. Make a note of what you find. If the system has two drives, select option 5 (Change Current Fixed Disk Drive) and choose the second drive; then use option 4 again to see how the second drive is partitioned. Again note what you find. Exit FDISK.

The Disk Administrator tool in Windows NT lacks some of the features of the Disk Administrator tool in Windows 2000 or Windows XP.

Formatting

All versions of Windows offer multiple ways to format a drive and thus make the drive capable of holding data. Most users choose to use one of the graphical methods of formatting in Windows. In Windows 9x, after you've partitioned a new drive using FDISK, the drive will show up in My Computer, but if you try to access it by clicking it, you'll get an error—preparing a drive takes two steps, remember: partitioning and *formatting*.

You can format a hard drive by typing **FORMAT X:** at a command prompt, where X is the letter of the drive you want to format. If you are already running Windows 98, simply right-click on the drive letter in My Computer and select Format to get the standard Windows 98 Format dialog box (Figure 8.15). The procedure here works the same way in Windows 2000 and XP, although the Format dialog box looks a bit different (Figure 8.16).

The Disk Management tool that comes with Windows 2000 and XP also performs disk formatting, but its capabilities reach way beyond formatting and partitioning.

Disk Management

The Disk Management tool that comes with Windows NT/2000/XP is the one-stop, do-it-all utility for working with hard drives using these operating systems. If there's something you want to do to a hard drive, Disk Management is the tool to use to get it done.

Windows 2000 and XP enable you to do some amazing things with your drives. For example, you can change the drive letters assigned to various devices, something Windows 9x doesn't allow. Even more amazing, Windows 2000 and XP enable you to implement a very special type of drive organization called **Redundant Array of Independent Disks (RAID)**. To allow this, Windows assigns a *drive signature* to each drive when it is installed.

• **Figure 8.15**   Windows 98 Format dialog box

Windows then uses this drive signature—invisible to you—to keep track of each of the drives installed in the system.

The first time you install a drive in a particular Windows 2000 or XP system and run Disk Management, Windows opens the Write Signature and Upgrade Disk wizard (Figure 8.17). The wizard asks if you want to put a signature on the drive—no question about it, you want to! It then asks if you want to upgrade the drive to a dynamic disk. In certain cases, you will want to choose Yes here also. For Windows to implement RAID, you must configure the drives as dynamic disks.

Dynamic Disks

Dynamic disks are a storage type unique to Windows 2000 and XP. You can do some cool things with dynamic disks, such as turn two separate hard drives into a single partition. Dynamic disk drives allow you to enlarge their partitions without first deleting the partition or losing data—something previously impossible without specialized third-party tools.

Regular drives are known as basic disks, to distinguish them from dynamic disks. When you convert a drive from a basic to a dynamic disk, there are no longer any such things as primary and extended partitions; dynamic disks are divided into *volumes* instead of partitions.

RAID

RAID arrays are multiple hard drives that work together to act as one drive with a single drive letter. There are seven types of RAID, numbered RAID 0 through RAID 6. Of those seven types, only three, RAID 0, RAID 1, and RAID 5, are commonly used. These RAID types correlate with various types of dynamic disks.

Dynamic disks support different types of volumes:

■ A *simple* volume uses space on a single disk; basically, it acts just like a primary partition.

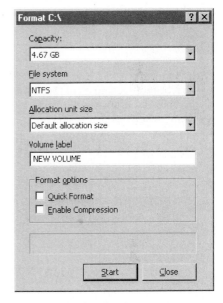

• **Figure 8.16**

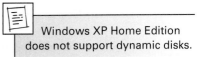
Windows XP Home Edition does not support dynamic disks.

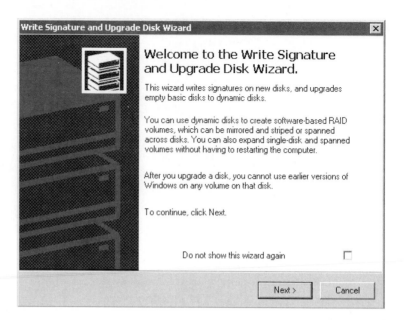

• **Figure 8.17**   Write Signature and Upgrade Disk wizard

Inside Information

Dynamic Disk Compatibility

Windows 2000 and Windows XP are the only operating systems that can read a dynamic disk, so you should be very sure that these are the only operating systems you'll be using before you upgrade from a basic disk to a dynamic disk. Never upgrade to dynamic disks on systems configured to boot more than one operating system, for example. Also note that if you need to remove a drive and put it into a system with an older operating system, if the drive is a dynamic drive, you won't be able to access the data.

■ A *spanned* volume is a simple volume spread across multiple disk drives; it acts like a single partition with one drive letter.

■ A *striped* volume is also known as RAID 0. Striping spreads out blocks of each file across multiple disks. Using two or more drives in a group called a *stripe set*, striping writes data first to a certain number of clusters on one drive, then on the next, and so on. Striping speeds up data throughput because the system has to wait a much shorter time for a drive to read or write data. The drawback of striping is that if any single drive in the stripe set fails, all data in the stripe set is lost.

■ A *mirrored* volume is also known as RAID 1. Using two drives, all data written on one drive is simultaneously written to the second drive. If one of the drives fails, the other can take its place. Mirroring is a very good way to preserve data if a drive fails, but throughput is slow because two read/write operations are required every time the drives are accessed. Data on mirrored drives is duplicated on two physical disks.

■ *RAID 5* is also known as striping with parity; it combines the best of RAID 0 and RAID 1. RAID 5 requires at least three hard drives. Basically, RAID 5 is striping using three or more disks, with fault tolerance added in the form of parity bits, which are also striped across the disks. If one the disks fails, its portion of the striped data can be re-created from the remaining data and the parity bits, as long as only of one of the disks fails. Because it is rare for more than one disk drive to fail at a time, RAID 5 offers safety while still allowing speedy drive access.

The benefits you receive from dynamic disks depend partly on the type you use. Striping enables faster access to your data, but because striped disks are optimized for speed, they're no more fault tolerant than basic disks. Mirrored disks provide wonderful fault tolerance but eat up large amounts of disk real estate. RAID 5 is the most broadly used type of dynamic storage because it combines the speed of striping and the fault tolerance of mirroring, but in a more space-efficient way using parity bits.

Upgrading to Dynamic Disks

To turn a basic disk into a dynamic disk, you can use the Upgrade wizard that starts automatically when you open the Disk Management utility after you install a new drive. You can also start the utility manually by right-clicking the drive and selecting the Convert to Dynamic Disk option (Figure 8.18). After upgrading, the Disk Management tool will indicate that the drive is a dynamic drive, as shown in Figure 8.19.

Dynamic drives are a type of storage, not a type of file system. Just like basic drives, dynamic drives can use FAT16, FAT32, and NTFS file systems.

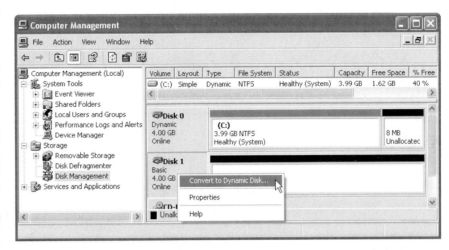

• **Figure 8.18**   Convert to Dynamic Disk option

Third-Party Tools

A number of excellent third-party tools are available to help you with partitioning and formatting chores. One of the most popular third-party tools is PowerQuest's PartitionMagic. PartitionMagic and other very advanced third-party tools are the Swiss Army knives of the drive partitioning and formatting world. Literally anything you need done to your drives, they can

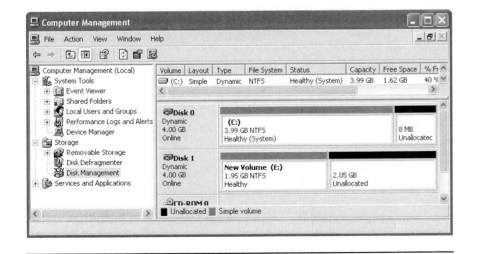

• **Figure 8.19**   Disk Management utility indicating that Disk 1 is now dynamic

do—and best of all, without destroying your data! PartitionMagic is discussed in more detail later in this chapter.

Working with Partitions Using the Disk Management Utility

Dynamic disk storage is the business standard these days, so it's something any good PC tech should be comfortable implementing. In this step-by-step exercise, you will use the Disk Management tool that comes with Windows 2000 and Windows XP to set up a disk with two partitions and then convert the basic disk partitions to dynamic disk volumes.

To complete this exercise, you will need the following:

- A computer system running Windows 2000 or Windows XP Professional with a second hard drive installed but *not* partitioned or formatted

Step 1

Have your system up and running in Windows. Go to the Control Panel and double-click on the Administrative Tools icon; then double-click on the Computer Management icon. In Computer Management, select Disk Management from the available utilities. Because you've installed a new, unformatted drive, the Windows wizard will appear. You're going to perform this task manually, so click Cancel. The Disk Management tool will display the new drive, but with a white bar on a red circle to indicate that it does not yet have a signature.

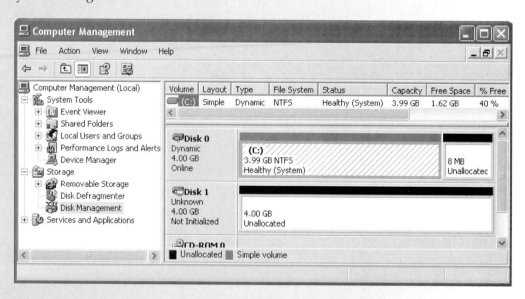

Step 2

Right-click the new disk and select Initialize Drive. After the drive is initialized, again right-click the disk, and this time select Convert to Dynamic Disk. After Disk Management converts the drive, right-click in the black area to the right of the disk area and select New Volume. This will start the New Volume wizard. Click Next on the first screen to display the partition types.

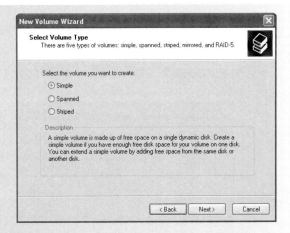

Step 3

Select Simple and click Next to display the Select Disks dialog box. This dialog box has two parts. The left side lists the available drives, and the right side lists the selected drives. By default, the disk you originally right-clicked is selected. At the bottom of the dialog box is the partition size selector. By default, it selects the entire drive. Reduce that amount by roughly half.

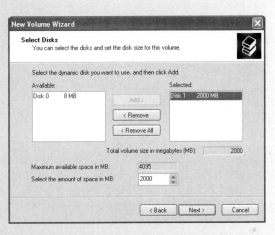

Step 4

Click Next to assign the new partition a drive letter. This is one of the more interesting screens. You can give the new partition a traditional drive letter, or you can make the new partition a *folder* on an existing partition. For this exercise, just accept the drive letter suggested and click Next.

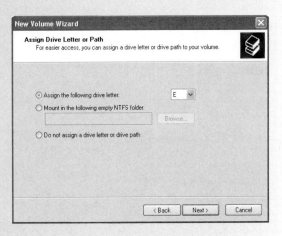

The final screen of the wizard prompts for the type of file format. Because you're running Windows 2000 or XP, NTFS will be selected by default. Accept NTFS and click Next. The wizard will display a summary screen. Click Next, and the new partition will appear.

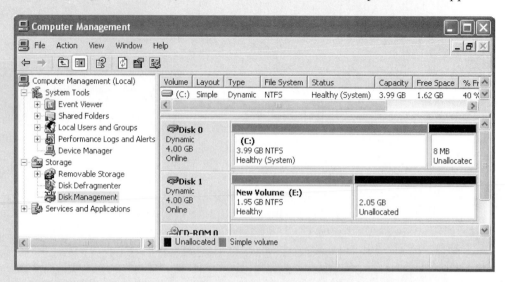

■ Hard Drive Maintenance and Troubleshooting

Hard drives are complex mechanical devices as well as electrical devices. With platters spinning at thousands of rotations per minute, they also generate heat and vibration. All of these factors make hard drives susceptible to failure. In this section, you will learn some basic maintenance tasks that will keep your hard drives healthy, and for those inevitable instances when a hard drive fails, you will also learn what you can do to repair them.

Hard Drive Maintenance

Hard drive maintenance can be broken down into two distinct functions: checking the disk occasionally for failed clusters and keeping data organized on the drive so that it can be accessed quickly.

ScanDisk

Individual clusters on hard drives sometimes go bad. There's nothing you can do to prevent this from happening, so it's important to check occasionally for bad clusters on drives. The tool used to perform this check is called **ScanDisk**. When it finds bad clusters, it puts the electronic equivalent of orange cones around them so that the system won't try to place data in those bad clusters. ScanDisk is one of the oldest utilities ever made for the PC market—ScanDisk was around back in the DOS days, and it continues to do its thing in the latest versions of Windows.

ScanDisk does far more than just check for bad clusters. It goes through all of the drive's filenames, looking for invalid names and attempting to fix them. It looks for clusters that have no filenames associated with them (we call these *lost chains*) and erases them. From time to time, the underlying links between parent and child folders are lost, so ScanDisk checks every parent and child folder. With a folder such as C:\TEST\DATA, for example, ScanDisk makes sure that the folder DATA is properly associated with its parent folder C:\TEST, and that C:\TEST is properly associated with its child folder C:\TEST\DATA.

The best part of ScanDisk is that it works so automatically. The trick is to know how to start it! In Windows 9*x*, you locate ScanDisk by choosing Start | Programs | Accessories | System Tools. You can also start ScanDisk by opening My Computer, right-clicking the drive you want to check, and selecting Properties to open the Drive Properties dialog box. Select the Tools tab and then click the Check Now button to start ScanDisk.

The Windows 9*x* version of ScanDisk gives you a choice between Standard and Thorough testing, as well as an option to have it automatically fix any errors it finds (Figure 8.20). For maintenance purposes, it's fine to use the Standard check. The Thorough check takes a long time, so you'll normally use it only when you suspect a problem. As a rule, you should also always check the Automatically Fix Errors check box.

To access Error-checking (a.k.a. ScanDisk) on a Windows 2000/XP system, open My Computer, right-click the drive you want to check, and select Properties to open the Drive Properties dialog box. Select the Tools tab and click the Check Now button (Figure 8.21) to display the Check Disk dialog box, which has two options. Check the box next to Automatically Fix File System Errors, but save the option to Scan For and Attempt Recovery of Bad Sectors for times when you actually suspect a problem.

Now that you know how to run ScanDisk, your next question should be, "How often do I run it?" A reasonable maintenance plan would include running ScanDisk about once a week. ScanDisk is fast (unless you use the Thorough option), and it's a great tool for keeping your system in top shape. However, disk checking isn't the only thing ScanDisk can do. As you're about to see, it's a powerful tool that can help you when things go wrong on a hard drive.

Defragmentation

Hard drives store files in clusters. Normally, the clusters used to store a file are contiguous (one right after the other), but as files get erased and rewritten, there are fewer and fewer contiguous clusters to write to. If your system cannot write files to contiguous clusters, it will save chunks wherever it can find empty clusters, often chopping a file into a large number of non-contiguous clusters. The FAT or MFT will keep track of the location of each cluster, but having to

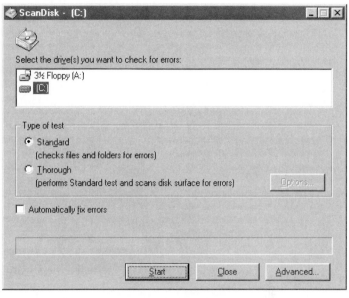

• **Figure 8.20**   ScanDisk options

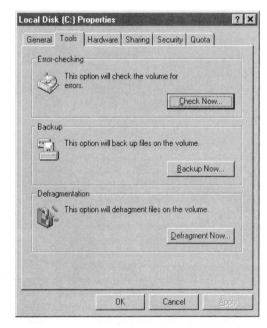

• **Figure 8.21**   Tools tab and Check Now button in Disk Properties in Windows 2000

Inside Information

Defrag

In the computer world, it's important to be familiar with the prevailing jargon. When discussing defragmentation, almost everyone refers to the process using the term defrag, as in, "I really need to defrag this disk—it's getting sooo slow!" Defrag utilities are almost as old as ScanDisk—you can find defrag programs beginning with the later versions of DOS. The DOS program was called DEFRAG, which is why PC techs use that term, and so does this book.

fetch pieces from all over the hard drive slows down access to your files. The solution to this is a process known as **defragmentation (defrag)**. Defragmentation is just what you'd think: file clusters are rearranged to minimize file fragmentation—that is, to maximize the number of files stored in contiguous clusters.

To access the Windows 98 Defrag program, choose Start | Programs | Accessories | System Tools | Disk Defragmenter. You'll be prompted to select the disk you want to defragment. After you've selected a disk, the defragging begins. Defragmentation can take quite a while, in some cases an hour or two for a very large, very fragmented drive on a very slow computer (although most of the time it can complete in under 30 minutes). If you want to watch the process, click the Show Details button to see the clusters get rearranged. It's fascinating to watch—kind of like watching paint dry to some, but sort of mesmerizing, too.

Simply running Defrag with the default settings is fine in most situations, but there are some specialized settings that you may want to employ. The Select Drive screen has a Settings button. Clicking this displays the settings choices you can use. The one option of interest is the Start Programs Faster option. This option tells Defrag to put all of the directory information at the beginning of the drive, which makes files load more quickly.

The Defrag tool that runs with Windows 2000 and XP is accessed via the Start button exactly as described for Windows 98. Although functionally

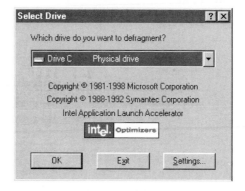

• Selecting the drive to defragment

Have you ever heard of Peter Norton? He's pretty famous in the PC world, and his original claim to fame is that he created the first versions of ScanDisk and Defrag.

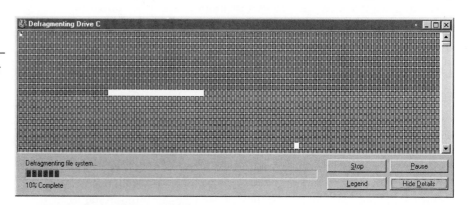

• Defrag running in Show Details mode

equivalent, it does look a bit different. No worry, though—it does the same job.

Defrag and ScanDisk are the two maintenance tools that everyone should run on their systems. As with ScanDisk, you should run Defrag once a week.

Disk Cleanup

Did you know that the average hard drive is full of trash? No, we're not talking about the junk you intentionally put in your hard drive like the 23,000 e-mail messages that you refuse to delete from your e-mail program. We're talking about all the files that you never see that Windows keeps for you. Here are a few examples:

- **Files in the Recycle Bin** When you delete a file, it isn't really deleted. It's placed in the Recycle Bin just in case you decide you need the file later. It's quite possible that you could check your Recycle Bin and find 3GB worth of files. That's a lot of trash!

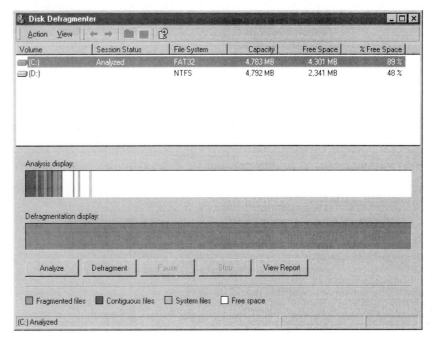

• Defrag in Windows 2000

Defrag can also be accessed through a drive's Properties dialog box in Windows 98, 2000, and XP.

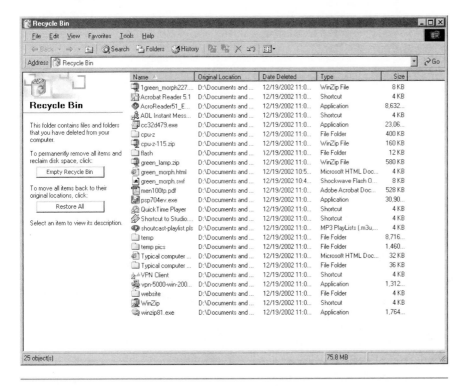

• Recycle Bin

- **Temporary Internet files** When you go to a web site, Windows keeps copies of the graphics and other items so that the page will load more quickly the next time you access the page. You can see these files by opening the Internet Options applet on the Control Panel. Click the Settings button on the General tab and then click the View Files button.

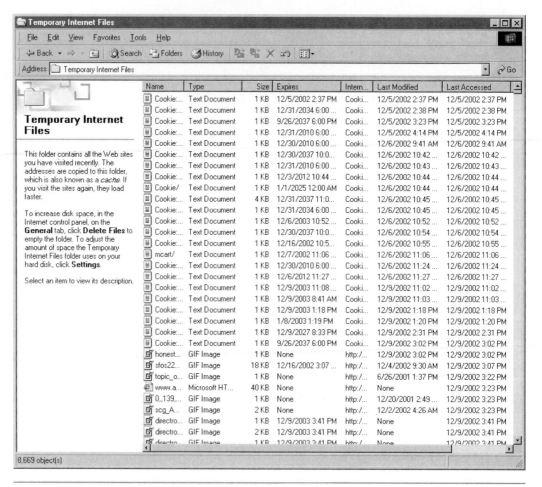

• Temporary Internet Files in Windows 2000

- **Downloaded program files** Your system always keeps a copy of any Java or ActiveX applets that it downloads. You can see these in the Internet Options applet by clicking the View Objects button on the General tab. You'll generally find only a few tiny files here.

- **Temporary files** Many applications create temporary files that are supposed to be deleted when the application is closed. For one reason or another, these temporary files sometimes aren't deleted. The location of these files varies with the version of Windows, but they always reside in a folder called TEMP.

Every hard drive will eventually become filled with lots of unnecessary trash. All versions of Windows tend to act erratically when the drives run out of unused space. Fortunately, all versions of Windows starting with Windows 98 have a powerful tool called Disk Cleanup. You can access Disk

Cleanup in all versions of Windows by choosing Start | Program | Accessories | System Tools | Disk Cleanup.

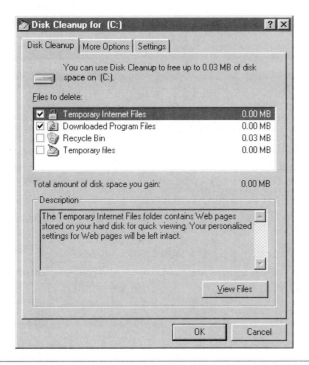

• Disk Cleanup in Windows 2000

Disk Cleanup gets rid of the four types of files just described. Run Disk Cleanup once a month or so to keep plenty of space available on your hard drive.

Troubleshooting

There's no scarier computer problem than an error that points to trouble with a hard drive. In this section, we look at some of the more common problems that occur with hard drives. These issues can be divided into three categories that correspond to the tasks for installing a drive: physical problems, system setup problems, and partitioning and formatting problems.

Physical Problems

Physical problems are rare but devastating when they happen. If a hard drive is truly damaged physically, there is nothing that you or any service technician can do to fix it. Fortunately, hard drives are designed to take a phenomenal amount of punishment without failing. Physical problems manifest themselves in two ways: either the drive works properly but makes a lot of noise, or the drive seems to disappear.

All hard drives make noise—the hum as the platters spin and the occasional slight scratching noise as the read/write heads access sectors are normal. However, if your drive begins to make any of the following sounds, it is about to die:

■ Continuous high-pitched squeal

- Series of clacks, a short pause, and then another series of clacks
- Continuous grinding or rumbling

Back up your critical data and replace the drive. You should do this immediately if you detect these or other symptoms of drive failure, because in most cases of drive failure you may have enough time to back up your critical data before the drive becomes completely unusable. Not always, but there have been cases where some critical files were able to be backed up prior to the drive becoming completely unusable. Don't delay! (And it should go without saying that you should have had backups *before* your hard disk had problems!)

You'll know when a drive simply disappears. If it's the drive that contains your operating system, the system will lock up. When you try to restart the computer, you'll see this error message:

```
No Boot Device Present
```

If it's a second drive, it will simply stop showing up in My Computer. The first thing to do in this case is to fire up the System Setup program and see if Autodetect sees the drive. If it does, then you do not have a physical problem with the drive. If Autodetect fails, shut off the system and remove the ribbon cable, but leave the power cable attached. Restart the system and listen to the drive. If the drive spins up, you know that the drive is getting good power. In most cases, this is a clue that the drive is probably good. In that case, you need to look for more mundane problems such as an unplugged power cord or jumpers incorrectly set. If the drive doesn't spin up, try another power connector. If it still doesn't spin up and you've triple-checked the jumpers and ribbon cable, you have a problem with the onboard electronics, and the drive is dead.

System Setup Problems

Electrical surges can cause your System Setup program to lose the hard drive information. Just reboot the system to verify that Autodetect still works and save the system settings.

Partitioning and Formatting Problems

Partitioning and formatting problems are by far the most common cause of hard drive errors. These problems sometimes manifest themselves in system lockup, but more often they manifest themselves in errors that seem to indicate a hard drive problem. Here are some examples:

- Data error reading drive C:
- Cannot copy file…
- Error copying file to drive D:
- No disk present

There are literally hundreds of these types of errors. The important thing to appreciate is simply that they are hard drive errors. When you have a formatting problem, the first tool to try is ScanDisk. Run ScanDisk in the Thorough mode. ScanDisk will fix most formatting errors. In fact, Windows will often run ScanDisk automatically if it detects a problem, most often after an unplanned shutdown.

If the problem persists after you run ScanDisk, go to the web site of your drive's manufacturer and download the diagnostic tool for your type of drive. These tools, known as low-level formatters, always run from a bootable floppy. They will often fix a problem that gets by ScanDisk.

PartitionMagic

As mentioned earlier in this chapter, a software product called PartitionMagic from PowerQuest is a veritable Swiss army knife of hard disk maintenance. With this program, you can do many things to a hard disk that are difficult or impossible using the built-in tools provided in Windows.

```
Microsoft ScanDisk


Because Windows was not properly shut down,
one or more of your disk drives may have errors on it.

To avoid seeing this message again, always shut down
your computer by selecting Shut Down from the Start menu.

ScanDisk is now checking drive C for errors:




◄ Exit ►

38% complete  ▐███████████░░░░░░░░░░░░░░░░░▌
```

• ScanDisk running automatically after an unplanned shutdown

There are a number of hard disk maintenance or reconfiguration tasks that can only be accomplished in Windows by using the following general procedure:

1. Back up all essential data files.

2. Repartition the disk as desired.

3. Reformat the partitions as needed.

4. Reinstall the operating system.

5. Reinstall all applications.

6. Restore critical data files from backup.

As you might imagine, this series of steps is not for the faint of heart. Not only is there the risk that you might miss backing up a critical file and lose it forever, but the procedure is also extremely time-consuming. So instead, you can use PartitionMagic to make the same underlying partitioning or formatting changes without needing to remove everything from your hard disk and essentially start all over again.

PartitionMagic is an easy-to-use program that can perform the following general tasks:

- Change the file system used on a partition. You can change directly between FAT16, FAT32, and NTFS (Windows only includes the ability to convert from FAT to NTFS but not vice.versa, and not between FAT16 and FAT32).

- Expand or shrink a partition.

- Create and delete partitions.

- Redistribute free space between partitions.

- Change the cluster size used by NTFS.

> PartitionMagic is for computers running a client operating system, such as Windows 2000 Professional, Windows 98, or Windows XP Home or Professional. PowerQuest sells a slightly different product called ServerMagic that must be used for server-oriented operating systems, such as Windows 2000 Server.

> Before using PartitionMagic to make any changes to the disk of a production computer, make sure you use PartitionMagic's built-in rescue disk program to create diskettes that can aid in recovery if something goes wrong. And even though PartitionMagic is a very reliable program, you should always back up important data before making any changes.

In the following step-by-step, you will learn PartitionMagic's main functions as you create space for a new partition on an existing system, format the new partition, convert it to a different file system, and finally remove the partition and re-expand your original partition.

Repartitioning a Hard Disk with PartitionMagic

For this exercise, you will need the following:

- A computer running Windows 2000 or Windows XP that has a single partition with at least 20 percent free space

- PartitionMagic 8 installed

Step 1

From the Start menu, open PartitionMagic. The opening screen will show you an overview of your disk configuration. For example, here you can see a system that has a 120GB single NTFS partition. (You can also see in the illustration a small utility partition, which your machine may or may not have. If it does, you can and should ignore it and avoid changing it.)

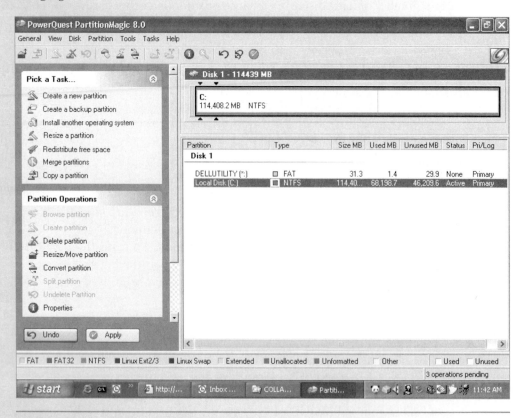

- The main PartitionMagic screen showing the existing partitions

Step 2

Right-click on the partition to be changed and choose Resize/Move from the pop-up menu. You will see the Resize/Move dialog box shown in the next illustration.

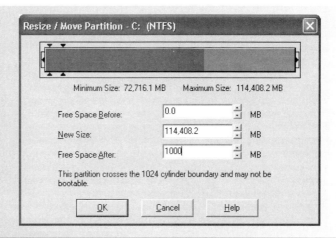

- Resizing the original main partition to make room for a new partition

Enter a value in the Free Space After field equal to about 5–10 percent of the original partition, after assuring yourself that the original partition has at least 20 percent of its capacity available. Click the OK button to save the new setting. (The settings you make are not committed until later).

You can see that there is now free space after the existing partition. You can also see the free space in the partition listing window.

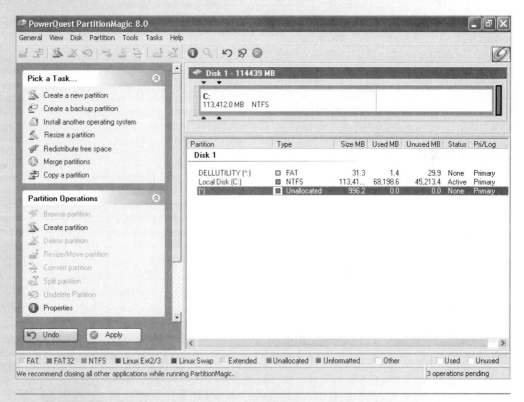

- Unallocated space is now available for the new partition.

Step 5

Right-click on the free space area after the original partition and choose Create from the pop-up menu. You see the Create Partition dialog box shown in the illustration.

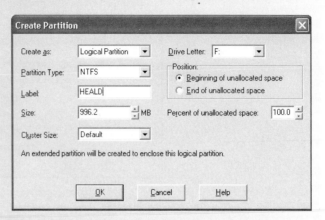

- Creating a new partition in PartitionMagic

Step 6

Using the fields shown in the Create Partition dialog box, set the new partition to be a logical partition formatted as NTFS. Set the cluster size to default. You may, if you wish, assign a partition label of your choosing to the new partition. You should also ensure that the drive letter that will be assigned to the new partition follows all existing drive letters on the system you are working with. This will help avoid, for example, programs not finding CD-ROM disks or shortcuts to existing drive letters. Click the OK button to proceed.

Step 7

You will now commit the pending changes. To do so, pull down the General menu and choose Apply Changes. You will see a confirmation dialog box that lets you see the detailed changes that will occur when you click Yes (click the Details button to see the changes first).

Step 8

You will see one final confirmation message letting you know that the system needs to reboot to carry out the changes. Click OK, and observe the system as the changes are applied. The process will take from 5–30 minutes depending on a number of factors, like the speed of the computer, the speed of the disk drive, how many files need to be moved to make room for the new partition, and so forth. When the process is done, the system will restart once more and then should boot normally.

Step 9

When PartitionMagic has completed the process and the computer has booted, you can browse the new partition with My Computer. If you wish, you can copy files onto it; it's a fully functioning NTFS partition in every respect.

Step 10

You will now convert the new partition's file system to FAT32. To do so, right-click on it in PartitionMagic and choose Convert from the pop-up menu. You will see the Convert Partition dialog box.

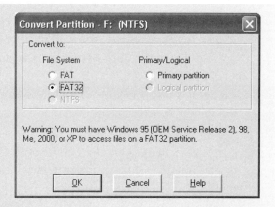

- Converting the new NTFS partition to FAT32

Ensure that FAT32 is selected and click the OK button. You will see a warning that some filenames may have to be renamed in the process (different file systems support long filenames in different ways). Click OK after reading the warning dialog box. Then, use the Apply Changes command in the General menu to carry out the conversion immediately; because there are few, if any, files on the new partition, the conversion usually completes very quickly. You can open the new partition's properties in Explorer to confirm that the file system conversion has completed.

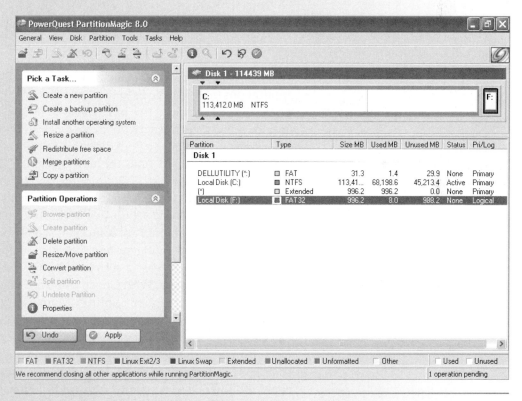

- The new partition is now added, and is FAT32

You will now destroy the new partition and then expand the original partition to its original size. To begin, right-click on the new partition and choose Delete from the pop-up menu. In the Delete dialog box, choose Delete and click OK. (In some cases you may want to use Delete and Secure Erase if you want the contents of the partition to be over-written and made unrecoverable. This isn't important in most cases).

Step 13

Right-click on the original partition and choose Resize / Move from the pop-up menu. In the Resize / Move Partition dialog box, set Free Space After to 0, and then click OK.

Step 14

Apply the changes by using the Apply Changes command in the General menu. A re-boot is not necessary for this operation, so just click OK and the changes are applied immediately.

You've now completed this step-by-step. You resized an existing partition, created a new partition in the freed space, formatted it as NTFS, converted it to FAT32, and then reversed all the changes. As mentioned earlier, these changes would be far more time-consuming and fraught with risk without a tool like PartitionMagic.

Norton Ghost

Norton Ghost is a software product produced by Symantec that has the ability to create an image file of everything on a system's hard disk and then can later restore the image to re-create the system to the point in time when the image was made.

While Ghost can be used as a method to back up systems, its primary utility in a corporate setting is based on two essential tasks.

First, for companies that have many computers that are exactly the same (from the same maker and with the same components), you can set up a base system with the operating system, all patches, all customizations, and all applications that are to be used throughout the company. Ghost is then used to create an image file of this base system. The image file is normally stored on a file server over the network or on a CD-ROM or DVD. Then, for all the other similar computers, a boot diskette with Ghost on it can be booted, and the image file restored onto the new system. This process occurs fairly quickly, usually in about 15–20 minutes, and aside from starting the process, no intervention is required. When complete, the computer is booted and it then is completely set up, just as the base system was. If you've ever had to set up a large number of computers, you know that normally the process of installing operating system, patches, customizations, and applications usually takes at least a couple of hours, with intervention required throughout the process. With Ghost, instead it takes about 20 minutes per system, with no intervention required. Moreover, a staffer can be trained to create systems using a Ghost image very easily. Doing all of the setup tasks by hand requires a checklist of tasks and much more training on the part of the person performing the installations.

Second, Ghost is also useful for companies that maintain fleets of note-book computers that people who travel occasionally can borrow for their trip. Using Ghost, each notebook can be set up once, an image created, and then when it is returned, it can be returned to its pristine state by restoring the image file onto the system. This helps keep company data secure, because travelers often leave copies of sensitive files on such notebooks, and also ensures that the system remains in a fully functioning configuration for each person who uses the computer.

Creating and Restoring a System Image with Ghost

For this step-by-step, you will need the following:

- A computer running Windows that has Ghost installed

- An attached CD-R writer and a blank CD-R disc
- A blank diskette

Step 1

You will first set up a boot diskette with Ghost on it. Start Ghost and move to the Ghost Utilities section.

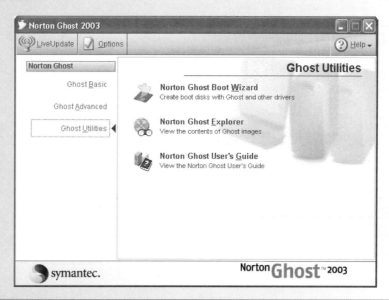

- Norton Ghost Utilities screen

Step 2

Click on the Norton Ghost Boot Wizard. You will see the Boot Wizard dialog box. Choose Standard Ghost Boot Disk and click Next.

- Creating a boot diskette with Ghost

You now see the Additional Services dialog box. If you are using a SCSI-based CD writer, make sure to select the Include Adaptec ASPI drivers option. The other options are not needed for this exercise, but are for using other types of storage devices and adding drivers for those devices to the Ghost boot diskette. Click Next to continue.

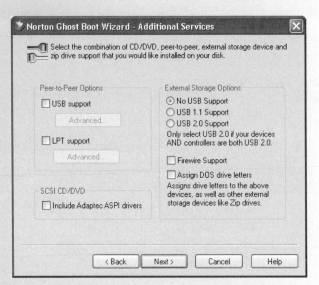

• Choosing various options for the boot diskette in Ghost

Step 4

Choose Use PC-DOS and click Next to continue. Accept the default location for Ghost, and click Next to continue; then accept the defaults for the diskette set to be created and click Next. On the Review dialog box, click Next. The diskette set is then created.

Step 5

Now you will use Ghost to create an image of your hard disk partition. From the main Ghost screen, move to the Ghost Basic section and choose Backup to start the Backup Wizard. Click Next to move to the partition selection dialog box.

Step 6

Under the Source section, choose the partition you want to back up. Normally, this is your main system partition. Under the Destination section, choose Recordable CD or DVD. Click Next to continue.

Step 7

Continue clicking Next or Continue (there are several confirmation screens you will see) until you arrive at the Task Summary screen. Then, click Run Now to begin the backup process. The computer will restart, and the backup will be created using the DOS-based Ghost program. When complete, the CD will eject, and the system will restart.

Step 8

To restore the system, you will use the Ghost boot diskette you created earlier in this step-by-step, as well as the image CD you just created. To begin, reboot the computer using the diskette you created.

Step 9

The DOS-based Ghost program starts automatically from the boot diskette. In some cases, your mouse may not work, so instead it's best to use the keyboard to navigate the display. (You use a combination of the TAB, arrows, and ENTER key). Press ENTER at the first splash screen to enter Ghost.

Step 10	Choose Local, and press ENTER; then choose Partition, and press ENTER. Next, choose From Image since we will be restoring from an image file, and press ENTER.
Step 11	Move to the Look In field at the top of the dialog box (it's presently showing your A: drive) and press ENTER to open the drop-down listing of drives. Choose the CD drive and press ENTER. Press ENTER again to select the drive and display its Ghost image files.
Step 12	Select the Ghost image file and press ENTER to continue. Choose the source partition and press ENTER. Select the local disk to restore to and press ENTER.
Step 13	Select the local partition to overwrite with the image file contents and press ENTER to continue. Be very careful not to select a different partition that has data you want preserved; the partition you select will be completely overwritten with the contents of the Ghost image file.
Step 14	At the final warning, if you're comfortable that you've selected the correct drive and partition, choose Yes and press ENTER. The restore then proceeds. Usually, it takes about the same time to restore an image file as it took to create it.
Step 15	After the restore is complete, you will see a final dialog box. Choose Reset Computer and press ENTER to reboot.

Your system should boot back into Windows. If you're restoring to the system from which you created the image, you won't notice any difference; however, you should realize that the partition was backed up to the CD, and completely rewritten. If you had, say, 10 or 50 new computers that your company just purchased, you could use this process to set them all up the same way as the base system from which the image was created. As you can see, Ghost can be an enormous timesaver for corporate IT departments.

Chapter 8 Review

■ Chapter Summary

After reading this chapter and completing the exercises, you should understand the following.

Describe How Hard Drives Store Data

- All hard drives have a make and a model, and this is important information to know.

- The smallest storage area on a hard drive is called a sector. Every sector stores 512 bytes.

- All hard drives must be partitioned.

- Windows systems have two types of partitions: primary and extended.

- Each partition has in effect its own personal card catalog, called a file allocation table (FAT).

- Three file systems are used on Windows PCs: FAT16, FAT32, and NTFS.

Physically Install a Hard Drive in a PC

- EIDE is the most common drive technology used in PCs today. EIDE drives use 40-pin cables.

- ATA66 and higher-speed drives need a special 80-wire cable. Even though the cable has 80 wires, it still has only 40 pins.

- The actual drive connection on the motherboard is almost universally called the controller, although in reality it is only a connector for the EIDE cable.

- One EIDE controller can support a maximum of two ATA devices. If two EIDE drives are on the same controller, one must be set as master and the other as slave.

- Almost all hard drives have two EIDE controllers on the motherboard. They are called the primary and the secondary controllers. This allows a maximum of four ATA devices in a single PC.

- Almost all System Setup programs have an Autodetect feature that tells the BIOS all of a drive's geometry settings.

- The original IDE standard supported a maximum drive size of 504MB. The LBA standard increased the maximum drive size of 8.3GB. The INT13 Extensions standard increased the maximum drive size to 137GB. The ATA-6 (Big Drives) standard increased the maximum drive size to 144 petabytes.

Configure a Newly Installed Hard Drive

- You partition hard drives during the installation of the operating system. Windows 9x systems use the FDISK utility to partition drives. Windows NT, 2000, and XP use the Disk Management program.

- Any time you delete a partition, all data on that partition is lost.

- FAT16 supports a maximum partition size of 2GB. FAT32 supports up to 2 terabytes. NTFS also supports partitions up to 2 terabytes.

- Windows 2000 and XP Professional have a new type of drive configuration called dynamic disk. Dynamic disk drives must be used if you want to take advantage of special features such as RAID or drive spanning.

- The three most important types of RAID are RAID 0, RAID 1, and RAID 5. RAID 0 is also known as a striping. RAID 1 is also known as mirroring. RAID 5 is known as striping with parity.

Maintain and Troubleshoot a Hard Drive

- ScanDisk and Defrag are the two most important tools for maintaining a healthy hard drive.

- ScanDisk primarily looks for bad clusters. ScanDisk also looks for invalid file and folder names.

- Defragmentation is a process in which file clusters are rearranged to minimize file fragmentation. All versions of Windows have a utility with this capability.

- All versions of Windows since Windows 98 have a tool called Disk Cleanup to remove unneeded files that accumulate during normal operation of the PC.

Reconfigure a Hard Drive Using PartitionMagic

- PartitionMagic is a software package that can make extensive changes to an existing hard drive's configuration.

- Using PartitionMagic to reconfigure a hard drive's partitioning or file system, you don't have to back up a hard disk, erase it, reconfigure it, and then reinstall and restore all of your data. Changes can be made to a system without disturbing its contents.

- Even though PartitionMagic is very reliable and dependable, you should always back up critical data before changing a hard disk's configuration, just in case.

Prepare and Deploy System Images Using Symantec Ghost

- Symantec Ghost is a product that can create an image file containing everything installed onto a computer.

- An image file created by Ghost can be used to quickly duplicate a base system's complete setup onto a large number of similar target systems much more quickly and easily than setting up each target system by hand.

Key Terms

ATA speed ratings *(346)*
cylinder *(340)*
defragmentation (defrag) *(364)*
dynamic disks *(357)*
Enhanced Integrated Drive
  Electronics (EIDE) *(346)*
extended partition *(341)*
file allocation table (FAT) *(341)*

geometry *(339)*
logical drive *(341)*
master *(347)*
master boot record (MBR) *(342)*
master file table (MFT) *(343)*
NT File System (NTFS) *(343)*
partition *(341)*
platter *(339)*

primary partition *(341)*
read/write head *(339)*
Redundant Array of Independent
  Disks (RAID) *(356)*
ScanDisk *(362)*
sectors per track *(341)*
slave *(347)*
track *(347)*

Key Term Quiz

Use the Key Terms list to complete the sentences that follow. (Not all terms will be used.)

1. _____ is a tool that checks for bad clusters and lost chains on a hard drive.

2. _____ are multiple hard drives that work together to act as one drive with a single drive letter.

3. The best file system used by Windows XP is _____.

4. Each partition has its own personal card catalog, called a/an _____.

5. The _____ is a tiny piece of code that helps the operating system load the correct partition.

6. A group of tracks of the same diameter going completely through a hard drive is a called a _____.

7. The circular paths where data is stored on a hard drive are called _____s.

8. A/an _____ is a discrete electronic chunk of a hard drive that is used as an underlying structure for organizing data on the drive.

9. A drive's _____ determines where it stores data on its stack of disks.

10. Extended partitions must be divided into one or more _____s.

Multiple-Choice Quiz

1. What are the three components of hard drive geometry?
   a. Cylinders, platters, and heads
   b. Heads, tracks, and sectors
   c. Cylinders, heads, and sectors per track
   d. Sectors, platters, and cylinders per track

2. What is the maximum number of primary partitions that Windows XP allows on a single hard drive?
   a. 1
   b. 4
   c. 8
   d. 32

3. What obsolete file system was used by DOS and Windows 3.1?

   a. FAT8

   b. FAT16

   c. FAT32

   d. FAT64

4. What term is used universally to describe all drives in the ATA-2 through ATA-5 standards?

   a. ATAPI

   b. ATA

   c. IDE

   d. EIDE

5. When two devices share a single ribbon cable, one of those devices must have its controller turned off. What is that device called?

   a. Secondary

   b. Passive

   c. Slave

   d. Dependent

6. What is the name of the tool used to partition a disk manually on a Windows 9x system?

   a. FDISK

   b. Defrag

   c. Partition

   d. ScanDisk

7. What type of dynamic disk storage is known as RAID 0?

   a. Striped

   b. Segmented

   c. Mirrored

   d. Spanned

8. Which RAID level uses striping with three or more disks and fault tolerance added in the form of parity bits?

   a. RAID 0

   b. RAID 1

   c. RAID 4

   d. RAID 5

9. How many read/write heads would a hard drive with 12 platters require?

   a. 12

   b. 24

   c. 48

   d. 60

10. Each sector on a hard drive stores how many bytes of data?

    a. 1

    b. 16

    c. 32

    d. 512

11. The Master Boot Record looks for what partition to boot from?

    a. Primary

    b. Secondary

    c. Active

    d. Extended

12. What is the name of the super-FAT used by the NTFS file system?

    a. NT File Allocation Table

    b. Master File Table

    c. Extended File Allocation Table

    d. NT File Administrator

13. What is the current method for transferring data between a hard drive and RAM?

    a. Ultra Direct Memory Access

    b. Programmable Input/Output

    c. Advanced Memory Attachment

    d. Integrated Drive Access

14. How many drives can a single EIDE controller support?

    a. 1

    b. 2

    c. 3

    d. 4

15. How many wires are there on the two types of ATA cables?

    a. 34 and 50

    b. 40 and 40

    c. 40 and 80

    d. 50 and 80

Essay Quiz

1. Write a set of instructions laying out the basic steps involved in partitioning and formatting a hard drive. Be sure to cover the steps in order and explain your terms.

2. You are assigned to handle maintenance for your boss's computer. Part of this responsibility involves keeping her hard drive in good working order. Write a memo detailing the various hard drive maintenance tasks you wish to perform. Explain why you need to do each one, and how often.

3. Your coworker comes to you for help. He just changed offices and set up his computer on his new desk. When he opened My Computer to access his second hard drive, it wasn't there! Write an essay explaining how you would troubleshoot this problem. Include any questions you would ask your coworker.

4. You have just given four of your coworkers new PCs. Each of the PCs has the hard drive partitioned into a C: drive and a D: drive. Your coworkers have never seen a drive with two partitions and are confused. Create an e-mail message explaining the two partitions and the benefits they might provide.

5. As the new PC technician at your company, you are shocked to discover that your predecessor did all the hard drive defragging and disk scanning herself, spending hours moving from one drive to the next. Create a short e-mail message explaining to the users that they can use these two tools themselves and provide a series of steps to show them how to run these programs.

Lab Projects

• Lab Project 8.1

Partitioning can be a far more complex affair than the basic single primary partitioning described in this chapter. Placing multiple partitions on a single drive allows you to organize your data more effectively and makes backup easier. Using a system with a hard drive that you can erase, try some of the more complex types of partitioning.

❶ Add one extended partition to the hard drive and then create two logical drives in the extended partition.

❷ Add two extended partitions to the hard drive and create a single logical drive in each one.

❸ Add one extended partition to the hard drive and create four logical drives in it.

• Lab Project 8.2

You should occasionally check a drive to see if it needs maintenance. This process often allows you to catch small errors on the drive before you begin losing data. Check the hard drive on a computer in your classroom to see if it needs maintenance.

❶ Run ScanDisk on the hard drive. Record the results.

❷ Have the Defrag program analyze the drive. Record the percentage of the drive it reports as fragmented.

❸ Compare your results with those of other students. Are the classroom systems well maintained?

❹ Create a maintenance plan for the classroom systems to keep the hard drives in good condition.

Securing a Network

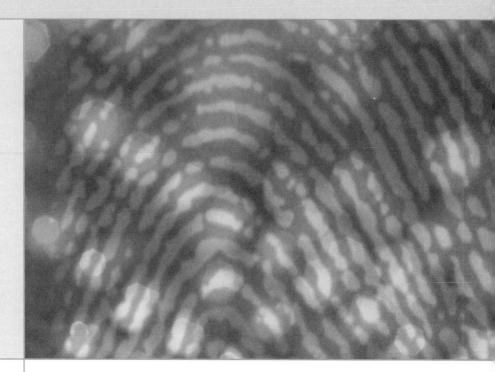

When we speak of security, the first image that usually comes to mind is one of door locks and alarm systems. In the physical world, these controls, in addition to armed guards and TV cameras, are very evident aspects of our security. These are things that protect and deter. Some controls protect our possessions by preventing the thief from stealing them, and other controls deter the thief because of the likelihood of being apprehended, convicted, and punished.

In the same manner, we must place controls on our computer networks. We use network controls, such as passwords, access control, firewalls, and antivirus software, to protect our networks from various malicious activity. The same devices may deter people from intruding on a network.

Unfortunately, it is impossible to protect networks completely. As with all sorts of security precautions, it comes down to cost and usefulness. Spending more money on a myriad of security devices may make a network more difficult to damage, but it may be unaffordable and may make the network too hard to use. Thus, security is a constant balancing of risk and cost. **Risk** is the likelihood that damage or injury may occur, and we can limit risk only to the extent that we can afford to do so.

Identifying Threats to Networking Security

Threats to the security of a network can come from inside the network as well as outside. Generally, a `threat` is someone or something that could inflict damage or injury. More specifically, for a threat to be worth our attention, the potential attacker requires motive, means, and opportunity. This means that there has to be a reason for the attack and that there must be some way for the attacker to make the attack (means and opportunity).

Who has the most knowledge and access to the systems and network of any company? The employees and other authorized users, of course. This means that internal threats are potentially the most common and the most dangerous.

Of course, you cannot ignore the external threats. `Hackers`, individuals who use their knowledge of computers to do harm, often just for fun, are a threat to any network. When you speak of securing a network, you must pay attention to both types of threats.

Internal Threats

All right, you already know that there are insiders who may seek to do harm to computer networks. Keep in mind that not all insider security issues are malicious. It is just as possible, and more likely, that an insider will cause a security problem by accident. Think of the employee who accidentally deletes an important file. The file may be critical to the operation of the company, but it is now gone. The employee did not intend to cause harm but, for whatever reason, managed to destroy the file.

In comparison, it might have been infinitely more difficult for an outsider to delete that important file. The file was likely on an internal server (with the appropriate security in place) and on the network. The outsider would have needed a lot of information, and possibly even some help, to gain access to the file. However, the employee, due to his or her trusted status in the organization, was able to delete the file accidentally.

Any security strategy designed to combat internal threats is comprised of three primary components:

- Account security
- File and directory permissions
- Practices and user education

The following sections detail how each of these components can be used to secure key systems and the network itself.

Account Security

Maintaining account security means preventing unauthorized individuals from gaining access to an account on the computer or network. The primary defensive measure, in this case, is `identification and authentication` (I&A). I&A is the security mechanism that allows a computer to uniquely identify the person who is attempting to log on or perform an action.

 It is often difficult to specifically identify threats to an organization. This is because people who wish to cause harm also try to hide their intent and their actions. In most circumstances, it is sufficient to know that there are bad people in the world and that having a business or even just an Internet connection can make you a target of such individuals.

 Some controls (like locks on doors) are expected to be there. Other controls are not expected, but certain conditions in the system or network may require them. As you go through this chapter, think about which controls fall into the "expected" category and which do not.

Methods of Authentication   As it turns out, identifying a person is the easy part—you just assign user IDs and names to each person on your system. The harder part is providing a mechanism for the user to prove that she is who she claims to be.

A person can prove his or her identity in three ways:

- By something the person knows
- By something the person has
- By something the person is

The first option, something a person knows, usually involves a password or personal identification number (PIN). To prove his or her identity, the person tells the computer system the password. Since only one person is supposed to know the password, the computer authenticates the person and allows access. This is the cheapest and easiest method of authentication and is also the most widely used.

The second option, something a person has, can be as simple as a credit card or driver's license. For very sensitive computer systems and networks, a smart card is used. These cards have computer chips in them that allow information to be stored. Since only one person should have the card, the person is authenticated because he or she possesses the card. This type of mechanism can be stronger than the use of passwords, but it also tends to be expensive, as each card costs between $25 and $100. If you think about organizations with tens of thousands of employees, you can see how quickly the cost skyrockets.

Biometrics involves using unique human characteristics for authentication—something the person is. The following characteristics can be used for authentication:

- Fingerprints
- Hand geometry
- Retina scans
- Facial geometry
- Voice prints

Figure 9.1 shows a picture of a hand geometry device (commonly called a *palm scanner*) that is used to grant access to a data center. The unique hand geometry of authorized individuals is recorded ahead of time. When a person requires access to the data center, the system compares the person's hand that is placed on the scanner with the record of authorized hands in the database. If the hand matches, the individual is allowed into the room.

Biometrics are expensive and there is some resistance to their use by employees (placing your head into a device and having a laser look at your eye is not the most comfortable feeling). They are also inappropriate for use in situations where the organization cannot physically control access (such as when a person makes a purchase across the Internet).

If you have the option, it is best to combine mechanisms, such as combining the use of a password and a smart card. This way, if the smart card is lost or stolen, an intruder with the card would still not know the password and could not get into the system.

Some people and civil rights groups have objected to the use of some types of biometrics, including fingerprints. Before you introduce such a system into your environment, make sure you understand the objections that may be raised.

• Figure 9.1   Hand geometry is one form of biometrics that is commonly used for physical access.

Strong Passwords   Since passwords are by far the most common type of authentication mechanism, it is worth taking a few minutes to look at how to choose a strong password. First off, passwords provide good authentication when they are kept secret. This means that they should not be written down or shared with coworkers. Sharing passwords is hard to prevent, but there are things that can be done (see the "File and Directory Permissions" section that follows).

Preventing employees from writing down passwords involves a combination of education and having the employees select easy-to-remember passwords. Do not fall into the trap that says easy-to-remember passwords are also weak passwords. This is not the case, as you will see in a minute.

Strong passwords have the following characteristics:

- They are hard to guess even if the person knows you.
- They are hard to discover using brute force.

If a person chooses a password that has something to do with himself or herself, it may be easy to guess. Thus, choosing the names of family members or pets, or the name of an interest, are generally not good choices for passwords. Likewise, passwords that are short or that can be found in a dictionary can be easily discovered using brute force (which will be explained shortly).

So how can you choose strong passwords? In reality, this is an easy thing to do. Passwords should be at least eight characters in length and contain a mixture of uppercase and lowercase letters, numbers, and special characters.

Of course, passwords should also be easy to remember so people don't write them down. Stringing multiple words together and substituting numbers for letters can help users create good passwords that are easy to remember, like these:

- Time4Lunch
- Itsmy1ife (note that the letter *L* is replaced with the number *1*)

Strong passwords can also be created by choosing the first letter of an easy-to-remember phrase:

- TbontbtitQ (To be or not to be, that is the question)
- oibLTibs (One if by land, two if by sea)

Breaking Passwords   Passwords are not so much broken as discovered. As was stated, strong passwords are hard to guess and hard to discover by brute force. Weak passwords are often discovered through simple guessing at the password prompt. Of course, this type of activity can be prevented through the use of ■password lockouts■. Most computer systems allow administrators to set the maximum number of failed password attempts that are to be allowed. After this number, the computer system locks the account so that no further attempts can be made.

Unix systems generally limit passwords to 8 characters in length by truncating the password after 8 characters. Windows systems allow longer passwords (up to 14 characters).

If you need to see how well your users understand the use of strong but easy-to-remember passwords, walk around your office area and look for yellow post-it notes on monitors or under keyboards. Don't forget to look at the ceiling above the desks. Some enterprising users may write their passwords on the tiles above their chairs!

Setting the Password Lockouts on Windows 2000

Setting the password lockouts on Windows 2000 is a good practice as it prevents password-guessing attacks. In the following steps, you will use the Windows 2000 Administrative Tools to set the password lockout for the system.

To complete this exercise, you will need the following items:

■ A computer running Windows 2000

■ An account with administrator access to the system

Step 1

Log in to the system using the administrator account or another account with administrator access.

Step 2

Click the Start button and select Settings | Control Panel.

Step 3

Double-click the Administrative Tools icon.

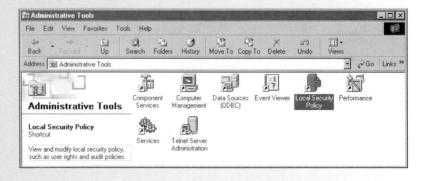

Step 4

Double-click the Local Security Policy icon, and select the Account Lockout Policy option under Account Policies.

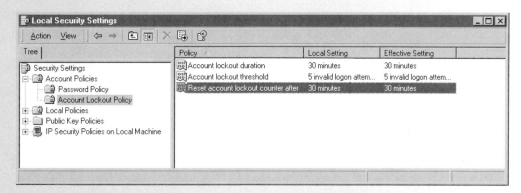

Step 5

Set the Account Lockout Duration by double-clicking the Account Lockout Duration item in the right panel. The lockout duration is the amount of time (measured in minutes) that the account will be locked out after some number of failed login attempts has been detected. The duration can be set as high as 99,999 minutes. Setting the duration to zero minutes will lock the account until it is reset by the system administrator.

Step 6

The Account Lockout Threshold option sets the number of failed login attempts that will be allowed before the lockout occurs. A number between three and five is usually appropriate for most environments.

Step 7	The last configuration item to set is Reset Account Lockout Counter After _____ Minutes. This item tells the system how long to track the failed login attempts. For example, setting this value to 30 minutes means that the system will count failed logins within a 30-minute window in order to lock the account. If the lockout threshold is not reached during that time frame, the lockout will not occur.
Step 8	Close all of the windows by choosing Cancel.

Passwords are normally stored in an encrypted format on computer systems. The encryption system used is one-way, so that you cannot get back to the original password by knowing the encrypted version. This is to prevent anyone who might see the password file from discovering a password.

Passwords that are difficult to guess can be discovered through a brute force attack. A **brute force attack** means that the attacker tries every possible combination of letters, numbers, and special characters to obtain a password. This may be done one of two ways: The attacker tries to log in with every possible combination of passwords (which would presumably be defeated by the account lockouts) or the attacker obtains the password file or copies of the encrypted passwords. The attacker encrypts each potential combination in the same manner as the system normally does and compares the results to the encrypted password. If the two match, the attacker has the correct password.

Clearly, this type of attack would be very time consuming and tedious to do by hand. To overcome this difficulty, several password-cracking programs have been developed. If the attacker can obtain the password file (called passwd, or the shadow password file—usually called shadow—on Unix, or the SAM file on Windows), the password-cracking program can be used to try to discover the passwords by brute force.

Figure 9.2 shows the results screen of L0phtCrack. (Note that the second character is a zero, not the letter *O*). This is one of the better programs for cracking passwords, and it can be obtained from www.atstake.com/research/lc/index.html. With such a program, it is possible to attempt every possible combination of letters, numbers, and special characters. Obviously, the more combinations that are attempted, the longer it takes to run, but the more complete the results will be. Once the attacker has the password file, it is impossible to prevent him or her from obtaining the passwords.

It is also possible to obtain encrypted passwords from the network as they are communicated between systems. This activity is called **sniffing** the wire. Often the passwords will not be encrypted here, and no cracking is necessary. Windows passwords are encrypted as they cross the network, however.

> Even the administrators of the system cannot look up passwords. If a password is lost or stolen, the administrator must change the user's password to something like "password" and set the account to require the user to change the password on the next login.

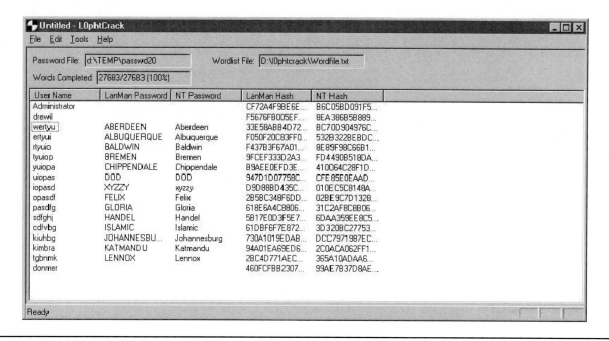

User Name	LanMan Password	NT Password	LanMan Hash	NT Hash
Administrator			CF72A4F9BE6E...	B6C05BD091F5...
drewil			F5676FB005EF...	8EA386B5B889...
wertyu	ABERDEEN	Aberdeen	33E58ABB4D72...	BC70D904976C...
ertyui	ALBUQUERQUE	Albuquerque	F050F20C83FF0...	532B322BEBDC...
rtyuio	BALDWIN	Baldwin	F437B3F67A01...	8E89F98C66B1...
tyuiop	BREMEN	Bremen	9FCEF333D2A3...	FD4490B518DA...
yuiopa	CHIPPENDALE	Chippendale	B9AEE0EFD3E...	410064C28F1D...
uiopas	DOD	DOD	947D1D07758C...	CFE85E0EAAD...
iopasd	XYZZY	xyzzy	D9D88BD435C...	010EC5C8148A...
opasdf	FELIX	Felix	2B5BC348F6DD...	02BE9C7D1328...
pasdfg	GLORIA	Gloria	618E6A4C8B06...	31C2AF8C8B06...
sdfghj	HANDEL	Handel	5B17E0D3F5E7...	6DAA359EE8C5...
cdfvbg	ISLAMIC	Islamic	61DBF6F7E872...	3D320BC27753...
kiuhbg	JOHANNESBU...	Johannesburg	730A1019EDAB...	DCC7971987EC...
kimbra	KATMANDU	Katmandu	94A01EA69ED6...	2C0ACA062FF1...
tgbnmk	LENNOX	Lennox	2BC4D771AEC...	365A10ADAA6...
donmer			460FCFBB2307...	99AE7B37D8AE...

• **Figure 9.2**   The main L0phtCrack screen

File and Directory Permissions

File and directory permissions (part of what is called *authorization* in many systems) allow the computer to identify which user IDs have access to what files. This is also called access control. Access control can be very granular, thus allowing only certain individual users access to a particular file or directory, or they can be established for groups of users.

Access control is a mechanism that is used to restrict what authorized users can do on a computer system. Establishing proper access controls can prevent users who do not have access rights to a file or folder from accidentally destroying or disclosing information and files. However, access control will not prevent an authorized user from disseminating information to others.

Windows Systems   Windows has the ability to set access control permissions at a very detailed level. Figure 9.3 shows the permissions that are available. As you can see, for each individual user or group in the domain, you can set any number of permissions on each directory or folder.

In normal circumstances, permissions are set on directories. The groups of users that need to have access to the files in the directory are identified, and only these groups are given access. Some groups may be given read-write or full control, while others may be given only read access.

Linux Systems   Linux systems (like most Unix systems) do not have the granularity of access controls that are found on a Windows system. On Linux systems, permissions can be set for the owner of the file, for the group, and for the world. For each of these three, read, write, and execute permissions can be granted.

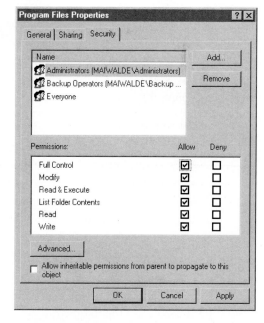

• **Figure 9.3**   Windows allows significant flexibility in access control configurations.

To see the permissions on a file, issue the command **ls -l**, and you will see something like this:

```
-rw-------  1 emaiwald  ppp        0 Nov 22 15:49 test.file
```

The permissions on `test.file` allow the owner read and write access. You can see this by the first set of characters. For this exercise, ignore the first hyphen (-). Positions 2–4 indicate the permissions for the file owner. In this case, `rw-` means that the owner has read and write permissions. If the owner had execute permissions, the fourth space would have an *x*. Positions 5–7 show the permissions for the group, and positions 8–10 indicate the permissions for everyone on the system or the world.

To change the permissions, you use the command `chmod` followed by the type of access and the category of access. For example:

```
$chmod 777 test.file
```

This command grants read, write, and execute privileges to all three categories (owner, group, and world). The three 7s represents the type of access to grant to each category based on this system: 4 gives read access, 2 gives write access, and 1 gives execute access. The number entered in the command is the sum of the access to be granted. Therefore, 7 means that read, write, and execute is granted (4 + 2 + 1 = 7). If only read and write access were to be granted, the number would be 6(4 + 2).

Practices and User Education

Technical security controls, such as password configurations and access control, can help an organization manage the security of its networks. However, such technical security controls can only go so far. These controls are based on the expertise and diligence of the system and network administrators, and because administrators are human, something likely will be forgotten or missed at some point that will open the computer systems and network to compromise.

Security Policies An organization's security policies define the expected level of security that is to be configured. These policies also define acceptable behavior for employees and users of the computer systems and networks.

Policies come in all shapes and sizes (some organizations do have one-page policies) and must be tailored to the culture of the organization. The following is a list of the areas that should be covered in an organization's network security policies:

- System configuration
- User authentication (such as passwords)

Try This!

Setting Permissions on a Folder

It is important to know how to set permissions on files and folders in Windows 2000. Try this:

1. Log in to the computer with a regular account that can create files on the local system.

2. Use My Computer to bring up the list of files and folders on your system.

3. Create a new folder for this exercise. (Don't change something on the system that might cause it to malfunction!)

4. Select and right-click the new folder. Select Properties from the list, and you will see a dialog box that provides general properties for the folder.

5. Click the Security tab and you will see who has what rights or permissions on the folder.

6. By adding individuals or groups to the list, you can establish the permissions that each group or user has to the folder.

- Access control configurations

- Network connectivity (how the internal network can be connected to the Internet)

- Computer and Internet use

- E-mail use

- Incident response (what to do when someone breaks into your systems)

- Disaster recovery (what to do when very bad things happen)

Overall, these policies provide the basic instructions for the administrators to do their jobs.

Security Awareness As mentioned earlier, it is very important to explain the need for security to your employees. Changing the password requirements without teaching your employees about the new requirements is a sure recipe for disaster.

When most people think of security awareness, they think of long, boring, required training classes. While classes are certainly part of it, they are not the only part, and they do not need to be long and boring. A good length for a basic class is less than one hour. Ideally, this would occur over lunch and would include videos as well as a presentation.

In addition to training classes, the awareness program should also include posters, newsletter articles, and e-mail reminders. The choice of how to use these parts of the program depend upon your organization. Get human resources or your public relations departments involved!

Audit Trails It is considered good practice for each server to keep an **audit trail**. An audit trail is a log that records certain security-related events that occur on a computer system. These events may include logins and logouts, system shutdowns and reboots, or even access to certain files. The audit log can be very useful in reconstructing events after a problem or concern has been identified. Keep in mind, however, that auditing can also generate a vast amount of information. Auditing every file access on a system is usually a bad idea, but auditing access to a file full of very sensitive information may give you an idea of who was trying to access the file.

It is good practice to record the following events in the audit trail:

- Successful logins

- Failed logins

- Successful logouts

- Failed logouts

- Successful management actions

- Failed management actions

- System events

- Failed access attempts

> If your organization does not have policies of this sort, don't just buy a book and copy the policies. Policies must be tailored to the organization.

> Commonwealth Films (www.commonwealthfilms.com) sells a large number of training videos. Many of them are useful for security-awareness training classes.

Chapter 9: Securing a Network

391

Try This!

Turning on Audit Trails in Windows 2000

It's important to know how to turn on audit trails in Windows 2000. Try this:

1. Log in to a Windows 2000 system as administrator or as a user with administrator access.

2. Click the Start button and select Settings | Control Panel.

3. Double-click the Administrative Tools icon.

4. Double-click the Local Security Policy icon.

5. In the left panel, expand the Local Policies item and select Audit Policy. Look at the list that is displayed in the right panel.

6. Double-click any of the items and you will be presented with a screen that allows you to configure the auditing for this type of event.

7. Go through the list and turn on the audit for the events that you would like to log.

8. Close the audit configuration screen.

9. Open your Event Viewer by clicking Start, Settings | Control Panel. Then choose Administrative Tools and double-click Event Viewer.

10. Choose Security Events in the left pane and you will see the events you turned on being logged.

The exact events that are tracked should be defined by the security policy and reflect information that is important for the organization.

It is also good practice to review your audit trails periodically. Unfortunately, audit trails that are generated by computers are not the easiest things to read. Creating or finding a tool that will automate the review of audit trails is best.

External Threats

Internal threats may be more dangerous, but, luckily, few insiders are likely to do malicious harm. External threats are more numerous, and hackers tend to attempt to cause harm when they are able to compromise a system. The good news is that external threats tend not to have the necessary access to compromise the system. Thus, they must somehow first gain access.

Front Door Attacks

The most common type of external attack is for a hacker to identify vulnerabilities on any of the organization's systems that are on the Internet. These systems may include mail servers and web servers, as well as network devices such as routers. We will call these types of attacks *front door* attacks because they attempt to exploit vulnerabilities in the organization's public face.

The Hacker's Attack   A hacker looking for a system to compromise is likely to search large portions of the Internet. This means that port scans will be used to find vulnerable systems. A **port scan** is a probe used to identify systems that are running services that may be vulnerable to attack. For example, if the hacker is looking for web servers to attack, he or she will search for systems that respond on port 80 (HTTP). Once these systems are found, the hacker will attempt to identify whether the system is vulnerable to attack. This may be done by simply issuing a bogus command across the connection. The web server at the other end will (in most cases) helpfully identify itself.

When a potentially vulnerable system is located, the hacker will launch an attack, with several potential outcomes:

- A web server might be defaced (the hacker changes the home page of the system).

- The system might be compromised so that the hacker is able to log in to the system.

- A service running on the system may cease to function.

Any combination of these things may occur, as they are not mutually exclusive. If the hacker is able to log in to the system, it is likely that he or she will drop what is called a `rootkit` on it. A rootkit is a set of programs that will aid the hacker in returning to the system and hiding his or her presence. Once a rootkit is on a system, it is very difficult to completely remove it. Usually it is best to rebuild the system from scratch.

Network Protections Protecting a network from external threats means that you must start with proper network architecture. Figure 9.4 shows a basic network layout. The router and firewall can both help protect the web server and the internal network. The router is a network device that is designed to pass traffic, but it is possible to configure access control lists on the router so that certain unwanted traffic is blocked or dropped rather than passed on. The access control lists could drop such things as inbound telnet traffic or traffic that is targeted at ports that are not used.

The `firewall` is a network security device that can be configured to allow certain traffic through. Firewalls will drop all traffic by default—they must be configured to pass traffic that is necessary for

Determining Which Web Server Is Running

Techniques such as determining which web server is running can be very useful for debugging as well as for gathering information. This exercise shows how easy it is to gather such information. Try this:

1. Log in to your system as a normal user.

2. Find a local web server or one on the Internet. You can do this by looking for a system named *www.<your domain name>*. Most companies use *www* as the name of their web servers.

3. Choose Start and Run. Type **cmd** when the computer asks you what you want to run. This will bring up a command prompt window.

4. Type the following:

   ```
   $telnet <web server> 80
   ```

   Telnet is used to establish an interactive session with a system. The *80* at the end of the command tells the telnet client to connect to port 80 on the web server. Replace *<web server>* in the command with the name of the web server that you have located.

5. Once the client connects, type the following:

   ```
   http /1.0 Get
   ```

   Then press ENTER two times. In most cases, you will get back some text that indicates a bad page request. Embedded in the response, though, may be some information about the web server in use. For example:

   ```
   HTTP/1.1 400 Bad Request
   Date: Mon, 25 Nov 2002 19:49:34 GMT
   Server: Apache/1.3.27
   Connection: close
   Content-Type: text/html; charset=iso-8859-1
   ```

   In this case, the web server is running Apache version 1.3.27. See what you can find.

business. In Figure 9.4, HTTP traffic must get to the web server so that the information on the web server can be made available to the Internet. E-mail must also get to the mail server so that the organization can receive mail. The firewall would be configured to allow this traffic. However, traffic to other ports would be blocked, since there is no reason for anyone on the Internet to connect to ports other than ports 25 and 80. Similarly, all traffic bound for the internal network would be blocked, as there is absolutely no reason to allow external systems to connect to sensitive, internal systems.

Through the use of basic security tools, such as firewalls and router access control lists, you can prevent hackers from targeting vulnerabilities that may exist in services that people on the Internet do not need to access.

Patching Vulnerabilities Perhaps the most important thing you can do to a network or system to protect it from hackers is update vulnerable software.

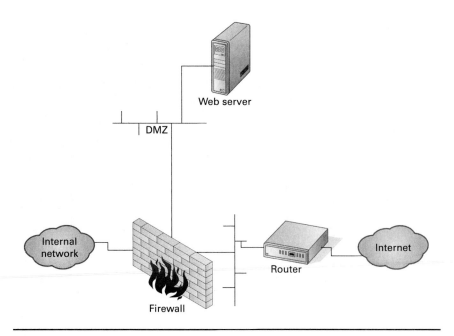

• **Figure 9.4**   Basic external network security protections

Today, software has become so complex that it appears to be impossible to eliminate programming errors completely, and some of these errors lead to security vulnerabilities that could allow a hacker to take control of the system. The only defense is to stay up to date on the vulnerabilities and patches, and update the system on a regular basis.

Many sources can provide information on vulnerabilities and patches. In fact, the manufacturers of operating systems and software usually provide mailing lists to keep you updated. Other organizations also provide this information. These are two of the major ones:

- Computer Emergency Response Team (CERT)—Provides a mailing list on major vulnerabilities and patches (`www.cert.org`)

- Security Focus (now part of Symantec)—Provides several mailing lists on software vulnerabilities (bugtraq), computer incidents (incidents), and others (`www.securityfocus.com`)

Patching systems can take time, but the protection that it affords the organization is well worth the effort.

Step-by-Step 9.2

Upgrading a Windows 2000 System

Microsoft has provided an easy-to-use web site where you can upgrade the software of any Windows system, including Windows 95, 98, 2000, and XP. The procedure is very simple, and the web site walks you through all of the necessary steps.

To complete this exercise, you will need the following items:

- A Windows computer (either 95, 98, 2000, or XP)
- An administrator login to the system

Step 1

Log in to your computer as an administrator or equivalent.

Step 2

Start Internet Explorer, enter **http://windowsupdate.Microsoft.com** in the Address field, and click the Go button. Note that you will have to allow Internet Explorer to run ActiveX scripts for this site to work properly.

Step 3

Click the Scan for Updates link and wait as the scripts identify the necessary upgrades for your system.

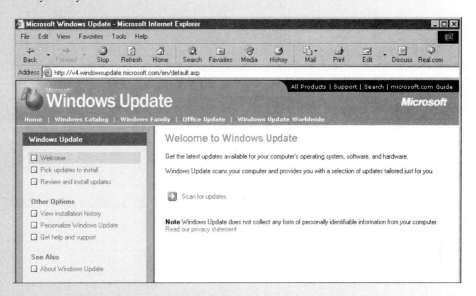

Step 4

Click the Review and Install Updates link so that you can choose which updates to install.

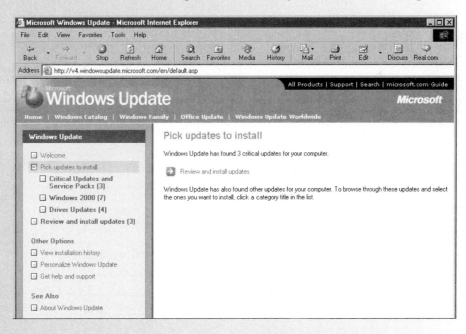

Step 5

Carefully review the list of updates that you can download and install. Some of them may have to be downloaded and installed separately. This information will be included in the descriptions. Also be aware that some of the updates can be rather large. If you have a slow connection, you may need to download one or two updates at a time. After you make your choices, click the Install Now button to begin the installation.

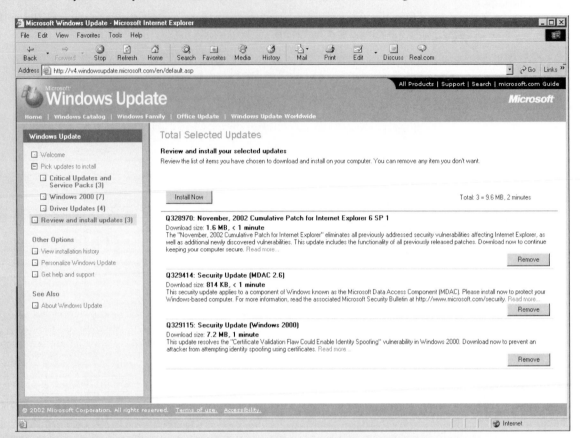

Step 6

After installation, it may be necessary to reboot your system for the updates to take effect.

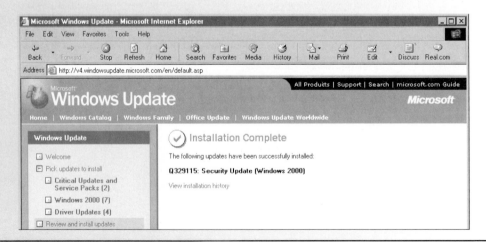

Back Door Attacks

We have talked about hackers coming through the front door. While this is one way in for hackers, it is not the only one. Keep in mind that hackers want to gain as much access as they can while hiding their true identities. Often, the best way to do this is to come in the back door—there are ways to get information or access to computer systems other than just attacking the security of the computer system. Here are some back door approaches:

- Physically breaking into the facility
- Using a remote access connection
- Using a wireless network access point
- Using social engineering to trick an employee into giving out information

Physical Security   The longer a person works with computers, the clearer it becomes that physical access to a system is a key component of security. If a hacker can gain physical access to a system, it is likely that he or she will be able to take control of the system. Therefore, the physical security that is provided around your organization's computer systems is as important, if not more so, than the network security.

In real life, physical security measures are fairly simple:

- Locate sensitive systems in a data center that has good physical access controls.
- Limit the access outsiders have to the organization's facilities so that they cannot use employee computers or attach their own systems to the network.

Following these basic principles will prevent the majority of physical access threats to your systems.

Remote Access Security   In an effort to allow remote or traveling employees to access internal resources, many organizations have implemented some type of remote access solution. Whether this is a dial-up solution or a virtual private network (VPN) over the Internet depends on the particular situation of the organization.

If these access points are properly secured—meaning that appropriate care has been taken to use strong authentication systems—there is usually little additional risk to the organization. However, sometimes remote access via dial-up phone line is not centrally controlled by the organization, and departments or individual employees establish their own remote access points. Too often, this is simply a single phone line into a single computer running pcAnywhere with no authentication. A configuration such as this allows anyone who finds out about the phone number to take control of the computer and act like a legitimate user of the organization's network.

One of the security tests that Lauren ordered performed against the SinkRSwim Pools network is called a penetration test. This is a test that looks for vulnerabilities in the computer and network systems of an organization. In some cases, the organization actually asks the testers to exploit a vulnerability to gain access to sensitive information. Ricky was part of a team that was testing the organization. Lauren gave Ricky the address of the firewall and web servers to try to penetrate, and he performed basic tests against these systems and found no obvious vulnerabilities. However, further examination of the web page showed fax and phone numbers.

Using the phone numbers, Ricky proceeded to war-dial approximately 1,000 phone numbers similar to them. War-dialing is an attempt to find

Inside Information

Updating Linux

Updating Linux systems is not as easy as updating Windows systems because there are many flavors of Linux, and each system may include software from several other vendors. It is usually best to periodically visit the web sites of the distribution you are using. For example, www.redhat.com *will provide updates and patches for the Red Hat Linux distributions. These updates will usually cover any software that is included in the original distribution.*

Once you have found the updates you want, you will need to download them and install them. Keep in mind that some vendors (such as Red Hat) also provide utilities to help you through the process. The Red Hat utility is called up2date, and it will start an interactive session that will walk you through the update process.

phone lines that are being answered by computers. Any time a computer answers a phone, a note is made of the number and attempts can then be made to gain access. Usually, automated programs are used to dial huge groups of numbers.

The next morning Ricky came in to find that the computer had found four numbers that responded with modem carriers. He tested each and found that one was a computer with pcAnywhere running and no password. From there it took the team only a quick five minutes to access the computers on SinkRSwim's internal network that contained the organization's most sensitive information.

Wireless Networks   In the past, controlling physical access to the office space of the organization usually controlled the physical access threat. Unfortunately, wireless technology now allows the organization's network to leak outside of the physical office space. The installation of a wireless hub may allow access to the network from outside the building or on other floors of the same building.

If wireless technology is installed, tests should be performed to determine exactly how far the signals travel. Be sure to check parking lots and other floors in the building. Unfortunately, the existing security measures associated with wireless networks have proven to be less than effective, allowing outsiders to gain access to internal networks. Figure 9.5 illustrates two of the potential dangers.

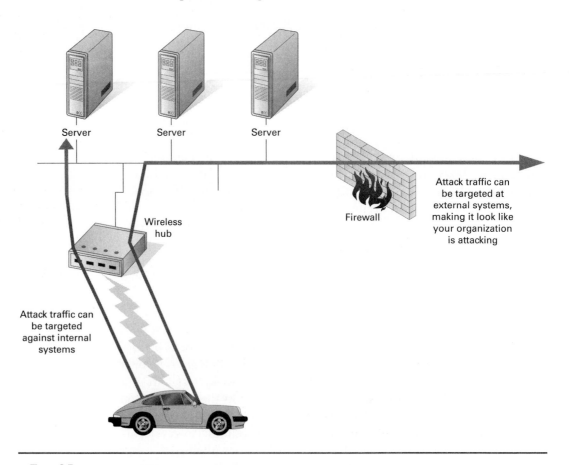

• **Figure 9.5**   Wireless security dangers

At the very least, if wireless networks are to be used, they should be segregated from the main internal network by a firewall and should require strong authentication. Also, try to keep track of how far your wireless network travels, as it may go farther than the parking lot!

Here are some other recommendations for using wireless networks:

- Monitor internal systems just as you monitor external systems, and use internal Intrusion Detection System (IDS) if possible.

- Understand the range and security features of your wireless systems.

- Use a VPN on your wireless networks.

- Use a firewall to limit access from your wireless networks to your internal networks.

- Identify valid MAC addresses and exclude all others from your wireless networks.

Social Engineering   Social engineering can be used to to gain unauthorized access to computer systems through non-technical means. A hacker may use lies and deceit to gain passwords or other information about the network. Consider the following conversation:

Hacker	"Hi, my name is John and I am with the Help desk. I am calling to solve a little problem with your computer."
Employee	"Gee, what kind of problem?"
Hacker	"Oh, nothing serious. Just a little unnecessary traffic. I just need your password so I can clear it up."
Employee	"OK, my password is g34hjuk8."
Hacker	"Thanks. I will take care of it and call you back in a few minutes to reboot your system."

Based on this conversation, how many of your employees will provide their passwords? Normally, the answer is about 60 percent (or even more!). The hacker may also take the role of an employee who needs remote access—the hacker tries to convince the help desk that he needs to provide a password or change an existing password. Remember that help desk employees are trained to be helpful.

The only way to combat this type of attack is by educating the users and help desk staff. Make sure that scenarios like this are included in the awareness training. A key point to make to employees is that the help desk will never ask for their passwords, since they already have all the access they need.

Denial of Service

A denial of service (DOS) attack is an attempt to prevent the legitimate use of a resource. This type of attack can be carried out with a pair of wire cutters or a backhoe, or it can be a sophisticated network-flooding attack. Most of the DOS attacks today take the form of some type of data flood on a network. This attack uses up all of the available bandwidth on a network and thus prevents legitimate traffic from reaching the computers on the network. The end result of this type of attack is that the legitimate users of the server cannot reach it, and it therefore appears to be down.

Inside Information

Working with the Physical Security Department
Computer and network security is not an area where you can work in a vacuum, and physical security is a good example of this. Normally, the job of physical security is separate from that of computer and network security. Therefore, in order to secure the organization's network and computers properly, the administrators must work with the staff charged with physical security.

Discuss the potential physical threats to the computers and networks with the person in charge of physical security. Identify which employees should be allowed into the data center, and discuss the potential for a visitor to access the network. This type of cooperation can help you in your career.

Have a help desk staff person participate in the awareness training program. This way he or she can relate firsthand what types of questions the help desk might have.

More recently, hackers have used large numbers of compromised servers connected to the Internet in what is called a `distributed denial of service (DDOS) attack`. The DDOS attack makes use of the compromised systems to increase the amount of traffic in the flood and thus take down larger connections or even multiple systems (see Figure 9.6).

DOS attacks do not have to be made against bandwidth. Attacks are also made against particular services (such as the web server or mail server). These types of attacks can be just as devastating as a bandwidth attack.

You can employ few methods to protect against DOS attacks. A DOS vulnerability that is caused by a software problem can be patched, but an attack against bandwidth is impossible to prevent. Any response by the victim also requires assistance from their Internet service provider (ISP) and the upstream providers. Even then, it may not be possible to stop the attack.

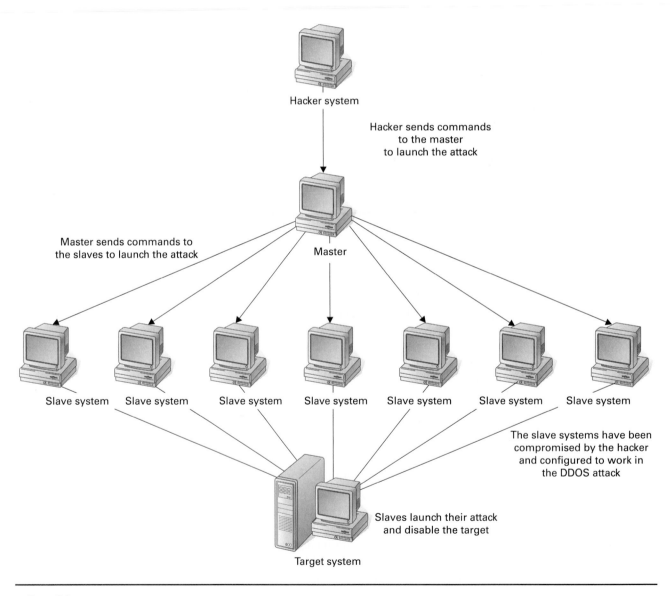

Hacker system

Hacker sends commands
to the master
to launch the attack

Master sends commands to
the slaves to launch the attack

Master

Slave system Slave system Slave system Slave system Slave system Slave system Slave system

The slave systems have been
compromised by the hacker
and configured to work in
the DDOS attack

Slaves launch their attack
and disable the target

Target system

• **Figure 9.6** A distributed denial of service attack

Viruses, Worms, and Other Malicious Code

Malicious programs are a significant security issue to all organizations. At the very least, these programs eat up staff time. At the other end of the spectrum, these programs can be very destructive or they can be used by hackers to gain entry into an organization's computer systems. Two useful sites that offer information about these malicious programs are McAfee Security at `www.mcafee.com` (makers of antivirus products) and Symantec at `www.Symantec.com` (makers of Norton AntiVirus). Both sites have searchable archives of malicious programs, where you can find fixes and the characteristics of the programs.

Types of Malicious Programs

There are three general types of malicious code: viruses, worms, and Trojan horses. Each has its own characteristics.

Viruses   A `virus` is a program that piggybacks on another program—viruses are not programs that exist on a system by themselves. By attaching themselves to another program and hiding there in spaces not used by the original program, they cause themselves to be run anytime the infected file runs. Macro viruses attach themselves to word processor documents and files for other programs with macro programming capabilities.

Viruses propagate through the sharing of files—executable files (.com or .exe files) or, in the case of macro viruses, document files. They can be shared through FTP sites or web sites, or simply by transferring disks between computers. These types of programs can be destructive or passive. Examples of viruses include Michelangelo and Melissa.

Worms   `Worms` are programs that execute on their own and use their own code to propagate. Generally, worms are programmed to exploit vulnerabilities on computer systems. Depending on the sophistication of the worm, it may do any of the following:

- Choose targets randomly or from a predefined list.

- Examine the target by searching for particular programs or vulnerabilities, or just attempt to exploit the vulnerability no matter what the target is.

- Send messages back to its creator about a system that has been compromised.

In effect, worms are automated forms of hacking, and they can compromise many systems in a very short period of time. Examples of worms are CodeRed and SaAdmind.

Trojan Horses   A `Trojan horse` is a program that pretends to be something it is not. Normally, the Trojan horse program is accompanied by some type of social engineering that attempts to make the recipient execute the program. If you look back at two recent Trojan horse programs, you can see how this was done:

- **ILOVEYOU**   The ILOVEYOU Trojan horse came as an e-mail message from someone that you knew. It pretended to be some type of love message, and that was a sufficient enticement to cause many people to open the file. Opening the file caused the script to run and propagate itself.

- **AnnaKornikova** The same method was used with this Trojan horse, but instead of pretending to be a love message, the e-mail indicated that it was a nude picture of the tennis star Anna Kournikova.

Preventing Infections

It shouldn't surprise anyone that the most important way to prevent malicious code infections is to have proper antivirus software installed and configured. However, user education is also important. Users need to be taught that e-mails with unexpected attachments should be treated with suspicion and not opened immediately. With that said, the following sections offer some recommendations for dealing with malicious code at various points in the infrastructure of an organization.

Servers Servers, especially file servers, should have antivirus software installed. This software should be configured to examine the entire file system for malicious code on a daily basis. It is best to configure these scans to begin in the off hours, as the scans can use a fair amount of the system's processing power.

Desktop Computers Desktop computers are the most likely location for a malicious code infection to begin, so the installation of antivirus software here is more critical than on the servers. Periodic checking of desktop computers can be difficult, since many employees turn their systems off when they go home for the night. Instead, all desktop systems should be configured to scan files as they are opened. This will allow the antivirus software to identify malicious code even if the employee disregards your recommendations and opens the e-mail attachment. This configuration will also catch files that are moved between work and home.

E-Mail E-mail is increasingly the medium of choice for spreading malicious code, which means you can watch for it and stop it before it gets to the desktop computers. Several products are on the market that will scan all incoming (and outgoing) e-mail messages for malicious code as they move through the e-mail server. If any is found, the e-mail is quarantined and not passed on to the destination without first being cleaned. It is usually easier to keep one antivirus installation configured and up to date than to try to keep every desktop properly configured and maintained.

Try This!

Checking Your Antivirus Configuration

Checking your antivirus configuration is a useful exercise, because an appropriate configuration can save you much time and aggravation. Try this:

1. Log in to your computer as administrator.

2. From the Start | Programs menu locate your antivirus program and start it up. This will bring up your user interface.

3. Look for a setting called "Realtime protection" or something close to that.

4. Check to make sure that the software is checking for malicious code in real time.

5. Once you have determined this, check to see what types of files are being checked. Many antivirus packages will default to checking only executable files, such as those with .com and .exe extensions. This configuration will not catch macro viruses. To catch macro viruses and other such malicious code, make sure the software checks all files.

Updating Antivirus Databases No matter which antivirus software an organization purchases, the antivirus database must be kept up to date. Every major antivirus vendor provides a mechanism to update the databases with the latest information. It should be noted that if the latest information is not installed with the software, the software will not detect the most recent malicious code.

Do no rely on employees and administrators remembering to update their own databases. Even the most well-intentioned employees will forget from time to time. Instead, configure the antivirus software to check for updates automatically and install them if an update is found. Make sure the software does this at least once per day.

Planning a Secure Network

As you might imagine, creating a secure network is not a five-minute task—it takes planning, testing, and constant awareness. A secure network begins with a definition of the security requirements, and it continues with the development of policies and awareness training of employees. Even if you have a good plan, though, bad things can still happen, and you must be prepared to deal with them.

Identifying Requirements

When developing a secure network, you must begin with security requirements. Security requirements fall into four basic areas:

- **Confidentiality** What information must be kept from unauthorized individuals? This requirement will affect the need for network security devices, as well as access control on files.

- **Integrity** What information must be protected from unauthorized changes? This requirement will affect the need for network security devices, as well as access control on files.

- **Availability** What information, systems, or capabilities must be ready for use? This requirement will affect the need for redundant systems and communications, as well as backups and alternative locations for disaster recovery.

- **Accountability** What information do you need to have about what has happened? This requirement will affect the need for authentication (so you know who was there) and audit logs (so you know what they did).

Together, the requirements in these four areas will drive the design of your network and the configuration of your systems.

Planning for Disaster

Planning for a disaster is a necessary part of building and maintaining a secure network. Disasters are events that cause massive damage to the organization's infrastructure. In most situations, this means that the organization's primary data center or site is no longer usable for business. When such a situation occurs, it is madness to expect employees to respond without a previously developed and tested **disaster recovery plan (DRP)**.

A complete DRP should take into account everything from the computer equipment and communications needs of the organization to where the employees will sit and work. This is not to say that every organization requires a backup site that can come online in minutes. Depending on the requirements for availability, the organization may not require such a response.

Meeting the availability requirements is often very expensive, as it may require duplicate equipment and an alternative location. These are costs that your organization may not wish to incur.

When developing the DRP, make sure that the organization understands who has the authority to initiate the plan. In most cases, this is obvious. In others, it is not. For example, a few years ago there was a major ice storm in the northeastern United States and eastern Canada. Many electric towers were taken down, and power to Montreal was cut. One organization in the city had a backup generator all set and ready to go. However, the managers of the organization were concerned about the supply of diesel fuel. They considered initiating a disaster response and contacted their hot site vendor. Unfortunately, they had not kept the configurations at the vendor up to date, and thus they could initiate the DRP only with the loss of some services. Clearly, the decision to initiate the DRP in this case needed to be made at a very high level in the organization.

This example also points out the need for testing the DRP. If the DRP had been tested on a regular basis, this problem could have been identified and corrected before a real disaster occurred.

Step-by-Step 9.3

Creating a DRP

Look around at your classroom configuration, or choose another network you know. You will use that network in this exercise.

To complete this exercise, you will need the following items:

- A pad of paper and a pencil

Step 1

Identify the components of the network. List the number and types of servers, desktop computers, routers, firewalls, printers—everything you can see. Be sure to note the make and model of the servers and the amount of memory and disk space. Also identify the operating system and the applications that run on each system.

Step 2

Try to prioritize the systems that you have listed. Take into account the use of each system and the dependencies. For example, a web server may be the most critical item because people on the Internet must have access to it. In this case, the network connections are also critical, because without them no one will be able to reach the server.

As part of this prioritization, identify how long each system can be down before it impacts business or operations.

Step 3	Find an alternative location for your computer systems. Ideally, your organization will have a facility that is somewhat remote from the current facility, and perhaps it can be an alternative location for the computer equipment. Remember that the site must have adequate space, power, climate control, physical security, and communications in order to work well as an alternative site.
Step 4	Develop a plan for getting the network back into operation at the new site. Take into account the amount of time each system can be down. Do you purchase duplicate equipment to keep at the alternative location, or will you try to procure this equipment after the disaster has occurred? This choice will depend on how quickly the systems must be returned to service and on your budget. Develop plans based on an unlimited budget and also on a very small budget. What is the smallest budget you can get away with?
Step 5	You have identified what you will do and how much it will cost. What do you need to do on a regular basis to make sure your plan stays up to date? If the network changes—if a new server or device is added, for example—what has to happen to the plan?

Which members of the staff must know about the plan? How will you keep these employees involved in the plan so that they will remember what to do next year? |

Backing Up the Network

Small disasters are likely to occur more frequently than big ones. Small disasters include hard drive failures, accidental file deletions, and system crashes. In these cases, restoring a single file or an entire drive is required, rather than declaring a disaster and moving to an alternative location.

File backups are an important part of managing the security of a network. However, these can also become prohibitively expensive if not done properly. At the high end of the cost spectrum, each server could be configured with backup drives in a RAID (redundant array of independent disks) configuration. There are five levels of RAID (levels 2 and 4 are not used, however), and each provides advantages for protecting data. However, while RAID protects against the loss of data resulting from a disk failure, it is expensive (additional disks must be purchased, along with a RAID controller) and it does not prevent the accidental deletion of files.

The alternative to RAID for protection from disk failure is to back up the files onto tape or another disk. This has the added advantage of protecting files from accidental deletion (since they can be restored from tape). Tapes also tend to be less expensive than RAID configurations.

The schedule of backups needs to be well thought out. In most cases, a full backup (meaning that every file is written to tape) occurs once a week, and incremental backups (which record only the changes since the last backup) occur every day.

Tapes need to be stored in a secure location because if something were to happen to the data center, the information on the tapes would be needed to rebuild operations. Therefore, you should normally move tapes offsite as soon as possible. Some organizations provide offsite storage and pick up and deliver tapes, allowing you to rotate the tapes on a daily basis.

Inside Information

Computing Backup Requirements

In most cases, organizations will take incremental backups on a daily basis and full backups weekly. Examine your servers and estimate the tape requirements for this backup schedule.

Now consider that you will want to keep some of the tapes offsite, following a regular rotation. A standard procedure is something like this:

- *One weekly set of backups is kept offsite at all times and rotated weekly.*
- *At the end of every month, a full backup is retained for a year.*
- *At the end of every year, a full backup is retained for a year (or more, depending on legal requirements).*

Now, how many backup tapes will you need?

Chapter 9 Review

■ Chapter Summary

After reading this chapter and completing the exercises, you should understand the following.

Identify Threats to Your Network

- Threats require motive, means, and opportunity.
- Employees or insiders are the most dangerous threats because they have means and opportunity.
- Hackers have sufficient means and motivation to attack your network. The only thing they may lack is the opportunity.
- User authentication must use at least one of the following: something known, something possessed, or a personal characteristic.
- Strong passwords can be constructed by using combinations of uppercase and lowercase letters, numbers, and special characters.
- Passwords are normally discovered through the use of a brute force attack.
- Access control mechanisms can be used to limit access to sensitive files.
- Technical security is not sufficient to protect a network. You must also have a security policy and educate users.
- Audit trails can be used to reconstruct events and thus can help in investigating security incidents.
- Hackers usually attempt to identify systems, services, and software before attacking.
- Once a vulnerability is identified, a hacker will exploit it and place a rootkit on the system.
- Firewalls are a basic component of a security architecture.
- Patching vulnerabilities is an important part of overall security.
- Physical security is necessary to protect overall computer security.

- Remote access via dial-up phone lines or a VPN can also be used by hackers to attack a network. Make sure such systems are protected by appropriate authentication.
- Wireless networks can extend beyond the physical confines of the building and can provide another means for hackers to gain access to your network.
- Hackers may use social engineering techniques to trick your employees out of information such as passwords.
- Denial of service attacks can take many forms, but all of them deny access to important systems or information.
- Malicious code often costs organizations significant time to clean up and remove.
- Antivirus software on desktop computers, servers, and e-mail systems is the best defense against malicious code.
- Antivirus signatures must be updated on a regular basis to make the antivirus software effective.

Plan for a Secure Network

- Requirements must be identified in the areas of confidentiality, integrity, availability, and accountability before a secure network can be constructed.
- Disaster planning is important for the availability of the network and systems.
- Proper disaster planning must include all key systems and information.
- Disaster planning is not a one-time exercise but must be updated every time a new system is added to the network.
- Backups are a necessary part of network security.
- Backups are used to reconstruct files after a disk failure or unintentional deletion.

■ Key Terms

access control *(389)*
audit trail *(391)*
biometrics *(384)*
brute force attack *(388)*
denial of service (DOS) attack *(399)*
disaster recovery plan *(403)*

distributed denial of service (DDOS) attack *(400)*
firewall *(393)*
hackers *(383)*
identification and authentication *(383)*

password lockouts *(385)*
penetration test *(397)*
policies *(390)*
port scan *(392)*
risk *(382)*
rootkit *(393)*

sniffing *(388)*
social engineering *(399)*
threat *(383)*
Trojan horse *(401)*
virus *(401)*
war-dial *(397)*
worms *(401)*

Key Term Quiz

Use the Key Terms list to complete the sentences that follow. (Not all terms will be used.)

1. _____ is dialing a large set of phone numbers in order to find computers that answer.

2. An attack that seeks to render systems or information unavailable is a(n) _____.

3. The starting point for a good security program is _____, which determines how systems will be configured.

4. A security device that is used for network access control is a(n) _____.

5. A(n) _____ is an individual with motive, means, and opportunity.

6. _____ is used to prove to the computer who you are.

7. A program that piggybacks on another program is called a(n) _____.

8. Listening in to a network to gather passwords is called _____ the network.

9. A security test that is used to identify security vulnerabilities is called a(n) _____.

10. The most effective way to discover passwords is through a(n) _____.

Multiple-Choice Quiz

1. What are the primary impediments to complete network security? Choose all that apply.
   a. Cost
   b. Usability
   c. Hackers
   d. Risk
   e. Threats

2. To be credible, a threat must posses motive, means, and
   a. Knowledge
   b. A computer
   c. Hacking tools
   d. Opportunity
   e. A vulnerability

3. Internal threats are dangerous because
   a. They are employees.
   b. They posses knowledge of which systems are most important.
   c. They posses motivation.
   d. They possess unauthorized access.
   e. They can be compromised.

4. The three types of authentication information are
   a. Something a person knows
   b. Something a person is
   c. Something a person wears
   d. Something a person does
   e. Something a person has

5. Which of the following is not a type of biometric system?
   a. Fingerprints
   b. Retina scan
   c. Voice print
   d. Facial geometry
   e. Password

6. Which of the following is the most widely used form of authentication?
   a. Fingerprints
   b. Smart cards
   c. Passwords
   d. User IDs
   e. Retina scans

7. Two characteristics of good passwords are that they are hard to guess and
   a. They are hard to discover using brute force.
   b. They are eight characters in length.
   c. They change every 45 days.
   d. They are made up of uppercase and lowercase letters.
   e. They include numbers and special characters.

8. Access control is used to
   a. Prevent hackers from gaining control of a system
   b. Prevent legitimate users from looking at files they are not authorized to see

c. Preventing employees from crashing systems

d. Preventing unauthorized users from conducting a port scan

e. Preventing users from encrypting files

9. Audit trails should be

a. Deleted weekly

b. Stored with other files

c. Reviewed regularly

d. Held for evidence

e. Not created

10. Before attacking, a hacker will look for signs of

a. A vulnerability

b. A web server

c. A port scan

d. An employee

e. Sensitive information

11. The most critical task that can be performed on a network to prevent a hacker from gaining access to a system is

a. Creating a firewall

b. Patching systems

c. Educating users

d. Creating policy

e. Capturing audit trails

12. Wireless networks can cause problems in securing networks because

a. Existing wireless security features are better than the rest of the network.

b. VPNs are not used.

c. War-dialing can find the wireless nodes.

d. Many wireless networks are unpatched.

e. They extend the network outside of the physical building.

13. Which is the most effective means of preventing virus infections?

a. User education

b. Patching systems

c. Using antivirus software

d. Creating appropriate policies

e. Conducting penetration tests

14. Security requirements should be identified in which of the following areas?

a. Confidentiality

b. Integrity

c. Availability

d. Accountability

e. All of the above

15. Backups are needed in addition to disaster recovery plans because

a. Tapes are included in disaster recovery plans.

b. The recovery of a single file is a less frequent requirement than the move to an alternative site.

c. Disaster plans re-create sites, while backups assist in the recovery of files.

d. Disaster recovery plans may not work.

e. Disaster plans must be constantly updated.

■ Essay Quiz

1. Compare and contrast the inside versus outside threats. List two ways in which inside threats can be thwarted. List two ways outside threats can be thwarted. Describe the similarities and differences between the two types of threats and the ways in which you can defend against them.

2. Using Amazon.com as an example, describe which security requirements you feel are most important and explain why. Think of the information that they must have to accept an order, the requirements on the information as it

goes through their system, the ability to know who ordered what, and the need for the site to be responsive to customers.

3. Describe the requirements that must be examined when choosing an identification and authentication system. In your discussion of the issues, be sure to include the level of trust, the cost, and other logistical issues.

4. Access control systems can become unmanageable if not used properly. The most common concern with access control is providing individual access

(or denying individual access) to each file. Propose a policy for managing access to files across an organization that is both easy to manage and appropriate from a security point of view.

5. In a certain organization, the security director determined that it was very important to track how administrators were using their access to systems. He decided to implement an audit policy to do this. Describe the events that should be audited in such a situation and what information each type of event will provide to the security director.

Lab Projects

• Lab Project 9.1

Security awareness is an important part of any good security program. The most important part of awareness is getting the information to the employees in a meaningful manner. You have been given the job of creating a security awareness program for your organization, which is an online retailer selling outdoor apparel. Outside of the shipping and warehouse staff, the majority of employees use computers on a daily basis. These employees include office staff, customer service representatives, buyers, and IT staff members.

To complete this exercise, you will need the following items:

■ Your networked Windows XP Professional workstation

■ Sketch pad and pencil

❶ Identify the parts of the awareness program (that is, what you will use to get your message of security across to the employees in each group).

❷ Determine the material to be covered in each part of the program.

❸ Outline how the material will be presented for each group.

• Lab Project 9.2

Your organization is investigating wireless technology. As part of the investigation, you have been asked to identify security issues. One issue that you identified was that the signal may be available outside of the facility. In order to provide hard data to management, you establish a wireless hub and use a wireless interface card in your laptop to check the range of the device.

To complete this exercise, you will need the following items:

■ A computer running Windows 2000 XP Professional with a wireless NIC

■ A wireless hub

❶ Check the ability to connect to the network both inside the building and outside.

❷ Record your results and present the results to management.

❸ Identify and test protective measures to limit who can access the wireless network.

❹ Present these measures as recommendations on how wireless technology may be used.

INDEX

clients
    configuring for Windows 2000
        Server, 211–214
    thin clients, 243–244
client/server e-mail, explanation of, 5
client/server networking
    advantages of, 2–3
    versus client/server database
        systems, 3
    disadvantages of, 3
    overview of, 1
    relationships in, 2–3
coax cable, description of, 13
collision domains, relationship
    to hubs, 12
collision packets versus data packets,
    25–26
columns, creating for application-
    assessment table, 18
commands
    entering in NetWare 6 server
        console, 116–117
    for file management in Linux, 54
compression
    explanation of, 111
    rules for NetWare 6, 113
concentrators, functionality of, 12
conductors, relationship to coax cable, 13
confidentiality, relationship to network
    security, 403
CONFIG command in NetWare 6,
    description of, 118
console commands in Novell NetWare 6,
    listing, 87
ConsoleOne utility in NetWare
    Administrator, features of, 93
contexts for trees, revealing during
    Novell Client installation, 98
Copy backups, explanation of, 234
copying, files in Linux, 57–58
cp command in Linux
    description of, 54
    using, 57, 61
CSU/DSU (channel service unit/data
    service unit), explanation of, 7
CTRL commands, using with pico, 55

◼ D

Daily backups, explanation of, 234
data packets versus collision packets,
    25–26
data recovery, performing, 368
data-link layer of OSI model,
    overview of, 9
DDoS (distributed denial of service
    attacks), occurrence of, 400
decimal and binary, converting between,
    299–300
default gateway addresses
    overview of, 297
    pinging, 317
Defrag program in Windows 98,
    accessing, 364–365
defragmentation, explanation of, 364

desktop, preparing for users in Windows
    NT 4.0 Workstation, 177–179
device drivers
    providing for Windows NT 4.0
        Workstation installation, 166
    verifying during Novell NetWare
        6 installation, 82
DHCP requests, configuring during
    Linux 7.3 server installation, 41
Differential backups, explanation of, 234
Digital Equipment Corp. Unix utility
    vendor, web site for, 281
dir command versus ls in Linux, 51
directories
    changing in Linux, 59
    in NFS, 103–106
    relationship to file sharing, 4
    setting in NWCONFIG.NLM, 122
disasters, planning for, 403–404
discovery process
    relationship to BDCs in
        Windows NT Server 4.0, 155
    relationship to NetLogon
        service, 252
Disk Cleanup utility, using, 366–367
disk drives, relationship to file sharing, 4
Disk Management utility
    formatting hard drives with,
        356–357
    using with partitions, 360–362
DISPLAY NETWORKS command in
    NetWare 6, description of, 118
DISPLAY SERVERS command in
    NetWare 6, description of, 118
Distinct Corp. Unix utility vendor, web
    site for, 281
domains, relationship to Windows NT
    Server 4.0, 154–155
DOS. *See* MS-DOS
DoS (denial of service) attacks,
    occurrence of, 399–401
DOWN command in NetWare 6,
    description of, 117
drive initialization, confirming during
    Linux 7.3 server installation, 38
drive letters
    mapping to NetWare server
        volumes, 100–102
    mapping to shared folders
        (Windows NT 4.0
        Workstation), 185–186
drivers
    installing for Novell NetWare 6, 79
    installing for Red Hat Linux
        servers, 35
    setting in NWCONFIG.NLM, 122
DRPs (disaster recovery plans),
    developing, 403–405
.DSK NLM type, description of, 119
DSL lines, capacity of, 7
DSREPAIR (directory services repair),
    running in Novell NetWare 6, 87
DSREPAIR.NLM, description of,
    119–121

dynamic disks
    compatibility of, 358
    features of, 357
    upgrading to, 359

◼ E

/e switch in winnt.exe or winn32.exe,
    result of, 143
EIDE cables, types of, 347
EIDE (Enhanced Integrated Drive
    Electronics)
    relationship to hard drives,
        346–347
    versus SCSI, 346
Emacs editor, features of, 56
e-mail, overview of, 5–6
e-mail servers, purpose of, 11
enterprise considerations in Novell
    integration, 277
ERP (enterprise resource planning), 7
Essay Quizzes
    for Configuring Hard Drives, 381
    for Connecting Client
        Workstations, 290
    for Designing a Network, 31
    for Networking with Novell
        NetWare 6, 128
    for Networking with Unix and
        Linux, 74
    for Networking with Windows
        NT, 193
    for Securing a Network, 408–409
    for TCP/IP, 337
    for Windows 2000 Server, 241
/etc folder, contents of, 59
Ethernet, choosing as network type, 24
Everyone group in Windows NT 4.0
    Workstation
    managing, 181
    user rights for, 182

◼ F

–F switch for ls command in Linux,
    description of, 54
/f switch in winnt.exe or winn32.exe,
    result of, 143
FAT partitions
    purpose of, 341–342
    removing from Windows NT
        Server 4.0, 157–158
    removing Windows NT boot
        loaders on, 80
    removing Windows NT Server 4.0
        from, 158–159
FAT16 and FAT32, features of, 342–343
fault tolerance in Windows NT Server 4.0,
    overview of, 133
FDISK
    removing partitions with, 34–35,
        75–77
    using, 356
    using to install Windows 98 on
        hard disks, 353–355

■ X

INTERNATIONAL CONTACT INFORMATION

AUSTRALIA
McGraw-Hill Book Company
Australia Pty. Ltd.
TEL +61-2-9900-1800
FAX +61-2-9878-8881
http://www.mcgraw-hill.com.au
books-it_sydney@mcgraw-hill.com

CANADA
McGraw-Hill Ryerson Ltd.
TEL +905-430-5000
FAX +905-430-5020
http://www.mcgraw-hill.ca

**GREECE, MIDDLE EAST, & AFRICA
(Excluding South Africa)**
McGraw-Hill Hellas
TEL +30-210-6560-990
TEL +30-210-6560-993
TEL +30-210-6560-994
FAX +30-210-6545-525

MEXICO (Also serving Latin America)
McGraw-Hill Interamericana Editores
S.A. de C.V.
TEL +525-1500-5108
FAX +525-117-1589
http://www.mcgraw-hill.com.mx
carlos_ruiz@mcgraw-hill.com

SINGAPORE (Serving Asia)
McGraw-Hill Book Company
TEL +65-6863-1580
FAX +65-6862-3354
http://www.mcgraw-hill.com.sg
mghasia@mcgraw-hill.com

SOUTH AFRICA
McGraw-Hill South Africa
TEL +27-11-622-7512
FAX +27-11-622-9045
robyn_swanepoel@mcgraw-hill.com

SPAIN
McGraw-Hill/
Interamericana de España, S.A.U.
TEL +34-91-180-3000
FAX +34-91-372-8513
http://www.mcgraw-hill.es
professional@mcgraw-hill.es

**UNITED KINGDOM, NORTHERN,
EASTERN, & CENTRAL EUROPE**
McGraw-Hill Education Europe
TEL +44-1-628-502500
FAX +44-1-628-770224
http://www.mcgraw-hill.co.uk
emea_queries@mcgraw-hill.com

ALL OTHER INQUIRIES Contact:
McGraw-Hill Technology Education
TEL +1-630-789-4000
FAX +1-630-789-5226
omg_international@mcgraw-hill.com